CW00926587

Borderline Books
free books - free minds
borderlinebooks.org

THE WOMEN WHO SAVED THE ENGLISH COUNTRYSIDE

THE WOMEN WHO SAVED THE ENGLISH COUNTRYSIDE

MATTHEW KELLY

YALE UNIVERSITY PRESS
NEW HAVEN AND LONDON

Copyright © 2022 Matthew Kelly

All rights reserved. This book may not be reproduced in whole or in part, in any form (beyond that copying permitted by Sections 107 and 108 of the U.S. Copyright Law and except by reviewers for the public press) without written permission from the publishers.

All reasonable efforts have been made to provide accurate sources for all images that appear in this book. Any discrepancies or omissions will be rectified in future editions.

For information about this and other Yale University Press publications, please contact:
U.S. Office: sales.press@yale.edu   yalebooks.com
Europe Office: sales@yaleup.co.uk   yalebooks.co.uk

Set in Adobe Caslon Pro by IDSUK (DataConnection) Ltd
Printed in Great Britain by TJ Books, Padstow, Cornwall

Library of Congress Control Number: 2022930463

ISBN 978-0-300-23224-0

A catalogue record for this book is available from the British Library.

10 9 8 7 6 5 4 3 2 1

MIX
Paper from
responsible sources
FSC
www.fsc.org   FSC® C013056

CONTENTS

CONTENTS

ILLUSTRATIONS

Chapter opener illustrations by Sarah Young.

Plates

1. Front page of *The Times*, 22 February 1967. The Times Digital Archive. *The Times*, Front Page: 22.02.1967 News UK & Ireland Limited [22.02.1967].
2. Landscape of Dartmoor horses disturbed by a helicopter, by Sylvia Sayer, 1968. Kate Ashbrook Private Collection. Courtesy of Kate Ashbrook.
3. Portrait of Octavia Hill, by John Singer Sargent, 1898. National Portrait Gallery / NPG 1746. © National Portrait Gallery, London.
4. 'Ide Hill, Kent, to be secured to the Public', 1899. Illustration for *The Graphic*, 12 August 1899, Bridgeman / LIP1042935. Look and Learn / Illustrated Papers Collection / Bridgeman Images.
5. View from Toys Hill in the Sevenoaks district of Kent, England. Marcin Rogozinski, 2013. Alamy / E6H5YY. Marcin Rogozinski / Alamy Stock Photo.

Maps

ACKNOWLEDGEMENTS

I am grateful to the many people who have helped this book come together. To friends and colleagues at Northumbria for their support and inspiration, especially Charlotte Alston, Lilian Armour, David Gleeson, Kay Howell, Daniel Laqua, Tom Lawson, James McConnel, Brian Ward, and the members of our ever-expanding Environmental Humanities Research Group. To Ben Anderson, Jeremy Burchardt, Katrina Navickas, Gale Pettifer, Paul Readman, Linda Ross, Ian Waites, and all the contributors to the 'Rural Modernism', 'Decommissioning the Twentieth Century', and 'Changing Landscapes, Changing Lives' projects, from whom I learn so much. To my PhD students Louis Holland Bonnet, Ciaran Johnson, and Nick Pepper, for keeping the day job so exciting and rewarding. To Dagmar Schäfer, Director of the Max Planck Institute for the History of Science in Berlin, and Wilko Graf von Hardenberg: I wish other pressures had allowed me to take up a longer fellowship. To Clare Alexander, my inestimable agent, to Julian Loose, for his faith and editorial direction, and to all at Yale, from the marketing team to Frazer Martin and Lucy Buchan, who patiently kept me on track as the book went into production. To Neil Gower, for the charming yet clever cover, to Sarah Young for the lovely chapter openers, to Jenny Roberts, a peerless copyeditor who mostly managed to save me from myself, and to Amanda Speake for the meticulous index. To Bethany Hamblen at Balliol and Alexandra Healey at Newcastle for giving so generously of their time and enabling access to archival material during the Covid-19 lockdown. To the National Trust for allowing me to quote from the Octavia Hill and Beatrix Potter letters. To Robin and Frances Dower, without whose kindness and generosity this book would have been so much less, and to Kate Ashbrook, who talked with me about Sylvia Sayer, shared images, and deserves her own chapter. To Martin Conway, Roy and Aisling Foster, Ultán Gillen, Neil Gregor, Leonie Hicks, Ian McBride, James McConnel, Caoimhe Nic Dháibhéid, Colin Reid, Katie Ritson, and William Whyte for their long service in the field. Special thanks to Josie McLellan, the most astute and energising of confidantes these past 25 years. And, finally, to Katarzyna Kosior, to whom this book is dedicated. She lived this project for as long as I did, enduring months of lockdown and online teaching, and yet still brings such joy to all we do together.

MK, Tynedale
January 2022

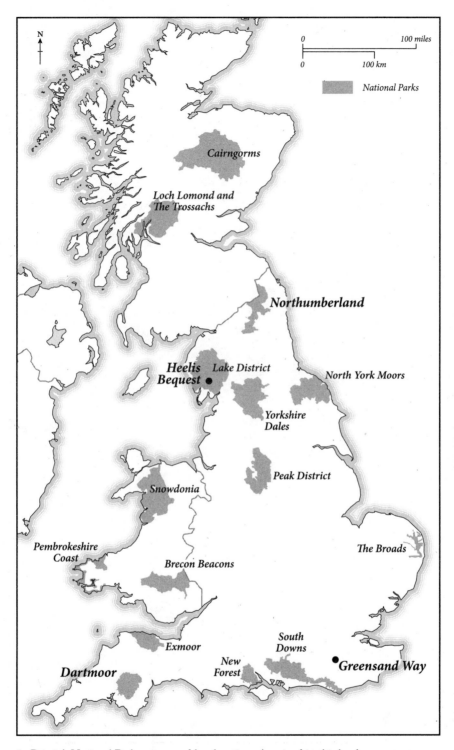

1. Britain's National Park system and key locations examined in this book.

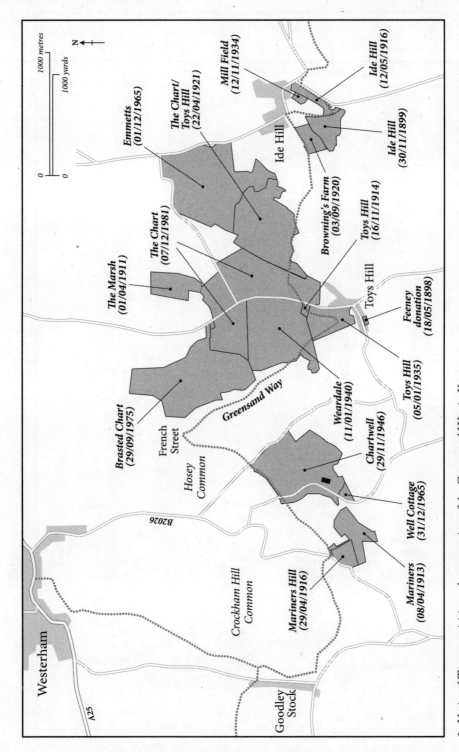

2. National Trust acquisitions along a section of the Greensand Way in Kent.

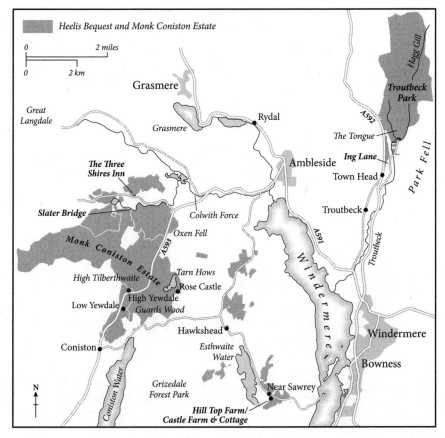

Heelis Bequest and Monk Coniston Estate

0   2 miles

0   2 km

Great Langdale

Grasmere

Grasmere

Rydal

Hagg Gill

Troutbeck Park

A592

The Tongue

Ambleside

Ing Lane

The Three Shires Inn

Town Head

Park Fell

Slater Bridge

Colwith Force

Oxen Fell

Troutbeck

Monk Coniston Estate

A593

A591

Tarn Hows

High Tilberthwaite

Rose Castle

High Yewdale

Low Yewdale

Guards Wood

Troutbeck

Windermere

Hawkshead

Coniston

Esthwaite Water

Windermere

Bowness

N

Coniston Water

Grizedale Forest Park

Near Sawrey

Hill Top Farm/ Castle Farm & Cottage

3. Map showing much of the land Beatrix Potter bequeathed to the National Trust or purchased on its behalf.

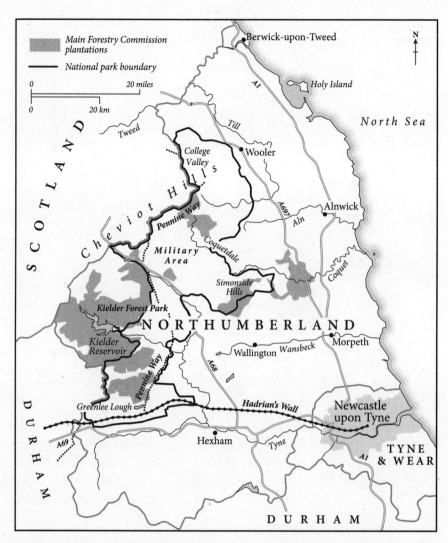

4. Map of Northumberland showing the boundaries of Northumberland National Park and other key locations mentioned in the text.

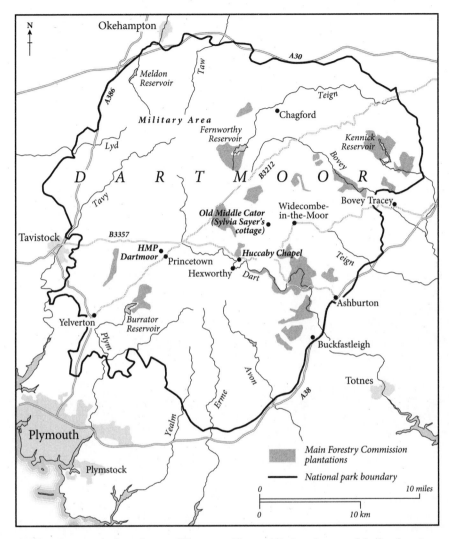

5. Map showing the boundaries of Dartmoor National Park and some of the key locations associated with Sylvia Sayer and her activism.

Introduction
The Four

On 22 February 1967, the front page of *The Times* was dominated by an image of a woman taking a photograph of a helicopter winching an artillery piece. An apparently unconcerned soldier stands in the background; bleak, open moorland recedes towards the distant horizon. This was Ringmoor Down on Dartmoor. The noise and menace of the military helicopter contrasts with the poise and composure of the civilian woman. First published in the *Western Morning News*, the photograph later migrated to the annual report of the Countryside Commission.[1]

The Times captioned the photograph 'Woman on the warpath at Dartmoor', but its subject was not an anonymous individual captured by an enterprising press photographer. This was a photo op, likely staged, but no less affective for that. The woman was Sylvia Sayer. That day, she exercised her right to access common land in protest at the use of Dartmoor National Park by the Ministry of Defence as a training ground. Her action highlighted how the military did not have the authority to prevent her from walking across the down. Ordinary people, she insisted, should not be inhibited from exercising their rights by the military's intrusive and intimidating presence. Sayer's attention-seeking action, entirely peaceful, was typical of her long tenure as chair of the Dartmoor Preservation Association. An ardent proponent of national park principles, she believed the

1

military's use of the parks should be subject to closer controls. Ideally, it should be expelled altogether. Only then could the qualities of the landscape be preserved from further harm and public rights of access guaranteed. This was but one apparently harmful use of the moors that exercised this most determined of campaigners.

By the early 1960s, Sayer was familiar to government ministers and Whitehall civil servants. Regular appearances at contentious planning inquiries and in the letter pages of the broadsheet newspapers had made her a figure of note. Her lucid, hand-written letters, sometimes accompanied by photographs evidencing her complaints, could not be ignored. She was equally the bane of senior army officers, Forestry Commission officials and water authority managers. Their every move on Dartmoor was subject to her scrutiny. If she opposed their plans, and she frequently did, she knew how to deploy the tools at her disposal to disrupt their smooth implementation. Equally, she could align her work with the priorities of the national park authorities, national or regional, chivvying them along, but she readily expressed her displeasure when they failed to live up to their purposes, as she thought they frequently did. From her stone cottage in a tiny Dartmoor hamlet, she orchestrated numerous campaigns that combined her verbal eloquence, combativeness and grasp of legal statute and planning processes, placing her among the most effective post-war environmental campaigners and lobbyists.

Despite this, little is known about Sayer today. The unveiling in December 2019 of a memorial plaque in the tiny chapel at Huccaby, at the heart of Dartmoor National Park, was a private family affair.[2] An attentive visitor might notice the discreet memorial stone marking the life of this most dynamic personality. Sayer is not alone. Many environmental campaigners have suffered this fate. If we are to understand not just the history of environmental campaigning in modern Britain but also the slow rise of the now near-universal environmental consciousness, we need to know more about activists like Sayer and the contexts in which they worked. To begin to understand

Sayer's broader historical significance is to begin to see why the migration of this grainy photograph from the regional and the national press to an official publication was more than just a testament to Sayer's brilliance as a publicist or the power of the image itself.

Sayer is one of four women examined by this book who helped make environmental consciousness. As activists, they worked to preserve the English landscapes they valued most from modern developments and to protect and increase rights of public access. Despite the significance of their work, there is no established historical narrative into which the four can be politely integrated. To make sense of their work is to start to tell that very story. They were agents in the making of this history. As Sayer's encounter with the army helicopter indicates, their actions could be disruptive, but to understand the effectiveness of the four we need to see how it primarily rested on steady, day-to-day work. This work helped establish the landscape designations and access rights that underpin the management of the English countryside today. The labour of committee meetings, report drafting, fund-raising and lobbying was just as important to the development of environmental rights, including rights of access, as iconic mass actions like the Winter Hill trespass of 1896 or the Kinder Scout trespass of 1932. The four contributed to this great work. They helped fashion arguments still heard today. Without their work, more land would be enclosed, more land would be built on, more footpaths and access to open spaces would have been lost. They helped guarantee what rights of access to the countryside we enjoy today. Aspects of the four might now be found politically or socially uncongenial, and sometimes their purposes were short-sighted, but it is hard to trace their achievements without coming to recognise the debt we owe them.

Let's meet the four. They can be classified according to a simple typology: the Public Moralist, the Philanthropist, the Technocrat and the Activist. Octavia Hill was a public moralist and reformer of quite astonishing range and commitment. Her historical reputation as a prominent Victorian, housing reformer and co-founder of the National Trust is long-established. Beatrix Potter is famous throughout the world, known during her lifetime and since for her children's books and association with the Lake District. Shy in youth and adulthood but a diarist and opinionated correspondent, Potter worked in close partnership with the National Trust and became one of the organisation's most important benefactors. Pauline Dower, sociable and exceptionally well-connected, channelled her radical energies into work for the post-war social democratic state as the longest-serving and most senior woman on the National Parks Commission. She did not achieve a high public profile during her lifetime but as a public servant helped establish the fundamentals of the national parks system. Sylvia Sayer, clear-headed, energetic and of unusual resolve, helped define pressure group politics in the post-1945 era, but is now little remembered even in those places where once she made so much noise.[3]

All four shared a determination to preserve their favoured patches from modern threats. They objected to untrammelled private developments and the construction of public infrastructure in places associated with natural beauty and public access. In the main, their preservationism was predicated on the defence of what they considered traditional country occupations, particularly farming based on the exercise of common rights. For Potter and Sayer, upland grazing regimes did not just create the charismatic landscapes they sought to protect but were somehow naturally determined as their proper use. More generally, the four were convinced that the experience of urbanisation and industrialisation alienated humanity from nature, having a terrible effect on human wellbeing, diminishing our capacity to even recognise our unhappiness. If public and private developers were the immediate enemy, they were symptomatic of a much greater force, the birth and development of industrial modernity. No place or person, however isolated, was safe. Only eternal vigilance could keep modernity's encroachment on humanity and nature at bay.

Although the four saw themselves as locked into an unending contest with the forces of modernity, they should not be caricatured as reactionary. They advocated forms of environmental citizenship that identified land as public goods from which flow collective rights. The political struggles they helped foment sought to deliver forms of environmental justice that were quintessentially modern, resolving into a simple if contentious question: who has the right to determine how land is used, and what political, social and cultural ramifications flow from how we answer this question? All four believed that the rights of private property should be limited by the needs of the wider community. If landholders did not extend their universe of obligation beyond their immediate self-interest, if the protection and production of vital public goods – health and happiness – could not be delivered through voluntary action, then legal or democratic processes should be brought to bear on the problem.

To tell their stories takes us from the birth pangs of modern preservationism in mid-Victorian Britain through to the institutionalisation of nature conservation in the late twentieth century. In what follows, the roles played by small, voluntarist organisations are related to the development of powerful national institutions like the National Trust, the national park authorities and the Forestry Commission. Through the lives of the four, we can see the gradual shift from voluntarist to statist principles. Hill and Potter, investing their hopes in the National Trust, represented the liberal and voluntarist ethos predominant before the 1930s, whereas Dower and Sayer, committed to national park principles, represented the social democratic, statist ethos that gathered strength after 1945. It was not a coincidence that the government which created the National Health Service in 1948 established the National Parks Commission in 1949.

The long lives of these women also show how difficult it is to adapt to changing times and new ideas. Theirs were unconventional careers, with no set retirement age, and each saw ideas and principles that seemed radical in their youth and held sway over their middle age come to seem outmoded. From the perspective of the early twenty-first century, the absence of an ecological dimension to the thinking of the four is most striking. All four possessed a good knowledge of flora and fauna, but they were not ecologists or nature conservationists even by the standards of their own time and tended to express their concern about threats to the natural environment in terms of aesthetic or cultural rather than ecological loss. Visual aesthetics mattered to them, reflecting the powerful historical legacies of romanticism and the picturesque. Potter, of course, was an artist of genius, but given these priorities it was not coincidental that the other three were also trained artists: Hill under the strict regime imposed by John Ruskin, Dower and Sayer in the more bohemian atmosphere of art college in the 1920s. More specifically, Sayer's retirement as chair of the Dartmoor Preservation Association in 1973 coincided with a shift in the focus of environmental politics away from landscape preservation towards a more scientific conservationism and an environmental ethos preoccupied with earth systems theory, the transnational consequences of industrial pollutants, and the extinction threats faced by 'charismatic megafauna' like pandas, whales and tigers. Since then, of course, the consequences of the carbon economy, particularly as manifest in anthropogenic climate change, has come to dominate the environmental agenda. Powerful though this paradigmatic shift was, it should not obscure how politically generative the work of the four had been.

All four enjoyed privileged upbringings and could leverage class-based advantages just as class-based sensibilities and political commitments affected the development of their environmental politics. That much will be evident in what follows. But in the lives of the four, matters of class and privilege intersected with those of gender. Their work was not understood to be 'women's work' – plenty of men did committee work in this period – but their status as women was central to their experiences and, in some cases, how they conceived of their work.[4] Advantages and disadvantages were conferred on each by being, so to speak, the only woman in the room. This could be isolating but it also gave the four licence to challenge existing mores and assumptions. It is true that Hill's way of working partly reflected her adherence to the Victorian ideal that men and women should occupy 'separate spheres', but by presenting the work she provided for women as 'domestic', she helped expand the scope of respectable women's work outside of the home. Sayer, by contrast, believed she had to confound gendered stereotypes if her arguments were to get a fair hearing: 'From the start I knew there was a disadvantage in being a woman. Some of the old councillors hate being corrected by a woman and I was always well informed and not emotional.'[5] The four were neither confined by the clubbable expectations imposed on men nor subdued by the spurious 'rational' or 'common sense' arguments often used to defend vested interests. No glass of whisky in the avuncular atmosphere of the club brought these women into line.

At times the four invite an attitude of wry amusement, but tone as well as argument help make a historical narrative. It is tempting to call them 'indefatigable', 'indomitable', 'spirited' and 'doughty'. These terms can enliven a text with characterful associations but should be used with care. Gendered cliché is undermining. Similarly, class stereotypes can be as problematic, as they too can be entertaining. In the nineteenth and twentieth centuries, activist women were often caricatured as eccentric, unflatteringly referred to as blue stockings or dismissed as upper-class busybodies, theatrical figures who were a bit posh, a bit barmy, with nothing better to do than bother the authorities with shrill claims that failed to grasp realities. When a man says, 'that bloody woman', to use a mild form of the demotic, he almost always means a woman who has trespassed on what he takes to be his domain or has challenged masculine authority. In their various ways, the four did just this. They should be recognised as effective political agents who helped recast what was constituted legitimate political authority in modern Britain.

To understand the strength of the four's commitments, we need to understand the places they sought to protect. This book takes the reader to Octavia's Kentish retreat, to Beatrix's Lakeland home, to the country mansion of Pauline's Northumberland childhood and to the Dartmoor cottage of Sylvia's adulthood. Hill, Potter, Dower and Sayer were highly networked, they did not work alone, but the history of activism surely demonstrates that the conviction and energy of a few unusually committed individuals, willing and able to do hard organisational and intellectual work, can shift the parameters of debate, ensuring marginal voices are heard in the centres of power. It is essential to the quality of our democracy that this continues. For this reason alone, the activist lives of the four is of enduring interest.

OCTAVIA HILL

Gathering in the Givers

Octavia Hill

Gathering in the Givers

In July 1912, shortly before her death aged 73, Octavia Hill wrote an appeal on behalf of the National Trust, or to give the organisation its full name, the National Trust for Places of Historic Interest or Natural Beauty. Published in the letter pages of *The Times*, Hill asked for donations to buy a small plot of land at Mariners Hill, a wooded promontory overlooking the Kentish Weald. Access to its magnificent eastern views was threatened by developers. The purchase would join a string of 'salient promontories' across Kent, Surrey and Hampshire saved by various bodies from enclosure by housing developers, and would adjoin small plots that Hill had helped the Trust acquire over the previous decade, creating a continuous stretch of woodland with guaranteed public access.[1] As the Trust had said of an earlier acquisition, it would 'prove not only a valuable "view point" in itself, but, being thus approached by paths on several sides, may form the centre of a beautiful walk'. On a clear day, views over the Weald, Ashdown Forest and the South Downs allowed 'glimpses here and there of the sea'.[2] In 1904, 'viewpoint' might not yet be established as a singular noun, but the Trust already conceived of its growing property portfolio as promising visitors a spectacular experience.

Hill told her readers that the asking price for the eight-acre plot was £1,550, about half the development value of the land, thereby making the crucial point that the price was presented as philanthropic.[3] As this

11

suggests, by its very existence the Trust had established a new way of thinking about the disposal of private property, and its campaigns often claimed that a bargain could be had if donors acted quickly. Given the Trust's later readiness to accept donations of big houses and country estates in lieu of death taxes, it is important to recover a sense of the Trust's high purposes in these early decades and the particular significance Hill attached to land purchase by public donation. The decisive role she played in the Trust's founding in 1894 formed part of her work to establish new notions of the public good in the age of capital. She vigorously promoted the idea that the public had rights of access to open spaces – and the health-giving benefits access delivered – that extended beyond the rapidly diminishing provision sustained by common rights or customary rights of way. By applying abstract principles derived from natural theology to the specific historical circumstances of the British people, especially the urban poor of London, she argued that landowners had obligations to the common good that should influence how they chose to dispose of their property. Hill promoted what is now called environmental justice.

In the 1870s and 1880s, Hill framed the claim that people had the rights of access to open spaces in terms of the specific generational experience of the urban poor. In the wake of rapid urbanisation and industrial development, and all that this did to transform the lives of working people, came the need for fields 'reminding men and women long lost in the whirl of London, of child days and places where they were born'.[4] Establishing urban parks was an urgent necessity, and Hill's commitment to this cause was inflected by her own experiences. During childhood, she suffered her own wrenching separation from the rural when her father was declared bankrupt, forcing the family to move from Cambridgeshire to London. By the 1890s, she was at least as preoccupied by the negative effect suburbanisation and privatisation had on the countryside, including the loss of what she characterised as natural landscapes, and this drove her commitment to the development of the National Trust. Her focus now fell less exclusively on the needs of the urban poor and broadened to establish an agenda based on the patriotic notion that the English landscape was a timelessly beautiful common possession of all classes.[5] As her mother wrote in 1897, Hill's 'heart is chiefly interested just now in saving *beautiful* spots in England, securing them in their beauty for future generations'.[6]

Those promontories across south-east England were therefore not acquired or donated simply because they boast breathtakingly beautiful views. Proximity to London, at a time when the railway network was expanding and working people had more leisure time, gave the hills additional utility; nearness to London made 'their breezy heights accessible to the pedestrian, the cyclist, and to the many families who value lovely country and have no gardens or but small ones'.[7] Hill insisted the provision of these health-giving qualities, denied to ordinary people by the developing market for urban and suburban residential and commercial property, was central to the National Trust's purpose. Her priorities were evident when the Trust contemplated the purchase of Barras Nose near Tintagel, an extraordinary volcanic bluff on the north Cornish coast. Although Barras Nose was not near to a densely populated urban centre, Hill nonetheless advised that Canon Hardwicke Rawnsley, a key National Trust collaborator, amend his appeal for donations so it 'dwell a little on the breeze and beauty of the space as well as on its historic and poetical side'.[8]

Hill's initial turn to what became known as the Open Spaces movement was prompted by the rapid expansion and development of London. Roads connecting Westminster and the City to outlying villages like Hampstead had been ribboned with housing. Developers soon looked to the spaces in between, stringing terraced housing across open country belonging to landlords keen to cash in. Huge strips of land were also taken over by the railway companies, as Dickens famously depicted in *Dombey and Son* (1848). Hill was acutely alert to the fact that landowners sought to persuade commoners to barter away their rights so the land might be sold free of entail. She feared impoverished commoners would sell their rights for 'a bag of coal at Christmas', a symbol of the exploitation of people who did not understand the value of their rights.

Hill was notoriously wary of systematic state intervention and did not advocate the appropriation of private property. She believed it was legitimate for citizens to work principally to protect their local interests, largely through a combination of voluntary donation and conventional market mechanisms. In this respect, she promoted a variant on the liberal principle that the pursuit of selfish interest could deliver public goods. At the same time, she recognised that some communities were better equipped than others to protect their own interests, a tendency she thought had been compounded during the nineteenth century by the ghettoisation of the urban poor. As more and more people were confined to smaller and smaller spaces, so their ability to discern the full ramifications of changes to land use diminished. It was thus morally incumbent on those who could see to act on behalf of people whose circumstances ensured they could not know better. That she wrote that each 'should give and give only to that which interest him or her' did not mean she was passive in her attempts to persuade people of what should interest them.[9] She worked hard to 'gather in the givers' by helping to create the moral and intellectual environment that encouraged voluntary action and donation.[10] To adopt Stefan Collini's formulation, she was a 'public moralist', 'intensely preoccupied with the question of arousing adequate motivation in the moral agent'.[11] This perspective made establishment of the National Trust as much an intervention in the new politics of giving as it was of land and access. Happy the millionaire, she wrote, to 'find his buttercups more abidingly powerful and blessed than his sovereigns', but she was keener still to mobilise small donors, whether the £25 that under exceptional circumstances might be expected of the middle classes or the few shillings of the working man or woman.[12]

Cross-class fellowship and sympathy was foundational to Hill's concept of social action. From 1872, she addressed an annual letter updating her 'fellow-workers' on the movement's achievements and how its funds, mainly private donations, were used. These letters, which constitute her most significant body of written work, mainly concerned the progress of the inner-city housing projects she oversaw, and the functioning of what was later referred to as the 'Octavia Hill system', but Hill's use of the term 'worker' equally applied to her Open Spaces work. It did not denote a class identity within a stratified society – hers was not a sociological usage – but a person engaged in a set of prescribed activities in the interests of a common cause. Campaigning was a component of this work, but Hill's fellow-workers were not agitators in the sense that they sought to put pressure on the government or individuals to act or behave in ways contrary to their immediate selfish interests. Rather, their fellowship created the circumstances that enabled their work to be done. Hill's housing workers were predominantly women and she had firm ideas about the suitability of women for what she judged to be 'domestic' work with the urban poor.

Hill applied the same principles to local authorities as she applied to individuals. Like most members of the Victorian middle class, she favoured permissive legislation that empowered but did not compel local authorities. Ratepayers should decide how their money was spent, but there was no reason why Hill should not seek to persuade elected public bodies to purchase land for public use, not least by exercising new powers to borrow money. London County Council's sensational acquisition of Epping Forest in the 1870s helped create a new sense of what was possible, but Hill considered smaller acquisitions equally important. Indeed, her acute sensitivity to the needs of elderly people and young mothers with small children challenged the ableist assumptions sometimes evident in the Open Spaces movement. Gently sloping hillsides, viewpoints and a fresh breeze were her priorities, which should be as easily accessible in urban open spaces as in the countryside. These priorities were evident in a speech she made about the politics of access and the Lake District. She outlined the need to preserve 'little winding ways, that lead us on by hedgerows and over brooks, through scented meadows and up grassy hill, away from dirty road, and into the silent green of wood and field'.[13] Contrast this accessible vision of an area associated with hardy hikers with James Bryce's failed attempts to secure the passage of his Access to Mountains (Scotland) bill in 1884, 1892 and 1908.[14] In 1898, we see her not in the Scottish Highlands conquering a Munro but joining celebrations to mark the opening to the public of Queen's Wood, adjacent to Highgate Woods in north London. The site had been purchased from the ecclesiastical commissioners through the joint action of a string of local councils and parish vestries.[15] In one of her last public statements, Hill celebrated how across Kent, Surrey and Hampshire various organisations, including local authorities, had either been presented with hills or had purchased them in the public interest:

> So important has it been felt to secure access for the ever-increasing population to some of these airy hillsides, commanding wide and beautiful views, that various localities have recently been actively engaged in organizing schemes for their preservation. Haslemere has purchased acres and acres of such land, Reigate is just completing the purchase of the beautiful area of Colley Hill. Finchampstead is initiating a similar scheme. Sevenoaks was last year presented by a generous donor with the well-known point of view called One Tree Hill.[16]

In contrast to the other women discussed in this book, Hill's work and her ideas have been the subject of sophisticated historical research and analysis. What follows prioritises the arguments she made, and the circumstances in which she made them – Hill could be intensely preoccupied by the detail of government legislation – but insight is drawn from the work of other scholars.[17] An important observation from an essay by Elizabeth Baigent provides a guiding thought for what follows. As Baigent reminds us, nineteenth-century

London was a place of constant animal–human interaction and the exposure of the poor to open space or nature was not as minimal as Hill often claimed. Consequently, to understand Hill's position we need to distinguish nature and open space from Victorian constructions of Nature and Open Space, phenomena which delivered a series of 'aesthetic, ideological and moral goods'.[18] A child might play happily in a piece of derelict land, but once that land was developed into a park and that same child played under supervision – as Hill insisted was necessary – the experience was radically transformed, taking on significant moral value. As she explained with respect to the Drury Lane 'garden' she helped establish in 1877, its opening times had to be limited because she didn't have access to funds needed to employ a 'sufficient force' to keep order 'in a garden among a population not yet trained to very civilised habits'.[19]

Hill helped to popularise the idea, long a staple of public health thinkers and activists, that environments act upon human beings, for good and for ill, and she helped translate into practical work the idea that the natural environment could have a reformatory effect on the individual.[20] Convinced that all citizens had a right of access to health-giving open spaces, she grappled with the distinction that many Victorians drew between the deserving and undeserving poor. At times she tacked towards non-doctrinaire positions, cautiously promoting the idea that access should not depend on citizens adhering to middle-class behavioural norms. Like many metropolitan Open Space campaigners, she tended to overlook the interests of those who knew the land through work and relied on it for their livelihood, but as she turned her attention to places beyond London, so she paid a little more attention to the rights of the rural poor.

Friendships and networks underpinned Hill's Open Space campaigning. One way to trace those connections is to take an annotated walk through her beloved Kentish hills, where her legacy is strongly manifest in the patchwork of designated sites, including much National Trust land, that allows access today. Such a designation archipelago is broadly characteristic of any pedestrian passage through an English landscape today. The campaigns that Hill helped orchestrate for the preservation of the Lake District were framed in terms of national public goods, but her interest in this short stretch of Kentish hillside stemmed from personal commitments. Mariners Hill was one of four promontories between Oxted in the west and Sevenoaks in the east acquired by the National Trust in this period. Each is a spur on the Greensand Ridge, a sandstone formation resting on wealden clay that runs across Surrey and Kent.[21] More intimately, Mariners Hill is part of a short stretch of wooded hillside between the villages of Limpsfield and Ide Hill known locally as Chartlands, a name derived from the old English for rough country. Since 1884, when Harriet Yorke, Hill's companion, built Larksfield, a substantial house overlooking the village of Crockham Hill, Chartlands had provided Hill with a rural respite from her work in London. In 1890, Yorke reluctantly bought a Mariners Hill site for £800 to protect access to Westerham Commons on the understanding that it would soon pass into the care of an organisation like the National Trust. Was it to repay this outstanding debt that Hill, in her final year, appealed to the readers of the *The Times*, exercising exactly the enlightened self-interest she encouraged in others?[22]

Given that later sections of this book focus on the charismatic upland landscapes designated as National Parks in the post-war years, it is especially important to be reminded of how walks in suburban areas are especially constrained, charting an interstitial route through a mosaic of private interests. An attentive trip through Hill country in the twenty-first century demonstrates how, over the past century or so, freedoms have been preserved or established often thanks to the accumulation of various scraps of land by the Trust and other bodies. In its unsystematic development, this designation archipelago reminds us of Hill's opposition to state intervention, whether with respect to the alleviation of poverty and its associated problems or in her Open Spaces work. The Trust owns much open access land and has been particularly important to preserving great stretches of beautiful but agriculturally marginal coastline from development, but it remains a membership organisation and depends on individual philanthropy. The Trust does not seek to deliver a universal public service but remains the product of the late Victorian liberal milieu Hill did so much to shape. Each step we take today validates the work they did then.

A Visit to the Hill Country Archipelago

Railway lines reached Sevenoaks in 1868, with a branch line to Westerham opening in 1881, and to Oxted in 1884, making Chartlands easily accessible to visitors from London.[23] Hill's friends and collaborators would be met at the station and taken by brake to Larksfield. I've travelled by car and I'm staying near Itchingwood Common, a partly wooded 23-hectare site a little below the Greensand Ridge. I plan to walk up to Limpsfield Chart and then follow the Greensand Way from Mariners Hill to Toys Hill via Crockham Hill village and Chartwell, Winston and Clementine Churchill's former home, also a National Trust property. The summer academic conference season has made the last few weeks hectic and I'm feeling guilty about my carbon footprint, conscious of the trans-atlantic flights and the long, fast stretches on the M1. Setting off for the first of several days on foot feels redemptive, a form of detox, every clean day somehow neutralising the emissions binge of the previous weeks. I know this is illusory, but on a bright, sunny July morning like this, with the promise of a hot day to come, it is hard not to feel right with the world. This euphoric buzz, this involuntary smile – wellbeing itself – is a feeling Hill politicised, coming close to arguing that it was a human right.

As I leave Itchingwood Common, my mind starts to unclutter. It's liberating, reassuring: this middle-aged brain still functions once the stress and tension abate. Thoughts idly flick between a conference paper about how exposure to the natural world challenges the 'hedonic reversion' thesis and whether the right of two commoners to graze a pony and take one cord of wood per annum from Itchingwood Common is still exercised. I take the bridleway off Itchingwood Common Road across the small northern spur of the common before passing through the yard of Tenchleys Manor, an L-shaped house of sixteenth-century origin. Beyond, the bridleway narrows as it traces a line up the steepening hill between the fenced woodland of Tenchleys Park on my left and the fenced grazing land on my right. I am suddenly confined, channelled, my rights precisely defined, a little less free than I was. This sensation intensifies as I come within a few hundred metres of Kent Hatch Road. Here are large private homes, with beautiful gardens, walls and hedges. Footpath markers proliferate, taking me on a twisting, interstitial route through private property. Removed footpath signs and damaged plastic markers charge each step with political significance: by my passage, I assert a right. Not far from here, Hill had contested the 'no thoroughfare' notice placed by Rev. John Colquhoun (1831–1917), owner of Chartwell and scion of a distinguished Scots family.[24] 'He and his son met us coming through on Saturday & he looked *very* black at us, but said not a word. He will not I think stop us but it seems hard on others.'[25] This gives me purpose and I feel a little defiant, almost hoping I will be challenged. I am no closer to people's private spaces than I would be walking down a street in a city, but here it feels different. Rural boundaries are permeable; spatial politics works differently.

Passing into Limpsfield Chart, a 350-acre site owned by the National Trust, changes the atmosphere. Part of Limpsfield Common, the site was donated to the Trust in 1972. I'm not convinced those brief moments of inward agitation were entirely unwarranted, but here my rights cannot be questioned. The site has an interesting history. William the Conqueror confiscated the Manor of Limpsfield and passed it to Battle Abbey, which it held until the Reformation when Henry VIII had it forcibly passed into private hands. As part of the Titsey Estate, it became the property of the Leveson-Gower family when William Leveson-Gower married Catherine Maria Gresham in 1804.[26] Major Richard Henry Gresham Leveson-Gower (1894–1982), an Old Etonian, having spent his formative adult years in the army and the City, took up the management of the estate in 1949 and with it the chairmanship of the Limpsfield Chart Golf Club, a position he held until his death. Between 1973 and 1976 the estate was bisected by the M25 (partly following the line of Westerham branch line, closed in 1961) and much of the estate, including the eighteenth-century house, is now north of the motorway. Anticipating the estate's partition, Leveson-Gower donated Limpsfield Chart, now south of the M25, to the National Trust in August 1972. To enable the transfer of ownership, the Trust raised £72,000 as an endowment fund through a mix of private and local authority donations, including £7,500 from the Rural District Council of Godstone, £5,000 from the General London Council, and donations of £1,000 from the London Boroughs of Bromley and Richmond-upon-Thames, Surrey County Council and Caterham and Warlingham Urban District Council.[27] Hill would have approved of the modest financial gestures by the London councils. Reviving an ancient ceremony, Leveson-Gower cut a sod of turf and handed it to the Trust's Director-General. Leveson-Gower died without issue and the remainder of the estate went into trust and is now open to the paying public.

Today, the National Trust manages Limpsfield Chart in collaboration with the volunteers of the Friends of Limpsfield Chart. Historicising their activities tells us much about current conservation priorities and management strategies. In 1809, the Board of Agriculture described Limpsfield Common as follows:

Between Godstone and Westerham in Kent, 'contains 480 acres.' The west side of it is a poor sand; but towards the middle, the soil improves to a loam of good staple. 'Heath, furze, and in some parts, beech, birch, and oak coppice-wood, thrive well on it; but the copyholders claiming a right to turn in cattle, as well as a privilege of weeding the wood,' prevents the timber from reaching any considerable size.[28]

This was a characteristic judgement of a board whose brief was to assess the extent of the country's natural resources and recommend how they could best be exploited. Common rights were often considered to hinder progress, in this case the development of a valuable timber supply. By contrast, on Limpsfield Chart today the Trust seeks to prevent self-seeding scrub and trees from consuming open heathland that has not been maintained by the exercise of grazing rights for the past 70 years. Bracken, gorse, oak, sycamore and birch that encroaches on historic heathland is removed to make space for new heather growth, while the thriving holly understorey of the older woodland is cut back, along with the thinning of birch, Scots pine and small oak, to open the forest floor to a wider range of plant and animal species. Restoring lowland heath and increasing woodland biodiversity is considered good conservation practice. In this case, conservationists seek to reproduce the effect of an obsolete human system of natural resource extraction. By this thinking, self-seeded trees need controlling if a series of woodland and heathland management objectives are to be met.

The woodland *is* lovely, and I take up the Greensand Way, following the designated footpath through Limpsfield Chart and into the High Chart. The handsome metal plates of the Greensand Way assure me of my rights as a pedestrian but a trio of notices inform me, as I pass into the land of Squerryes Park Estate, how complex the picture really is. A 'Polite Notice' says I'm not free to wander these woods at will but must stick to the 'Public Rights of Way' detailed on the section of OS map reproduced on the sign. I'm also reminded that the Wildlife and Countryside Act 1981 protects property as well as nature: it's 'an offence to uproot any wild plant without the landowner's permission. This includes the foraging of mushrooms, nuts or foliage within this property'. Walkers inspired by a certain kind of nature writing, take note. The second notice says that people wishing to ride here must purchase a permit, particularly if they want their insurance to be valid, and the third says the owner is in receipt of EU and DEFRA funding through the English Woodland Grant Scheme, administered by the Forestry Commission to support the creation or management of woodland. Something of the complexity of pre-Brexit rural Britain, as yet little changed since the UK's departure from the European Union, is neatly captured by this smorgasbord of permission and restriction, the statutory protection of propertied and unpropertied, and public subsidy spent in collaboration with a state agency. It's an unusually legible example of the public–private partnerships that can shape a pleasant walk in the country.

Simpler circumstances are found across the boundary between Goodley Stock and Crockham Hill Common, a 92-hectare site to its south. The woodland is continuous, and both are part of the Squerryes Estate but whereas the former contains public rights of way, the latter has been managed since October 1925 by the local authority under the 1899 Commons Act.[29] Public access is guaranteed but subject to byelaws displayed on dilapidated metal signs at the road entrances. It is hard to imagine who would have stopped to read the small print when it was legible, but the significance of the sign is as much symbolic as it is precisely legal.

Larksfield is situated on the southern border of the common. Yorke and Hill chose the site partly because they hoped the acquisition of the freehold would help them defend the common if threatened by the Lord of the Manor.[30] Elijah Hoole, Hill's favourite architect, built the house, extending it in the 1890s to include guest rooms and a balcony looking south over the Weald. Hill captured something of the site's appeal and the success of the house in a letter: 'It is on very dry soil, about 700 above sea-level, gets sun from morning to night, has magnificent views, & much lovely open heath land around it, – the fires all burn well, & though it is open to wind it is not cold being well-built & sunny.'[31] She especially loved the garden, describing to her mother the pleasure she took in nature's agency: 'it is so delightful to watch what nature has done, now that she has taken possession of the ground, what lovely and various things she has set in it'. Roses, foxgloves, white clover, golden lady's finger, buttercups, potentilla, crimson clover, pink mallow and sweet briar had all taken hold. The peace and tranquillity of Larksfield seemed to dissolve the barrier between human and non-human nature and Hill experienced 'a sort of fraternal nearness with tall grass and stately and lovely flowers'.[32]

Expectations thus roused, it is disconcerting that the casual visitor today is confronted by high box hedges. But for the chimney pots, the house is wholly barred from view, while the reputably magnificent views of the Weald enjoyed by Hill and Yorke are entirely obscured. The irony couldn't be greater. The three and a half acres immediately adjacent to Larksfield were donated to the Trust in 1904 and, in the Council report for that year, it was presented as a place to walk and for the viewpoint. The gift is now attributed to Hill, but it was recorded by the Council as having been made 'anonymously' through Hill, in language that was unmistakably hers. Making the gift was a 'fitting mode of perpetuating the memory of those who in their lives have shewn at once an appreciation of Nature and a desire to make a permanent gift to those who have no beautiful parks or gardens of their own, and whose lives are spent in the gloomier and more sordid surroundings of a great city'.[33] Similar claims were made when Hill facilitated the donation of a further eight acres at Crockham Hill to the Trust in 1907. The Council reported that the land both commanded a 'very extensive and beautiful panorama stretching across the Weald of Kent' and gave access to a little copse wood and the 'not inferior joy which a varying carpet of wild flowers can give', a right appreciated by villagers and walkers from further afield. 'The number of houses springing up on every side testify to the popularity of the district,' the Council commented, 'and are a tangible proof of the importance of securing for the public these "view-points", as they have been called, before they are appropriated for the sites of private houses and gardens.'[34]

Today, laurel hedges, electronic gates with cameras and expensive SUVs reflect the tremendous affluence repeatedly encountered in this stretch of suburbanised countryside and the desire of owners to maximise their privacy. Just as negotiating a gravel drive hardly requires particulate-heavy, diesel-powered, off-road capability, so hedges up to two metres in height do not require planning permission. The angular monotony of the hedges mark a harsh contrast with the irregular, semi-natural woodland – all bramble and fern – the other side of the drive. In the past, the gardens at Larksfield were opened under the National Gardens Scheme, a charity run since 1927 to facilitate occasional public access to notably fine gardens.[35] Feeling alienated, I walk down Smiths Lane into Crockham Hill village more than usually conscious of the large, private houses barring views of the hill I'd walked up an hour earlier. Hill teaches us to look and experience differently, sensitising us to the privileges of ownership.

Crockham Hill celebrated its most famous resident with a village sign erected on the Golden Jubilee of Elizabeth II, marking the lives of two notable modern women in one. Hill is portrayed in profile, rather as the monarch is on coins, above which a roundel portrays an image of the village as pastoral idyll. Agricultural labourers sheave, the pub is busy with outside drinkers, children play, and the church, flying the Cross of St George, dominates the village. Above the roundel is the symbol of Kent, a bucking white stallion, and its motto, 'Invicta' or unconquered, a reference to the legend that William the Conqueror treated with the people of Kent rather than fight them. It is not altogether clear why this should be a source of pride. Nearby is a recent memorial stone to the staff and pupils of the London County Council Residential School at Weald House killed by German bombing in June 1944. Eight members of staff and 22 children aged between six months and two years were killed. The names etched into slate make for a simple, affecting memorial, commemorating the terrible trauma suffered by this community.

Holy Trinity, Crockham, an Anglican church built in 1842, helps date the first wave of Victorian settlement, and no Hill pilgrimage should bypass it. John Newman, continuing the work of Pevsner, sums up the modern history of the village and the place of the church in it with all the concision of his mentor: 'A promontory of the chart ridge, having superb views over the Weald. Early Victorian settlement justified building a church. The views were rediscovered from the 1870s, when the wealthy began to build mansions to catch them.'[36] Hill, a member of this second wave, is buried under a yew tree in the churchyard and inside the church a stone sarcophagus by the altar is topped with her outsized marble effigy. She is dressed in skirt, blouse and shawl, her feet rest on a pile of sizeable books, account ledgers rather than novels. Baigent says the 'flowing garb' alluded 'to a knightly crusader tomb'.[37] A revived taste for effigies was one aspect of the medievalism that left such a strong mark on the material culture of Victorian Britain and Hill's effigy reflected the sensibilities of that age. Few, though, represented single women, particularly non-aristocratic women, and this one, commissioned in 1913, was intended for Southwark Cathedral. A shortage of funds and the incompetence of its sculptor, one Miss Abbott, ensured it was not completed until 1928, by which time the aggrandising piety it represented had become a little outmoded.[38] Squeezed into Holy Trinity, the disproportionate presence of the sarcophagus gives this modestly sized church a mausoleum-like quality, and in some respects its presence here distorts the memory of Hill, exaggerating the importance of Crockham Hill in the broader context of her work. Southwark would have been more fitting.

The inscription on the sarcophagus remembers Hill as a housing reformer and a founder of the National Trust and she is credited with devoting 'her life to raising the bodily condition and renewing the spiritual strength of her fellow citizens'. As we'll see, this striking formulation largely chimes with Hill's writings and reflects early twentieth-century concerns about the condition of the British working class in the context of the UK's imperial and global wars. The small stained-glass window commemorating her life and the centenary of the foundation of the National Trust again pictures her in profile, though this time the younger version is chosen: a secular saint in this Anglican space. The window is divided into two parts. On the right, factories and inner-city housing are depicted in gloomy blues and purples; on the left, brightly lit Lakeland land-scapes and Palladian architecture are represented in bright yellows and greens. A tree straddles the divide, its trunk and roots are on the side of rural sweetness and light, a third or so of its branches on the side of urban darkness. The left-hand scene captures much that is associated with the National Trust – the Lake District and stately homes – though it is important to note that the Trust became closely associated with great houses long after Hill's death. Indeed, at one point she threatened to resign from the Trust when she sensed that its priorities were shifting from land to buildings. When Yorke died in 1930, a statement read on behalf of Ramsay MacDonald, the Labour prime minister, at a National Trust memorial dinner, focused entirely on the preservation of the countryside, alluding not at all to the great houses which came to dominate later percep-tions of the Trust.[39] A stained-glass window can only offer a simplistic, schematic view of more complex issues, so there is no need to judge the window too harshly, but it nonetheless misrepresents Hill's ideas, diminishing what was most progressive about her thinking. Hill rejected any simplistic dichotomy between rural good and urban bad, investing much of her energy in making urban environments better.

Hill's grave is placed prominently to the right of the gate and the path leading to the church porch. On the gravestone, Hill is named second, after her sister Miranda (1836–1910) and before Yorke (1842–1930). The burial axis is perpendicular to the path and the headstone is erected at the path end. Contrary to convention, the simple inscription on the headstone faces outwards, towards the path. It is positioned to be noticed. Of the church's three monuments to Hill, this headstone carries most meaning. Unmarried sisters were often buried together, and the stone might be read as no more than a manifestation of spinsterhood, but the addition of Yorke attests to the importance of female friendship to Hill's life and work. Hill's promotion as a symbol of the National Trust and as a singularly important woman risks obscuring her position in a dense network of volunteers and campaigners, many of whom were women.

Hill's commitments had their origins in family. Her father, James Hill, was a fervent Owenist, but it seems that the maternal line exerted a more powerful influence.[40] Hill's maternal grandfather, Dr Thomas Southwood Smith, a Unitarian minister and sanitary reformer of national and international repute, was close to the social reformer and utilitarian philosopher Jeremy Bentham and his disciple Edwin Chadwick. Smith delivered the lecture over Bentham's corpse before its notorious public dissection, as demanded by Bentham's 1827 pamphlet 'The Use of the Dead to the Living'.[41] Hill's mother, Caroline Southwood Hill, was part of a radical Unitarian, early feminist tradition. In the late 1830s she ran the *Star in the East* with her husband, which declared itself equally concerned with women's and men's rights, but her principal work was as a highly prescriptive educationalist. She was influenced by the Swiss educationalist Johann Heinrich Pestalozzi (1746–1827), taking from him the importance to child development of time spent in the open air alongside more conventional pedagogy. The purpose of education, she argued, should be the 'development of a sound body, of a sound mind, of a Christ-like spirit, or, as St. Paul calls it, charity'. By this Pauline reading, charity is not giving to the poor, but a Christian disposition that abnegates all ego, 'suffers long', 'rejoices in the truth', 'is kind' and 'endures all things'; an effective education would leave the child open to the workings of this Christian spirit.[42] The family led a rather peripatetic life, but when James Hill's business ventures failed in 1840, Caroline Hill took her five daughters to her father's household in London, where once old enough they were expected to combine their education with paid work. In Octavia's case, this began aged 14 when she became her mother's assistant at the Ladies Guild, a co-operative workshop in Holborn, and was given responsibility for the ragged-school girls aged between 8 and 17 who were employed there.

The move to central London was a seminal moment for Hill and her sisters, exposing them to the huge social challenges the city faced and her grandfather's progressive circle of friends. It was at her grandfather's house in 1853, aged 15, that Hill first encountered John Ruskin, the extraordinarily polymathic art historian, social critic and proto-environmentalist. Ruskin later employed Hill as a copyist before encouraging her to embark on 'practical work' and financing her early housing projects. The Hills attended services at St Peter's Church, Vere Street, London, where the theologian and friend of her grandfather, F.D. Maurice, preached (more below), while among the progressively minded young women Hill met at St Peter's were the Garrett sisters. All would leave a strong mark on the Victorian period. Elizabeth (later Anderson) worked with Hill at the Working Women's College, an offshoot of Maurice's Working Men's College, and became Britain's first woman doctor; Millicent (later Fawcett) became a leading women's suffrage campaigner; and Agnes and her cousin Rhoda, influenced by the Arts and Crafts Movement, were later feted as the first women to establish an interior decoration firm. Hill's later housing projects also brought her into contact with Henrietta Rowland (later Barnett), the girls education reformer, and Beatrice Potter (later Webb), the social scientist and Fabian.[43]

Octavia's mother lived with her until her death in 1902, exerting a powerful influence over her life and thinking. This appears to have been particularly felt in the early 1860s when Hill became intensely attached to Sophia Jex-Blake, a pioneering woman medic. In a letter to her sisters, Hill described Jex-Blake as a 'bright, spirited, brave, generous young lady living alone in true bachelor style'.[44] Sophia attended Hill's book-keeping classes in 1860. Hill was 20, Jex-Blake was 18. Their friendship, later the source of some speculation, made Hill 'merry as a grig', as she told her sister Miranda that April.[45] Hill invited her friend to join their household, but this arrangement ran aground when Jex-Blake came into conflict with Caroline Hill. Hill hinted at the problems in her last surviving written mention of Jex-Blake.[46] Jex-Blake left, and Hill renounced the friendship for good, seemingly never to look back.

Although it's unclear what happened, it seems likely that Hill bowed to the will of her mother, perhaps mindful of her father's mental collapse and therefore alarmed by the passion the friendship unleashed. In any case, her family suppressed all memory of the affair. Letters were destroyed or kept out of the public eye. Early hagiographical work on Hill made no allusion to the friendship. Jex-Blake's biographers have since established her record as a successful campaigner for the right of women to access medical training, ensuring she takes her place among the pioneering women of her generation and is not reduced to an intriguing curiosity in Hill's early life.[47] Recent times have proven less deferential. A scene in the play commissioned by the Trust to mark its centenary in 1995 saw Hill kissed passionately by Jex-Blake. As a theatre critic summarised the play, 'A lesbian called Sophia Jex-Blake yearns for the young Octavia Hill, whose heart belongs to the aging John Ruskin, who in turn rejects her for the still younger Rose La Touche'.[48] More carefully, Caroline Morrell suggests 'the costs of the sort of emotional upheaval that Sophia brought to her life outweighed the joy and excitement that she clearly got from the friendship'. Hill placed duty towards family above all others.[49]

Other significant female friends reflected the Highgate circle of Unitarian radicals and Christian Socialist circles that Hill moved in as a young woman. Full justice cannot be done to their significance, but these are names to conjure with. Among them was Jane Nassau Senior, sister of Thomas Hughes, the author of *Tom Brown's School Days* (1857), and daughter-in-law of the influential political economist Nassau William Senior, and the feminists Emily Davies and Barbara Leigh Smith (née Bodichon), cousin of Florence Nightingale.[50] Hill had much in common with these mid-Victorian feminists, described by Helen McCarthy as believing 'emphatically in the spiritually redeeming nature of work for both sexes'; Hill might also be located within what Noel Annan described in a famous essay as the 'intellectual aristocracy'. Tracing these connections can become almost an end in itself.[51] Each marriage, friendship or organisational affiliation generated new ties of affection and intriguing connections, generating an ever-denser social network presided over by glamorous upper-class figureheads. If Hill's friendships initially reflected family links to progressive causes – Hill was briefly governess to Hughes's children – they increasingly reflected her own achievements and standing. Over the course of her lifetime, her involvement in numerous organisations, often at their moment of genesis, largely reflected her conviction that the betterment of society could be achieved through civic engagement rather than state intervention. Friendships among like-minded women were the product of a moment in history when a growing number of pioneering middle-class women, particularly but not exclusively unmarried women, became active in progressive and philanthropic causes, sometimes feminist, that relied on women's voluntary labour and were often thought dependent on particularly female qualities.[52]

Hill insisted, for instance, that her rent collectors were women: 'Ladies must do it, for it is detailed work; ladies must do it, for it is household work.'[53] This statement is dense with meaning. Hill understood rent collection not just as a financial transaction dictated by the market, but the dominant vector of a relationship bound by rights and responsibilities on both sides. Jane Garnett argues that

Hill was strongly influenced by the distinction John Ruskin drew between kingly and queenly qualities and how these shaped everyday life. Queenly power, Ruskin argued, 'is for rule, not for battle, – and her intellect' is 'not for invention or creation, but for sweet ordering, arrangement, and decision'.[54] But rather than reading this as designating biologically determined male and female roles, Garnett argues that Ruskin intended that qualities he revered like gentleness, courtesy, patience, hope, carefulness and accuracy, though gendered by social critics as female, could be applied positively to workers of either sex.[55] This aspect of Hill's belief system chimed with her sympathy for the anti-systematic theology of F.D. Maurice. In *Social Morality* (1869), Maurice argued that:

> The free and brave Spirit is the Spirit of charity and truth, the Spirit which fights in us with our selfishness; a Spirit which makes men feminine, if feminine means courteous, deferential, free from brutal and insolent pretensions; but which also gives women manliness, if manliness means the vigour to live for the cause of Humanity and die for it.[56]

Whether or not Hill fully embraced these challenging readings of gender or, to put it a different way, whether she regarded these subtleties as particularly useful in practice is another question. Her writings suggest she often witnessed considerate and loving behaviour by fathers that might be construed as feminine, but she held to the view that masculine and feminine qualities mapped onto men and women. She gave her clearest expression of her views in July 1910 in a notorious letter to *The Times* on the question of women's suffrage. Regretting the necessity of this foray into the 'political world', her letter developed into an extraordinary screed premised on her belief that 'men and women help one another because they are different, have different gifts and different spheres – one is the complement of the other', meaning 'they become one in marriage and one also in friendship and in fellow-work'. Hill was unconvinced that the advent of two million women voters entering 'the arena of party struggle and political life' would improve the quality of the men elected to parliament, as some suffragists argued, and instead calculated the cost to the country as being the diminution of women's good 'influence and inspiration' and their diversion from their 'noble and helpful service' caring for 'the sick, the old, the young, and the erring, as guardians of the poor, as nurses, as teachers, as visitors'. By this 'out-of-sight, silent work which really achieves something, a great blessing is conferred on our country'. Hill's expression of separate spheres theory captures the archetype so well that her peroration is worth quoting at length:

> Let the woman seek the quiet paths of helpful real work, be set on finding where she is wanted, on her duties, not on her rights – there is enough of struggle for place and power, enough of watching what is popular and will win votes, enough of effort to secure majorities; if she would temper this wild struggle, let her seek to do her own work steadily and earnestly, looking rather to the out-of-sight, neglected sphere, and she will, to my mind, be filling the place to which by God's appointment she is called. I believe there are thousands of silent women who agree with me in earnestly hoping that no Woman's Suffrage Bill will pass.[57]

Many people shared her views, including a significant if diminishing number of women, and her position, its wrongness notwithstanding, had evident ideological coherence, expressed with an authority born of her experience of a lifetime's philanthropic work. Her position rejected the anti-suffrage position that women should be denied the vote on the grounds that they possessed neither the intellectual ability nor the emotional stability to exercise it rationally. Instead, her argument was strongly based on her understanding of women's distinct abilities and preferences, for she evidently believed

33

women made an important contribution to society at large, including in professional capacities. That she did not express her convictions in party-political terms is true enough, and it might seem disingenuous that she saw her letter as a rare intervention in 'politics', but if we are to understand Hill on her own terms, the distinction she drew between 'politics', as a properly male occupation, and philanthropy and new forms of public life, as open to both men and women, which included work for the National Trust, must be grasped.

I leave the church and trudge back up Crockham Hill, determined to press on to Mariners Hill and its legendary view. In the middle of Crockham Woods, I come upon The Warren, a gorgeously scruffy house that has somehow escaped gentrification. Beehives tucked in by the side of the house evoke the Crockham Hill of the village roundel. Digging around the internet tells me that the chair of the Crockham Hill Women's Institute lives here – somehow fitting. The house has had strong Hill connections. In the 1880s, it belonged to Charles Edmund Maurice, son of F.D. Maurice, and Emily Southwood Maurice, Hill's sister, poet and later editor of Hill's early letters.[58] Ernest and Elinor Carrington Ouvry later occupied the house and held eight hectares or so of the common. Ernest, of Huguenot background, matriculated at Wadham College, Oxford in 1885 and later became a solicitor. He acted for Hill and was recipient of a letter from her declaring that 'beanfeasters', 'roughs' and 'noisy children' should be kept off National Trust land. Hill's outburst might well have been triggered by Ouvry's concern about what the transfer of Mariners Hill to the National Trust would mean for his quality of life. In April 1916, he sold his own land at Crockham Hill Common to the National Trust, completing its existing holding on the site.[59] Elinor was the youngest daughter of Charles and Gertrude Lewes (née Hill) and Hill's niece. Here was another connection to the 'intellectual aristocracy'. Charles Lewes was the son of George Lewes, who had an open marriage and lived with Mary Ann Evans, the writer better known as George Eliot.

34

Another Mariners Hill site, some 15 acres, was donated by Florence le Marchant Tupper (1864–1956) in 1913. She was the only child of Lieutenant-General Sir Gaspard le Marchant Tupper, veteran of the Crimean War, commander of the garrison at Woolwich and landscape artist. His work, including scenes from Crimea and 'Views of the West Indies', occasionally come up for sale. He left Florence much of his £220,000 fortune and, apart from her National Trust donation, she also gave to the National Gallery.[60]

During the walk through the woods, pleasant indeed, I'm filled with anticipation. Before the famous view at Mariners Hill, I expect to come upon a sixteenth-century cottage and four acres of enclosed land, comprising a mix of old garden and grassland. I'm in for a shock. In 2010, Sevenoaks District Council permitted the demolition of the cottage and the construction of a five-bedroom house with pointy eaves in its place. A new garage was refused planning permission, though later applications for a triple garage, an ornamental fishpond and a tennis court or football pitch laid with astro turf were approved. A basement, wherein lurks a cinema, makes the property's footprint subterranean too. A carefully tended lawn has replaced rough grass-land, and walls and high hedges enclose the whole site.[61] Where there was once a continuum between woods and garden, the site more clearing than enclosure, there are now sharp boundaries and ecolog-ical loss. That Sevenoaks District Council permitted this develop-ment immediately adjacent to a site that looms large in the history of public access to beautiful places is striking. As I round the south-east corner of the site, I am confined to a strip of land little wider than a footpath, hedge behind and a barbed-wire fence in front. Brooding on these issues, I don't notice immediately how wide the cumulus hangs, how azure the sky and how thickly the woodland of the Weald ribbons the land below to the far horizon. It's transfixing.

Chartwell, Winston Churchill's former house, also in the hands of the National Trust, sits below the hill. The café serves coq au vin, cooked to Churchill's favourite recipe, and tasty though it is, I can't quite believe this is the real thing. A pint of champagne might be the missing accompaniment. I have a quick look around the house and garden, conscious all the time that I need to press on. Iain Sinclair's mordant description of the place – and Churchill's watercolours – can't be beaten, though I feel more generous-spirited than he.[62]

The walk to Toys Hill passes through an interesting mix of woodland and field, though the path running around the northern perimeter of Chartwell is exceptionally narrow: a wooden fence on one side, a wire fence on the other – interstitial again. Toys Hill itself is a good patch of woodland and common, mostly acquired by the National Trust over the course of the twentieth century through a mix of donation and purchase. The viewpoint itself and four adjacent cottages were donated in May 1895 by Mr and Mrs Richardson Evans in memory of their nephew Frederick Feeney. A site of just 0.23 hectares, its importance far outweighed its size in this pioneering phase of the Trust's history. A now familiar story was told about the acquisition. The membership had long 'desired that it should secure one of the headlands of Kent and Surrey overlooking the Weald, and commanding a view of the hills, as these promontories are being rapidly purchased for building and enclosed'.[63] Active management, however, was needed if the site was to fulfill its full social potential. Hill wanted to address overcrowding in the cottages, and she wondered if two further cottages ('much needed') could be built on the plot. She also planned to donate a well to Toys Hill village and to create a fenced terrace with a seat ('like the places one sees abroad – projecting terraces to see a view').[64] The decision to build a well and place a memorial stone at the site recording that the land was given as a memorial to Mr Feeney did more than just record a debt and a purpose. At the Trust's 1898 AGM, the acquisition of Toys Hill was presented as the first example of the Trust's idea that memorials might now take the form of beautiful scenery or land commanding beautiful views preserved for the public.[65]

These hopes were not misplaced. The Trust acquired the remainder of the site 45 years later. Although sometimes misremembered as being a gift by the Earl of Stanhope, the site was in fact acquired by purchase thanks to a substantial bequest.[66] The story goes something like this. In 1905, the Earl of Stanhope (a staunch Tory) gave the site to his youngest son, Philip Stanhope (1847–1923), later 1st Baron Weardale, sometime Liberal MP, peacenik, internationalist, pioneering supporter and president of the Save the Children Fund, and opponent of women's suffrage. In 1906, Philip built a 145-room mock Tudor mansion named Weardale Manor on the site – Stanhope is a village in Weardale, County Durham – from where he and his wife, Countess Alexandra Tolstoy (1856–1934), entertained in some style during the summer season. Although this was the kind of private development Hill chafed against, in 1914, and in rather obscure circumstances, Philip donated an exhausted gravel pit now used as a car park, but it took a more significant bequest to bring the whole site into the ownership of the Trust.[67]

When Philip died without an heir, ownership reverted to the Earl. Soon after, the Countess supervised the sale of the house contents, including Chippendale and Louis XVI furniture, in a six-day public sale – such sales often fascinated the general public – and the house was left to decay, succumbing to wet and dry rot, bad plumbing, and neglect.[68] It had once been 'difficult to imagine a more charming spot', but by 1930 Weardale Manor stood as a 'most melancholy example of the vanity of human desires'.[69] Redemption came in 1937, when William Alexander Robertson, barrister of the Inner Temple, made the kind of grand gesture Hill had encouraged. He left the Trust close to £50,000 in memory of his brothers killed during the Great War for the acquisition of sites within easy reach of London. Norman Cairns Robertson was killed in action during the Battle of the Somme in July 1916 and Laurence Grant Robertson in a German military hospital as a prisoner of war in April 1917.[70] The Trust duly embarked on a spending spree across south-east England, evidenced by obelisk memorials to the Robertson brothers erected at Dunstable Downs, Frensham Common, Sharpenhoe Clappers, The Devil's

Punchbowl, Hydon's Ball and Heath, Netley Park, Birling Gap and, yes, Toys Hill, where three cottages and 71 acres were acquired for £6,200 in collaboration with the Countryside Trust Ltd.[71] Much about the Toys Hill transaction characterised the fate of grand country houses made economically unviable by changing times. A big house demolished, its building materials sold off in local sales and the land sold on. There's little doubt Stanhope benefited from the Trust's peculiar commitment to this stretch of land. Some terracing and a water tower, converted into a bat hibernaculum, are all that now recall Lord Weardale's pre-war hubris.[72]

The walk from Toys Hill to Ide Hill through the Octavia Hill Woodlands (donated to the National Trust by Sevenoaks District Council in 1981) and Scords Wood (purchased by the Trust for £500 from Charles Hoskins Master in 1921) is fascinating.[73] Scords Wood had been part of Henden Manor since the thirteenth century, enjoying a rather chequered history during the tyranny of Henry VIII, and since changing hands several times. Master's donation preceded his decision to sell the remainder of the estate in 1926; later owners included film producer Sir Michael Balcon, credited with giving Alfred Hitchcock his directorial break, and Robert Spear Hudson, Churchill's Minister of Agriculture during the Second World War, who led the 'Dig for Victory' campaign (he set a good example and dug up the garden); today, the remaining land is worked as a dairy farm.[74] To fully appreciate how exciting Scords Wood is today, the pedestrian must not skirt its southern edge along the Greensand Way, but take the paths weaving through the wood's core.

Scords Wood is not ancient woodland according to the standard definition. Native woodland, rich in lime and oak, was cleared 1,000 years ago. Since then, heathland predominated and evidence suggests that from the thirteenth century the Brasted Chart villagers exercised rights of pannage, gathered peat and firewood and quarried chert for their roads and buildings. After enclosure, it was managed for beech on the crest and coppiced oak on its slopes, crops harvested for firewood and use in charcoal manufacture. From the 1930s, the wood was left to its own devices until the great storm of October 1987. About 90 per cent of the woodland was damaged, going from almost closed canopy to just 2 per cent cover; about 5 per cent of the ground was upturned by fallen trees. In general, public pressure to 'repair the damage done' by the storm persuaded the government to incentivise the clearance of fallen trees with bulldozers and burning, followed by replanting. Elsewhere on Toys Hill this approach compacted the soil and caused erosion, encouraging the widespread establishment of dense birch thickets. Scords was treated differently. And this was not a matter of chance. We know much about the history of Scords because prior to the storm the site had already been studied by scientists at King's College, London.[75] In the light of the storm, their work took on new significance. As their research had established, to return the character of the woodland to its pre-storm condition would be to restore a neglected relic of nineteenth-century commercial forestry.

Instead, the National Trust has allowed 50 acres of Scords to respond naturally to the calamity. Dead trees and still living fallen trees were left in place – crowns of fallen trees covered nearly a quarter of the ground. Willowherb and foxglove quickly colonised what had previously been unvegetated leaf litter, for they do well on bared acid soil and well-lit conditions. By the fourth growing season, birch seedlings and holly had established itself, fungi and invertebrates were thriving on deadwood, and hard fern was making the most of the root pits. By the 11th growing season, most fallen trees were dead, brambles grown over the crowns, and bracken was dominant, but beech had sprouted, a spindly oak or two had established itself, and on open ground birch was vigorous – some 700 saplings were counted in 1999. English Nature's conclusions left no room for uncertainty:

It is now clear that woodland regeneration has established well in areas left to natural development, and that here the small-scale mixture of habitats, including closed birch thickets, bramble-filled open spaces, piles of decaying dead trunks and crowns, and the few sprouting pollards and trees and other native tree regeneration, represents a far superior wildlife habitat and at no cost.[76]

In 2017, on the 30th anniversary of the storm, the National Trust claimed a success. Having embraced decay as 'an integrated part of life', it celebrated the diversity of Toys Hill as 'a mosaic of different habitats', as a place of 'light and shade', now thriving thanks to how 'nature is self-destructive and self-healing at the same time'.[77] For much of Britain's woodlands, October 1987 was a missed opportunity, not so Scords Wood, where a form of self-willed nature has taken hold. What Hill would have made of the regeneration of the wood we can only guess, but the transition from cultivated beech to natural-growth birch woodland carries its own historical significance. This is not the restoration of 'native' woodland – that has been gone for 1,000 years and will remain so – but instead the creation of a new, ecologically rich habitat. Birch is likely to become less predominant, as oak and other species become more established, but not all of this future is predictable. And it is for this reason, modest though these 50 acres are, that they feel so alive. Here all is tangled, understorey thrives, trees grow not in stands, regimented into compartments, but where they take hold; this is woodland before forestry, messy, chatty, a class before teacher arrives. I tear myself away, over-stimulated, for there is one more promontory to see.

If the subsequent acquisition of land by the National Trust at Mariners Hill and Toys Hill transformed these places from relatively modest plots with spectacular viewpoints into extensive woodlands, Ide Hill retains something of its original character. It is relatively isolated and, according to the Woodland Trust, does constitute an ancient woodland, albeit significantly diminished by the 1987 storms.[78] As the National Trust Council reported in 1899, the 15-acre site and timber had been offered for sale at £1,750 and Miranda Hill committed to buy it on the understanding that the Trust would raise the money to buy it from her. 'The importance of preserving this beautiful hillside for the public use,' insisted the Trust once again, 'in a district which is rapidly becoming suburban, cannot be exaggerated.'[79] A year later, Lucy Fowler and Mrs Wharvie stumped up the cash.[80] Another relative of Hill and another greensand location provides the postscript to this tale. One Tree Hill, the other side of Sevenoaks, was named after a solitary hornbeam said to be visible from the English Channel. It was a part of Lord Derby's Tonbridge Estate. Negotiations lasted several months before, in 1911, Dr and Mrs Jameson Hurry of Reading were able to present the site to the Trust in memory of Alderman Arthur Hill, Mrs Hurry's father, four times mayor of Reading, and a half-brother of Hill.[81]

This annotated walk through the Hill Country Archipelago provides much evidence of how the confluence of familial attachment, political commitment and moral suasion – perhaps pressure – generated the rights of access enjoyed today. Such a phrase, 'rights of access enjoyed today', might sound a little bland, pietistic even, and a degree of discomfort might be felt about the debt owed to a group of privileged Victorians and their descendants. But it must now be clear that this walk can only be taken because of their actions. This pattern is repeated throughout the English landscape. Small beginnings, scraps of land acquired here and there, have acted as a starter. Designated long-distance footpaths, like the Greensand Way, are a case in point. Originating in a pragmatic stitching together of existing footpaths and often hard-won new rights of way, they chart apparently immutable ways through, their naming conventions creating new ways of imagining the landscape. They make encounters with landscape legible in terms of time and distance, guaranteeing freedoms that are linear and interstitial, measured in days to come or miles to go. Had I not briskly doubled back through the evening sunshine with my scribbled notes and photos, I could have continued east along the Greensand Way – it's 108 miles long – leaving the Hill

Country Archipelago behind but continuing to move through another complex landscape sequence. To understand these sequences, their historicity needs to be grasped. Ancient rights are preserved and new rights created because individuals made choices. Every permissive footpath opened or closed represents just such a choice. Hill's writings, and the historical context in which she wrote, provide a good place to start thinking about why these choices have been made and continue to be.

Arguments

In 1875, Hill became publicly committed to the Open Spaces movement. She joined the Commons Preservation Society (CPS; established 1865), remaining a member as it became first the Commons and Footpaths Preservation Society and then the Commons, Open Spaces and Footpaths Preservation Society, name changes which reflected the broadening and interlinking of the multiple agendas at work in the Open Spaces movement. Two developments that summer occasioned her first significant public interventions in the Open Spaces debate. Swiss Cottage Fields came up for sale and Richard Cross, Benjamin Disraeli's Home Secretary, placed his Artisans' and Labourers' Dwellings Improvement bill before parliament.

Swiss Cottage Fields was an area of open country just north of Marylebone and Paddington and close to Hill's housing projects. Hill's failed attempt to raise the £10,000 needed to buy the fields taught her an important lesson. Subsequent land purchase campaigns she helped orchestrate were launched only after a firm agreement was reached with the vendor to sell at an agreed price within an agreed timescale. Knocked by the Swiss Cottage Fields disappointment, she wrote privately of her decision to make the provision of 'small central spaces' her immediate priority, but in practice the defeat fired her enthusiasm for later campaigns to keep Parliament Hill, Hampstead Heath, Epping Forest and the commons of Wandsworth,

Tooting and Barnes open to the public and free from development.[82] The case she made for the purchase of Swiss Cottage Fields established a set of arguments she clung to in future decades as the scale of her ambitions grew, extending from London's immediate environs to charismatic landscapes further afield, as her focus shifted from the immediate needs of the poorest to a more general advocacy of the national benefits of public access to open spaces.

Richard Cross's bill was a response to the government-commissioned report 'Dwellings of the Poor', which was strongly influenced by the Charity Organisation Society (COS). Hill was a staunch member and subsequently advised on the bill's drafting and fed debating points to sympathetic MPs.[83] The Act made cheap loans available so local authorities could buy and demolish slum dwellings for development by commercial builders. Commonly regarded as central to Disraeli's social or 'One Nation' Conservative agenda, the Act delivered on commitments made at his famous Manchester and Crystal Palace speeches in 1872 and during the general election of 1874. Although some historians see 'more style than substance' in Disraeli's social policy, Jon Parry argues that the bill reflected 'the now-standard concerns of the moralistic middle classes who were seeking gestures to integrate the working man into the political system and ways to elevate his character and improve national efficiency, without challenging the foundations of the Victorian economy. In that sense, social legislation emerged out of a parliamentary and civil servant consensus.'[84] Responding to shifts in public opinion with modest but high-profile policy initiatives that enabled market mechanisms to deliver social goods is, of course, a typical Conservative tactic. Note Parry's characterisation of the legislation as a gesture. But with respect to the development of Hill's agenda, it was her linkage of Conservative legislation to the strongly liberal agenda of the Commons Preservation Society that was most significant to the development of her ideas.[85]

Hill directed her arguments to the middle-class liberal readers of *Macmillan's Magazine*. Like the *Cornhill* (established 1860), *Macmillan's*

(1859) typified the new generation of shilling monthlies that, following the abolition of the Stamp Act in 1854, broadened the readership for essayistic commentary on current affairs. At first glance, Hill's 'Space for the People' does not seem a particularly effective piece of campaigning literature. The threat to Swiss Cottage Fields is mentioned late in the essay and Hill's opening observations did not point towards a call for action. This indirect structure, however, allowed her to present her argument through affective reportage. To readers cognisant of the need for housing, and particularly sanitary housing for London's poor, building terraced housing on Swiss Cottage Fields was not obviously a bad thing. Hill therefore built her case gradually, developing her defence of Swiss Cottage Fields as open space by drawing on her experience as a housing reformer. She recalled times she had spent in dark, cramped, overcrowded slum housing, of back-yards that left her longing to 'pull down the flat blank wall darkening the small rooms' or to push it back to 'leave a little space for drying clothes, for a small wash-house, for the barrow to stand'. This is subtly gendered, of course, foregrounding the needs of housewives, and affec-tive in the sentimental emphasis it places on the difference just a little more space makes.

Hill explained that the social cost of confining London's working class to cramped, poorly ventilated housing was most visible on a hot summer's evening. Nearly every 'inmate' is driven outdoors, babies and children are everywhere, like an infestation, and 'the drinking is wildest, the fighting fiercest, and the language most violent'. As a visitor of refined sensibility and richness of experience, she felt things apparently denied to the men and women of the poorest neighbour-hoods. The light of the setting sun glancing across a red chimney pot invoked the 'sad thought of the fair and quiet places far away, where it is falling softly on tree, and hill, and cloud'. Places to sit, places to walk, and places where children could play were needed. The 'healing gift of space', Hill felt sure, would do more for these unfortunate people than any amount of philanthropic work among them.[86]

Hill demonstrated this by picturing Swiss Cottage Fields in bucolic terms as a 'green hilly peninsula', entered through 'a little white gate', where 'hundreds of working people' took their ease at the weekend, either walking there or taking a cheap short ride on the railway. These working people were probably not slum-dwellers, for she thought the shaming effect of poverty ensured the poor were 'shy of a neatly dressed public', but her description of Swiss Cottage Fields made an affecting contrast with conditions in the slum. She naturalised the behaviour of working people as 'spread over the green open space like a stream that has just escaped from between rocks', just as in other cases she described certain kinds of behaviour as almost instinctive, before offering a touching description of a family, and especially the mother, finding in natural surroundings the 'healing gift of space'. 'They just sit down on the grass; the baby grabs at the daisies, the tiny children toddle about, or tumble onto soft grass, the mother's arms are rested, and there she sits till it is time to return.' These vital moments of tranquillity were threatened by 'Acres of villas!'[87]

Hill's representation of Swiss Cottage Fields as a site of healthy recreation reflected changes in the lobbying position adopted by the Commons Preservation Society in the 1870s. Initially the CPS sought to prevent enclosure by using legal means to assert rights of common, and it successfully contested a string of enclosure attempts, sometimes by persuading the courts that apparently obsolete rights still had legal standing. These moves could be combined with direct action, as when Earl Brownlow forcibly enclosed 434 acres of Berkhamsted Common in 1866 by erecting two miles of iron fences. The CPS contracted 122 navvies to come up from London to tear them down, to the delight of the watching crowd. In the subsequent court hearing, the CPS won its case partly by establishing that the residents of nearby Northchurch had common rights, effectively imposing an injunction on any future attempt to enclose.[88]

It was soon evident that rights of common provided a limited basis for guaranteeing rights of public access. Rights of common applied to specific rights holders, usually holders of property adjacent to or near to the common, which did not grant rights of access to the public at large. And where customary rights of access to commons existed, a lord of the manor who wanted to enclose land needed only to have the enclosure commissioners dissolve the common rights with compensation paid, there being no legal protection for customary rights of access. Consequently, from the mid-1870s, the parliamentary lobbying of the CPS emphasised less the protection or restoration of traditional rights of common and more the present and future social benefits conferred by maintaining open space. This shift in emphasis had two more immediate basic causes and a consequence. First, the CPS bridled at the accusation that their tactics were disingenuous. As critics claimed, the organisation was not principally concerned with protecting pastoral uses of the common but wished to establish the public's use of the land as an interest that deserved protection under the law. The CPS believed the public who made use of land for recreational purposes should be recognised as a legitimate interest in any process that might lead to a change in use or prevent customary access: a claim that remains contentious today and, to anticipate an argument made later in this book, a claim that granted the general public *locus standi* – that is, a legitimate interest – with respect to decisions that would affect access to common land. Second, the CPS could not afford to protect common rights on the basis of the market valuation of land. In short, legal protections were needed because funds raised by the CPS could not compete with those at the disposal of house builders seeking to buy out the rights of the semi-rural poor.[89]

This shift in priorities also reflected the nervousness of the CPS when faced by lower-class attempts to resist the dissolution of common rights (and the right to assembly), particularly when the authorities had embarked on a park-making initiative.[90] An emblematic example was the battle fought over Mousehold Heath, an upland on the northeast outskirts of Norwich and adjacent to the 'slum suburb' of

Pockthorpe. For centuries, the people of Pockthorpe had quarried sand, gravel and stone from the heath and, from 1849, they established small brick-making concerns. In the 1860s, drawing on a powerful tradition of organised radicalism, they saw off an attempt by Norwich town council to turn the heath into a public park, but in 1883, when suburbanising pressures were greater, a chancery hearing found in the favour of the city and the heath was enclosed in 1884. The heath was landscaped, footpaths were laid, and evidence of the use of the common by the Pockthorpe commoners were removed, making for an accessible yet aesthetically pleasing 'wild and rugged' place.[91] We do not know if Hill extended her universe of obligation to the commoners of Pockthorpe, but it is hard to imagine she opposed the transformation of the heath into a managed and regulated public park. To take another example, it is unlikely she felt much sympathy for the leadership provided by the Irish radical John de Morgan and his plebeian Commons Protection League during the popular conflict over the enclosure of Plumstead Common during July 1876.[92]

As these examples suggest, it seems likely Hill wanted to demonstrate the respectability of Open Space politics. This was reinforced by the centrality to her sense of environmental justice of the Christian notion that God had granted open space as a 'common gift to man'.[93] When this is not 'easily inherited', she wrote, 'it may be given by the state, the city, the millionaire, without danger of destroying the individual's power and habit of energetic self-help'.[94] And if Hill's politics are to be understood, the crucial distinction she made between inherited, communal rights and individual responsibility must be grasped. A happy life, to which all responsible citizens had a right, was possible for the poor of the city if it could be lived between collective and private spaces. The home, whether rented or owned, must be treated as an 'individual possession', for which the occupier was privately responsible, but the park or common was a 'common inheritance' that 'may be given without pauperising'.[95] If clear boundaries were maintained between the private and public domain, the public goods to which the people had a right could be delivered without creating welfare dependency, the quintessential fear of Victorian liberals. Just as she believed it was justifiable to evict tenants who did not pay their rent or look after their homes according to her exacting standards, so too she believed all members of the community had rights of access to open space.

In future interventions, Hill tended to emphasise voluntary action and individual moral responsibility, but in 'Space for the People' she clearly identified the state as a legitimate agent. It could deliver forms of restorative justice that would compensate the working classes of London for their lost inheritance. In doing so, she also recognised that voluntarist principles created a tension between the immediate desires of the activist and far-reaching social action. To bring about the 'refor-mation of our poorest people', the middle classes should be ready to both fight for their own patch – in her case, Swiss Cottage Fields – and take up causes on behalf of people poorly equipped to defend or establish their rights. The inability of the urban poor to fully recognise their own rights was a symptom of their degraded position, which made it incumbent on the middle classes to expand their universe of obligation towards those who could know little better. If, as Hill believed, all felt the nervous anxiety generated by modern urban life, the means of escape should not be the privilege of the few, but the right of the many, and to guarantee that right was to fulfil God's will:

> Our lives in London are over-crowded, over-excited, over-strained. This is true of all classes; we all want quiet; we all want beauty for the refreshment of our souls. Sometimes we think of it as a luxury, but when God made the world, He made it very beau-tiful, and meant that we should live amongst its beauties, and that they should speak peace to us in our daily lives.[96]

It is not clear whether she ever reconciled her rights-based argu-ments with the principle of personal responsibility. When the

Artisans' Dwelling Act was criticised for anticipating the replacement of slum housing with single-room homes, Hill was quick to defend an architectural strategy that provided the means for the poor to extend the size of their homes as their capacity to do so increased.

> As their habits and means improve, they will be able to take two, or even three rooms close to each other, and opening on to the same passage. If for the present the narrowness of their means, or their imperfect civilization, lead them to be content with one room only, surely it is a distinct gain that this one room should be clean, light, dry, and airy, instead of dark, close, and dilapidated?[97]

In absolute terms, Hill's relativist position can hardly be gainsaid but placing 'habits and means', or 'civilization' and 'means' into a position of equivalence made a larger moral claim, for here she fell back on the shibboleth that an individual's status in life, and more crudely their wealth or material comfort, was as determined by their character as by structural factors largely outside of their control. There was nothing particularly unusual about this belief. As was rather mordantly said of COS stalwart Helen Bosanquet's *The Strength of the People: A Study in Social Economics* (1902), it 'is a long sermon on the importance of character in making one family rich and another poor'.[98]

That said, Hill's commitment to philanthropic work meant that she accepted that the market economy did not necessarily reward virtue. If this failing created an obligation to provide charity rather than universalist state provision, to make charity conditional on virtue made private citizens like Hill the arbiters of what constituted a virtuous life. Crucial, however, was her belief that changing the environment could have a reformatory effect on the individual, what some scholars describe as 'associationist psychology',[99] a reminder that she did not see the moral condition of any individual as absolute or fixed. All had the potential to live better lives. During the parliamentary debates on the 1875 bill, Ughtred Kay-Shuttleworth MP quoted her view that slum clearance would diminish levels of criminality by literally breaking up 'those nests of thieves'. It was not, however, a simple matter of disrupting criminal space. According to Hill, the 'near presence of honest respectable neighbours makes habitual thieving impossible; just as dirty people are shamed into cleanliness when scattered among ordinary decent folk, and brought into the presence of light'.[100] Just as Hill believed art could have a morally uplifting effect, so too might the beautiful example of honest people; no meaningful distinction could be drawn between the religious and literal connotations of 'the presence of light'. Honest folk, like the men and women taking their ease on Swiss Cottage Fields, did not hide away. Open Space was happy, healthy and honest, Open Space exercises a positive effect on the bad.

Similar thinking was evident across a range of initiatives that caught Hill's attention. She attended the 'drawing-room meeting' in June 1876 during which Sir Charles Trevelyan promoted the idea that 'boarding out' (i.e. fostering) orphan pauper children, otherwise subject to the degraded environment of the workhouse, would improve them 'morally, physically, and mentally', advantaging the ratepayer by reducing pauperism and 'the State in adding to the wealth producers'.[101] In December 1881, she struck a similar note, explaining that the purposes of the Metropolitan Association of Befriending Young Servants was to help young women recently out of the workhouse 'with inherited defects of character and constitu-tion, and in which her tendencies have been repressed by necessary discipline' to meet 'the trials of life', particularly in domestic service.[102] Similarly, as a key instigator of the Southwark Cadet Corps, she was a signatory to a report cited by the National Rifle Association in February 1890. As the report explained, for 'working lads between the ages of 12 and 17' the 'effect of order and discipline on the lads has been surprising – rough, unruly, and unmanageable boys have become orderly, obedient, and well-behaved, and employers of labour testify to the benefit the lads derive from habits of discipline'.[103]

The circularity of these arguments is evident. If Hill was in the position to dispense charity, this must be a measure of her own good character and hence her qualification to judge the character of others and thus dispense charity. Altruism, where means allowed, was inherent to good character. It is easy to imagine why this notion of character could generate considerable anxiety among the Victorian privileged. Is my material comfort and position in life a just reflection of my character?[104] Equally, it can be seen why charity or philanthropy came to be considered an inadequate response to the enormity of the challenge posed by poverty. As social critics began to favour explanations of poverty that emphasised structural rather than moral causes, so the impersonal redistributive capacity of the state came to be seen to offer a solution to the basic unfairness of society. Social democracy was thus born out of the failures of liberal capitalism and the limitations of late Victorian philanthropy. Access to open space became an aspect of this turn to interventionism, of which the establishment of the National Trust in the 1890s was a stage in that development, though clearly not its full realisation. This, though, is to get ahead of the argument. It is now clear that Hill was convinced that (1) the environment could have a reformatory effect, (2) that the respectable poor had right to access open spaces, and (3) that the privileged were duty-bound to help provide this. In her next significant intervention, Hill added a crucial addition to her battery of arguments. The middle classes had to learn to see that the failure to adhere to middle-class behavioural norms by the respectable poor did not abrogate their rights.

Hill's 'Our Common Land', again published by *Macmillan's*, immediately registered this shift in emphasis. Whereas 'Space for the People' constructed working people as other, 'Our Common Land' was integrationist, questioning whether the social distinctions structuring Victorian social life were conducive to the common good. Aspects of her argument were derived from the legal work of George Shaw-Lefevre MP, long-time chair of the Commons Preservation

Society, but again she set the scene by drawing on her own observations, this time scenes witnessed in and around London on spring or summer bank holidays.

Bank holidays were still a novelty, having been legislated for by Gladstone's Liberal government in 1871. Time off on Easter Monday, Whit Monday, the first Monday in August and Boxing or St Stephen's Day were part of a growing culture of leisure stemming from regularised working hours. For the working classes, bank holidays complemented holy days and, since the Factory Act of 1850, the Saturday half-day, whereas for the middle classes long weekends were becoming a pleasant addition to the growing habit of taking longer annual holidays. Characteristically, Hill drew attention to the fact that bank holidays required that some public servants– especially the police – remained on duty in order to maintain regulated public spaces, while those likely to profit from the holiday trade were open for business.

Hill opened boldly. She admitted that 'few persons who have a choice of holidays' would choose to travel or take a 'stroll in the country' on a bank holiday because the mass exodus from London made conditions so unpleasant. 'Choice' was the key modifier here, immediately challenging the reader – as we would now say – to check their privilege. The roads were 'crowded with every description of vehicle', and 'every kind of public conveyance', including the railways, was full beyond capacity. Epping Forest could attract crowds of 50,000 people on a 'reasonably fine' Sunday.[105] But as Hill developed her case, it became clear that she did not intend to reify as absolute the different subjectivities of the middle-class reader and the working-class holidaymaker but to show that the holidaying masses of London took to the countryside on bank holidays to meet the same needs that compelled the middle classes hither at other times. Hill sought to help the middle-class reader see beyond quotidian behaviour it did not like towards the wider significance of the day. Whereas the liberal theorist J.S. Mill questioned whether the individual might be stirred to act against selfish inclinations by the idea of a universal but disembodied humanity,[106] Hill provided gentle instruction in the art of imaginative sympathy as a basis for social action.

> Yet in spite of all this, and in spite of the really bad sights to be seen at every public house on the road; in spite of the wild songs and boisterous behaviour, and reckless driving home at night, which show how sadly intoxication is still bound up with the idea and practical use of a holiday to hundreds of our people, how much intense enjoyment the day gives! how large a part of this enjoyment is unmixed good![107]

To truly see the 'swarming' quality of the crowd, 'undisciplined' and not 'always the gentlest or most refined', was to see that it was 'heartily happy'. Children 'untiringly' ran around; fathers 'affectionately' brought their wives 'a pot of ale' and their children 'sweetmeats'; 'great rough lads' with 'round, honest faces', who had walked long distances along dusty roads, 'beamed with rough mirth at every joke'. Again, she was particularly sensitive of the need working women, especially mothers, had for rest. Come evening and the journey home, a supervisory presence was maintained by 'the quiet figure of the mounted policeman' who kept a 'very tolerable order'. The inebriated working classes retained their respect for his authority. The open spaces of the bank holiday were quite rightly regulated space.

Hill's description was redolent of innumerable sentimental prints of lower-class Victorian life, but her purpose was not just to move her readers with a condescending evocation of Victorian working-class vitality, but to generate in them the 'imaginative sympathy' necessary if they were to contemplate the significance of those few hours spent in open space and the effort expended in getting there. Here Hill drew on broader currents at work in mid-Victorian society, influenced by Adam Smith's *The Theory of Moral Sentiment* (1759) and, more immediately, Ruskin's famous adage that 'The greatest thing a human soul ever does in this world is to see something, and tell what it saw in a plain way'.[108] 'To us,' Hill wrote, 'the Common or forest look indeed crowded with people, but to them the feeling is one of sufficient space, free air, green grass, and colour, with a life without which they might think the place dull.' To understand how conditions the middle class might find oppressive generated such pleasure, Hill urged her readers to adopt a relativist perspective. The working classes lived in cramped conditions in narrow streets; on entering the open spaces of forest or common they 'expand into free uncrowded space'. Once again, Hill identified herself as one of her readers, presenting the working classes as a single entity, almost a phenomenon of natural science, a homogenised 'them' to the individuals constituting 'us', the 'persons' who choose to avoid Epping Forest on a bank holiday. But then she steps away from the reader, takes up the position of intermediary, and reminds the reader that agency lay with them: 'Every atom of open space you have left to these people is needed; take care you lose none of it; it is becoming yearly of more vital importance to save or increase it.'[109]

The consequences that might stem from the failure to adhere to Hill's injunction is left unsaid, for a partial solution was potentially to hand. Hill's immediate concern, to which these reflections were preliminaries, was her judgement that the bill currently making its progress through parliament needed amendment. The bill was intended to encourage lords of the manor to permit public access to commons by making provision for its regulation. This provision was more significant than it might at first sound. As Hill argued, following current CPS thinking, protecting customary rights of access could be an effective means of securing their object of maintaining access, whereas to defend 'obsolete, ... often nearly valueless, customs' had little intrinsic value. Access campaigners, she argued, should place the defence of rights of access on 'its real grounds': it was 'for the sake of the health and enjoyment of the people, that the conscience of the nation supports the attempt to keep them open'.[110] As Hill warmed to her theme, she emphasised the linkages between nation, patriotism and 'native' rights, warning that as a small number of landowners accumulated an ever-larger proportion of the nation's land – she cited evidence that 710 persons owned a quarter of the land of England – she feared the patriotic sentiment of ordinary people would weaken. Privatising the 'common inheritance of us all as English men and women', she argued, undermined national unity. Note her deliberate inclusion of women. She asked if the absorption of smallholdings by large landowners and the passing of yeoman farmers diminished the sense that 'our people ... have any share in the soil of their native England', but ultimately she struck a more radical note, insisting that the more the land was held in common, the 'healthier' the individual and the greater the cohesion of the nation.[111]

The 1876 bill was a classic example of permissive legislation. It empowered but it did not compel, and Hill was concerned that the bill gave the lord of the manor little incentive to make provisions that would limit the future developmental potential of the land. Moral suasion, it seemed, would not always deliver necessary public goods. Hence she wanted the bill to be amended so that all future enclosures of common land would require the sanction of a dedicated parliamentary committee. The bill also made provision for urban sanitary authorities to purchase or receive as a gift the common rights of any suburban common, allowing them to be kept open to the public. This provision was promising but again Hill foresaw problems. The bill defined a suburban common as lying within six miles of a town of 5,000 inhabitants. This was no longer sufficient. Rapid expansion of the railway system had made commons of 20 miles distant accessible by day-trippers, transforming what constituted a town's hinterland. The boisterous bank holiday journeys to the 'open spaces' at Epping, Richmond, Wimbledon and Hampstead evoked by Hill might still have been largely reached by travelling *from* rather than *through* London, but she was acutely conscious of how rapidly London's geographies and its spatial politics were being reshaped.[112]

It is not a banal anachronism to highlight the difference between then and now. Hill's sense of impending change was central to her politics: like all Victorians alert to the consequences of Victorian dynamism, she had a strongly relativist sense of time and space.[113] She understood that the needs of Londoners could not and never had been fully met by the city's built footprint. As the population of the city grew, leading to higher concentrations of people in poorer areas and demands for new housing by the expanding middle class, the pressure on the city's 'open spaces', a phrase at this point still used casually by Hill, could only grow, taking on ever greater political significance. Thus Hill's preoccupation with the needs of the poor was increasingly joined by her awareness of how the growing desire of the professional middle class to own country homes in the city's hinterlands was closing land off from the relatively mobile lower-middle class. Is the 'privilege of space, and light, and air, and beauty', she asked, deploying a Ruskinian lexicon she was fast making her own, 'not to be considered for the small shopkeeper, for the hard-working clerk, who will probably never own a square yard of English land, but who cares to take his wife and children into the country for a fortnight in the summer?'. Where once the holidaymaker could walk on the commons, Hill asked, were they to be now confined to 'straight roads between hedges?'. Not only did the privatisation of common land deny people access to open spaces, but new developments in the suburbanised countryside reproduced the depressing characteristics of the city. The darkening effect of high walls and tall buildings in the city, so essential to Hill's repertoire of urban misery, was now echoed in the new hedgerows of privatised countryside, while straightened roads destroyed the natural irregularity so pleasing to romantic sensibilities.

A decade later, Hill amplified some of these views in a lecture delivered to the Kyrle Society. Established in 1876 by Miranda Hill, Hill's younger sister, and named after the philanthropist John Kyrle, the 'Man of Ross' eulogised by Alexander Pope, who bequeathed his birthplace as a public park, the Kyrle Society was predicated on a simple proposition: if the poor and the destitute could not be brought to beauty, beauty should be brought to them. Hill acted as the society's treasurer. Although hampered by poor organisation, provincial branches conducted valuable philanthropic work and, in conjunction with the Commons Preservation Society, the society's members worked hard to promote the Open Spaces agenda.[114] Hill's Kyrle lecture, 'Colour, Space, and Music for the People' provides useful insight into the activities of the Kyrle Society, particularly Hill's commitment to repurposing disused burial grounds as public parks, but it is perhaps most striking as a stark expression of the limits of her radicalism.[115] Her argument was predicated on a notional common humanity, and once again she repeatedly invited her readers to see their needs and expectations in terms of the lives of the poor, explaining that the public spaces shaping the lives of the poor, depicted as grim and miserable, should be understood as equivalent to the private spaces of middle-class domesticity. If the former were no less essential to the lives of the poor than the latter were to middle-class contentment, their condition should be a question of public concern. At the same time, she naturalised wealth disparity, suggesting its attendant poverty could only be mitigated by charitable efforts – the purpose of the Kyrle Society – rather than fundamentally challenged. What she thought might be done for the poor now seems breathtakingly limited.

Hill's argument was fundamentally religious. She distinguished aspects of life that give joy into primary and secondary gifts. First among the primary gifts is the 'loving guidance' and 'near presence of a Father', and for those who know how 'a thought of God transcends all sorrow and subdues all fear, the idea of there being *any* life which need be forlorn sounds strange'. The second great primary gift is family ties, a 'blessing' available to 'every man and woman who enters into the inheritance of love by the fulfilment of duty'. These claims were more than simple, homiletic pieties; they are fundamental to Hill's conviction that family duty and happiness are inextricably intertwined, making a fulfilling life open to all irrespective of their social circumstances: 'These two primary blessings, the power of entering into divine and human love, we all possess – high and low, rich and poor.'[116] Such sentiments might have satisfied an audience shaped by the moralising, individualist notions of self-help, but they were hardly an adequate response to the structural bases of poverty.

She then asks her audience to consider how 'unequally' 'secondary gifts' – 'music, colour, art, nature, space, quiet' – are 'divided', encouraging them to reflect upon the positive influence these gifts exercise over their own lives and to consider their absence in London's poor districts. She urges her audience to imagine the plight of a man injured while working in the docks. She accepted that a working man might be crippled by an accident at work and confined for life to his home or the workhouse, the employer incurring no further liability. How might those years be brightened, what might 'carry his thoughts anywhere away from his own blasted life?'[117] Pictures, perhaps, maybe a scene from Christ's life or a cottage scene reminiscent of his childhood? A scarcely credible response to such a loss, as many of Hill's contemporaries would have recognised, but note how Hill's supposition that a dockworker had enjoyed a rural childhood located him historically, making him subject to the forces of urbanisation and industrialisation transforming Britain. As the bourgeoisie suburbanised the breezy heights of an increasingly depopulated countryside, so the lower classes were sucked into London and elsewhere, their adult lives a long recession from the joys of a rural childhood. Condemned to 'the monotonous, dreary tints of the poor districts of London', the lives of working people became literally colourless, always in shadow, confined to small poorly lit rooms overlooked by high walls.

It need not be this way. Hill observes 'the effort of the prosaic English workman to procure pictures in gilt frames, wax flowers, or a red or green table cover', or how when not 'quite oppressed by toil and poverty, the father makes window-boxes for his nasturtiums, the girl puts on her bright ribbon, the mother hangs up the red curtain'. Hill sees these gestures towards colour as instinctive, answering a need to find in their lives some echo of the 'Father's bright world of beauty'. She invites her listeners to imagine their own domestic spaces stripped of colour or music and condemns indifference to the needs of those 'who show no evidence of want' as 'small and mean'.[118] 'Kindliness' only gets one so far, 'imaginative sympathy' is needed.[119] Unvoiced needs are not simply evidence of a silent stoicism in the face of want. Hill offered a more disruptive interpretation. To articulate need is a function of privilege. Hill did not describe the decision to establish the National Trust in terms of the categories established by the Kyrle lecture, but it surely attempted to correct, however modestly, the uneven distribution of 'secondary gifts'.

The National Trust

The *Times* newspaper remarked in 1887 that 'there are now almost as many Bills aiming at the preservation as at the appropriation of open spaces',[120] but despite the shift in how the Commons Preservation Society justified its priorities, it remained dependent on establishing the legal standing of existing rights. This was thrown into sharp relief by a conflict particularly congenial to the CPS that arose in the early 1880s. In 1884, Lord Sackville, owner of the Knole estate in Sevenoaks, Kent obstructed access to Knole Park. Sackville's ire was roused by the increased number of day-trippers accessing the park since the opening of the railway to Sevenoaks in 1862 and its improvement in 1868. Visitors in carriages and on horseback were particularly infuriating, though Sackville's obstructions also prevented access to perambulators and bathchairs. Crowds gathered on the nights of 18 and 19 June, tore down Sackville's new gate and staged a protest outside his house – men dressed as women pushing prams. The local constabulary was mobilised, Sackville made recourse to the law, but CPS lawyers successfully established the legal right of the people to access the park on foot. The Knole Park Bridle Road Defence Fund might have failed to have the right of way recognised as a bridleway, but Sackville could not but agree to remove new obstructions and the case established in law that he could not limit the number of visitors exercising their rights.[121]

Around this time, the CPS began to supplement largely defensive moves like the Knole case by encouraging the piecemeal acquisition of small patches of land for preservation purposes, sometimes by the CPS itself, sometimes by private citizens, all of which created an unwelcome management burden. Alleviating these pressures helped motivate Octavia Hill, Canon Hardwicke Rawnsley (another protégé of Ruskin) and Robert Hunter (a solicitor and prominent public servant who worked for the CPS) to establish the National Trust.[122] In 1884, Hunter circulated a paper on the subject, duly followed up with a meeting at James Bryce's house, but Shaw-Lefevre, not wanting to divert attention away from the CPS, poured cold water on the initiative. Hill and Hunter were drawing closer together. They founded the Kent and Surrey Committee of the CPS, more evidence of Hill's changing priorities, and when the Lodore Falls and the island of Grasmere in the Lake District came up for sale in 1893, Rawnsley headed to London convinced they needed to act. The triumvirate of Hill, Hunter and Rawnsley was in place. A meeting in November 1893 established the National Trust's provisional council.[123] Coverage of the meeting in the *Times* newspaper did not follow the dull but useful reporting convention of listing the people present and outlining the proceedings but instead gathered the material together into a short feature describing the Trust's aims before offering a broader commentary on the initiative, including a strikingly radical reading of its potential.

Devised 'to act as general trustee for all property intended for the use and enjoyment of the nation at large', the Trust would, *The Times* explained, 'accept from private owners of property gifts of places of interest or beauty, which can only be made if a perpetual custodian and administrator can be found'. Apparently 'highly commendable from a public point of view', the Trust would accept cash donations from the public and develop its capacity to raise money when 'a specially desirable bit of property' came onto the market, particularly 'to save it perhaps from the clutches of the jerry-builder'. The dig at the jerry-builder was a tad predictable. The article then broke with the Trust's position, arguing that the power of compulsory purchase could be justified if 'the public interest' could be invoked, just as it had been to enable the expansion of the railway network. Thus a new purpose for the state was imagined based on the idea that certain landscapes constituted vital infrastructure. 'We see no reason why for public purposes a bit of beautiful scenery should not be the subject of a forced sale under equitable conditions just as much as a bit of ugly country for a railway.' Preservationists, exhorted the newspaper, had to organise as effectively as the building trade; the land market had to be reimagined as a site of contestation between the private and public interests.[124] It is hard to think of a moment when the Trust itself struck as forceful a note. Compulsory purchase was off its agenda.[125]

The following July saw the inaugural meeting of the Trust. Enabled by the patronage of a large group of influential people, the meetings bore out Disraeli's assumption that no radical initiative could hope to succeed without aristocratic patronage.[126] To list those present, many of whom had been present the previous year, provides crude evidence of how the Trust's principal object – to hold property in trust on behalf of the nation – had become socially acceptable. Assembled at Grosvenor House under the presidency of the Duke of Devonshire was the Duke of Westminster, the Marquis of Dufferin and Ava, the Marquis of Ripon, the Earl of Carlisle, the Earl of Rosebery, Lord Hobhouse, George Shaw-Lefevre MP, James Bryce MP, Leonard Courtney MP, Mr Huxley, Sir Frederic Leighton, Mr Burt MP, Sir George Reid, the Master of Trinity, the Master of Balliol, the President of Magdalen, the Provost of Eton, the Principal of Owens College, Sir Henry Acland, Mr Watts RA, Mr Holman Hunt, Professor Herkomer, Professor Jobb, Mr Besant, Mrs Humphrey Ward, and others. A mix then of aristocrats, politicians, artists, heads of Oxbridge colleges, academics and a novelist, the 'intellectual aristocracy' in its full splendour.[127] The Trust enjoyed significant royal patronage. Princess Louise was the first of several royal patrons.

Hill, Rawnsley and Hunter led the charge, to the apparently vocal approval of the audience, their contributions inflected with their individual priorities or perspectives. To take the three in the order they spoke, Rawnsley hoped the Trust would establish a 'National Gallery of natural pictures'; Hill compared the organisation to 'St Francis of old' – it would be 'strong in poverty, and, like him, would ask for gifts'; Hunter hoped its properties might one day become legally 'inalienable', duly achieved by clause 21 of the National Trust Act 1907.[128] In a private letter to Sydney Cockerell, likely an attempt to collar him as secretary, Hill pondered the Trust's prospects and the nature of its work. 'I fear we want a great deal, and give next to nothing. Of course, it might grow, but then it might not. The work would be delightful to one who cared for it: all the good results of the Commons and Footpaths work, with little or no fighting.'[129] Thirty years of CPS work had left Hill and her associates seeking a less combative form of access politics.

There were reasons to be cheerful. The Light Railways Act passed by parliament two years later, although a rather obscure piece of legislation, provided intriguing evidence of the Trust's increasing political traction. The Act sought to lower the high transport costs faced by the agricultural sector by establishing a commission to enable railway construction and thereby avoid the costly private bill process.[130] This was a contentious development because it granted a body apart from parliament or the government the right to initiate the compulsory purchase of land.[131] Over the course of 1895–6, a dedicated lobby kept the pressure on the Board of Trade, the sponsoring government department, to push the bill through and, despite a packed parliamentary agenda, Arthur Balfour, the Conservative prime minister, ensured time was made for the bill and its Irish counterpart before the dissolution of parliament that summer.[132] The CPS lobbied the Board of Trade to add a clause to the bill to enable the protection of commons and open spaces. Instead, a clause was added to the Act – clause 22 – headed 'Preservation of scenery and objects of historical interest', which allowed objections to any draft order on the grounds that the undertaking would 'destroy or injure any building or other object of historical interest or injuriously affect any natural scenery'. Although the CPS declared itself satisfied with the clause, the Board of Trade's decision to adopt the language of the Trust diminished the clause's political charge by placing less emphasis on preserving rights of access to private land and more on preserving aspects of the national patrimony. Notable as the only time the phrase 'preservation of scenery' appears in British legislation, the insertion of the clause was evidence that the Conservative government did not find the agenda of the National Trust especially troubling.[133]

The significance of the Light Railways Act should not be underestimated. It was put to greater use in the towns and cities than in open country, but clause 22 goes some way towards demonstrating why in 'The Open Spaces of the Future', published in 1899, Hill attacked her theme with such confidence. Hill recalled work 'we' had done, happily claiming that much of the essential, pioneering groundwork had been laid. Vital open spaces had been preserved for the people in London, including Parliament Hill Fields, Clissold Park, Hilly Fields, Brockwell Park, The Lawn, Church Yard Bottom Wood, Golders Hill, Telegraph Hill and Epping Forest, demonstrating how Open Spaces societies, local bodies, City Parochial Charity Commissioners, the London County Council and private donors might continue the work. Similarly, numerous children's playgrounds had been provided by the London school boards, though the degree to which Hill insisted these should be closely regulated spaces now seems extraordinary. If the playground was a place of organised 'games, drill, of outdoor processions and festivals, and of gardening', she wrote, children were not 'tempted' by 'the degrading, but exciting, street'.[134]

Respects duly paid to past achievements, she could now propagate the new agenda prompted by 'the changed circumstances of modern life'.[135] Preserving larger spaces, particularly those close to London, must be attended to, for establishing formal public spaces had thrown into sharp relief the public's 'general and deep-rooted desire' for land 'preserved in its natural state'. They must cater to those who 'want a wood walk, even if it be sometimes a little muddy, who like the silence of a hill-top, and a marsh for the wild flowers, and which does not wish irregularities of slope or density of thicket smoothed away.'[136] She surely had her Kentish redoubt in mind as she considered how developments in transport and the suburbanisation of London's hinterlands meant 'unbuilt' land or 'unappropriated space' had to be secured before it was too late. Just as it was urgent to defend footpaths against enclosure, so legal means must be found to protect what gave the path value: 'the path is robbed of all its charms by the erection of high, black-pitched fences, which, though they leave the right of way, have deprived it of all its amenities'.[137]

Hill's use of the term 'amenities' to describe the public goods provided by footpaths is striking. In the twentieth century, particularly in the post-1945 years, this term became the standard way to identify rights of way, footpaths and access to open space as a service – an amenity – that the government, particularly at a local level, was obliged to provide and protect. It is more striking still that in Hill's letter of 1897, she explained that the question was less whether rights existed and more 'how the parish, district and county councils are going to fulfil the duties committed to their care as guardians of public rights'.[138] Were local authorities prepared to resist powerful interests? The middle classes, having extended their sense of civic duty towards those less able to defend their rights in the city, now must come to the defence of the rural poor, who 'have not knowledge, courage, money, or perseverance to protect the paths which were their common possession'.[139] In her letter of 1892, she wrote of her hope 'that the support of the country by South London, of the rural cottager by the suburban districts, and of both by an experienced London executive, may result in arresting the progress by which path by path, common after common, and roadside strip after strip, are being lost'.[140] This was a patriotic question: 'I think men love a country more when its woods, and fields, and streams, and flowers, and lakes and hills, and the sky that bends over them are visible.'[141] Hill came close to claiming that the remorseless advance of the propertied middle class literally diminished the material extent of the nation, but her radicalism should not be misconstrued. First, her patriotic rage against villa blight did not fundamentally challenge the rights of private property, but instead insisted that proper legal protections should be extended to existing rights; second, although she had become conscious of the needs of rural cottagers, she did not depart from the strong tendency of the CPS to see commons as amenity, caring 'little about those whose livelihood depended on the commons'.[142]

She ended this latest intervention on an upbeat note. Where the CPS contested the rights of new wealth, finding itself in perpetual conflict with house builders or landowners with capital to invest, the National Trust 'is happy in that it appeals to the generosity of men'. It could already boast holdings in Gwynedd, Cornwall, Kent and Sussex, as well as the Lake District (as discussed in the next chapter), all acquired either as gifts or through fund-raising. By taking land off the market in perpetuity, the National Trust made it 'free for all time to the step of every comer, a bit of England belonging to the English in a very special way'.[143]

The emphasis Hill now placed on wild, more natural spaces marked a departure from her established preference for managed urban parks. This reflected significant cultural shifts. Just as activists reimagined open space as Open Space, making it a political object, so too had nature become Nature, an amenity of benefit to all citizens. Still, the universalist implications of Hill's invitation to 'every comer' had its limits, and privately she looked to limit access to National Trust properties to those who had cultivated appropriate needs and sensibilities. As she explained in a notorious letter of 1903, the Trust 'by no means plan to give access to the tramp, the London rough, the noisy beanfeaster, or the shouting crowds of children, they offer no attractions for them, but plan to preserve the land in its natural beauty for the artist, the professional man, and such of the public as appreciate and respect natural beauty'.[144] She gave public expression to such thoughts, and others less attractive still, in her letter of 1891:

> Think of Kent and Surrey, the play places of our wearied Londoners – not of the rough who robs the bank of its primrose roots, but of the doctor and his wife, of the busy merchant; of these and all who, whether from Saturday to Monday at a country inn, or on a day's holiday, or for a week in small country lodgings, or daily, after their city duties, revel in beauty and quiet. Kent and Surrey are the home of many a simple English rustic, where he ekes out his low wages by having a donkey on the common, and cutting for his winter fire. How are we defending the inheritance of our land-less fellow countrymen? We are losing it, irrecoverably losing it, year by year. Only a handful of us are yet at work on the Kent and Surrey Committee of the Commons Preservation Society ... The agricultural labourers have found us out, and many a hard-earned shilling reaches us in postal orders from a village, many an illiterate but burning letter. But where are the educated workers? ... Why is all the energy to go into the slums of London, and none into the remote places from which our slums are fed; all to the free dinners and the pittance to the lazy unemployed; none to the honest rustic, who with difficulty

supports himself with the addition of fuel and pasture dependent on his common rights? How is it that the rural labourers have heard of this work, and that it has attracted so little attention from the richer country residents, or from educated Londoners?[145]

The London 'rough', 'the lazy unemployed', 'the shouting crowds of children': what could be tolerated in Epping Forest was not welcome on Hill's beloved Kent and Surrey hills. These strictures are not too surprising. Hill's politics had always been shaped by the distinction between the deserving and the undeserving poor. Given that she evicted tenants for the non-payment of rent or for anti-social behaviour, why would she think people of a similar character should be made welcome on National Trust land? It was not common land, it was not publicly owned, it was a form of private property to which the Trust could erect barriers to entry.

In her last major statement on the question, 'Natural Beauty as a National Asset' (1905), a commentary on the purposes of the National Trust and a synthesis of her own thinking, the liberal constraints that confined her radicalism remained in place even as she struck a national note. Her elitism was intact. Nominations to the Trust's governing body, she boasted, was made by the 'great artistic, learned and scientific foundations of the United Kingdom', such as the British Museum, the National Gallery and the Royal Academy, thus avoiding 'mercenary considerations', or vulgar populist imperatives.[146] She had become more expressly nationalist and Anglocentric: 'England is rich in natural beauty, and full of stately and picturesque buildings, beautiful in themselves, and recalling a great past, events and men who have made our nation what it is.'[147] And, yes, exposure to this combination of natural and national history could be 'ennobling'.[148] Her case was anti-utilitarian and she deployed the affective tropes developed in earlier essays, perhaps for the first time fully combining the Open Spaces, the Kyrle and the National Trust agendas to her characteristic blend of natural rights theory and natural theology to make the case for 'corporate action' to 'secure for all in common what each cannot provide for himself'.[149] The rights of the unpropertied had to be defended against the dynamics of the free market: 'How many there are who have no country seat, deer forest, or yacht, who in their well-earned holiday need rest and contact with nature! Forest and field, mountain and seashore are gradually passing into private hands, and being closed to the public as holiday folk increase in number.'[150]

But this was not to be the moment her rights-based argument finally embraced a fully fledged Christian Socialism. Her fear that her argument implied more than she intended is almost palpable as she fell back on familiar assurances and reified the virtues of 'a free-will offering'.[151]

Most of us are in no way urging that such purchases should lose their grace and spring and spontaneity by being made compulsory, nor, by being embodied in the nation's expenditure, press hardly on those who are struggling for absolute subsistence. We are not asking that such areas should be acquired by rate or tax, but that, by the voluntary combination of many, great and permanent possessions should be acquired for the people.[152]

Reputation

'To live here in sight of all this; to be able to point it out to his friends, to talk of it, to possess it!'[153] These are the thoughts of Soames Forsyte on first encountering Robin Hill, the site outside of London where he will build the house that will fail to save his marriage. Soames is a fictional character, the protagonist of *The Man of Property* (1906), the first volume of John Galsworthy's *The Forsyte Saga*, but it is tempting to imagine that Robin Hill is based on one of the new houses at Limpsfield. The reason for this is simple enough. *The Man of Property* is dedicated to Edward Garnett, Galsworthy's editor, and the Cearn, Garnett's 1895 Arts and Craft house at Limpsfield, was an important literary gathering place in the 1890s and 1900s.

The atmosphere at the Cearn could not have been more different than what Soames imagined for Robin Hill. Where Soames considered himself the bearer of a frugal, upstanding respectability, Garnett cultivated a rustic atmosphere of cultural experimentation and free love. Ford Madox Ford, D.H. Lawrence, Joseph Conrad and Galsworthy all stayed at the Cearn and it seems to have been particularly important to Lawrence, who worked on *The Trespasser* while there. He described the house, built by the 'smock-wearing, Fabian architect' Harrison Cowlishaw, as 'one of those new, ancient cottages'.[154] Cowlishaw married Garnett's sister Lucy and they bought Kiln Farm, at nearby Edenbridge. Limpsfield was, as Ford later put it, 'the extra-urban headquarters of the Fabian society'. Here, political exiles like the Russian Kropotkins and Stepniaks and Armenian Nazarbeks, and Fabians like Edward Pease and the Hobsons gathered, either at the Cearn or at the Champion, a converted double cottage owned by Sydney and Margaret Olivier. Olivier was very much of this world. A Fabian member of the Labour Party and a close friend of Sidney Webb, he was both closely associated with progressive causes and an employee at the Colonial Office, becoming Governor of Jamaica (1907–13) and serving as Secretary of State for India in Ramsay MacDonald's short-lived Labour government of 1924.[155] His daughters were members of Rupert Brooke's circle of ruralist skinny-dippers, dubbed by Virginia Woolf the Neo-Pagans. Daphne (1889–1950) later founded the first Steiner school in Britain, while Noël (1893–1969) inspired Brooke's 'The Hill' ('Breathless, we flung us on the windy hill, / Laughed in the sun, and kissed the lovely grass'). When Sidney and Beatrice Webb were looking for a plot of land and a cottage in the early 1920s, Pease urged them to come to Limpsfield and take the plot neighbouring his house. Instead, while teaching at a Fabian summer school at Hindhead, an early acquisition of the National Trust, Sidney Webb found Waterside Copse, near Liphook.[156]

In later years, Ford looked back on his time at Limpsfield in the 1890s with a wistful ambivalence that later became scorn. He wrote ruefully of a beardy time spent dressed in 'queer, useful or homespun clothes and boots', contrasting the late Victorian rebelliousness of those living 'among the geese, donkeys, goats and sheep of the gorse-covered commons' with the more prosaic hopes of the Edwardian years. Perhaps he was also thinking of the more rarefied daring of the Neo-Pagans, whose lives, lived through an ideal of Nature, were more decadent than they were outwardly progressive. By the 1930s, his view of his own past had hardened further still. His meeting with Conrad was the only worthwhile thing to come out of the 'mistaken search after high thinking' that took him to Limpsfield. The naïve 'agricultural enthusiasm' of his Fabian interlocutors, those cranky medievalists and back-to-basics romantics pursuing 'the life of the Intelligentsia as lived in the London suburbs', offered no meaningful or intellectually serious response to the social challenges posed by the time.[157]

Whether or not one shares Ford's contempt for his dalliance with the Fabian rustics, and recent biographies of Garnett evidence the extraordinarily positive role he played in the development of a host of writers, it seems remarkable that one can explore Octavia Hill's Kentish hills without stumbling across any reference to Garnett and his circle.[158] Certainly, Hill was an elderly woman by the time the Neo-Pagans were frolicking at Limpsfield and unlikely to take to free love or skinny-dipping, but it is as though the Victorians and the Edwardians were sealed off from each other, overlapping in time but enjoying parallel existences in space. It is neatly ironic that Hill's last essay, her 'Natural Beauty as a National Asset', was published in *The Nineteenth Century and After*. But as the Fabian dimension of this milieu throws into sharp relief, this was more than a generational divide. Hill's conversative moralising and her commitment to philanthropic work by apparently apolitical women was at odds with the Fabianism of Garnett's circle.

Beatrice Webb (1858–1943), for instance, was no more a skinny-dipper than Hill and she was among those women influenced by Hill in her formative years, but as a social researcher, a socialist and advocate of the cooperative movement, she and her husband Sidney reached for solutions that were statist and universal, having a huge influence on the development of the Labour movement. These differences were evident during their service on the Royal Commission on the Poor Laws (1905–9). Whereas Webb co-authored the famous Minority Report, Hill was aligned with the Majority Report, authored by Helen Bosanquet of the COS. The Majority Report accepted that 'something in our social organisation is seriously wrong' but endorsed the traditional view that pauperism was fundamentally a moral condition; the Minority Report argued that bad moral character was a consequence rather than a cause of 'social disorganisation' and advocated the creation of a network of comprehensive public services dealing with health, childcare, education and employment.[159] In his judicious comparison of the work Hill and Webb did for the commission, Lawrence Goldman uses Hill's questioning of witnesses to demonstrate her continued attachment to theories of pauperism that emphasised individual responsibility, observing 'her undiluted attachment to the outlook she held half a century before, and of her unwillingness to open her mind to the evidence of new social research that the Royal Commission encountered'.[160] If Hill's housing work aided thousands of people, and the number of philanthropic projects individuals might choose to undertake was of course unlimited, Webb looked to 'structural' approaches that would improve the lives of millions.

Hill's reputation as a philanthropist is captured by how her name has been deployed in parliamentary debates since her death.[161] A run of examples testifying to Hill's reputation as a philanthropist noted for the practicality of her work can be cited with respect to housing policy, particularly in the inter-war years. In 1919, she provided a precedent when moves were made to have a clause inserted into a housing bill requiring the name of the medical officer and the person responsible for maintaining the fabric of the building inscribed into every rent book; in 1927, the success of the 'Octavia Hill system' of supervision and maintenance was cited as evidence that few people had 'slum minds'; and in 1934, Hill's record was drawn on to make the case for transferring some 'working-class property from small private land-lords to responsible public or quasi-public ownership and manage-ment'. In 1930, the Labour peer Lord Parmoor recalled that 'the lady managers under Miss Octavia Hill and the rent collectors, though they demanded regularity and would allow no arrears, yet, by their care and understanding of human nature and of the nature of their tenants, introduced a spirit which was almost a revolution in social conditions in that district'. Hill's paternalism could provoke a fierce response, as in 1934 when Nye Bevan excoriated a Conservative MP's suggestion that a comparable system of home visitors might distribute welfare payments and subject recipients to 'impudent advice' about how to spend their money ('a characteristic Conservative speech').[162]

As Parmoor's speech indicates, much comment on the 'Octavia Hill system' was explicitly gendered and her example cropped up occasionally with respect to debates concerning the status of women. Bryce cited her arguments in December 1917 when opposing the extension of the franchise to women, and on the centenary of the 1918 Act admitting women to the franchise she was identified as a barrier to women's suffrage. More typically, she was seen as an excep-tional, exemplary woman, such as when the case was made for the admission of peeresses to the House of Lords in 1925 and 1946 or for equality of pay between men and women in 1935 or as a role model on International Women's Day in 2007.[163] Occasionally, favourable mentions were made with respect to her work for the Open Spaces movement or the National Trust, though she was also used as a stick with which to beat the National Trust, as when ques-tions about the Trust's governance and internal democracy were raised in 2001 – Chris Patten wondered what Hill, Rawnsley and Hunter would have made of the 'landed leviathan' the Trust had become – or in 2020 when opportunistic Tories criticised the Trust's landmark 'Colonial Countryside' project and its chair for expressing sympathy with the Black Lives Matter movement.[164]

In the middle decades of the century, obituaries recording the achievements of Hill's 'fellow-workers' provided repeated opportunities to remind readers of her achievements and example, and her name was kept before the public by assiduous younger collaborators like Sydney Cockerell, Director of the Fitzwilliam Museum in Cambridge. 1938, the year of her centenary, saw particularly lively press coverage, and on successive Sundays in February 1966 a series of five-minute broadcasts, 'Story: "Octavia Hill"', aired on the BBC.[165] The 150th anniversary of her first housing project was marked by the publication of *A Life More Noble: Reflections on Octavia Hill's Ambition of Nobility for All*, a collection of 90 short pieces by a potent mix of commentators, politicians, tenants and celebrities. Notwithstanding the unnerving contrast between the affective immediacy of the pieces by current housing association tenants and the comparatively laboured writing of the academics and politicians, it is an engaging collection, albeit one that overlooks Hill's Open Spaces work. That reflected the specific nature of the commemoration, but also the tendency to compartmentalise her immensely rich and complex public life. Keeping all those moving parts in view is indeed difficult, but as I have tried to show, there was a coherence to the evolution of her thinking that takes us from Paddington to Limpsfield and far beyond.

Hill was one of only three women invited in her own right to Victoria's Golden Jubilee service at Westminster in 1887. That's remarkable enough, and Ian Hislop is right to describe her as 'brilliant and brittle, inspiring and infuriating, dogmatic and yet an undeniable force for good', and it is largely the case that the potency of the less attractive parts of her politics were lost as they were displaced by new thinking.[166] The same might be said of our next subject. Valerie Vaz, Labour MP for Walsall South, was on to something in 2013 when she observed in a debate about housing and planning that a way must be found to 'maintain the spirit of Octavia Hill and Beatrix Potter and balance the need for housing with a protection of the countryside preserved for future generations'.[167]

BEATRIX POTTER

A Farm of One's Own

Beatrix Potter

A Farm of One's Own

The Bequest

In 1944, the National Trust informed its members of a spectacular acquisition: the Heelis Bequest. It comprised 1,638 hectares of land and property in the Lake District, located mainly in the vicinity of Lake Coniston, Lake Windermere and Esthwaite Water. It was by some distance the largest single Lake District bequest yet made to the Trust and dwarfed previous purchases enabled by fund-raising. And although not the largest bequest made to the Trust in this period – that laurel belongs to the Wallington Estate in Northumberland, bequeathed to the Trust in April 1942 by Sir Charles Philips Trevelyan – it was unique in other ways. Not only had the land and property been accumulated by its owner over the previous 30 years or so, but much of it was bought with the express intention of eventually donating it to the Trust. The estate came into the hands of the Trust not because of onerous death duties or as a public-spirited gesture by an heir, but as a purely voluntary, premeditated act.

Although the Heelis Bequest was complicated, comprising numerous properties, including fell, farm and house property, it can be divided into three parts. First, the fields and house property at Hawkshead and Near Sawrey, a stretch of territory skirting the eastern shore of Esthwaite Water, one of the smaller lakes in the south of the Lake District. Hill Top Farm, epicentre of the homage the National Trust now pays its most significant individual benefactor, lies at its heart. Second, Troutbeck Park, one of the District's largest enclosed sheep farms, occupies a tremendous site immediately west of the Kirkstone Pass, through which flows the eponymous Trout Beck. And, third, the Monk Coniston Estate, a large and complex property lying between the head of Coniston Water in the south and Little Langdale in the north, including land and property further west at Eskdale. Since then, the Trust has acquired adjacent properties, evidence of how the Heelis Bequest helped determine its later priorities.

H.B. Heelis is of course better known to the world as Beatrix Potter, the remarkable creator of *The Tale of Peter Rabbit* and other children's books. Her bequest ensured that she left her mark on the physical characteristics of the Lake District to a degree unmatched by any other modern figure. Neither Wordsworth nor Ruskin, for all that they influenced how people have thought about and experienced the region, had the inclination to acquire extensive tracts of Lake District land and property, and by those means seek to control its future. Their means – forms of cultural authority – were different, as were their times.[1] Potter's purchases were made possible, and she believed necessary, by the break-up or sale of big estates in the first half of the twentieth century, be they of aristocratic origin or the newer confections of Victorian industrialists. In this way, she was simply a member of a new generation of landowners, emblematic of the latest phase in the economic cycle whereby new wealth enables land ownership when older begins to fail. Potter's accumulation of significant personal wealth also had a historical context. She had two major sources of income. A northern industrial inheritance came to her in stages over the course of her life, and she earned a great deal as the author of a series of phenomenally lucrative children's books. The success of the books flowed from the confluence of a tremendous talent, changing attitudes towards childhood and the development of a globalised, consumer literary market, Anglophone and non-Anglophone, with its associated merchandising impetus, that benefited particularly from a powerful strand of transatlantic Anglophilia.

If Potter's acquisitiveness was not unusual, her intentions were. Her early land purchases at Near Sawrey were not philanthropic, but the acquisition of Troutbeck partially was, and the acquisition of the Monk Coniston Estate, the largest single component of the bequest, certainly was. Both Troutbeck and Monk Coniston were purchased with the intention of bequeathing them to the Trust. In this respect, Potter was the heir to Octavia Hill, purchasing to preserve, albeit on an unprecedented scale. But she was less motivated by other aspects of Hill's agenda. Potter took a principled position on maintaining public access to the fells, but in practice she was often pragmatic, using access as a way of diverting the public away from other types of agricultural land; she was not keen on day-trippers and could be privately ungenerous about overweight women in unsuitable shoes; and, in contrast to Hill, she placed little symbolic value on the collection of small donations from working people: she preferred quick transactions with single wealthy donors, enjoying high-powered negotiations. Moreover, as the scion of a wealthy industrial family, she found appeals to the public socially embarrassing: her mother's refusal to financially support her efforts on behalf of the Trust was a source of continuing frustration, and she often reminded contacts at the Trust how keenly she felt this. On one occasion, she told the Trust she might snap up a farm on their behalf at auction but could not be relied upon to pledge the same sum to a public appeal.[2] But she also thought market conditions encouraged bolder moves. 'Small purchases are a wasteful way of buying land', she wrote in February 1930. 'Large properties are down in value and unsaleable.'[3]

These preferences also reflected her reluctance to concede that a broader public interest was at stake, and she rarely celebrated the general social goods delivered by the Trust. To do so risked exposing the need for increased state intervention, which, as we will see, left her uneasy; moreover, she was temperamentally and ideologically unsuited to pressure group politics and played little role in the burgeoning National Parks movement. Instead, she framed her interventions in terms of the need to sustain certain forms of agricultural life in the Lakes, generally in the face of suburbanising pressures. New houses on small private plots of land in prominent locations were her bête noire. Her preservationism was predicated on a mix of aesthetic judgement and local priorities rather than a nationally orientated social progressivism.

As a property owner, Potter was no passive preservationist. She did not allow the Coniston Estate or Troutbeck Farm to continue as they supposedly ever had, and she was not the first preservationist to struggle to reconcile the romanticised image of the Lakeland farmer with her own attitudes towards the men she had to work with.[4] Blending a curatorial instinct with a dynamic mix of conscious modernisation and the revival of traditional practices, she was an active improver, keen to see her property portfolio brought under close supervision and effective management, introducing methods that she expected the Trust to maintain after her death. She helped establish Herdwick sheep as the quintessential Lakeland breed, though her influence in this regard should not be exaggerated. Her insistence that hefted flocks be maintained should be seen in the context of her commitment to restored buildings, tidy farmscapes and careful farm and landscape management. She was particularly keen on planting trees, regarding them as both improving the aesthetic value of her property and providing a useful resource; she recognised the commercial value of conifer plantations and did not necessarily regard their establishment as an illegitimate use of Lakeland. In this, she stood in stark contrast to mainstream preservationism, which in the Lake District gained much of its momentum from opposition to the Forestry Commission's expansionism.[5] Just as Potter produced a charming vision of English rurality on the page, so she endeavoured to produce a Lake District farmed according to her principles. Her

rigorously interventionist preservationism was modern in its determination to discipline her tenants, her employees and her land. Much
of this echoes Octavia Hill's vigorous paternalism.

Potter's approach to her three property groups was not inter-
changeable. She acquired them at different stages of her life, they
presented different propositions and her differing attitudes towards
them tell us much about her changing priorities. Hill Top made
Potter a hobbyist farmer, and though further land purchases transformed her holding into a more serious agricultural proposition, she
was never dependent on farming for an income; the death of her
father, her marriage and the purchase of Troutbeck made her a
substantial farmer and person of influence in the local agricultural
community; and the purchase of the Monk Coniston Estate made
her a preservationist responsible for a highly complex property portfolio. Something of this process of accumulation and expanding
responsibility is captured in the long-established biographical narrative that sees her transformation in middle age from Beatrix Potter,
the spinster writer and illustrator of children's storybooks, to Mrs
Heelis, the relatively anonymous but highly active fellswoman, farmer
and wife. In a sparkling biographical study focused on her early life,
Matthew Dennison argues that Potter's diaries suggest 'a young
woman engaged in a struggle for self-determination'. Potter's life can
indeed be presented as an appealing process of 'becoming', whereby
she achieved a form of realised, adult selfhood in response to a highly
privileged but unorthodox and somewhat repressive upbringing
during which her growing desire for autonomy and impactful activity
came into conflict with a powerful sense of obligation towards her
parents.[6] This metanarrative was recently popularised in a Hollywood
film.[7] A sense of what the Potter children were up against is evidenced
by her brother Bertram's decision in 1902 to marry a former mill
worker and live for 11 years a secret married life as a small farmer in
the Scottish Borders, during which he dutifully showed up for family
holidays and was elected to the Athenaeum, his father's club.[8]

It would be unfair to imply that Potter's biographers have neglected the Mrs Heelis years. Linda Lear's exemplary biography does justice to those years and a rich strand of Lakeland writing celebrates Potter's life as a fellswoman. Nonetheless, there remains a tendency to treat that part of her life as an addendum, if not a diminuendo. This is unsurprising, for explaining the provenance of the children's books is a compelling subject, but to project this as the dominant biographical theme of her life risks obscuring her other commitments and legacy.

By approaching Potter as a preservationist, this chapter seeks less to revise the 'becoming' narrative and more to provide a different perspective on its trajectory. It seeks not to demonstrate that the children's books were less important to her life than is often supposed, but to put them in their place as Potter achieved a sense of hers. Visitors to Hill Top today are reminded of how the intimacies of local places helped inspire the 'Little Books'. A visit to Hill Top and Lower Sawrey is a carefully curated experience: to see on the ground what is familiar on the page is affecting. But to reduce Potter's encounter with the Lake District to a source of inspiration for the books profoundly obscures the breadth of her activities.

However, a sharp divide should not be drawn between the young creative genius and the determined middle-aged and elderly farmer. Such an approach obscures the continuities in her life and her relatively late success. Her first book, *The Tale of Peter Rabbit*, was published in 1902 when Potter was 36, and she did not establish herself in the Lake District as a property owner until she was 39, developing her farming interests long before she ceased producing her 'Little Books'. Moreover, something of the satisfaction Potter found in establishing herself as a person of consequence in the Lake District flowed from her family identity and history. One of the farms that formed part of the Monk Coniston Estate had been owned by her grandfather, and she regarded purchasing the estate as a form of restitution, a manifestation of familial piety. What is more, her father, Rupert Potter, was one of the first life members of the Trust, providing the organisation with legal advice,[9] and family holidays brought Potter to the Lake District from a young age, when she came under the influence of Canon Rawnsley, a family friend. Potter's preservationism reflected an elective affinity that originated in family life.

Our engagement with Potter's later life is inhibited by her decision to stop keeping a journal in 1897. We do not know why she did this, but it certainly marks a watershed in any biographical treatment of her life. Thereafter, we know her less through her private thoughts and more through her actions, necessitating an approach to her life more reliant on inference and implication, particularly with respect to how her correspondence is read. Amanda Vickery argues that Florence Nightingale's passionate writings ask us to see public heroism as an inevitable reaction to a previous period of mind-numbing claustration.[10] Potter, by contrast, freed herself from familial claustration in middle age not for public heroism but for love, a companionable marriage and a purposeful anonymity. Despite the enormous success of her books, and despite her close work with the National Trust, Potter's modus operandi was private and enabled by private means.

Potter's final diary entry reflected on how 'it is odious to a shy person to be snubbed as conceited, especially when the shy person happened to be right, and under the temptation of sauciness'.[11] Shyness is one of the keys to unlocking her life. Perhaps this is all we need to know to understand her cleaving to the private realm. Eve Colpus, writing about a younger generation of contemporary women philanthropists, provides a richer context through which Potter's distinctiveness might be grasped. Colpus emphasises the powerful urge felt by elite women philanthropists to reflect upon their work *as women*, arguing that the relationship between their philanthropy and the felt moral imperative to render society service was bound up with notions of selfhood that rejected the earlier tendency to treat elite women's service as crude forms of compensation for privilege.[12] Potter did not engage in such reflections, probably did not regard herself as a philanthropist, and, one suspects, was impatient of both. Perhaps she was simply too busy working, perhaps this was a function of old age, perhaps the lively correspondence she maintained with a range of interlocutors was enough, perhaps she really was sui generis. She certainly did not gravitate towards identifiably women's causes, though she was conscious of how as a woman she had to work particularly hard to earn the respect of her neighbours. Nonetheless, Potter's decision to embed herself in Lakeland society, to manage her lands as she saw fit, and to act as the National Trust's agent on land she herself initially bought, carried a strong political charge.

Upbringing

The Tale of Peter Rabbit was an instant hit, selling more than 50,000 copies by the end of 1903. By 1905, Potter had added a further five titles to her roster of 'Little Books', including the tales of Squirrel Nutkin, Benjamin Bunny and Mrs Tiggy-Winkle. Eight further titles would follow before 1909. The sources of this extraordinary period of work and inspiration were varied. Most immediately, Potter's success stemmed from the moment she stumbled upon a way to deploy her powers as an artist, her knowledge of the natural world, her close observation of wildlife, especially small mammals, and her rather sharp eye and ear for human behaviour and its foibles. Without achieving that alchemy, neither inevitable nor seemingly the realisation of long-held ambition, Potter would likely have remained the obscure spinster daughter of wealthy parents.

That Potter had the time and space – as well as the resources – to nurture her talent cannot be separated from her exceptionally privileged if idiosyncratic upbringing. She was not under pressure to earn her living, and her shyness and temperament seemed to have militated against an early marriage. As a lawyer, her father was a member of London's professional class, but her family's Unitarian commitments and northern industrial roots ensured that they did not have an altogether secure place in London society. According to Lear, Potter's family on both sides were 'distinguished by their Radical political opinions, Unitarian convictions, extraordinary success in trade, and a discerning interest in the arts'.[13] To this might be added a sustained commitment to philanthropy, including a touch of Owenism, and a strong urge to convert industrial wealth into landscaped country estates. Edmund Potter, Potter's paternal grandfather, transformed a rundown cotton mill in Dinting Vale, Glossop, into the world's largest calico printing works. He married Jessie Crompton, a local woman of radical inclinations, and together they combined industrial manufacture, Unitarianism and close ties to the Manchester art scene with a powerful commitment to the benefits of the arts for working people. Potter adored Jessie. When Edmund became MP for Carlisle (1862–74) – his period in parliament coincided with Gladstone's great reforming ministry of 1868–74 – he established a home in London and acquired Camfield Place, a country estate of over 300 acres in Hertfordshire landscaped by Lancelot 'Capability' Brown. It was later owned by the romantic novelist Dame Barbara Cartland, who shaped its interiors according to her own aesthetic preferences. Edmund died in 1883, leaving an estate valued at £441,970; on Jessie's death in 1891 much of this passed to Rupert Potter, Beatrix's father.[14] Potter later recalled 'the feeling' at Camfield, of 'well-assured, indolent wealth, honourably earned and wisely spent'.[15]

Potter's mother had similar antecedents. Her grandfather, John Leech of Stalybridge, was a Unitarian cotton manufacturer. He too bought a country estate, pulled down the old house, and built Gorse Hall overlooking the town, which he duly stocked with contemporary British art, including a Turner. He died in 1860, leaving his wife Jane to a long widowhood dedicated to philanthropy. She converted Hob Hill, the first Leech home, into a Unitarian free school, which educated up to four hundred girls and infants and provided night classes for workers. Octavia Hill would have approved. Harriet, one of the Leech daughters, married Fred Burton, a wealthy cotton merchant who built Gwaynynog, an estate near Denbigh in Wales.[16]

Rupert Potter was the second son and his father approved of his decision to choose a professional career rather than enter the family business. He was educated at Manchester College by leading Unitarian progressives, where he excelled in the classics and ancient history. He took a degree at the University of London in 1851, becoming the first member of his family to graduate. His teachers included the Rev. William Gaskell, Professor of English History and Literature, and James Martineau, Professor of Mental and Moral Philosophy and Political Economy, both Unitarian luminaries and notably related to famous women, the novelist Elizabeth Gaskell (William's wife) and the political economist and writer Harriet Martineau (James's sister). Rupert Potter had some success at the bar, specialising as an equity draughtsman and conveyancer, and though not wholly dependent on earning his income, he made a good fist of this and some investments before benefiting from a series of large legacies from 1884. He was also a skilled artist with a particular knack as a caricaturist, and was strongly drawn to the arts world and the associated social opportunities London offered. A sure sign of his social standing was his election to the Reform Club and, more extraordinary still, to the Athenaeum, where one of his proposers was Sir Charles Eastlake, President of the Royal Academy, Director of the National Gallery and President of the Photographic Society of London. Rupert preferred the prestigious if culturally conservative intellectual milieu of the Athenaeum to the liberal politics of the Reform. His daughter benefited from these contacts.[17]

Helen Potter was not an altogether sympathetic figure, though much of what is known of her personality reflects the jaundiced views of her daughter. Helen's brittle personality cannot have been helped by the restrictions imposed upon married, upper-middle-class Victorian women. Historians have long questioned the truism that Victorian men and women inhabited 'separate spheres', but the one social group in which the ideology most structured their experience was that of the affluent middle and upper-middle class.[18] Helen Potter paid the visits demanded by 'the season', her bored, grown-up daughter often in tow, but her northern accent and religious nonconformity did not help her ambitions to get on in 'society'. Her snobbish ambitions were common enough and as a wealthy woman seeking conventional forms of social recognition an unconventional daughter inhibited by chronic shyness must have been a burden. Like her husband, she could paint and draw, 'accomplishments' easily downplayed as characteristic of affluent women of her time, though, as Lear observes, they indicate 'that Helen shared her husband's art enthusiasms and that she too had artistic talent that added to the sum ultimately inherited by both her children'.[19]

Dennison writes that Potter's diary, 'in details that are more often implied than explicit', contains 'striking portraits of Rupert and Helen Potter and intimations of the gulf between parents and child'.[20] Of one holiday, much of which Potter spent in solitary mycological pursuits – her preoccupation with fungi kept her busy in the mid-1890s – she wrote 'it is somewhat trying to pass a season of enjoyment in the company of persons who are constantly on the lookout for matters of complaint'.[21] She confided to her diary a different kind of frustration in 1896. Her lament that Unitarianism was a 'creed apt to be a timid, illogical compromise, and their forms of Service a badly performed imitation of the Church', might be read as a broader frustration with her family's station in life.[22] Potter's use of the definitive article – 'the Church' – alluded to Anglicanism, a hint perhaps of her growing Toryism and her growing sense that the family's Unitarianism was petty-minded and self-marginalising.

Potter drew and painted from nature and by copying from books since she was a small child. She took pride in being self-taught, developing a practice that reflected the artistic atmosphere of the family home, though she did receive lessons in drawing and watercolours from a Miss Cameron, a reminder that her parents did recognise and try to nurture her talent. Her influences were extensive if conventional; less conventional was the intensity of her commitment. Illustrated works of fiction or natural history sent her into raptures and she sought to emulate children's book illustrators like Edward Lear, Sir John Tenniel and Randolph Caldecott, and natural history illustrators from Thomas Bewick through to those of her own day, including the women artists who helped develop the genre. She was awed by the work of J.M.W. Turner, to her mind the greatest of landscape painters, but her preference was for small-scale, finely detailed intimate work, and her preferred medium was watercolour. This preference was reinforced when her parents took her to the Winter Exhibition of Old Masters at the Royal Academy when she was 16. Her first encounter with Reynolds, Gainsborough, Van Dyck and Titian was overwhelming but intimidation soon gave way to inspiration, beginning a phase of intensive gallery-going and note-taking. Expensive lessons in oil painting briefly complemented those she received from Miss Cameron, but the tension between the felt obligation to respond positively to the teacher's instruction and her increasingly strong sense of her own practice made her anxious. Diary entries indicate that she rationalised her response by distinguishing between technical proficiency, which could be taught, and innate talent, which could only be nurtured through solitary practice. Perhaps though, as she hinted in her diary, the teacher just wasn't very good.[23]

Potter had a seemingly insatiable curiosity about the workings of the natural world. Her parents tolerated the menagerie she and her brother Bertram established in their nursery, with its scarcely credible range of creatures, including several pet rabbits, a bat, birds, any number of insects – examined under a microscope – and small lizards. Dead samples were duly categorised and stored, apparently without squeamishness. Potter's close observations of the physical appearance and behaviour of her menagerie saw her realise her skill as a draughtsperson and painter of small mammals, plants and fungi. Human figures and large animals, such as horses, of a comparable standard eluded her.

Her later recollections of childhood were suffused with a powerful sense of scent and texture, her sensory receptiveness to the world's materiality being finely tuned. This sensitivity nurtured her powerful sense of place, a tendency reinforced by a childhood punctuated with regular visits to Camfield, Easter breaks on the south coast of England, long summer holidays at Dalguise in Perthshire, where she enjoyed a decade of summers from 1871, and then holidays in the Lake District from her teens into adulthood. Holidaying with her parents was an obligation she never overcame, but it is too easy to assume that this was necessarily burdensome. Long summer holidays gave her extended opportunities to pursue her natural history and artistic interests, and by these means she often met the people who influenced her development. Holidaying also nurtured her taste for landscape. Camfield Place, diligently manicured by Jessie Potter, contrasted with Dalguise, 'untamed and chimerical',[24] a contrast replicated to some extent at Hill Top and Troutbeck.

Potter was exceptionally lucky in her friends and mentors. To take just four examples, Sir John Everett Millais, founder of the Pre-Raphaelite Brotherhood, Royal Academician and society painter, was a friend of her father and a regular at Dalguise. Millais was married to Effie Gray, Ruskin's first wife (she of the notorious wedding night) and a Perthshire woman, the reason they all holidayed there. Potter regularly visited Millais's London studio with her father and the painter paid her the splendid compliment that she had that rare combination, a good hand and 'observation'. Millais's early Pre-Raphaelite work was a lasting influence. Potter fiercely admired its fine detail and the brilliance with which all aspects of the painting were in focus at once, creating an impression at once natural and artistically visionary. Lady Eastlake, wife of the Director of the National Gallery and President of the Royal Academy, was another friend of her father and advised him about who might help develop his daughter's evident artistic talent.[25] By contrast, Charlie McIntosh, an amateur naturalist Potter met on her Scottish family holidays, encouraged her turn towards more scientific work in the 1890s. Acting on his advice, and with some help from her father's contacts, Potter threw herself into mycological research and drawing. She succeeded in having a paper 'laid on the table' at the Linnean Society but further attempts to navigate this unfamiliar world saw her repeatedly rebuffed in a manner she found personally hurtful, demoralising and baffling. Why did the scientists at Kew Gardens not respond more readily to her carefully established theories? Without realising it, she had pitted herself against the increasingly professionalised habitus of scientific research and its attendant misogyny. The age of the amateur was rapidly passing.

Although she was soon in full retreat from mycological work, the episode was important in several ways. It was Potter's first serious attempt to engage with the adult world beyond her immediate family circle, wide though this was, seeking forms of recognition untainted by familial indulgence. Also, Potter's research, partly classificatory, is further evidence that her exceptional observational skills had uses beyond the whimsical representation of the natural world on paper. Her acute eye for detail would later be deployed with effect as a champion sheep breeder, seeing her develop a strong knowledge of the flock books. More immediately, this setback was one of the triggers that got her thinking about how she might prepare her drawings and stories for publication. A key figure in this process was the fourth and, for our purposes, the most important of Potter's friends and mentors, Canon Hardwicke Rawnsley.

Rawnsley had been a guest of the Potters in 1882 when they holidayed at Wray Castle, the neo-Gothic 1840s pile on the west bank of Windermere. He quickly found common cause with Rupert Potter and soon noticed the talent of his quietly productive teenage daughter, always to be found drawing or painting. Lear says that Rawnsley's influence on Potter is hard to document but no less certain for this;

Dennison reports that Rawnsley family lore had it that he was a little in love with her.[26] In any case, after the mycological episode, and more than a decade after they first met, Rawnsley was among those who encouraged Potter to develop her drawings and stories for publication.[27]

Rawnsley is a surprisingly elusive figure. He left extensive papers but still awaits a full-length biography; no historian has yet felt moved to tackle systematically his awful handwriting. Still, we know he acted as honorary secretary for the National Trust, and rare was the preservationist cause to which he did not lend his voice. Variously described as having a 'flashing intellect, robust curiosity and restless energy' and being 'idealistic and energetic but also aggressive and irritable',[28] Rawnsley was as ready to establish an ad-hoc committee as he was to write to *The Times*. Taught by Ruskin at Oxford, he had joined the famous North Hinksey road-building project as an under-graduate – alongside Oscar Wilde, among others – before working for Hill on her housing projects. Following a nervous breakdown, possibly triggered by his experience as a volunteer in a London hostel, he convalesced with friends at Windermere, living with his cousin Edward Preston Rawnsley, inheritor in 1875 of Wray Castle. These inauspicious circumstances provided Rawnsley with his life's work. He was ordained in 1877 and his cousin granted him the living of St Margaret of Antioch, the church at Wray-on-Windermere. In 1883, he became vicar at Crosthwaite, from where until his death in 1920 he practised his clerical duties, coordinated preservationist campaigns, wrote works of topographical and historical description and nurtured local artisanal skills.

Perhaps, then, the best way to make sense of Rawnsley's influence on Potter is to consider where he fits into the broader history of Lake District preservationism. Potter's decision to buy Lake District land reflected personal preferences and a wider set of cultural cues. The significance Potter attached to the Lakes saw the intersection of biography, family and a wider political and cultural context.

Viking Sheep, Rawnsley and Preservationism

Since the late eighteenth century, the Lake District has attracted artists, poets, writers and, in steadily increasing numbers, tourists. The first guidebook was published in 1778 and many more would follow, though the most influential was William Wordsworth's *Guide to the Lakes*, first published as a separate volume in 1822 and updated in 1835. As much a manifesto as a guide, it warned against disfiguring the landscape with conifer plantations and new houses and other buildings out of sympathy with the 'vernacular' architecture of the region, and celebrated the virtues of the commoning system and the 'republic of shepherds', a form of liberty threatened by agricultural improvement and political economy. By attributing the magnificence of the landscape to the way it was farmed, Wordsworth linked its preservation to a particular system of social organisation; he did not promote the myth that the Lake District is a wilderness untouched by human hand, but instead recognised that it was a 'cultural landscape' or a 'taskscape'.[29] As Wordsworth grasped, the Lake District's appearance and ecologies reflected how it was worked. Like all environments in the Anthropocene, it is a hybrid production of human and non-human nature.

Jonathan Bate argues that Wordsworth's *Guide*, probably his most read work in the nineteenth century, exemplified what he calls 'Romantic ecology', an environmental perspective focused on the materiality of the landscape, reflecting concern not just for how the landscape *is* but also for how it is *produced*. To recognise that Wordsworth conceived of the landscape as an ecology, as a dynamic system without a fixed or permanent character, and one malleable by human hands, gives a sharper edge to familiar lines like 'Nature never did betray / The heart that lov'd her' ('Tintern Abbey'). By challenging the convention that 'Romantic discourse attempts to seal itself hermetically off from materiality', Bate's work grounds Wordsworth in time and place, recovering his radicalism and placing his work in its proper context, that of agricultural improvement and enclosure.[30]

By this reading, Rawnsley and his collaborators were also Romantic ecologists, their preservationism stemming from their recognition that modern human activities threatened the Lake District's characteristics because changing how it was used would change what was produced. Holiday homes, for instance, constituted a new form of usage, generating new kinds of building and therefore a new kind of Lake District. Bate argues that Ruskin was the key figure here, 'for it was through him more than anyone else that the Wordsworthian ecology entered into a broader – and indeed explicitly political – nineteenth-century environmental tradition'.[31] Paul Readman agrees, stating that Rawnsley's generation got from Ruskin the 'idea that the preservation of "wild" nature – such as that of the Lakes – as a lived-in, inherited environment, was of vital social value, not least because exposure to this nature was of educative benefit to all in the here-and-now'.[32] Ruskin demanded not the restoration of a fanciful pre-modern purity but recognition that pre-modern survivals had something to teach moderns about healthy ways of living. Octavia Hill's Ruskinian impetus compelled her to take the message to the slums of the city, Rawnsley's to the lakes and fells.

Wordsworth did much to establish the idea that farming on Lakeland is dominated by commonage, but Kenneth Olwig reminds us that modern Lakeland comprises two types of landscapes that exist contiguously. The first is part of the 'English core area', composed of enclosed, individually owned private farms, little different in their legal underpinnings to industrial urban society; the second, part of a North Atlantic archipelago that includes the western coast of Scotland, the Faroe Islands, Iceland and Norway, is shaped by ideas and practices associated with commonage and a body of terms of Nordic origin.[33] On this basis, Lakeland might be equally associated with Dartmoor, an English upland boasting a different origin narrative but also strongly associated with Nordic place names, commons and large tracts of enclosed land.[34] Potter's Lakeland purchases included both types of Lakeland terrain and, as will become clear, she had a strong preference for sole ownership rather than common land.

Wordsworth also claimed that the magnificence of the Lake District and its cultural significance made it 'a sort of national property'. The implications of this are significant. By arguing that the rights of private property cannot be absolute in the Lake District, and to link the preservation of the landscape to the preservation of a way of life, Wordsworth identified the tension that has run through preservationist and conservationist debates about Lakeland ever since. In recent times, this has tended to resolve itself into the following questions. Should commoners be maintained by the state to conserve the landscape as they cease to be profitable farmers, on the grounds that well-managed grazing delivers valuable public goods, particularly with respect to tourism, the most dynamic component of the Lakeland economy? And if pastoralism is no longer profitable should significant stretches of Lakeland terrain be committed to other purposes, including managing it for biodiversity rather than as grazing land? Farmers tend to find the premise of these questions offensive, rejecting the notion that they should be paid to 'garden' Lakeland on behalf of visitors, though some mobilise the Wordsworthian case for their continuance as producers of much-loved landscapes. In some Lakeland places, most significantly the rewilding project at Ennerdale, such sensibilities have already been sidelined, often to public acclaim, though this transformation is enacted on land already transformed by the Forestry Commission. Conversely, what should happen when other pressures or influences lead landowners to change *how* a living is extracted from the land, departing from customary practices, which in turn affects the character of the land produced?

Early preservationist tracts like Wordsworth's *Guide* also remind us that the object of their concern was not yet necessarily identified as a distinct geographical place. An anonymous version of the text was first published in 1810 to accompany a series of prints by Reverend Joseph

Wilkinson published as 'Select Views in Cumberland, Westmoreland, Lancashire'. References to 'the Lake District', 'Lakeland' or 'the Lakes' need to be historicised. We might readily assume that the Lake District has long been imagined as a distinct upland region characterised by lakes, but prior to the designation of the Lake District National Park in 1950 no such place existed in a formal sense, it was simply parts of Lancashire, Westmorland and Cumberland. Technically, Potter's first 'Lake District' purchases were in rural north Lancashire. Cumbria was not established as a county until 1974, a consequence of the 1972 Local Government Act. Although it is implausible to suppose that before the late eighteenth century the geographical distinctiveness of the 'Lake District' had not been recognised, the region's reification as the 'Lake District', a singular entity, is a more recent phenomenon.

To grasp that the Lake District is a geographically distinct place requires a sophisticated regional, if not a national, perspective or imagination. Modern mapping and the development of increasingly sophisticated ways of representing the landscape, particularly with respect to visually encoding elevation, enabled the landscape to be comprehended in ways that far exceed the capacity of the human eye. Another form of imagined landscape was produced through topographical writing, such as Harriet Martineau's companionable loco-descriptive 'A year in Ambleside' (1850) and *A Complete Guide to the English Lakes* (1855).[35] Advertising and tourism promotion were another factor, but it took controversies provoked by the development of infrastructure for the value accrued by the Lake District became politically legible. In the 1870s, Manchester Corporation sought to convert Thirlmere into a reservoir, provoking fierce but ultimately futile resistance. Parliament approved the plans in 1879 and the work was completed in the 1890s. Harriet Ritvo argues that the campaign against the reservoir saw the 'Dawn of Green' in Britain.[36] In the 1880s, a more institutionalised form of environmental campaigning developed from successive campaigns against extending the railway network deeper into the district.[37] Schemes to connect Braithwaite station to the Buttermere side of

Honister Pass, to run a line down one of side of Ennerdale and to connect Windermere to Ambleside, were driven by the needs of the slate quarriers, by mineral speculation and by tourism.

Did the campaign against the Ambleside railway stem from a preservationist hostility to mass working-class tourism and reflect entrenched views about what constituted the proper way of enjoying Lakeland? The evidence is mixed. Ruskin, for instance, did not deny the working class their right to leisure time spent in beautiful, healthy surroundings, but he wanted them directed towards the immediate environs of their towns and cities rather than 'emptied like coals from a sack' into Keswick and Windermere.[38] Did Ruskin, as Wendy Joy Darby argues, wish to segregate the landscape along class lines?[39] Certainly, Ruskin was convinced parts of the working class were incorrigible, destined for the pub rather than uplifting sites and activities. The 'imaginative sympathy' evident in Hill's account of the Bank Holiday crowds at Epping Forest was not always evident in Ruskin's crabbed commentaries on the railways. By contrast, MPs representing working-class constituencies were among those ensuring parliament rejected the railway bills, complicating the claim that landscape preservation was a marginal, middle-class concern.[40] In any case, these conflicts were the first time the notion that the Lake District was a form of 'national property' had real political consequences. From the preservationist point of view, vigilance was now needed. In the aftermath of the Honister crisis, Rawnsley helped establish the Lake District Defence Society (LDDS). Based on the national membership of the Wordsworth Society (which included Ruskin, Tennyson, William Morris and the Duke of Westminster), the society was emphatically not driven by local people. Presaging later National Park politics, Rawnsley believed the LDDS was necessary if narrow local interests were not to trump the national and international importance of Lakeland.[41]

Disregard for local feeling was not at odds with the paternalist aspect of this campaigning. Rawnsley and his ilk did not seek to preserve the Lake District solely for men and women of their sensibilities. Modern developments also put at risk the character of the unspoiled 'Cumbrian and Westmoreland peasant', whose 'severely simple life' was not a sufficient defence against the seductions of commercial life, including the opportunities presented by tourism. Lakeland's 'native' people might have been 'the descendants of an ancient race devoted to liberty and a rustic way of life' but they were not its 'safest guardians'.[42] Nonetheless, Rawnsley's paternalism allowed that the fellsmen and women could be the authors of their own salvation if they could become conscious of the importance of their heritage and be given the means to resist the degrading blandishments of commercial society. Consequently, in 1883, Rawnsley and his wife Edith established the Keswick School of the Industrial Arts, which trained workers in the production of handicrafted goods made from wood, silver, copper, brass and linen.[43] Demonstrating that traditional manufacture might be profitable could act as a barrier against other commercial prospects. In his sermons, Rawnsley reinforced this message, trying to persuade the 'sons of Vikings who dwell in the homes of Britons of old' of their moral duty to uphold local traditions and revere and care for the land just as their ancestors had done.[44]

Identifying the 'native' population as of Viking ancestry was linked to another of Rawnsley's preoccupations, namely the idea that they shared these origins with Herdwick sheep. Herdwicks were integral to the Lakeland lives Rawnsley sought to preserve. His decision to establish the Herdwick Sheep Association in 1899 is often considered a key moment in the valorisation of these quirky, endearing animals as the quintessential Lakeland breed, but Rawnsley's celebrity should not be allowed to exaggerate his importance to this process. So, before looking more closely at Rawnsley's ideas about Herdwicks, their prehistory should be examined.

The Herdwick Sheep Breeders' Association, of which Potter was elected the first woman president in 1930, date their foundation to 1916, dismissing Rawnsley's earlier 'attempt'.[45] In actual fact, as Frank

Garnett's classic *Westmorland Agriculture, 1800–1900* shows, both organisations are part of a longer history. Garnett's survey of sheep distribution suggests that during the nineteenth century Blackfaced Heath sheep – to use Garnett's classification – were most numerous in Westmorland, but in the county's 'western hilly districts', which include iconic Lakeland territories, Herdwicks predominated, whereas Silverdales were preferred on the limestone fells to the south.[46] Herdwicks had been interbred with 'indigenous "black faces"', and Garnett insists that attempts made in the late eighteenth century to 'breed a pure race' were unsuccessful.[47] Notions of indigeneity are often problematic, but it is striking to note that Garnett regarded the Herdwicks as incomers. For much of the nineteenth century commentators thought Herdwicks could be 'improved' through interbreeding. Why this might be desirable is indicated by a prize-winning essay of 1852 by a Cumberland farmer. He argued that the breed were more possessed 'of the characters of the original race than any other in the country' and, as such, 'stands lowest in the scale of excellence, and shows no marks of kindred with any other race'.[48] Similar views were expressed following their appearance at the 1880 Royal Show in Carlisle. The *Field* noted that they 'look like the last remnant of, we won't say barbarism, but of very ancient and primitive sheep breeding'; another commentator insisted they were 'still susceptible of considerable improvement'.[49]

Over the course of the century there was a perceptible shift from an improvement discourse that looked askance at 'primitive' characteristics, which might be corrected with careful interbreeding, towards the valorisation of a Herdwickian racial purity, whose characteristics made them peculiarly suited to the harsh conditions of the fells. Even the purists acknowledged that weakness had been bred out thanks to careful management. The Penrith Agricultural Society (1833) was the first local society to offer prizes for Herdwicks; the Appleby and Kirkby Stephen Agricultural Society (1845) and the High Borrow Bridge Agricultural Society (1848) followed; Herdwicks were first shown in exhibition at the Royal Agricultural Society when it came to Carlisle in 1855, while the West Cumberland Fell Dales Sheep Association (1844) was particularly interested in the breed.[50] More organisations followed. The Troutbeck Herdwick and Other Sheep Association was established in 1868 and the Bampton Association for the Improvement of Mountain Sheep held shows between 1876 and 1898.[51] In earlier periods, Herdwick ewes were kept on the fells until unable to breed, sometimes for 16 years, but by the nineteenth century farmers began to sell Herdwick ewes to lowland farmers after four to six cropping seasons for breeding with Leicester, Wensleydale or Cheviot rams. The Herdwick-Cheviot mix produced a lamb that rapidly fattened, and the popularity of these 'half-bred sheep' or 'grey-faces' meant they too became a fixture at the shows, further evidence of the classifying urge of modern agriculture. Garnett's book is packed with descriptions of good agricultural specimens, culled from various authorities.[52] A story in *The Country Gentleman's Magazine* suggested these judgements were shaped by the racial discourses of empire: 'breeding flocks of Herdwicks are kept as free from strange alliances as the mares of Arabia, or high-caste hindoos', the breed had been improved through 'repeated acts of selection'.[53] A decade later, Daniel Gate found it 'deplorable' that so many Herdwicks were effectively left to fend for themselves on the fells, but attentive stockmen could work wonders in a short period of time, transforming an 'ill-developed, coarse-woolled animal' into 'well formed' sheep: 'in the place of "hempen locks"' was good wool 'eagerly sought after by local manufacturers'.[54]

The long-circulated myth that the Herdwicks were descended from a population of just 40 or so individuals which survived a Spanish shipwreck off the coast (sometimes identified as part of the Spanish Armada) was gradually superseded by the belief that they were of a more ancient origin, likely Viking, a precursor to the modern view that their origins lie in the Texel breed, originally from the Netherlands. The Spanish theory was dismissed by one authority as early as 1879, saying the likely place of origin was Denmark or Sweden, though

Rawnsley, who wrote prolifically if repetitively about Lakeland, rejected the Spanish tale late in the day.[55] In 1899, writing of Langdale Valley, part of the Monk Coniston Estate, he observed: 'Fiery-hearted creatures are these little Herdwick sheep, the Spanish blood is strong within their veins, they have not forgot the fury of the dread Armada, or the fury of the winds that drove them, so tradition has it, to our shore.'[56] By 1906, now under the sway of Viking theories, he had changed his tune. The 'very word Herdwick', he wrote, 'has a Viking ring to it'. The Spanish theory could now be dismissed.

> I believe that they are of much more ancient lineage as far as our fell stock goes, for it is much more likely that these creatures whose chief characteristics are the hairy mane and the wool-feathered legs that fit them to cope with the snow as they 'peckle' amongst the heather or beat grass for their food in winter time, came from a Northern climate rather than a Southern one.[57]

Five years later he elaborated on the theory, arguing that the 'termi-native' of the word Herdwick suggested 'a warrior breed', 'as hardy as the hardy Norseman himself', their 'ruffs' and 'Roman noses' evidently intended for animals who had to 'fend for themselves in snowy places, where grass was scarce'. These claims then gave way to a discussion of 'heafing' (a word, he wrote, of Danish, Swedish and Icelandic origin), the powerful sense a Herdwick flock has of its territory when out of the open fells.[58] That Herdwicks can be 'heafed' is one reason Herdwick stock-raisers place so much importance on inter-genera-tional continuity in their 'hefted' flocks. Herdwicks learn their 'heaf' from their elders, meaning great store was placed on flocks being 'tied' to particular grazing lands. Tradition has it that flocks belong first to the farm rather than the owner or tenant, so that when a farm changed hands so did the flock.

And what of the human descendants of Vikings, asked Rawnsley, turning his attention to the fellsmen and women? They too were heafed. Their instinct for home, like their Herdwicks, was strong; their word was their bond; once wed, they were 'true to contract'; they respected order; they kept their tempers but could bear a grudge; they were generally sober but had a 'natural hospitality' and festivities could 'awaken Viking echoes'; they were not artistic or poetic, but they shared 'the old Norseman's pride that prevented them giving way to sorrow', and they bore illness with 'patient heroism', had little fear of death – their burial practices Viking survivals – and their 'sense of an over-ruling Providence, which in Viking times was a sense of over-mastering fate' was very strong. Thankfully, the days of 'junketings from farm to farm' had faded away, though Parish registers – and here Rawnsley's choice of words was circumspect – preserved much evidence of illegitimate children. Rawnsley hoped 'young men may in the next generation think nobly of what is due to young women, and be more knightly and more self-restrained for Christ's sake'.[59]

This fanciful stuff, characteristic of the patrician outlook of many preservationists, comes perilously close to making essentialist racial claims about the people of the Lake District. Readman cautions against hasty judgement, arguing that late Victorian attitudes towards Viking influences tended to emphasise the benefits of what was loosely understood as inter-racial commingling, with some contemporaries suggesting that the injection of Viking blood had reinvigorated Britain's people.[60] Moreover, Rawnsley's interest in Viking influence was part of a broader culture turn towards reading landscapes historically, particularly through the etymology of place names, in a manner that could emphasise the benefit to Britain of past variety rather than the benefit of pure lines of descent. Something similar shaped Dartmoor preservationists, who from the 1870s emphasised Scandinavian influences on Dartmoor place names, adding to already complex origin narratives.[61] To Rawnsley, a sweeping Lake District view was powerful not just for its aesthetic beauty, but for how knowledge of its history made it 'storied ground', enhancing its national and therefore its preservationist significance.[62] Little evidence suggests

Potter was much interested in Rawnsley's musings on the Viking survivals in the personalities of her neighbours, but there was a clear alignment between his linkage of Lakeland's 'native' peoples with Herdwicks and Potter's determination to maintain the valley farms and hefted Herdwick flocks on the Monk Coniston Estate. Crucially, her preferences reflected not personal whim but established preservationist priorities.

The final factor conditioning Potter's decision to purchase was of course the presence of the National Trust in Lakeland. Prior to the First World War, it acquired a number of Lakeland properties, modest by later standards but signalling increased ambition. Apart from the small memorial raised by subscription to Ruskin at Friars Crag near Keswick in 1900, three principal purchases, made in 1902, 1906 and 1908, were lakeside sites acquired to maintain public access. As such, the purchases resembled the Trust's defensive Kentish purchases, and the appeals were made on similar terms. Brandelhow Park, a 106-acre site on Derwentwater, was acquired for £7,000 thanks to a campaign launched by Octavia Hill that quickly entered Trust lore on account of the donation accompanied by this note: 'I am a working man and cannot afford more than 2s., but I once saw Derwentwater and can never forget it. I will do what I can to get my mates to help.'[63] Hill attributed the purchase of 'lake-side, green with wood and meadow, grey with rock, and commanding view of purple mountain and blue lake' to the 'indefatigable energy and unwearied perseverance' of Rawnsley and the generosity of the people. She wrote:

> I kept receiving letters, one more delightful than the other; some
> from the young in their exuberance of life; some from the old, rich
> in memory; some from the rich, with solemn sense of duty; some
> from the poor, eager to contribute their mite; some from the north,
> from sense of neighbourhood; some from the south, in gratitude
> for holiday; some from America, from friends and in thought of

kinship and common inheritance of literature; some from our colonies and abroad in thought of English loveliness and dearness.[64]

Gowbarrow Fell on Ullswater, a 745-acre site famous for Wordsworth's daffodils, that includes the spectacular waterfall Aira Force, fine woodland and the famous viewpoint at Yew Crag, was acquired by subscription four years later. This time the Trust's campaign leaflet carried a stronger political edge. Lamenting how 'every year the land is more locked up in private ownership', it asked 'Why not nationalise the English Lake District?'.[65] The author of the pamphlet had perhaps been emboldened by the election of a Liberal government, though this was not the first time access campaigners had pushed for government intervention. Similar demands were made in the 1890s when the Muckross Estate in Co. Killarney, Ireland came on the market.[66] Hill emphasised the significance of the campaign in familiar terms. Gowbarrow 'may either be free to foot of man, woman and child of all ages, or appropriated to one or two families, and fenced off with barbed wire; shut off from artist, naturalist, hard-worked professional man, smoke-grimed city dweller, workman and child; of how £18 buys one acre of it for all time'.[67] Rawnsley later emphasised the historical importance of the site, listing its Neolithic, Roman, Viking and Arthurian associations.[68] Manesty Park, a 33-acre site almost immediately adjacent to Brandelhow Park, purchased in 1908, allowed the Trust to preserve from development much of the south-west shore of Derwentwater. Other acquisitions followed, including great reaches of open land: in 1923, the Fell and Rock Climbing Club vested the Trust with 3,000 acres of high fell at Great Gable in memory of 20 members who fell during the First World War; in 1925, A.C. Benson, Master of Magdalene College, Cambridge and Gordon Graham Wordsworth, grandson of the poet, agreed a price with Lord Leconfield for the transfer to the National Trust of the adjacent Scafell above 2,000 ft in 1925.[69]

Hill Top Farm

Potter acquired Hill Top Farm during this first period of the Trust's expansion into Lakeland. Contemporaries described the parish as a quiet place, 'not yet entered by the railway ... on the whole very secluded', characterised by 'scattered, rambling villages on broken ground' and a mix of mainly pasture, substantial woods and plantation, and some arable. The scenery was 'pleasing rather than grand' and 'summer excursionists', passing through Hawkshead en route from the Windermere Ferry to Coniston, could catch a glimpse of the school where Wordsworth was educated. Grumbles that modern architecture failed to take account of 'climate, history, geology' were beginning to be heard.[70] The Trust was not interested in properties like this. Hill Top was not on a lake, in a location well-known to visitors or riven with access issues. Potter's first purchase was a private decision, without immediate public significance. That would come later, and only retrospect makes Potter's decision to buy a small farm in 1905 significant to the later history of the Trust.

The purchase was also intensely private in another way. It was shadowed by grief. Potter's friendship with Norman Warne, her editor and the son of her publisher, had blossomed into love and she had accepted his proposal that July. While Potter was on holiday on the west coast of Wales, Warne had been taken ill, developing lymphatic leukaemia. He deteriorated rapidly and died just weeks after the engagement and while Potter was still away. Potter's family had strongly opposed her marrying into trade, which can only have compounded the pain brought by her loss. Nonetheless, she decided to go ahead with her plan to purchase Hill Top, made possible by her earnings and a legacy from her aunt. She negotiated with Frederic Fowkes, a local land speculator, who had bought the farm as one of several lots in September 1905 for £1,375. He sold it to Potter on 15 November for £2,805. To consider this transaction in isolation suggests that Potter had been exploited by an unscrupulous land agent, and she was convinced that her first independent financial decision had made her something of a laughing stock in the village.[71] But if compared to the famous kerfuffle caused in 1910 by the sale and purchase of Tattershall Castle, an unusual site in the Lincolnshire Fens, the transaction begins to look more typical of the manoeuvrings that occasioned the pre-war property market. Like Hill Top, Tattershall Castle came onto the market as part of a larger sale, though it was a historical curiosity rather than a working farm.

Peter Mandler tells the tale: in 1910 Lord Fortescue sold the castle to T.H. Hooley, a speculator, who offered it to Albert Ball, the former Mayor of Nottingham, for £1,125. Ball offered it to the National Trust for £2,000, which was declined, and it was soon in the hands of Hooley's creditors. The bank then offered it to the Trust for £3,000, again declined, after which the bank decided the best way to realise its value was to sell its chimneypieces separately. The Trust now mobilised, Rawnsley writing the inevitable letter to *The Times*, but this only served to increase the potential value of the castle's parts and the Trust's attempt to raise the vastly inflated purchase price of the chimneypieces through a public appeal was a flop. The bank sold the castle, minus its chimneypieces, to another dealer, reportedly for export to America. Once the fuss died down, Lord Curzon stepped in, bought the castle from the dealer for £2,750 and, with help from eminent friends, bought the chimneypieces for £5,155, acquiring for £8,000 what the Trust had been originally offered for £2,000. Curzon left the castle to the Trust in his will, duly fulfilled in 1926.[72]

The Tattershall Castle debacle demonstrated that people more experienced than Potter could fall foul of the property market, but what further insight does the case offer into Potter's purchase of Hill Top? At first glance, not a great deal, but in terms of Potter's later decisions, it did lead to significant developments. As Mandler explains, the passage of the Ancient Monuments Act in 1913 was intended to prevent such desecrations in the future on the grounds that the national interest dictated that certain buildings should be protected. The Trust had lobbied for the legislation, but in practice the Act proved to be toothless, reflecting the refusal by members of both houses of parliament to countenance a significant empowering of the state to either make significant interventions in the property market or impose effective planning controls over what owners could do to their property. Having a building scheduled as an ancient monument rarely prevented it from being sold or altered and might well have added to its market value.[73]

Potter, then, had entered the property market during a particularly febrile period. Tensions over the fate of large estates were becoming increasingly politicised, and the demon spectre of the American plutocrat loomed large in the preservationist imagination, the aristocratic house sale becoming emblematic of the time. Contents could be worth more than the building or the land, and on occasion entire rooms or staircases were dismantled for shipping. The 1913 Act gestured towards a stronger programme of state-enabled preservation, but little really changed. It is unsurprising that the Trust could not raise the money to purchase the chimneypieces – a pretty bizarre ask – but more generally the episode, including its legislative aftermath, demonstrated that purchase remained the only plausible protection against unwanted change. And more than this, although the available evidence does suggest that Curzon's patrician intervention particularly registered with Potter, its logic would be hers in future years: she too would be the wealthy individual who prevented harm when no other body had the resources to act.

This was for the future. For now, Potter had no intention of farming full time and she kept on John Cannon, the Hill Top tenant who lived there with his wife and two children, but she did embark on a string of improvements. She was amused to discover that Hill Top was effectively a pig farm, but this did not put her off, her eye for detail having found a new outlet. The garden was to be relaid, so it could be developed into a productive kitchen garden, and the house enlarged, allowing enough living space for herself and the tenant's family. She was soon taken aback by the impact of her improvements. As dictated by current fashion, her desire for a small lawn had been interpreted as a space large enough for a tennis court. She soon had Cannon dig it up for potatoes. And though pleased by the house, she was troubled by the visual impact of her improvements: 'The new works though doubtless an improvement are painfully *new*. Instead of the old winding road – with a tumble-down wall covered with polypody [creeping fern] – there is a straight wide road & a very bare wall. Also heaps of soil everywhere & new railings, they would show up less if they were tarred.'[74]

These were the characteristic laments of the absentee landlord and, aged 40, she again holidayed with her parents at Lingholm that summer. Feeling the pull of Hill Top, 20 miles to the south, that summer surely reminded her that neither the purchase nor the death of her betrothed registered a clear break with old routines. When she got to Near Sawrey in the autumn, work on the garden gave her great pleasure (and a ravenous appetite) and she was overwhelmed with offers of flowers and shrubs from her neighbours; less satisfactory were her dealings with local tradesmen, who made it clear that being a woman and an outsider was a double disadvantage. Still, with an air of ceremony, she lit her first fire in her new library in mid-October; more auspicious still, Cannon decided to buy 16 Herdwick ewes. There would be lambs at Hill Top in the spring.

Under Potter's supervision, Hill Top gradually became a picture-book small farm.[75] The Herdwicks, soon a flock of 31, the pigs, now 14 in total, and a gaggle of ducks and chickens were joined by six dairy cows and, in due course, calves and bullocks. Outbuildings were added, and existing buildings improved; the garden was developed (partly inspired by Gwaynynog, the house of her Leech relatives); and the farmhouse was furnished to a high standard. Hill Top did not function according to the usual constraints faced by a small farm, and Potter's ability to diversify its holdings reflected her own wishes rather than agricultural necessity. She could afford to buck the trend towards specialisation. The satisfaction she derived from these developments catalysed a period of tremendous creativity: the now 'Little Books' came thick and fast, their illustrations inspired by Hill Top and Near Sawrey.

Despite Potter accumulating additional parcels of land, Hill Top was not enough, and she was primed to buy when neighbouring Castle Farm came on the market in 1909. She acquired the house, a labourer's cottage, the outbuildings and 20 acres for £1,573, a good price, helped along by her decision to instruct W.H. Heelis and Son to handle the conveyancing. Castle Farm was contiguous with Hill Top and extended her property directly into the village. She now had an established position in this small agricultural community, but more significant still was that the transaction brought her into contact with William Heelis, one of the firm's two partners. At 38 years old, he was 'tall, quiet, rather handsome with an athletic build and an easy manner'; he rode a motorcycle and had an acute understanding of the Lakeland property market. Heelis would henceforth act for Potter and keep an eye on her interests when she was in London.[76] For example, subsequent to the purchase of Castle Farm, Heelis reached an agreement with the Ecclesiastical Commission that on the payment of six pounds, four shillings and two pence Potter would no longer be obliged to make the customary annual payment of four shillings, two pence and one halfpenny, the 'Minister's Salary', for the incumbent of the Benefice of Hawkshead. For Potter, these were insignificant sums, but by this small but characteristic gesture she sought to free herself of a financial obligation belonging to her lands in the parish.[77]

Castle Farm had been sold as part of the break-up of a tenanted estate, which raised numerous minor legal questions about the property related to neighbouring freeholds, particularly with respect to water. For example, Robert Holt Edmondson bought a section of the Castle Estate that was sandwiched by Potter's Bull Banks, where she had a water catchpit, and her Castle Field. Potter and Edmundson agreed that she could lay a pipe across Edmondson's land and he could draw water from her catchpit.[78] Similarly, when Ulverston Rural District Council wanted to extract water from a stream that flowed through her property, Heelis negotiated an agreement whereby the council would compensate her with two cattle troughs and connect her to the mains.[79] Further agreements over water supply were an inevitable feature of her later purchases, generating a complex skein of legal agreements and payments.

Potter and Heelis developed a companionable friendship, mixing business and pleasure as allowed by the demands of Potter's now elderly and frail parents (summer holidays remained an obligation), and in October 1912 Heelis asked Potter to marry him. She accepted, her parents disapproved (a country solicitor!), she bore their remonstrances and after much agonising about the timing – and some stress-related illness along the way – Beatrix and William were married in London in October 1913. They made Castle Cottage, suitably renovated (French windows and a veranda were added), their matrimonial home.

In the meantime, Potter had dipped her toes into some new areas of activity. In response to the political imbroglio provoked by the rejection of Lloyd George's 'People's Budget' by the House of Lords, Potter produced propaganda material in support of the Conservatives in the first of 1910's general elections. Like many agriculturalists, she did not believe free trade was in Britain's interest, a position at odds with her nonconformist Liberal upbringing. She was doubtless influenced by Tory arguments that the imposition of tariffs would revive the rural economy, though the evidence suggests she adopted this position partly to protect her more immediate interests.[80] German manufacturers accused of undercutting British producers included unofficial producers of Peter Rabbit merchandise, now an important part of her income. Her attempt to link her opposition to free trade to her opposition to legislation enabling a census to be taken of Britain's horse stock, which she took to be a harbinger of the likely conscription of horses in the event of war, was not altogether convincing, but it still reflected her contradictory attitudes towards the state. Protectionist on the one hand but opposed to regulation on the other, she had become quite the Tory.[81] Indeed, she contemplated intervening in the debate provoked by the government's decision to ban the presence or participation of children under the age of 16 in the knacker's yard during a slaughter. Children, she thought, had become too cosseted.[82] True she was middle-aged, but these modest forays into national politics were underpinned less by an ideologically coherent opposition to greater intervention by the state and more by that familiar rural notion that well-meaning metropolitan legislators do not understand the ways of the countryside.

Better known was her involvement in the campaign against the construction of an aeroplane factory at Cockshott Point on Windermere and the use of hydroplanes on the lake. The episode mobilised the National Trust, led by Rawnsley and Robert Hunter, and provided a rare example of Potter intervening directly in a classic preservationist campaign. Rawnsley helped get the campaign going with a letter to *The Times* in January 1912, which garnered swift responses from a string of local notables, including E.W. Wakefield, the principal protagonist; William Forwood, Commodore of the Royal Windermere Yacht Club; Arthur Holmes, Honorary Secretary of the Windermere Hydro-aeroplane Protect Committee (the ad-hoc group Rawnsley helped to organise); one H.B. Potter of Near Sawrey; William Knight of Keswick; and Hunter himself.[83] Privately, Potter wrote of 'a beastly fly-swimming spluttering aeroplane careering up & down Windermere; it makes a noise like 10 million bluebottles' and had 'caused a horse to bolt & smashed a tradesman's cart';[84] publicly, she countered Wakefield's claim that he was acting in the national interest by helping Britain to catch up in a technological arms race by asserting that his real aim was to establish tourist flights between Bowness and Grasmere. That might well have been true, although parliamentary exchanges implied that Wakefield's experiments had the approval of the Admiralty.[85] Potter's lengthiest intervention was a letter to *Country Life* magazine, which proved to be, in some respects, her most direct evocation of what she found most valuable about Lakeland life.

She stated her case against the hydro-aeroplanes not through conventional homilies about the peace and tranquillity provided by the Lake District, but instead she established the integrity of Lakeland life by treating the Windermere ferry as a synecdoche for the communities that lived near the lake. Quoting evidence from Swainson Cowper's *History of Hawkshead* (1899) of the ferry's continuous existence since the seventeenth century, she described what a tourist might see:

> the ramshackle, picturesque boat, heavy laden with the Coniston four-horsed coach and char-a-banc, or with carrier's tilt cart and bustling motor, or homely toppling loads of oak bark and hooper's swills, or droves of sheep or cattle. Farm-carts go down and across with sacks of wool and bark and faggots; they struggle homewards with loads of coal. Everyone uses the ferry.

This is not a vision of Lakeland as outside of time, devoid of the mechanical hand of early twentieth-century modernity – there is the 'char-a-banc' and a 'motor' – but it is Lakeland as taskscape, a place of practical considerations, of the movement of people and material. Potter could imagine horses on land becoming accustomed to the whine of the engines, but she could not imagine them remaining calm on the ferry as the hydroplane swooped over them.[86] Twenty years later, she took a similar line on the new generation of motorboats, the 'bottom of the lake' being the best place for them.[87]

Potter closed with a line from Wordsworth's poem 'There was a Boy', about the receptivity of a child to nature's agency. In this simple, affecting lyric, Wordsworth recalls a boy who would stand on the edge of Windermere and mimic the hooting of the owls. The owls respond 'with quivering peals, / And long halloos, and screams, and echoes loud / Redoubled and redoubled; concourse wild / Of jocund din!'. But when all falls quiet, the boy sometimes hears something else, the essence of the place. He dies aged 12 and Wordsworth describes standing mute before his grave on summer evenings, reflecting on how the landscape itself had worked upon the boy's sensibilities. It seems far from coincidental that Potter chose an excerpt from a poem in the same tradition as Wordsworth's more celebrated 'Michael', for both poems explore not only nature's affect upon the human imagination, but more specifically the affect this had on a gnarled old shepherd and a sensitive but uneducated Lakeland child, neither of whom were privy to the counsels of Romanticism. This small gesture aligned Potter closely with the peoples of the Lake District rather than with the national agenda of the preservationists, and it seems significant to her later activities. When she attempted to mobilise a petition against the hydroplane, something of her political naïvety was evident in her disappointment at finding her Liberal rather than her Conservative London contacts more receptive. The communal interest must not trump the entrepreneur. A few months later, she gleefully wrote to her publisher that 'the roof of the hydro hangar has blown in, & smashed two machines'.[88]

Potter remained in Rawnsley's ambit – she was a committed member of the Footpath Association – but she was also increasingly drawn into more conventional rural activities. In 1912, she was elected as a Representative Freeholder to the Landowners' Community Association, an organisation mainly concerned with local land management questions, particularly with respect to the upkeep of roads, timber and property boundaries.[89] It is not to be confused with the Central Landowners' Association, founded in 1906 to defend land interests against the apparent growing threat from the land nationalisation lobby.[90] In 1913, she acted as a judge at a trussed poultry contest at the local agricultural show.[91] Not long after, she bought Sawrey House Estate, adding 66 acres (and a tarn) to her holdings, making

Hill Top more viable as a Lakeland farm. Potter, like Hill, had never been fashionable in her dress, but now she positively embraced the apparent freedoms country living provided, adopting an unconventional but practical style, setting her apart from other Lakeland women. Her wooden clogs and heavy tweeds became something of a uniform, and were not always thought becoming by local people for a woman of her class.[92] But perhaps more than anything else, the experience of war saw her develop the outlook of a countrywoman. Cheap imports before 1914 had placed pressure on agricultural prices – hence her embrace of protectionism – and the benefits that stemmed from the increased prices paid for agricultural produce during the war, including the new subsidies paid for converting pasture to arable (Potter had 160 acres under plough), were offset by the intense pressures stemming from labour shortages. Potter accepted this as a necessity of war – like many young men in the community, one of the Cannon boys had enlisted – but she was incensed that women agricultural workers were attracted by relatively high wages in munitions factories, as she lamented in an anonymous letter to *The Times*.[93]

Potter's war was personally hard. Her father died in 1914 (she received a quarter of his estate, some £35,000) and her brother Bertram, to whom she had always been close, unexpectedly succumbed to a cerebral haemorrhage in June 1918, possibly brought on by his alcoholism; she was also constantly irritated by delayed royalty cheques from Warne, which culminated in financial scandal in 1917; but her plight cannot be compared to that of a typical Lakeland farmer and, in April 1917, she once again expanded her interest, leasing Hawkshead Field, a 66-acre farm that included a house, cottage and outbuildings, for seven years at £52 per annum.[94]

Troutbeck

Potter's acquisition of Troutbeck Park Farm in 1923 marked a new departure. Her reason for buying was simple. The farm was coming on the market and risked being planted with holiday homes: 'one red tiled bungalow' placed in a sensitive spot, she thought, could destroy an area.[95] It was a common preservationist concern. H.H. Symonds wrote that 'everywhere the green or greenish tint of the native roofing slate is warm and fresh and cheerful, in key with the fell-sides; to introduce the blue or purple Welsh slate, or red tiles, or red asbestos roofing composition, "tiled" in a lozenge pattern, is a sin'.[96]

Troutbeck was a large farm, totalling 760 hectares (1,875 acres), which she added to with new purchases in the following years. It was evidence, if more evidence was needed, that her accumulation of land in the Lake District went beyond her desire to fully participate in its agricultural life. She bought Troutbeck Park fully intending to bequeath it to the National Trust, and she made the requisite change to her will shortly afterwards. And just as she actively sought to improve Hill Top and Castle Farm, so too with Troutbeck. Her attachment to Troutbeck Park reflected its unusual characteristics. At first glance, Troutbeck looks like open fell and could be mistaken for common land, but the valley through which the Trout Beck flows is enclosed land, whose outer boundaries date back to its 'impark-ment' by the Cistercians of Furness Abbey in the thirteenth century. 'Imparkment' was a response to increasing population and grazing pressures – at its height, the monks and lay brothers of Furness Abbey kept thousands of sheep. Inside the park, landowners preserved deer for the hunt; outside the park, commoners and men of lower social status could hunt for fox, hare and rabbit over extensive common grazings.[97] Troutbeck's later conversion into a sheep farm made it unusual in being entirely self-contained: the farm, the enclosed fields and the rough grazing form the same freehold. Something of the pleasure Potter took in Troutbeck Park stemmed from the fact that this allowed her to do more or less as she pleased. Once, that is, she'd dispensed with the sitting tenants, whom she considered neglectful and disreputable, and dealt with the bad case of liver fluke that had infested the flock. She'd once come upon a dog feasting on a sheep's carcass left to rot behind the house.[98] It is worth emphasising this: although celebrated as a champion of traditional Lake District farming, and particularly for the role she played in the valorisation of Herdwicks, Potter did not feel a particular commitment to her tenantry or the commoners. She frequently criticised tenants for their slovenly ways, and on more than one occasion was especially critical of 'Herdwick shepherds'. She tended to prefer employees to tenants and liked to offer potential employees twice the going rate to induce them into her employment, further evidence of the empowering effect of her money. Troutbeck, then, was managed by Jimmy Hislop, initially supported by Tom Storey as a full-time shepherd, and, for 19 years at lambing time, Joe Moscrop, a Border Country bachelor of farming background.

It is easy to be a little awed by the great sweep and isolation of Troutbeck's location. In *A Complete Guide to the English Lakes* (1855), Harriet Martineau included a celebratory description of Troutbeck, 'the most primitive of the frequented valleys in this district'. Even on the gloomy day I walked its length, when visibility was reduced at times to just a few metres, the effect of its dramatic valley setting, 'scooped out between the ridges', was palpable.[99] Closed in to the north by the forbidding massif of Stony Cove Pike (763m), overlooked to the west by Ill Bell (757m) and to the east by the famous Kirkstone Pass (455m), the Lake District's highest major road, it is hard not to adopt an environmentally deterministic outlook: the parameters of this place seem defined by nature, notwithstanding that its present limits are consequent upon a set of decisions made by the Cistercians in the thirteenth century. Looking down from Troutbeck village or Town Head – as popular with tourists as with wealthy second-home owners – the valley seems flattened, but as I descend Ing Lane into the flat bottom of the valley below Troutbeck Park my perspective changes as the fells rise about me. For now, on the flat bottom of the valley, the going is easy. Small fields, enclosed by slate stone walls and barbed-wire fences, tidily grid the marshy rough grazing both sides of the beck. Herdwicks predominate, but there are also Bluefaced Leicesters and, in one field, two languorous rams graze among the ewes, working up some energy. A mole catcher has displayed his deeds: little pink snouts are spiked onto barbed wire, giant forepaws becoming skeletal as the corpses rot. At the entrance to Troutbeck, a notice tells of environmental projects undertaken on the farm co-funded by the British government and the European Union. Silage bales tightly wrapped in purple polymer are stickered with big, quirky faces. Would Potter have been amused?

Little indicates that this is an iconic National Trust site. The farm buildings are unexceptional and weather-worn, though no more so than might be expected of any working farm; under bright sun, the white-wash would appear less lime-tinged by damp climate and harsh weather. As Martineau wrote, 'dwellings of too glaring a white' are tempered with 'weather stains'.[100] The Troutbeck soundscape is particularly affecting. Potter wrote of it:

> Troutbeck Tongue is uncanny, a place of silences and whispering echoes. It is a mighty table-land between two streams. They rise together, north of the Tongue, in one maze of bogs and pools. They flow on either hand ... and re-unite beneath the southern crags, making the table-land almost an island haunted by the sounds that creep on running waters that encompass it.[101]

Since 1975, Troutbeck Park has been designated a Site of Special Scientific Interest (SSSI) on account of its rich flora. In the yard behind the farm buildings, Herdwick lambs are gathered in a muddy enclosure: chocolate-brown fleeces, white faces, stubby horns and puppy-like air.

I skirt the Tongue to the east, following the path by Hagg Gill, one of Potter's streams, through glacially smoothed terrain. Spoil heaps from the disused quarries loom above, eerie reminders of how this spot once echoed with industrial activity, producing a very different soundscape.[102] Herdwick ewes and their lambs, descendants of the 'heafed' flock Potter sought to preserve, are walled in on the bumpy humpy hillside to my left. They chew, seemingly quizzical, apparently less nervous around human beings than other breeds. Walking through wintry Lakeland fields, I've been followed by small flocks of Herdwicks, a metre or so from my heels but never close enough to be touched.

As the farm buildings become obscured by the Tongue and the temperature drops, the sedge, the mire and the snaking slate walls provoke a familiar, happy solitude. I am the 'lone enraptured male' identified by Kathleen Jamie in her coruscating critique of a certain kind of nature writing, and I reflect on this, mindful too that Potter – and many Lakeland farmers – make no necessary distinction between places of work and places of natural beauty.[103] Ascending Park Fell, my lonely rapture becomes mild anxiety as the encroaching mist reduces visibility to just a few metres and my breath quickens. I've not walked here before and must trust the map, the path and my sense of direction, but as landscape features become obscured by mist so tracking my progress on the map is correspondingly tricky. Retracing my steps would be easy, but I know catching sight of the beacon at Thornthwaite Crag will allay my anxiety. A figure strides out of the mist. We exchange pleasantries about the sinister turn in the weather and he's reassuring, saying regular posts now mark the way to the beacon. And so they do, successively taking form. The beacon, a thick, chimney stack of slate, is suddenly visible, and I'm soon exchanging relieved smiles and fresh pleasantries with walkers who have followed St Raven's Edge from the Kirkstone Pass. I scrawl 'whoop!' in biro on the OS map, a mnemonic to a minor ordeal.

On a clear day, the views are expansive, north towards Ullswater and south down the valley to Windermere, but today all is greyish white. I might have seen what was once George Grizedale's farm at Hartsopp, contiguous with Potter's northern boundaries and on her to-buy list, but she lost out when it came on the market in 1926. The sale thwarted her 'dream' to make all the land between the Kirkstone

Pass and the Haweswater catchment into 'a reservation', for although she thought the land as 'unbeautiful as Lakes can be' – 'judicial planting' might help – it was one of 'the few corners of the district not exploited'.[104] She later hoped that the Forestry Commission would buy up land on Kirkstone Pass because new plantations would 'improve that bleak scenery' and make a reservation around Troutbeck and provide shelter.[105] This placed her outside of the preservationist mainstream, which was locked into a process of fraught negotiation with the Forestry Commission in the early 1930s and in 1935 saw the commission agree not to seek to afforest the central area of the Lake District, including Troutbeck and its immediate surroundings.[106] More modest ambitions, however, were paying off. She had bought a strip of land directly adjacent to the Kirkstone Pass, cutting off land from the road belonging to a Mrs Poole by Troutbeck. She now need only wait for the old woman to die, for no one else could wish to buy it. She also had her eye on contiguous fields owned by four neighbouring farmers.

Potter's comments formed part of a longer letter describing the progress she'd made at Troutbeck Park.[107] It revealed a lot about her ambitions and methods. 'After very great trouble' the tenant had been got out and she decided not to let the farm again. The land and 'sheepstock' were in a 'derelict and unhealthy condition', mosses and drains needed clearing, and the fencing was in a poor state. She planned to plant trees, including larch for use as fencing posts (walls were too expensive), though for the time being she relied on thinnings from her small Sawrey plantations. She had already planted five acres of larch at the Park and she planned to plant Scotch firs on Hall Hill, to the front of the house, presumably as shelter. She also wanted oaks on the south side of the Tongue and behind them Scotch fir, birch and larch, telling Samuel Hamer, Secretary to the National Trust, to note this should she not live to see it done. Her planned improvements meant she needed someone who understood dry stone walling and how to look after plantations. She would not take on anyone without checking the condition of his existing tenancy. '*Herdwick men are untidy farmers*', she wrote, and sometimes 'annoying men'. She turned down several applications from prospective tenants, in one case because she thought him unlikely to be conscientious and reliable, but more particularly because she anticipated a new tenant likely to be disgruntled by her plans. What she really wanted was employees and she soon gathered an expert team she could trust to build up the flock of about 1,100 'pure bred heafed Herdwicks', a 'landlord's stock' of about '700 ewes, 180 twinters [two-winter sheep], and 220 hoggs [male or female lambs before shearing]'. At this stage, she was reluctant to write numbers into her will because some tenants 'dislike a large tied stock' but she argued 'there must always be a large landlord stock at the Park' for the practical reason that 'the tops are not fenced'. She described the Trust as inheriting the 'landlord part of me' and 'my executors the tenant part'.[108]

Her urge to show Herdwicks saw her persuade Tom Storey to work with her at New Sawrey to help breed prize-winning examples. Conventional wisdom had it that Herdwicks were not suited to softer country, but Potter and Storey demonstrated that Herdwicks thrived on a good diet in easier country, and she won many first prizes over the next decade. In essence, Potter's experience indicated that while Herdwicks might out-survive most breeds in harsh uplands this doesn't preclude their thriving in less testing conditions. Again, financial advantage helped, and she generally got her way at livestock auctions. It is appealing to imagine the close attention she paid to flock books and her exceptional eye for animal anatomy, honed by decades of close observation as an artist, paid off, the artist and the fellswoman finding common cause. Tom Storey was less convinced, and there is a somewhat weather-worn anecdote about her failing to recognise her own sheep at a country fair. In any case, she took great pleasure in her achievements, crowing about the success of her ewes in September 1930: 'We were at Keswick yesterday & Windermere today Hawkshead tomorrow – my old ladies are tired of motoring in the lorry; but we still sweep the board. It is getting awkward!'[109] That year, she was made the first woman president of the Herdwick Sheep Breeders' Association and the men that dominated the shows soon acknowledged her expertise and prevailed upon her to act as judge. On being elevated to the chair, a 'jolly old farmer' toasted her as comparable to a 'first prize cow'; on another occasion a friendly but inebriated farmer enthusiastically clapped her on the back, sending her flying. Still, hers was a double achievement: she had successfully penetrated a world notoriously dismissive of incomers and had done so as a woman.[110]

Further evidence of the satisfaction she gleaned from her new enterprise is evident in the letters she wrote to Joe Moscrop. Early each year she struck up correspondence in anticipation of lambing, seeking to induce him to come with an account of the progress made on her farms and asking advice about how they might proceed. Business-focused but not businesslike, these letters differed from those addressed to Hamer, revealing a different side of her personality and a different way of using the written word. Her concerns were those of any attentive farmer, but there was more to these enchanting letters than a simple accounting. She detailed the appearance and character of her stock, the progress and behaviour of her sheepdogs, the wildlife found on her farms, and more besides, including comments on the mid-Victorian radicals Cobden and Bright, whom her father had known, and the passing in 1936 of George V: 'don't you think', she asked, 'it is to the credit of human nature that a plain honest – not a very clever man should have gained so much love and respect?'. Each lamb successfully birthed was an achievement, affirming that she was doing good work: there is something of the new entrant enthused by early successes in these letters. And notwithstanding her determination to be treated as a phlegmatic and pragmatic farmer, and her sometimes abrasive efforts to present herself as such, she ascribed to her animals distinctive personality traits and developmental trajectories, whether writing of a restless bull, of 'bonny' yellow calves 'playing like lambs', or her attempts to produce manageable pups from Lassie, her favourite but 'excitable' sheepdog. Introducing Lassie to a 'slow quiet dog' did not have the desired effect and the resulting pups took 'after the bitch in disposition'.[111] James Rebanks, Herdwick farmer, heritage consultant and author of two best-selling accounts of the life of a Lake District fellsman, loves these letters and it is easy to imagine why.[112] The delight Potter once took in her nursery menagerie was now found in her fells and her farms, somewhat intractable adults replacing tricky parents or nannies; and just as in her Little Books she created a rustic ideal, so now she sought to establish a great stretch of Lakeland, cast according to her ideals of good husbandry and landscape management. Commercial success, bolstered by a very substantial inheritance, permitted her to maintain a continuum between her childhood, middle years and old age, between the nursery, the Little Books and Troutbeck: the page had become the landscape, her money and her employees the watercolours, but she kept tight hold of the brush.[113]

The scramble down from Thornthwaite Crag into the valley is testing. It is steep, and the scree is brutal. Crows caw a desolate soundtrack to a desolate scene. Potter disliked the birds, once mentioning in a discussion about the persecution of birds of prey that crows were a far greater threat to farming interests. They were egg stealers and would pick the eyes out of live sheep. Buzzards, by contrast, were 'farmed' at Troutbeck because they dealt with field mice, 'which eat a surprising amount of herbage up on the fells'.[114] My blurry photos catch me in motion, more concerned for getting the descent over than with posterity. I scribble 'Hard' on the map. At Thornthwaite Mouth, the lowest point of the ridge, the path up Stony Cove Pike beckons but I plunge down back into the valley, the full length of Troutbeck Park before me. The mist now lifts a little, and the scene, doused with moisture, is compelling. Rawnsley would remind me of the Cistercians, the quarrying, the hefted flock, but up here little evidence of the farm is visible, the buildings obscured by the top of the Tongue, and notions of timelessness seek to blind the historicising eye. At the same time, I'm a little intimidated by the distance before me, alert to how the lifting mist has revealed the fading light of an autumn afternoon and I should probably get cracking. 'Galumphing, which is partly jumping and partly galloping,' advises Arthur Ransome, 'is a quick way of going downhill.'[115] I tighten the straps on my small rucksack and galumph down Park Fell Head, gravity providing me all the momentum I need, strained thigh muscles checking my progress. I could do without landing flat on my face.

Notions of timelessness are quickly banished. A mini tongue, crevassed by the Trout Beck and a tributary, is the site of a new plantation. The National Trust has planted oak, rowan, holly, alder, willow, aspen, hawthorn, bird cherry and birch as part of a broader aim to improve tree cover on its vast holdings across the district, generating new habitat, flood defence and greater biodiversity. If the woodland is to take hold, the sheep need to be kept out, and the saplings are encased in plastic guards and fenced in.[116] As these trees mature, an arrow-head shaped copse will come into being, aligned with the contours of the fell and pointing to the trees that dash the brook downstream. Further on, in the flush meadow shadowed by the Tongue, the ground flora appreciably enriches, teeming today with fat brown fox moth caterpillars. It is exuberant, a botanist's paradise, but in my amateurish way I quickly lose track of the great variety of species. The slew of Latin names that comprise the SSSI site description delineate how the 'flushed grassland and fen vegetation' becomes 'woodland variant rush pasture' in the wet alder wood that skirts the west side of Trout Beck. The flora is more unruly than is captured by the technical description.[117]

The content of Potter's letters to Hamer were not confined to Troutbeck. Her self-appointed role as watchdog saw her alert Hamer to developments she thought should concern the Trust, and she expected the Trust to act against developments she judged at odds with its principles. For instance, she thought holiday camps a 'wholesome sign of the times', but in 1925 was roused by the prospect of Swiss-style chalets on Mickleden Beck below Langdale Fell. 'If people are going to be allowed to put nasty sham chalets into peaceful solitudes,' she wrote, 'I can only repeat my heartfelt wish that all the heads of the valleys and roots of the mountains were in the hands of the Trust.'[118] Her faith in the Trust would never really abate. She explained that she did not get involved in the recent Langdale sales because the farms were not immediately adjacent to the fells ('a Naboth's vineyard in the way'), admitting that the appeal of Troutbeck was that it had 'no common rights' and included the high fells. In the same way, she hoped the National Trust would one day acquire Brotherilkeld at Eskdale, another substantial valley-head farm – prior to visiting 'the top end', she'd thought Eskdale 'a fussy full-of-lodgings-&-toy-railway place'.[119] She kept tabs on other developments. She was quick to write to Hamer when she learned that Bridge House, a small but iconic seventeenth-century building in Ambleside that straddles Stock Gyll Beck, had come on the market: 'Not beautiful; but it will be looked for, & missed, if it goes down.'[120] Gordon Wordsworth led the successful campaign to raise the £1,200 needed to secure the house for the Trust in 1926. As the poet's only surviving grandson and resident at The Stepping Stones, Ambleside, it is probable that he recognised the importance of the Trust's work after seeing the contents of Rydal Mount (his grandfather's former home) auctioned off following the death in 1920 of Violet Fisher-Wordsworth, Wordsworth's great-granddaughter.[121]

The National Trust's decision to appoint a dedicated land agent in the Lake District marked a significant step in its development as a professional property management trust with a significant salariat and strong regional governance structures. It was logical that Lakeland, as the site of the Trust's largest concentration of holdings, would be the initial locus of these organisational experiments.[122] Potter got wind of these discussions in 1929 and again offered Hamer unsolicited advice, writing three hasty letters in the space of a week. She feared that the Trust would appoint a local man from within the agricultural community, particularly someone who had already worked as a land agent, whom she doubted would properly protect the interests of the Trust. An outsider was needed, preferably 'a gentleman', possibly an ex-navy officer, or 'a university man not afraid of dirtying his hands', who had professional expertise and was genuinely 'interested' in the work. Above all, he needed to be a 'superior man with more than a merely local interest', boasting 'a clear head, a good presence', and 'above politics and squabbles'. 'The typical agent,' she added for good measure, 'has all the faults of the idle rich, with bumptiousness added.' Potter was not keen on the type: she found local land agents rude, condescending to her as a woman and prone to drink. Appoint an agent of this type, she joked, and she 'would turn socialist and vote for a National Park and the office of Works!!'. They needed someone whom the local people would respect. 'Our Westmorland lads are rough,' she argued, 'but you have no idea how sharp they are to reckon up whether a man is a gentleman or not.' Not even her husband, whose name had been mentioned, was up to the job.[123] Bruce Thompson eventually got the job, a decision Potter would in some ways come to rue.

Monk Coniston Park Estate

The Heelis collection, held by the Lancashire Archives, includes a file titled 'Monk Coniston Park Estate, 1916–1929'. It contains numerous legal documents concerned with the inheritance of the estate within the Marshall family, its mortgage liabilities and evidence enough of the financial pressures that meant the Marshalls wanted to sell. Three lengthy schedules detail the component parts of the estate, several hundred entries depicting a complex mix of meadow, plantation, house property, enclosures, coppice, pasture, slate quarries, roads, waste and intake land. More broadly, the schedule lists a mix of fell, plantations and farms, including some large stretches of common land, notably Tilberthwaite High Fell (Tilberthwaite

Allotment, 777 acres), Little Fell, Holme Fell (296 + 136 acres), Tom Heights (172 acres) and part of Coniston Moor (181 acres). In the main, the western and north-west side of the estate is common land, and land to the east and north-east of Coniston Water was tenanted.

Setting aside the common land to the west, a circular walk of the estate is not much further than the Troutbeck loop – the north–south axis of both estates is about four miles – but the experience is radically different. Visitors like Monk Coniston's variety, including honeypots like Tarn Hows, but Potter wrote gloomily of a 'bewildering place', 'no bigger than the Park but more bother'. Her gaze onto the landscape was managerial rather than leisured and she saw a lot of problems.[124] As I set off from Coniston Far End, planning an inexact beating of bounds, I'm excited by the prospect of a varied and intimate landscape, agricultural, post-industrial, touristic and human in scale. If at Troutbeck I experienced the Burkean sublime, today I expect the rustic and picturesque.

I pass through the woodland and rank grass that edge Yewdale Fells, marvelling at the Dog House, a nineteenth-century folly built by the Marshalls for their fox hounds, and the grand old oaks that frame the western wooded slopes of Yewdale and the White Gill waterfall. The sound of distant rushing water suffuses the scene. Potter valued the estate's timber as a commercial asset and was alert to the danger of it being felled and sold before the sale completed, but she considered the old oaks at Guards Wood, the backdrop to this scene, as sacrosanct. The larch would mature into a valuable cash crop, but under her management the oaks at Guards Wood, a site from which she hoped the public could be excluded, would be preserved.[125] As at Troutbeck, conservation broadleaf planting has been taken up here; the site is peppered with saplings encased in their plastic tubes.

A National Trust noticeboard introduces the estate. The Marshalls, a Leeds family, made their industrial fortune from flax, converting some of that enormous wealth into a country estate. 'Marshall was a man of the Victorian Age and his vision of the Lake District was influenced by the fashion for idealised landscapes', the noticeboard reads. 'If your estate lacked tall trees, limpid lakes and pretty cottages you simply had them installed, until by brute wealth and creative flair you were the envy of your neighbours.' Potter's environing at Troutbeck was modest by these standards and I like the wry admission that the estate now looked after by the Trust was an exercise in landscape production: the rich man installing large-scale features just as someone might a shower, while to group 'brute wealth' with 'creative flair' is refreshingly honest. Nineteenth-century industrialists were the Medici of their time, the land their canvas, as estates across the country now attest.[126]

By the 1920s the Marshall finances were in bad shape. Monk Coniston House was sold off first, and in 1929 the family were said to be desperate to sell the rest. The price was rumoured to be anything between £15,000 and £18,000. Potter entered into a remarkable agreement with the Trust. She would buy the whole estate, sell to the Trust a substantial portion as soon as possible, but act as land manager for the whole, and bequeath the rest in due course. Quite how the Trust would raise the money and how the estate would be divided was unclear, but Potter was determined to drive a hard bargain.[127] As she occasionally reminded the Trust, it was she who took the risk, for there was no guarantee of how quickly the Trust might raise the requisite funds – Potter was unsure how long her capital would be tied up in the property.

Her business-like approach to the ensuing negotiations with the Trust also reflected the fact that the area did not arouse a heartfelt commitment. Tilberthwaite and Tarn Hows were the 'plums' and Holme Ground was of 'sentimental' value because her grandfather once owned it, but otherwise she had 'no feeling of affection for Coniston'. The estate was 'bewildering' and she wrote frankly of her preference for 'a single large valley like Troutbeck', but could see the landscape appealed to the public.[128] She was little perturbed in October 1929 when she learned that the Forestry Commission had apparently already reached an agreement with the Marshalls to purchase the estate, threatening the extension of the commission's massive conifer plantations at Grizedale and Furness to Langdale. This fell through, partly thanks to bureaucratic inertia on the part of the commission, and Potter, a private buyer, could move quickly and decisively. She was more concerned that a small, half-acre plot of land at Tarn Hows, to be sold separately, would be purchased because the 'old building material' on the site and its size gave 'scope for an unsightly bungalow'. The Marshalls wanted £500 for the site, but eventually settled for £425, which Potter conveyed directly to the Trust.[129] It is still striking to read that she thought the afforestation of Tilberthwaite Fell, Holme Fell and Tam Craggs would be 'no great disappointment' if the Trust could reach an agreement with the commission that would save the 'little green farms' and the estate's 'scrubby timber'.[130]

As already noted, Potter did not subscribe to the panoply of preservationist concerns, regarding modern forestry as a legitimate use of the land. We have seen how she often regarded trees, whether deciduous or evergreen, as timber, a valuable, renewable asset, requiring long-term investment and management. Her purchases were principally intended to prevent threats to the valley farms and, most decidedly, new building, including the 'suburban' development of Coniston.[131] In the 1920s, the auguries were clear. The bus service between Coniston and Ambleside took people through Yewdale, opening up the area to visitors and potential purchasers of building plots. She found new houses built above Shelworth Bridge, which reached the edge of the estate, objectionable, including a particularly offensive bungalow with red tile roofing, and she feared this presaged an unpleasant future should the estate fall into the wrong hands.[132] That which Hill feared the railways would do to the Kentish Weald in the 1890s, Potter feared the motor car would do to the Lake District in the 1920s.

Throughout the 1930s, Potter lamented high visitor numbers, reported instances of bad or foolish behaviour to Hamer and complained about the increasing number of charabancs clogging up unimproved tracks, lobbying the Rural District Council to prohibit their use of certain roads.

The priority Potter attached to the valley farms did not simply reflect preservationist commitments. Given her retention of the portion of the estate the Trust was unable to purchase, she did not want a substantial proportion of her capital bound up in non-productive land or property. The land she planned to retain had to generate rent, whereas the Trust would initially buy primarily the fells of the western half of the estate. Acquiring land at Troutbeck remained her priority, and she wanted to retain the financial flexibility to respond quickly to other opportunities. Her approach to the estate also reflected an underlying ethos. She did not want the Marshalls to know of her plans until the deposit was paid, or her role in the Trust's acquisition of the estate to be publicised; she disliked 'public begging' and did not relish a fund-raising campaign to buy her out, preferring private approaches to potential major donors. She could be dismissive of small-scale donations, failing to share Hill's sense of their particular virtue, though this partly reflected personal sensitivities about her mother's wealth: people might ask why Helen Potter had not stepped in.[133] Helen Potter's refusal to support these efforts frustrated her daughter, who once wryly commented that her mother 'might feel stirred to send a trifle! – only she has just had the car varnished'.[134] Her involvement was to be presented by the Trust as a 'deal', maybe a 'gamble', but not as 'a Quixotic public spirited action', and she found 'odious' any suggestion that the 'appeal' was intended to 'relieve' her of a financial burden.[135]

The National Trust annual report for 1929–30 had indeed praised her 'great public spirit' for buying the estate and offering to sell it to the Trust at cost.[136] These sensitivities briefly came to a head two years later when she was named against her wishes as the purchaser, on behalf of the Trust, of Thwaite Farm which adjoined Monk Coniston. She wrote furiously to Hamer to say that in response she and William had shelved plans to make a substantial donation to the Trust when her mother died, raging that G.M. Trevelyan – prominent Trust patron and historian – needed to be told.[137] Her ire soon passed, as it was wont to do, but this was not the last time she criticised Professor Trevelyan, whom she did not think had good business sense.

The crossing over Yewdale Beck is edged with a low but monumental wall, a relic of the estate, and the little row of white-washed cottages at Low Yewdale, built for the families of quarrymen and a little bit scruffy, epitomise rustic ideals. Potter had thought Yewdale 'frightfully untidy', but she admired its 'picturesque scrub' woodland and was impressed that Marshall had resisted the temptation to sell off building plots, preventing encroachment on the site.[138] As I walked through Yewdale towards Tarn Hows, where I would join the Cumbrian Way, a magnificent rabbit hunkered down in an ancient apple orchard overgrown with fern and bramble.

Tarn Hows was peat bog until the middle of the nineteenth century when Marshall built a dam, converting three small tarns into a sizeable artificial lake, which he stocked with fish, and laid out with footpaths and carriageways. It is a short walk from Monk Coniston House. Designated an SSSI in 1984 on the strength of its diverse aquatic flora, Tarn Hows gives striking evidence of how an artificial landscape can acquire conservation value.[139] Its management today exemplifies how traditional landscape use is revived to create the conditions that once allowed particular flora and fauna to thrive. In particular, the netted carpet moth, a priority species in the UK Biodiversity Action Plan, feed upon touch-me-not balsam, which will only grow at Tarn Hows if the woodland floor is sufficiently open to light. Consequently, for a few weeks every winter Belted Galloways are let into the woodland to create the conditions that allow touch-me-not balsam to grow. The complexity of the SSSI designation contrasts sharply with the emphasis placed on this single species, its progress a synecdoche for a more complex mosaic of conservation practices. The public is also told how the alder coppice at Tarn Hows, once managed to guarantee a plentiful supply of char-coal for the iron smelting industry and long since neglected, is being coppiced again to create the light-filled woodland conditions that allow wildflowers, birds and butterflies to thrive.[140]

Potter might have snootily found Tarn Hows 'too theatrical ... like scene painting' but its popularity with visitors was long-estab-lished and the Trust found it an attractive proposition for donors.[141] Sir Samuel and Lady Nancy Scott, already significant benefactors, were keen to purchase the site on behalf of the Trust. They recalled their children enjoying picnics at the Tarn and wished to be associ-ated with a distinct and popular site. Potter liked and admired the Scotts but could be condescending in private: 'He wants to say he has bought the Tarns – they all want to do that.' On completion of the donation, she suggested Hamer give Scott 'something he can frame and hang up!'[142] At the end of 1930, Potter and the Trust faced a few tense months when the Marshalls put a 0.6-acre site on the market at Tarn Hows, providing 'scope for an unsightly bungalow'. Potter engaged Mrs Marshall in a game of brinkmanship she eventually won by refusing to increase her bid of £425 to £500.[143]

I circumnavigate the Tarn to the west, passing near Rose Castle ('an ugly dry well-built small house', according to Potter),[144] and come upon the magnificent spectacle of a farmer summoning his herd of Belted Galloways. 'Hieeee!' he cries, and the beasts come, galumphing, keen to get their share of 'cake', a highly nutritious feed distributed from his quad bike.

North of here, the ground is marshy and undulating, gradually ascending to the Cumbrian Way. The path cuts a passageway through terrain profuse with moss, fern, liverwort, oak and a heavy grass and herbage weave. Dry stone walls thick with moss structure the land-scape; lichens form patterns on bedrock exposed where shallow peat has eroded. The contour-conquering, technical proficiency of the walls is awe-inspiring, but as I take misty breaths, sensing the natural exuberance of this sodden place, it is hard not to be impressed by the claim that this landscape once supported a biodiversity comparable to the rainforests. Ferns always signal the primeval, and here they seem a vestige of past riches. Potter wrote of her preference for this end of the estate and, as was her wont, she expressed this through purchase, having her eye on a small patch of land that had come on the market.[145]

On the footpaths through Oxen Fell I feel my botanic ignorance more acutely, for here the walls and hedges add further richness to the mix. A 50-year-old commemoration bench is being gradually reclaimed by ferns, grasses and lichen. Closer to Colwith Force (force is a Lakeland term for waterfall), a National Trust sign fills in some of the gaps. The moist climate and acid soils encourage sessile oaks, supporting an understorey of birch, holly, rowan and hazel, richer soils adding ash, wych elm and cherry to the assemblage. The only management required is the removal of non-native trees and control of sheep and deer densities to encourage regrowth. Almost as an afterthought, the text adds that the Trust is keeping adjacent land free of grazing so that natural regeneration can occur.

Colwith Force is a place of sharp contrasts. Water torrents foam through a narrow ravine, gravity releasing a tremendous shock of stored energy. It's loud and brash. Immediately adjacent, steady flows of clear water are funnelled from the disused gunpowder works at Elterwater. The works have been closed since 1930, at a cost – according to Potter – of 80 jobs, which she feared would ruin Chapel Stile and Elterwater. The closure pricked her conscience for she was aware that purchasing Monk Coniston would deny some of the men jobs with the Forestry Commission.[146] The multi-levelled complex of channels, some dug into the earth and lined with slate and concrete, is thick with moss and lichen, a gentle encroachment that cannot obscure how earlier water engineers have inscribed a near irreversible trace onto this landscape.

An old sign, once duck egg blue, is bolted to a gate with rusty screws. It asks walkers to stay in single file to avoid damaging crops grown in a herb-rich meadow, but post-industrial signifiers are none-theless thick on the ground as I skirt the northern boundaries of Potter's estate and turn south entering quarry country. The beck feeding Colwith Force is crossed at Slater Bridge. It is divided mid-stream by a stone mound. Great slate flats and rusty railings take the pedestrian to the centre, at which point the bridge becomes arched, formed as though from stone vertebrae, a rack of ribs. A commemoration plaque remembers one who had loved this spot. Further on, I admire the dark green door and white-wash of the Yorkshire Ramblers' Club hut at Low Hall Garth. Formerly a farmstead cottage, it is now leased to the Club by the Trust.

From here to Low Tilberthwaite, the history and atmosphere of Troutbeck finds an echo in old quarry roads shadowed by moody spoil heaps. In the 1930s, and in contrast to Troutbeck, the quarries were still working, adding another responsibility to the estate's new manager. 'A lot of the quarrymen are reckless scamps especially the Welsh strain', Potter wrote.[147] The once-massive scale of these operations is evident all around, though nature again is making a come-back. Moss, lichen, shrubs and trees are transforming spoil heaps into habitat. Potter wondered if part of this terrain – Atkinson Ground – could be sold for shooting.[148] Below, at High Tilberthwaite farm, a territory more agreeable to Potter, the yard is clogged with Herdwicks just taken down off the fell. A collie or two mills about, their work done, tails aslant. Less celebrated ruminants graze the in-bye land. Potter took particular satisfaction in the Lake District Association having taken responsibility for managing access to Tilberthwaite Ghyll and keeping the bridge in good repair. She thought it a 'nasty place', attractive to 'a different class' of visitors, 'fat women off chara's [sic]' who 'might fall through the bridge'.[149]

The public road connecting Holme Ground to the main road at High Yewdale trails off a little to the north at Hodge Close quarry; add to this how Holme Fell masks the site to the east and woodland encloses much of the rest and the farm feels private in a manner not dissimilar to Troutbeck. The strength of Potter's sentimental attachment to the farm is hard to gauge, but as I complete my perambulation I find it easy to imagine how a family association with this extraordinary landscape could be powerfully affecting.

Planning

Potter's scathing view of visitors to Tilberthwaite Ghyll should not obscure the serious access issues raised by the Trust's acquisition of the Coniston Park Estate. Tricky questions were raised about visitor expectations that a conventionally owned agricultural estate did not have to resolve, at least not in the 1930s. Potter recognised that Monk Coniston could not be treated as a private estate and had to be managed according to the spirit intended by the Trust, but the uniqueness of the estate as a Trust possession – 'a large mixed property' – raised new 'conundrums', exposing the tensions between preservationist, access and estate management agendas and priorities. She sought advice from the Trust. Could the quarry tenants put up 'no admittance' notices, treating transgressors as trespassers? Could a farmer be justified in locking a gate to protect livestock, particularly where there was a history of visitors leaving it open? And could she bar entry to new plantations, which could only become established if the public and livestock were kept out? Camping also needed to be regulated. Padlocks were as problematic on Trust property as unfettered access. Walling up certain gateways was one solution, as was discouraging access by not erecting a sign drawing attention to the Trust's ownership of a farm or land, as at Thwaite, but Potter recognised that ad-hoc solutions were not sufficient and systematic signage dealing with a range of factors was necessary.[150]

A great concern was the risk of fire. Potter worried that work at a plantation near the Tarns meant that there was effectively '100's of cartloads of twiggy thinnings, most inflammable and most tempting to kettle-boilers'. A fire could spread quickly, destroying fine hardwood timber. Discarded glass bottles were also a fire risk.[151] Signage raised aesthetic concerns. Like Clough Williams-Ellis, whom we'll encounter in later chapters, she disliked enamel signs.[152] This 'unpleasing substance, sadly vulgarised' was likely to be 'conspicuous in this slate country', she wrote, saying it evoked 'adverts and town parks'. The cream and chocolate enamel signs proposed by the Trust were not the best option. An 'old fashioned wooden board' was preferable, though she recognised enamel's hard-wearing utility, especially if the alternative was tin. Most problematic were the ad-hoc signs placed willy-nilly at the roadside by tenant farmers diversifying their businesses by offering accommodation or teas.[153] Her aesthetic snobbishness extended to the Trust's Yew Tree tearoom, where she hung some watercolours of Lindeth How as a defence against 'gifts of rubbish' the Trust might be otherwise forced to accept – a view over Grasmere by Cuthbert Rigby of Ambleside was acceptable.[154] But she also realised that signage could have a positive function. By directing visitors to popular viewpoints and facilities their movement through the estate could be managed. She developed an increasingly institutional eye, wishing to see notices standardised across the estate according to National Trust norms.

Above all, Potter was concerned with traffic management and, more particularly, road improvement issues over which she had little direct influence. Steadily increasing volumes of motorised traffic meant pressure to widen roads, erect signs and convert gravel roads to macadam. Potter did not dismiss the needs of motorists, but she disliked these developments, and was frustrated that there was little she or the Trust could do to prevent them. Most roads were owned and managed by the county council and, in the main, the council sought to improve infrastructure rather than impose restrictions. New players in this growing culture of motoring, like the Royal Automobile Club and the Automobile Association, worked with the local authorities to improve conditions for their members. Inevitably, Potter thought they did not understand Lakeland, and she disliked the RAC's mustard-coloured signs. Despite wanting more restrictive byelaws, particularly with respect to access by charabancs, grumbling to the Trust was as much as she did. Perhaps she was right to think that Trust workmen could provide immediate solutions, such as creating passing places in the place of thorough-going widening schemes, but on this issue, more than any other, she was out of time. Her opposition to the Trust's decision to convert some of its private gravel roads to tarmacadam had little effect, and it was hardly helpful to say of a tenant at Thwaite wanting a road with a camber to enable drainage that she ought to buy some rubber boots. Where she could expect her will to prevail was with respect to Troutbeck; the access road was only to be ever used as such, and not opened to charabancs.[155]

She was also determined that the public's right to access the estate be placed on a proper legal footing. The Rights of Way Act 1932 required that maps showing public rights of way be agreed between landowners and the local authorities. Once again, we see legislation creating a loose obligation that relied on local initiative. Rights of way had to be claimed, putting pressure on local civil society organisations to initiate the process. Unsurprising, this method of establishing right was seen to favour the landlord. Indeed, Potter established that no public rights of way existed on the Monk Coniston Estate, rights of access to footpaths being limited to occupants of one sort or another. The National Trust allowed access on a permissive basis, but that's a quite different legal basis. Potter might be judged sharply for the satisfaction she took in this outcome, though her purposes were less to govern pedestrian access and more to establish a firm legal basis for keeping out another new threat – motorcyclists.[156]

A clear expression of her continuing faith in the Trust was her response to a town planning scheme published in December 1930. She went to see it at the town clerk's office in Windermere and was soon writing to Hamer of its provoking foolishness. She recognised that it constituted an attempt to 'give some control over disfiguring erections' but was concerned that 'it almost reads like an incitement to residential planning'. Sections marked white on the map indicated sites suitable for three-acre housing plots and included land in front of the Tongue, confirming Potter's earlier fears about the site, and the road frontage on the Kirkstone Pass that she had already bought. In her view, three-acre plots were too big for a garden, the likely result being 'an untidy shrubbery wood of conifers, and a road frontage of laurel hedge', and too small for a farm. 'The National Trust,' she declared, 'is the only salvation for the Lake District.'[157] In a similar vein, she explained to Rawnsley's widow Eleanor why 'there are great advantages to farm under the Trust'. Having no income tax or death duties to pay, it allowed more money for repairs and greater security for good tenants.[158]

More pertinent were her scattered comments on the National Trust's purposes and the growing pressure on the state to become an agent in the preservation of the English countryside. Potter's conviction that the National Trust was 'the only salvation' for the Lake District helps contextualise her negative outbursts about proposals circulating at this time about the Lake District being designated a national park. She was surely aware that a conference at Manchester in October 1929 had established the Lake District National Reserve Committee, an impressive grouping that included representatives of the National Trust; the Campaign for the Protection of Rural England (CPRE); the Commons, Open Spaces and Footpaths Preservation Society; the Lake District (South) Regional Planning Committee; the Lake District Safeguarding Society; the Cumberland and Westmorland Antiquities and Archaeological Society; the Ramblers' Federation of Liverpool, Manchester and Sheffield; the English Lake District Association; the Cumberland Nature Club; the Fell and Rock Climbing Club; the Cumbrian Regional Planning Committee; and the Society for Checking the Abuse of Public Advertising.[159] This intersection of local and national bodies was exactly the kind of development shaping preservationist politics in the 1920s and the growing consensus that a greater role should be played by the 'State' in the protection of 'rural amenity' and, in particular, the new emphasis placed on the 'science of planning'.

The Committee testifies to how the National Trust operated within a political context shaped by an emergent activist culture driven by networking, organisational cooperation and the crafting of agreed positions and statements. The trigger for the formation of the committee, however, was specific. It was a response to the Labour Government's decision to instruct the Addison Committee to prepare a report on how a national parks system might be established in Britain. For two years, a wide range of statutory and voluntary bodies presented evidence to the committee, generating the most extensive investigation into the condition of rural Britain undertaken to that date. Justice cannot be done here to the vast corpus of material collected, much of which can be consulted at the National Archives, but an examination of the National Trust's submissions with respect to the Lake District makes clear how advanced its thinking had become.

The Reserve Committee made two submissions.[160] Addison was reminded that the Lake District had been long recognised as a geographical unit, had no distinct existence for local government purposes, and the idea that it needed special protection was not new. Coordinated action was difficult because the area straddled three county boundaries, five or six urban district councils, and seven or eight rural district council areas. Lakeland could only be accorded the protection it deserved if it was treated as 'one single and indivisible unit' and managed according to 'national perspectives'. A new management structure, funded by central government, should treat open fell country as 'untouchable', though Addison conceded that the commoning system already afforded significant protection; the real threat from developers was to 'Dale land' where 'life should be preserved, and encouragement given to good sheep farming'. Potter would have agreed – Troutbeck was dale land – and she shared the Committee's insistence that building restrictions should be strong

and planning permission granted only for necessary farm improvements and the 'maintenance and possible increase of simple accommodation for mountaineer and rambler'; further development of
existing industries, such as quarrying and afforestation, might be
allowed 'in special cases'.[161]

Much preservationist ire was directed against new energy infrastructure, including overhead power cables and the wirescapes of
modern rurality, and the Reserve Committee was no exception.
A stand had to be taken against modern encroachments, limiting the
actions of the water and electricity companies, and the mining, quarrying and aviation industries. Potter, of course, had objected to
aircraft flying over Lake Coniston and she complained bitterly that
electricity cabling was 'turning Coniston village into the semblance
of a birdcage' – the electrical engineer overseeing the development
was a petty despot. Some encroachment on Trust land was necessary,
that much she conceded, but she hoped electricity would not reach
Near Sawrey, describing the electricity pylons erected at Blawith as
'squat erections, almost uglier than the tall variety'; she was a little
smug that the cabling required to bring electricity from Coniston to
Hawkshead would be buried.[162] When the grid eventually reached
Sawrey, she refused to admit electricity to the house but allowed it to
penetrate her shippons, or cow sheds, telling Tom Storey that 'The
cows might like it'.[163]

Inevitably, the United States national park system loomed large in
the Addison discussions. Vast landscapes had been placed in the
ownership of the federal government since the first parks were established at Yellowstone and Yosemite in 1872 and 1890. The Reserve
Committee conceded that it was implausible that the whole district
should be taken into some form of public ownership, either by the
state or the National Trust, or leased in its entirety to the National
Trust, but that these options were worth considering was symptomatic of the changing parameters of the debate. Early twentieth-
century commentators rarely noticed that the idea that the US

national parks preserved 'pristine wilderness' ignored the violent displacement of the indigenous population that had helped shape their natural characteristics.[164] In any case, the Reserve Committee advocated the introduction of enhanced planning regulations, proposing that 'the whole District should be scheduled and placed as regards matters of amenity under the jurisdiction of a special Commission'. The Committee suggested that this new public body should comprise representatives of government departments, the local authorities, and the amenity associations, such as those that comprised the Reserve Committee. Sometimes to the irritation of civil servants and elected politicians, the amenity societies insisted that they were representative bodies and therefore had a right to a formal role in decision-making processes.[165] Taking shape were the ideas that underpinned the post-war national park authorities, the precursor of late twentieth-century stakeholder political culture.

Did Potter approve? When the National Trust was faced with the challenge posed by raising the money to buy Monk Coniston, she was adamant that the campaign should not be exploited by those talking 'nonsense ... about this National Park rubbish!'.[166] This outburst was clearly provoked by the maelstrom of ideas brought into circulation by the Addison hearings. On another occasion, she disparagingly referred to national park thinking as 'socialist', an ideology towards which she certainly felt a deep aversion. Back in 1924, she was particularly exercised when Beatrice Webb, whose maiden name was Beatrice Potter, was mistaken for herself. Conscious that this mistake might have commercial implications, she wrote to Warne, 'if the Webbs are going to become prominent along with our new rulers, the error had better be contradicted; for I do not think that nice old fashioned people who like my books would like them quite so much if they believed them to be of socialist origin'.[167] So it can be inferred that she was at best ambivalent about the National Trust's case that the preservation agenda and the protection of amenity could only be fulfilled through systematic state intervention. She cannot have been happy when John Bailey, chair of the Trust's Executive Committee, and G.M. Trevelyan, member of council, proposed that the government buy the entirety of the Lake District's 'development rights'. By this means, land values would be stabilised because they would be effectively fixed according to current usage rather than development potential. Significant upfront costs would ensure low costs thereafter, they claimed, but if such a sweeping intervention was impossible, they would – naturally enough – settle for a government-financed purchase fund of £100,000 per year, allowing the state to accumulate a significant estate on behalf of the nation.[168] Potter might have stomached the latter, but the emphasis the Trust now placed on state intervention rather than individual philanthropy sat less easily with her Tory instincts. She certainly shared the Trust's account of the negative impact of the motor car on the countryside and sympathised with their complaint that new roads were 'destroying old villages and old trees, quiet fields and stately parks' but, as we've seen, her solution to the problem of charabancs clogging up the narrow unstable lanes of the Monk Coniston Estate was not widening and metalling but restriction. She no more approved of improved roads than she did of pylons – she lamented the decline of wheelwrights, loathing the new-fangled use of rubber tyres on carts and wheelbarrows.[169] Doubtless she was pleased that the Trust prioritised the preservation of the Lake District, followed – but not too closely – by Dartmoor and the South Downs, and much of the Trust's following statement would have had her nodding in agreement:

Again the State has hitherto taken few or no steps to preserve the beauty of the most exceptional features of the English landscape. Quarrying destroys famous hills; garish bungalows, housing a few people, ruin many square miles of those English downs which have no parallel elsewhere; factories and gas works and sewage stations are carelessly allowed to be placed where there is no particular reason for placing them and many particular reasons for not doing so; promiscuous advertisements disfigure our fields and roadsides and even disgrace some of the most historic and beautiful spots in the country. The State looks on at all this: and by its own action does nothing at present to prevent it.[170]

Equally likely, she recognised the virtue of protecting land 'for the sake of the preservation of their wildlife whether of birds, animals and insects, or of trees, plants and flowers', and she would have shared the Trust's view that, on these grounds, public access sometimes needed to be restricted. Again, though, it seems doubtful that she would have thought nature conservation was the proper duty of the state as opposed to benign landowners.

Addison recommended that the government establish a national park system. New planning authorities would be given special powers with respect to protecting the amenity value of particular landscapes. This chimed with the Trust's case and was favourably received in government. However, the Labour government collapsed as a consequence of the economic crisis it faced after the Wall Street Crash in 1929. The establishment in 1931 of the Conservative-dominated National Government saw plans to establish national parks in Britain stymied by a combination of austerity and an ideological reluctance to empower a new national government agency. Nonetheless, across the House of Commons it was recognised that development pressures raised pressing questions about weakness of planning regulations in the countryside. The law had not kept up with the pace of change. Consequently, in 1930–1, parliament discussed the Rural Amenities bill, a private members' bill promoted by Sir Hilton Young MP, that sought to prevent the further 'uglification of the countryside' by bringing 'a reasonable measure of forethought', otherwise planning, to its development. Young equated 'uglification' with the 'urbanisation of the country', which included ribbon developments, the mixing of domestic, commercial and industrial buildings, advertising hoardings and petrol stations, exactly the kind of disfigurements famously traduced in Clough Williams-Ellis's *England and the Octopus* (1928). Forms of decline (the break-up of great estates and agricultural depression) and new forms of affluence, including increased mobility ('private motor car, the motor omnibus, and the commercial motor vehicle'), accounted for these pressures, which Young insisted the bill sought to manage rather than suppress.[171]

Potter would have nodded along to the hyperbole of Lady Cynthia Mosley, Labour MP and first wife of the notorious Sir Oswald Mosley: 'Think of the prodigal waste of a lovely tract of countryside that is utterly ruined by one glaring red roof, a whole hillside spoilt for good and all by some hideous bungalow put down at the wrong place.'[172] Young withdrew the bill to make way for the Labour Government's Town and Country Planning bill, duly lost to the dissolution, before a watered-down version was passed by the National Government in 1932. Ministers then spoke of the 'desecration' threatening the 'quiet beauty' of the countryside by 'indiscriminate building', and MPs welcomed provisions to protect the 'natural and created beauty of England' from jerry-builders. Not only had the 'growth of mechanised transport and rural electrification' brought uncontrolled ribbon development of the 'bungaloid type', but increased road building and regular bus services since the war had made it 'extremely difficult to point to any land which is not likely to be developed in the near future'.[173] As new transport and energy technologies and networks made rural Britain more accessible, the logic of the modern state dictated that planning provisions would be extended.

Conservative politicians insisted that the Act met the needs identified by Addison, but although it permitted local authorities to impose planning regimes on valued rural environments, it neither imposed obligations nor established the means to bring a national parks system into being. This was permissive legislation in the nineteenth-century tradition. And by empowering all local authorities rather than mandating some local authorities, the Act was not considered an adequate response to the principle that certain select landscapes should be protected because they were of especial national significance.

Potter was open-minded about the prospect of a new planning authority specifically for the Lake District. She thought county councillors often made decisions about places they did not properly understand, and landlords did themselves no favours in the court of public opinion by simply opposing all suggestions: they needed to participate in public discussions so the scheme might be guided into 'sensible channels'. She clearly disliked schematic approaches like zoning – the strategy also being pursued for forestry – but she thought a new authority that could take a case-by-case approach might be a boon.[174] For example, it was 'a shame' the Trust could acquire Mounsey's Intake but could not prevent a Miss Roberts from selling a £10 plot for a bungalow opposite.[175] Reflecting on the debate in a letter to Eleanor Rawnsley, she wondered what her husband would have made of recent developments, some 'for good, for evil, and for doubtful good'. She saw the value of 'this new widespread interest in the overworked new word "amenity"', recognising it created a form of value that chimed with her priorities, but still she wrote 'personally I mistrust and definitely dislike some recent feelers towards a new policy'. She'd come to believe that the preservation of the 'character of the Lake District' depended on good landlords and was particularly critical of smallholders inclined to sell off sheep stock, cut all the scrub timber, and concentrate on hens.[176] She fell back on National Trust shibboleths, convinced that the 'Canon's original aim for complete preservation of as much property as possible by acquisition was the right one for the Lake District'.[177]

The Trust, however, could not rely on its buying power alone. In the 1930s, it built on its experience of working with Potter by developing new preservationist strategies less dependent on its capacity to purchase or the slow-moving machinery of planning legislation. It sought to work with purchasers ready to enter legally binding restrictive covenants that would require the Trust's written permission before certain developments could take place. In effect, the purchaser was required to agree in perpetuity to a reduction in the development value of the land, meaning future returns on the investment were largely limited by its existing use.[178] Such agreements still relied upon the cooperation of sympathetic individuals or institutions. Agreement was reached on this basis with the owner of 500 acres of land adjacent to Tarn Hows, but more important was the agreement entered into by Balliol College, Oxford when in 1934 it looked to invest a legacy of £10,000. For the Trust, the timing was good. Martin Marshall had placed his Buttermere Estate on the market, which included Crummock, Loweswater and Buttermere Lakes.[179] The Trust hoped to enact a process comparable to Potter's acquisition of the Monk Coniston Estate. It would raise the necessary cash but ultimately looked to retain and manage the open land and sell to the partner – in this case Balliol – the valley farms, which would then accrue a modest, but respectable return on the rental value.[180] In the event, the Trust were unable to raise enough money to make the whole purchase, but Balliol agreed to separately purchase seven farms and two houses and enter into a simultaneous covenant with the Trust.

The key figures in the Balliol transaction were A.D. Lindsay, the Master, and C.S. Orwin, the Estates Bursar. They make an intriguing combination. Lindsay believed that the state had a duty to guarantee that all citizens enjoyed a decent quality of life, which meant restraining the worst excesses of self-interest, but his idealism posited that the political and moral leadership of the Labour movement could enable this by nurturing the best aspects of human nature rather than by imposing state controls.[181] Octavia Hill might have found his brand of Christian Socialism congenial. Nor was Lindsay's interest in the Lake District entirely impersonal. In 1926, he had bought the cottage at Low Ground, an isolated spot on Birker Fell near Eskdale and when elevated to the peerage in 1945, he took the title 1st Baron Lindsay of Birker. Orwin, by contrast, combined his responsibilities at the college with his role as director of Oxford's Institute of Agricultural Economics. He published extensively on agricultural history, including *The Open Fields* (Oxford, 1938), and wrote a series of interventions on the need to rationalise British agriculture.[182] Other key players in the transaction included G.M. Trevelyan, who purchased Gatesgarth as part of this process and scrawled letters to Lindsay about the kind of arrangement that would suit the Trust, and Henry Williams, the Bishop of Carlisle, an Oxford man keen on Balliol's involvement, who provided local intelligence.[183] Lindsay and Williams were among other academic and literary figures with strong Lake District connections who signed a public letter opposing the afforestation of the estate.[184]

Crucial to the historical significance of the transaction was what the college's understanding of the rental value of farms revealed about changing perceptions of Lake District farms as businesses. Existing rents were high if the farms were considered solely as agricultural propositions, but the college's enquiries established that these were already diversified businesses. The more valuable of the farms offered teas, overnight accommodation and basic camping facilities, provisions the college thought could be further developed.[185] Potter might look askance at such activities, which could be disincentivised by lowering rents, but these diverse income strands underpinned the market value of the farms and Marshall was not obliged to sell to a buyer willing to agree to the restrictive covenants. By covenanting to preserve the valley's 'amenities' by not erecting any building (accepting those of agricultural use), posting advertisements or signs, or establishing conifer plantations, Balliol's offer of £12,000 recognised the limited scope for increasing the income derived from this extensive property. Moreover, despite concern about certain tenants, the college also undertook to maintain the seven farms as going concerns and to keep the existing tenants in place, assuming they wished to remain so. Rationalising the seven farms as agricultural businesses was firmly off the college's agenda.

Retirement

By the mid-1930s, Potter was feeling her age. 'I am written out for story books,' she wrote in 1934, 'and my eyes are too tired for painting, but I can still take great pleasure in old oak – and drains – and damp walls – oh the repairs. Such are the problems which occupy my declining years.'[186] Though determined and resilient, she'd never been physically strong and, at 70 years old, she tired more easily and found the hills difficult.[187] A series of minor operations weakened her further still. Reactionary attitudes were setting in. She made glib links between the growing international crisis and domestic policies. She was rightly pessimistic about the international situation and rueful about the hopes invested in the League of Nations, apparently more likely to lead to war than prevent it, and wild outbursts occasionally marred personal letters. In the event of a European conflict, she hoped they would 'exterminate each other', allowing 'England the Colonies and the States', should they survive, 'to rule – *really* rule by power, not by preaching a better world'. Her social attitudes were not very progressive either. Had the money 'wasted on the dole ... been spent at Vickers', the aircraft manufacturers at Barrow, 'this country might have stood independently', though she doubted whether the men of Maryport (a depressed coastal town north-west of Keswick) wanted to return to work. Migration would suit them better. Still, she recognised that Hitler was a 'brutal raving lunatic' and Chamberlain an incurable optimist, and she was darkly ironic about a friend's enthusiasm for Mussolini, becoming increasingly concerned by the deepening European crisis in early 1939. She ticked Moscrop off for making light of the international situation.[188]

In 1936, Potter announced her decision to retire as the National Trust land agent for the Monk Coniston Estate. She pledged to give her successor, Bruce Thompson, 'any information which may be useful to the management of the Trust's Coniston estate'.[189] Early letters were helpful, but she quickly became frustrated with Thompson's conduct and took to writing to the Trust's national secretary to make known her discontent.[190] She thought Thompson tardy with repairs and wrong to erect new fences at Thwaite – he didn't understand the needs of livestock or visitors – but most enraging was his management of the estate's forestry. Her most eviscerating letter was in response to his decision to fell a stand of old oaks at Thwaite, sell the Tilberthwaite coppice to a firewood dealer, and clear scrub and coppice at Holme Fell. Her fury was premised on her understanding of good forestry practice and the Trust's commitment to preserving natural beauty. Thompson might be inexperienced, with 'no sense at all' and 'not capable of learning', but the problem was more fundamental. It is 'impossible to inculcate a pictorial sense of trees arranged in landscape', she raged, 'when imagination is a blank'. The Trust did not take her criticisms altogether seriously but was keen to placate its most important benefactor. A little diplomacy was required. Her last letter to Thompson, written in March 1942, was brusque but civil, packed with advice about estate matters.[191]

Potter died on the night of 22 December 1943. Her final letters were as much preoccupied with her children's books as they were with day-to-day estate management, though the peoples suffering another winter under occupation were on her mind and she summoned up the energy to complain about the 'neutrals': Turkey, Ireland ('Eire') and Sweden. Her last recorded letter was a simple note of friendship to Joe Moscrop, the shepherd who had enabled her achievements as a Herdwick farmer and knew more than most about what this meant to her: 'Very far through, but still some kick in me. Am not going right away at present. I write a line to shake you by the hand, our friendship has been entirely pleasant. I am very ill with bronchitis.'[192]

Potter once observed that the Monk Coniston Estate had 'no history'. It had been 'collected' by the Marshalls who bought up 'small . . . expensively priced' properties.[193] Bit by bit, she transformed this assemblage of individual holdings into a functioning estate, all described in meticulous detail in letters to the Trust.[194] By promoting what she considered good habits among her tenants and tidy, well-maintained farmscapes, she recalled Octavia Hill's attachment to managed parks. The self-discipline required to produce good farmscapes went hand in hand with the production of good people. Her will, effectively the last letter she addressed to the Trust, attempted to prolong this process, projecting into the future a history for her estates. 'As far as possible' the land should be let and managed on the same basis she had, the house property 'at moderate rents to the same class of tenants' and the farms 'at moderate rates to good tenants'; sheep stock on the fell farms should remain 'pure Herdwick breed', and she specified the number to be hefted at Troutbeck. £5,000 was placed in trust, to be used as necessary to maintain or expand the estate.[195]

The simplicity of her will hardly does justice to the complexity of the work she bequeathed to the Trust or the difficulty it sometimes faced adhering to her strictures. In 2005, the Trust was condemned as having betrayed Potter's wishes when it broke up the High Yewdale farm tenancy and distributed the land to three existing tenancies because it no longer considered the farm financially viable; in 2016, the Trust attracted further bad publicity when it bought the land and sheep belonging to Thorneythwaite Farm but not the farmhouse. Both acts of consolidation saw the loss of another Lake District tenancy with implications for hefted Herdwick flocks, though whether the Yewdale decision contravened Potter's 'as far as possible' is as open to debate as whether the Trust's recent commitment to nature-friendly farming is compatible with the Lakeland ideal Potter helped establish. More certain is that the magnificence of the Heelis Bequest consolidated the position of the National Trust in the Lake District. From this firm basis it could proceed to acquire the further holdings that would make its membership the most significant landowner in the history of England's most celebrated landscape.

Potter's last piece of published writing had nothing to do with pressing matters of estate management or the politics of the moment. 'The Lonely Hills' was published in May 1942 in *The Horn Book Magazine*, an American literary magazine for children. Writing of how 'music strikes chords of memory', Potter's elegy gave patchy expression to her love for the landscapes and people of Lakeland. She recalled the English folk dance revival, the music and dance of local pageants and even dancing on the stone floors of her farmhouse kitchen, providing rare insight into her enthusiasm for Lakeland custom and the joys of domestic life. But it was her turn from the human to the non-human that was most affective: in an anecdote that blended whimsy with credulity, she proposed that the urge to respond to music with dance is not confined to the human world.

> Another time all by myself alone I watched a weird dance, to the music of Piper Wind. It was far away in that lovely wilderness behind the table-land on Troutbeck Tongue. In the midst of this waste of yellow bent-grass and stones there is a patch of green grass and stunted thorn. Round the tree – round and round in measured canter went four of the wild fell ponies. Round and round, then checked and turned; round and round reversed; arched necks, tossing manes, tails streaming. I watched a while, crouching behind a boulder. . . . I stood up. They stopped, stared, and snorted, then galloped out of sight.[196]

A magical moment of apparent inter-species recognition. The fell ponies meet the gaze of the lone enraptured female with a dose of huffy equine camp. Conjured up in old age and out of the depths of war, the encounter magics the reader not just to those uncanny hills but also back to the Potter nursery and the fascination with the natural world that began it all.

PAULINE DOWER

'Inconspicuous Good'

Pauline Dower

'Inconspicuous Good'

Pauline Dower looks, and is, a countrywoman, with a swinging stride that takes her easily over rough country, and long-sighted eyes that seldom need the fieldglasses she carries. She could have been a farmer, and indeed took an agricultural diploma with a view to running her father's Northumberland estates, but marriage intervened. During the two years of fieldwork that resulted in her husband's report, she was his chauffeur and constant companion – 'I was the dog it was all tried on,' is how she puts it.[1]

This extract is from a short profile published in *The Times* in January 1958. It marked Pauline Dower's promotion to the role of Deputy Chair of the National Parks Commission, the body established in 1949 to designate National Parks and Areas of Outstanding Natural Beauty in England and Wales and act as their advocate in Whitehall and beyond. Dower was the longest-serving and highest-profile woman to serve as member of the commission, and one of only two commissioners to retain their place from its inception in 1949 until the membership was restructured in 1966 prior to its supersession by the Countryside Commission in 1968.[2] Despite this exceptional service, she attracted little press coverage and has been largely forgotten as one of the pioneering figures in the development of Britain's national park system. Even this friendly profile piece was inconspicuous, coming at the bottom of page 11. Perhaps this was simply because the commission, described by Dower as doing 'inconspicuous good', was always a minor component of the post-war state bureaucracy and Dower's promotion made her a salaried public servant rather than a prominent public figure. Indeed, the day-to-day work of the commission might seem less immediately appealing than the heroics of the campaign that brought it into being. Few commissioners were public figures, most were at best fringe members of 'the Establishment' – the people, characterised by Noel Annan, who made 'Our Age' – and the period of Conservative government between 1951 and 1964 is rarely noted for the dynamism of domestic politics.[3]

Dower's relative obscurity nonetheless also carries a gendered charge. When the *Manchester Guardian*, a self-consciously progressive newspaper, announced the membership of the commission, Pauline Dower was referred to as 'Mrs John Dower'. Representing wives as appendages of their husbands was a long-established convention, obscuring women's identities and, in Pauline Dower's case, the significant contribution she made to public life. Need it be said that 'Dower' in this chapter indicates Pauline Dower, its principal subject, rather than her husband? The work Dower did for the commission is sometimes evident in the archival record, especially when she played a leading role in a particular matter, and this chapter's treatment of her work for the commission will be built around those processes. Much of the time, however, she was one of 11 unpaid commission members, a relatively anonymous team member whose individual contribution is not so clear. Her work was defined by statutory processes and to emphasise the hard, persistent work these processes demanded invites a more sympathetic portrayal of the commission than has been made in the past.[4] Still, despite the statutory framework and the rigidities of planning processes, much of the work of the commission was haphazard, relying as much on individual initiative as it did the routine that might be imagined to define work for the state. The commission was under-resourced and overstretched – its administrative support was dedicated but inadequate – but to focus on Dower's work helps recover something of the pioneering spirit and day-to-day commitment that established the essentials of the national parks system.

Dower's public purposes cannot be separated from those of her husband or the preservationist and access commitments of her family, particularly her father and uncles. Both *The Times* and the *Manchester Guardian* observed that Dower's place on the commission reflected the work she did with her husband on the two National Parks reports that paved the way for the 1949 Act.[5] The Dower Report (1945) is quite obviously indelibly associated with Dower's husband John, who went on to help draft the Hobhouse Report (1947), and Dower's place on the commission would almost certainly have gone to him had he not died of tuberculosis in 1947. Her place was a courtesy extended to a grieving widow, but it was not an obligation. Lewis Silkin, the Minister of Housing and Country Planning, might easily have overlooked her, not least because she was a woman, and she might well have been replaced, as happened to other commissioners. That this did not happen means we can be confident that her place reflected the faith men in power had in her abilities and commitment.

A Trevelyan

Dower's late husband was not the only factor that helps explain her seemingly impregnable position on the commission. Her family background, by any standard, was extraordinary – and this too throws into sharp relief the peculiarity of her subsequent neglect. She was a Trevelyan, a direct descendant of the family of Whig-Liberal politicians and historians centred on the 13,000-acre family estate at Wallington Hall, near the village of Cambo in Northumberland, described by David Cannadine as having been 'governing England, and governing India, for generations'.[6] Dower's role on the commission did not simply reflect her Trevelyan or her Dower identities, but how her marriage brought together the two great forces that drove the national parks lobby in the inter-war and post-war years, and indeed the broader development of Attlee's Labour Party. The National Parks and Access to the Countryside Act was of a piece with the legislation that gave the UK the National Health Service. Both had their origins in the same social democratic or socialist democratic political milieu. Dower represented the radical liberal/ socialist 'Right to Roam' commitment, salted with a little noblesse oblige, and her husband John the new technocratic faith in state planning; to put it another way, the Dower marriage saw the confluence of liberal progressivism, a strong dose of inter-war socialism, and faith in the capacity of the state to deliver beneficial social goods.

How did Dower represent her family background and upbringing? In the early 1980s, she was interviewed by the National Trust in the library at Wallington – the clock ticked in the background, chiming the quarter hour – and repeated some of the same material in her pamphlet, *Living at Wallington*.[7] The next few pages draw on these retrospectives, piquant detail shedding light on her attitudes towards the family, particularly its radicalism and the decision to sign over the Wallington Estate to the Trust in 1941. At the time, Dower had written to her father, Sir Charles Philips Trevelyan, to say it was 'what I've wanted all along, you showing the way', and she was especially pleased that he was doing it in his lifetime, becoming the Trust's 'first tenant' at Wallington.[8]

First things first. Dower pronounced 'Trevelyan' with short vowel sounds, rendering it 'Trivilian'. This reflected as much the family's Cornish roots at it did her upper-class background. She pronounced the 'ca' in 'Newcastle' as in 'cat' rather than 'car', though without any Northumbrian inflection. As full-length biographies of Macaulay, his brother-in-law Charles Edward Trevelyan and great-nephew G.M. Trevelyan make clear, Dower's brief account of her family's history could hardly do it justice. She was at ease with the order of things, not least because she had a Whiggish faith in progress and her family's singular contribution to its advance. The Wallington Estate, after all, was in the hands of an organisation tasked with preserving it in the interests of the nation, so what she remembered – or chose to emphasise – has its own significance. The decision to hand Wallington over to the Trust tends to be pitched by the Trevelyans as driven by progressive political commitments, though avoiding onerous death duties was on Sir Charles's mind.[9] Still, it is indisputable that the campaign that brought the National Parks Commission into being had been catalysed by a suite of organisations that at one time or another enjoyed the patronage of the Trevelyans, including the National Trust, the Youth Hostel Association, the Ramblers Association and the Campaign for the Protection of Rural England.

Dower takes the listener deftly from the nineteenth century and the worlds of Macaulay and his nephew Sir George Otto Trevelyan, another Whig historian and Liberal politician, through to the late twentieth century. A powerful sense of continuity animated Dower's recollections, ensuring the relatively distant past seemed near-present, as when she observed that her grandfather, Sir George, had known Pauline, Lady Trevelyan, after whom Dower herself was named. In the 1850s and 60s, Pauline had made Wallington a centre for the arts and, thanks to the famous Pre-Raphaelite murals at Wallington, a site that reifies the centrality of Northumberland to British national identity. The murals decorate the Central Hall, formerly a courtyard, but roofed over by the Newcastle architect John Dobson in the mid-1850s. Dobson sought to emulate an Italian Renaissance palazzo and took inspiration from John Ruskin's *The Stones of Venice* (1851–3). Ruskin was an occasional visitor to Wallington and his delicate 'Wheat, Wild Oats, Cornflower and Yarrow' are among the flower paintings forming part of the Hall's decorative scheme. Dominant, however, are the eight historical murals, painted in 1857–61 by William Bell Scott, the North's pre-eminent Pre-Raphaelite. They provide an episodic history of the county that begins with an image of the Roman Wall replete with Roman sentries and local workers and culminates in a complex image of the Industrial Revolution.

The murals warrant a closer look. The broadly Whiggish epic they trace focuses on nation building and highlights the region's centrality to the conversion of Britain to Christianity ('King Egfrid and Cuthbert'), the passage of wisdom from generation to generation ('The Death of Bede') and the gradual overcoming of, first, regional lawlessness and anarchy in the late medieval period ('Spur in the Dish' evokes the 'riding and rieving') and, second, the damaging effects of factionalism in the early modern period ('Bernard Gilpin'). All of this points to an account of the integrationist benefits of religious toleration and political progress. A Victorian audience might see in the 'Descent of the Danes', depicting a Tynemouth community, secular and religious, in flight, an allusion to contemporary ideas about the racial intermixing that had created the hardy spirit of the British people. This strength was manifest in Bell's celebratory painting of 'Grace Darling', the daughter of the lighthouse keeper who helped her father rescue passengers from the paddle steamer SS *Forfarshire* wrecked off the Northumberland coast in September 1838. The most powerful and most reproduced image was 'Iron and Coal', Bell Scott's complex allegory about the imbrication of industrial development, the free press, education and liberty. The scene is set on Newcastle Quayside. In the background, the new High Level Bridge and a loaded keel (a barge for transporting coal); in the foreground, men hammer iron into shape and a young girl studies maths. Allusion is made to the Armstrong munitions factory in Newcastle, given a tremendous fillip by the Crimean War (1853–6), and Garibaldi's military victories in the Italian *Risorgimento*, a cause célèbre among liberals and radicals. Fifty years later, G.M. Trevelyan established his reputation as a historian with a trilogy of works on Garibaldi.[10]

Dower was not comfortable talking about the political career of her great-grandfather, Sir Charles Edward Trevelyan. She passes over his notorious Minute on Education (1835) – it made the case for Anglophone education in India on the grounds that Arabic and Sanskrit literatures were worthless – and makes a relativist defence of his catastrophic decisions as Assistant Secretary to the Treasury during the Irish Famine. By contrast, she spoke with affection of her grandfather, Sir George Otto Trevelyan, recounting both his political career and something of the intimacies of family life – it is with George Otto she begins *Living at Wallington*. He had known 'Trollope's London', told Trollope's stories as though they were true, and had served in Gladstone's cabinets. Under his watch, a steady stream of liberals, radicals among them, came to Wallington, though Dower was unsure if Gladstone was ever a house guest. She recalled with affection how her grandfather read to her in 'Old English Greek' from Macaulay's 'great copies' of Homer, translating it into English along the way, and took his grandchildren on 10-mile drives in the brougham over the iconic hump-backed bridge to the south of the house – motorists are instructed to sound their horn as they approach – and onto Shieldhill and the beautiful view north of Wallington and the clock tower. Dower really hit her stride, however, when talking of her father, Sir Charles, and his brothers, George Macaulay, the historian, and Robert, the poet. They were a 'splendid trio', known for their 'startling, loud Trevelyan laugh'. Surviving photographs suggest close fraternal bonds.

Sir Charles entered parliament as a Liberal in 1899 and Dower remembered his principal interests as education reform and British misrule in Ireland. During the 'parliamentary season', a phrase reminding us that a political career can be as social as it was political, the whole household – family members, servants, dogs and cats – decamped by wagonette and train from Cambo to their London house at 14 Great College Street, the street immediately adjacent to parliament. Dower remembered the parliamentary season as an endless run of dinner parties enabled by the house having its own division bell. On its first ring, the men would stir; on its second, they'd contemplate heading for the House; on its third, they'd make a run for it, and having fulfilled their modest party-political duties, would swiftly rejoin the women. Winston Churchill occasionally dined at Great College Street, dominating conversation. So far, so very Trollopian.

Her father's social and political position was complicated by his opposition to the First World War, which was of a piece with his growing commitment to socialism and internationalist ideals. George supported the war, but the brothers were sufficiently 'devoted to each other' to prevent a break. Indeed, for all that the Trevelyan dinner table was animated by vigorous discussion, politics was somehow avoided and literature and history predominated, George taking to extremes the supposed Trevelyan aversion to small talk. 'He was very, very remarkable,' recalled Dower, 'and very formidable, more formidable than my father.' Charles's decision to send his children to Sidcot, a co-educational Quaker school in Somerset, reflected co-ed commitments picked up on a youthful trip to the United States with Beatrice and Sidney Webb, and the likelihood that no public school would accept his children on account of his 'pacifism'. Dower recalled his response to the Russian Revolution. 'I remember him drawing me to his knee and saying, "the greatest thing has happened since the birth of Jesus Christ, the Russian people have risen and are freeing themselves", that's what it meant to him.' After the 1914–18 war, Charles was elected for Newcastle Central as a Labour MP and served as minister in the MacDonald governments. One evening at Wallington after the 1939–45 war, Nye Bevan, just back from 'Russia in Stalin's day', spent two hours outlining 'a terrible picture of repression and massacre'. 'Well, Nye,' said Sir Charles, 'I don't believe a word of it.'

Dower's parents were 'most devoted' to the constituency, and she admired her mother's philanthropic work during the high unemployment of the Great Depression, though she skates over Molly Trevelyan's own political commitments. Molly was president of the

Northumberland Women's Liberal Federation, was in favour of women's suffrage and undertook a range of philanthropic roles throughout her life, becoming well-known throughout the county. It seems Sir Charles expected her to subordinate her political ambitions to his own and she campaigned energetically on his behalf during elections.[11] Dower claims, a little fancifully perhaps, that her mother helped poor families get on top of drunkenness to ensure the fathers did not drink away what little money they had. The Wallington Estate had been 'dry' since 1846, though a little beer or cider was allowed on occasion. Both Sir Charles and George were patrons of the Youth Hostel Association (YHA), established in 1930, George being its first president. Following her grandfather's death in 1928, when Dower was 22 and newly engaged to John, her father inherited the estate and the baronetcy, and the family moved the short distance from Cambo to Wallington, 'a very exciting move, all done with estate carts'.

By this time, Dower had studied Agriculture at Reading, spent a year at the Central School of Art in London, where she became an accomplished student in watercolours and etching, had tried shepherding, and taken to the lanes of Northumberland on a motorcycle, clad in leather and goggles. Born in 1905, the eldest daughter of six, she was close to her father and his clear favourite. He hoped she would eventually run the estate and allowed art school as an indulgence before she took on responsibilities for which her diploma in agriculture at Reading was preparation. Dower was also close to her aunt Gertrude Bell, her mother's half-sister, a remarkable figure, traveller, archaeologist and diplomat, who could not fail to inspire a clever, energetic young woman.[12]

Dower's marriage celebrations fell on 3 September 1929, Cromwell Day, and broke the period of mourning at Wallington. George Trevelyan, asked to toast the bride's health, gave a 'tremendous speech' about Cromwell, pleasing Dower, an unabashed Cromwellian, but her status as bride was forgotten as toasts were drunk; George's friend, the young historian Arthur Bryant, followed with 'a cavalier speech', but he too forgot the bride; eventually, someone remembered the purpose of the feast and Dower got her dues. She and John slipped off soon afterwards. Dower's marriage disrupted her father's hopes that she would one day take over the estate. As her mother drily observed on the birth of her first grandchild in 1931, 'matrimony cut across a great many professions'. On completing her training on a farm in Ayrshire, Dower had returned home, set to help farm the estate land: 'She bought 300 pigs. The pigs came on Wednesday, her suitor came on Thursday, and on Friday she was engaged. She is now engaged on a much greater task and is preparing for one still greater.'[13]

In the 1930s, Sir Charles opened Wallington to casual visitors and for use by socially progressive organisations like the People's Theatre of Newcastle and the Workers' Educational Association. Attics became dormitories and on occasion upwards of 20 people stayed. Dower remembered her father being very keen on encouraging young people to read, debate and form opinions. The lively picture Dower painted of Wallington as a family home is just as striking:

> The first summer we were here, he opened it free at weekends, Saturdays and Sundays from 2–4.30, and we simply took turns showing people around the house. Not very much was open because we were such a large family, we were all over everywhere, but we showed the entrance hall, the dining room, drawing room and central hall; I don't think we showed this room, which was a family sitting room ... Well, we couldn't have cleared up all our knitting and sewing, games and puzzles and all that sort of thing.

When asked about whether the decision to hand the house to the Trust was the right one, she was emphatic in her response:

> Absolutely. Absolutely, I think it has really fulfilled what my father wanted, from two points of view, both from the point of

view of the actual care of the house, which is superb, and of the estate too, and also of course it enabled the whole of the estate to remain as one community, which was my father's purpose in giving the village and the outlying hamlets and all the farms, the whole thing; he gave 14,000 acres taken entire to keep the community together. And . . . from the point of view of the public . . . they have this splendid place open to them. . . . I think we all felt very strongly that father's point of view that nobody had the right to own and enjoy all the beauty there is at Wallington, all the seemliness at Wallington, without sharing it with people, that was the base of his wanting to give it to the Trust.

When John Dower challenged his father-in-law to set an example by handing Wallington over to the National Trust in his lifetime and become Wallington's first National Trust tenant, Charles admitted his reluctance, declaring himself 'an illogical Englishman'. This anecdote was later served up to explain the apparent contradictions that shaped inter-war Trevelyanism, that mix of great privilege and progress.

John Dower enjoyed a comfortable upbringing in Ilkley, West Yorkshire, during which he developed his love of the Yorkshire Dales, especially Malhamdale. His father, Robert Dower, a Methodist lay preacher and director of a Yorkshire steelworks, had been at Cambridge with the Trevelyan brothers and had been invited by Charles to Seatoller in the Lake District to join the famous Man Hunt, an invitation extended in 1925 to his son, John, who in due course met Pauline, daughter of the 'master of the hunt'. The hunt is the stuff of Trevelyan lore. As David Cannadine describes it, each Whitsuntide from 1898, 'the finest flower of the new Liberal intelligentsia descended on the Lake District. . . . They were divided into hares and hounds, and for three days they hunted each other over the fells'.[14] After Cambridge, where he read History and Architectural History, John was articled to Sir Herbert Baker's busy architectural practice in London and then briefly with Charles Voysey before setting up his own architectural practice. At the same time he was drawn into the study of town planning under the influence of Patrick Abercrombie, Britain's first professor of architecture, doyen of mid-century town planners and founding member of the CPRE. John's architectural projects included the YHA hostels at Malham in Yorkshire, Eskdale in the Lake District and Bellingham in Northumberland, and he established himself as part of the broadly left-wing planner-architect elite that did so much to shape public debate about landscape use in the 1930s. He worked for the CPRE on a series of landscape surveys in 1929, contributed maps showing possible national park boundaries for the Addison Committee, and worked closely with the leading left-wing think tank Political and Economic Planning, writing or contributing to 16 of its 'broadsheets'. In a voluntary capacity, he combined his work for the politically cautious CPRE with work for the more radical Friends of the Lake District, and he was keen to ensure that lines of communication remained open between the two organisations as tensions arose over the most effective way to respond to the Forestry Commission's expansionist ambitions in the area. His preternatural talent as a writer of lucid and clearly organised prose made him a tremendous asset to the national parks movement. When the principal amenity organisations gathered in Central Hall, Westminster in 1935 to revive the national parks agenda, he drafted its key statement *National Parks: An Appeal*. This led to the formation of the Standing Committee on National Parks, for which he wrote *The Case for National Parks in Great Britain* in 1937. Axiomatic to the standing committee was that the government should establish a National Parks Commission to exercise planning control over a newly designated national parks system. John was convinced that the proposed commission should not focus largely on preventing developments, but must play a positive planning role, helping to deliver a high quality of life for residents, enabling a good experience for visitors and ensuring necessary developments took as their guide 'the form and dispositions of the existing buildings, especially those of the seventeenth and eighteenth centuries'.[15] John Dower was as much a planner as a preservationist.

Aged 37 when the war broke out, John was determined to join up, but was invalided out of the army in October 1940. While he convalesced with his family, friends in Whitehall kept him abreast of developments regarding post-war planning and he was soon invited to join the small team of experts under Lord Reith established by the Ministry of Works in early 1941. At this stage, John lived in London, but Dower and the children were evacuated to Kirby Malham in the Yorkshire Dales. We cannot know if he contracted TB during his brief but arduous war service overseeing the strengthening of Dover's defences or if the disease had lain dormant in him for many years – the final diagnosis, in Dower's words, of 'incurable TB' was made in October 1942 – but either way it is hard to read David Wilkinson's meticulous reconstruction of his work for the Ministry, including much politicking, without being conscious of the gruelling impact of his declining health.[16] This gives a tragic dimension to the production of his epochal National Parks Report of 1943, published in 1945 once resistance from the Ministry of Agriculture, the Ministry of Health, the War Office, the Admiralty and the Treasury was overcome, and then the central role he played in the translation of these ideas into the policy proposals of the Hobhouse Report.[17] The intellectual focus and coherence of his letters during this period and the close editorial attention he paid to the draft report would be impressive under ordinary circumstances but against the backdrop of his rapidly deteriorating health they are all the more remarkable.[18]

Dower enabled her husband to do his work, and occasionally accompanied him on his surveying, taking the wheel of their open-top Vauxhall coupé, but her involvement in the research and writing should not be exaggerated or sentimentalised. Theirs could be a companionable marriage, another way in which their lives were progressive, but the extensive letters Dower wrote from Yorkshire to her parents during the war, and especially those confiding in her father, revealed growing strains within her marriage.

John's frequent absences from home due to work meant Dower spent significant periods alone with her children and she often felt isolated and lonely. Although John conceded she found 'her complete rustication and domestication rather trying at times', when home she thought him either occupied with his work, unwell or prone to treat those times as a holiday.[19] Dower was especially unhappy during Christmas 1943, when he did not help with the domestic chores, and afterwards confessed she was glad he was well enough to be away for work. Occasionally she admitted to feeling frustrated by his inactive presence when he was unwell, though like her parents she worried that he made a relapse more likely by never allowing himself to fully recover before resuming work.[20] Mundane issues could create significant tensions. The old stove in the house they rented demanded a daily diet of coal and constant cleaning and, by Dower's account, John constantly put off having it replaced. He finally arranged for its replacement with an Aga in the spring of 1943. 'For all my devotion to John etc. etc.,' she wrote to her mother, 'I have no intention of becoming a social & nervous wreck because of avoidable overwork; I will *not* spend all my day working & have to cut out all mental & social activity, as I'm having to do.'[21]

These tensions did not just arise from Dower's grievances as a hard-pressed housewife, witness to her husband's interesting career, though that would be reason enough. Resentment at the mundane marital and maternal duties that dominated her life was intensified by the growing tension between her husband's politics and her politicisation as a Russophile socialist and desire to become a Labour activist. She touched on these issues in letters to her mother, fearing her isolation might turn her 'into a fanatic of some sort', but in letters to her father, in whom she found a kindred spirit, she sought advice on how to manage her political awakening and its personal consequences. Her remarkable letter of September 1942, a feminist *cri de coeur*, captured the anguish stoked in her. Exposure to new ideas saw her come to see John's work as limited by outmoded pre-war thinking, evidence of the conservative nature of the post-war settlement then becoming apparent.

It's really this friction between what my whole nature urges me to do (working for Socialism in whatever way I can) & what my sense of duty & family wisdom advises me to do (striving to look after the house & children & John, & remaining a nice, unthinking housewife) that gives me these recurrent bouts of extreme nervous tiredness, I believe. I seem to be living a Jekyll & Hyde existence simultaneously, not tidily in turns but all the time, my mind working furiously on political & social issues at the same time as organising family life. And I see no other prospect; because though I can & do delegate much of this routine work to this nice girl, Ann Redfearn, who comes in for 5 days a week, I can't delegate, even if I wanted to, my job as John's wife or mother of his 3 children. It seems perhaps silly therefore to bother [?] make a good 'politician'; I see things too directly, too 'black & white' as John says, with no subtleties & little patience. (Just as in painting, I like things clear & clear-coloured) & find it hard to understand why people won't face up to Socialism but turn away afraid of it & of its implications – even though for long I did the same myself. Perhaps as I get more chance to meet & talk with ordinary people I shall get plenty of grey rubbed into my clear colours & the fine edge of my beliefs well blunted. How much use I can be to the Labour Party I don't know. A friend of mine said the other day 'If you can't convince John of the rightness of Socialism how can you expect to convince other people?'. And momentarily I was persuaded that he was right; but on thinking it over, I think that John's & my minds are so fundamentally different that I could never set out to convince him; whenever I try to say anything about politics or social questions he uses his very clear, trained brain to test me with practical questions of which he cannot expect me to know the answer, & then says that I know nothing about it; & yet though I retire miserably snubbed, I *know* that I have in me a flame of an ideal higher than all his comfortable, tidy planning & ideas of reconstruction based on the same old 1939 world. But trying to talk to him only makes us both uncomfortable, he because he hates anything like emotion, I because it makes me rebel against his cold imposition of his mind on mine. It's rather a silly situation that my 'coming to life' like this should have as result the making extremely difficult of my relations to John; because I find it excessively hard to find anything to talk about though I'm bursting with talk, living in this place. But what am I to do? I'm still hesitating about joining the Labour Party solely because I find it quite impossible to talk it over with John; I've not ever been able to tell him anything about Laski's meeting.[22]

Sir Charles assured his daughter of her intellectual abilities, comparing her transformation to that of the young Beatrice Webb, another brilliant woman who made a rapid political conversion in early adulthood. 'She's wonderfully like you,' he wrote. 'You are both honest and hard as nails, whether or not you end up in the same street.' She was bound to be shaken psychologically and emotionally by the suddenness of her new commitments, he explained, the very rapidity of her conversion attesting to her intelligence. Guided in part by her father, a strenuous advocate of the Webbs' notorious apologia *Soviet Communism*, she voraciously read books, pamphlets and socialist periodicals.[23] She was impressed by Harold Laski, the Labour activist (Party chairman 1945–6) and academic who combined Stalinist sympathies with recognition of the possible necessity of revolutionary violence; by contrast, she was unconvinced by G.D.H. Cole's guild socialism, but his 'diagnosis of different types of mental wake-up in individuals & of policy' in *Europe, Russia and the Future* (1943) helped 'clarify' her 'own position'. Britain's fundamental problems, she now saw, stemmed from the dominance of the 'profit motive', the essential selfishness of the propertied classes, and how 'this English way of compromise & evolution, our insistent and persistent insularity, our habit of self-congratulation' acted as a barrier to radical change. Her father couldn't have agreed more and took every opportunity to remind his daughter of his contempt for the upper classes and faith in the working classes to grasp the coming opportunity to inaugurate a new era. Unsurprisingly, her view of the British Empire had also soured and, again egged on by her father, she wrote of her growing 'hatred of all our British, imperial way of life', particularly the distortions fed to the British people by a complicit media. Impressed by Nehru's 'fine mind', and mindful of her father's professed belief in racial equality, she exclaimed 'to think that we insist the Indians are "unreasonable" people or uneducated!'.[24] Above all, though, she was awed by the Russian war effort – she always wrote Russian rather than Soviet – which she thought explicable in terms of its superior social system.[25]

Her Tory landlord's outrage at her decision to take in a German refugee left Dower menaced by the threat of eviction and provided a convenient symbol of everything that must be overcome. Her father advised her she was secure for the period of the lease and affirmed the justice of the distinction she drew between the Nazis and all Germans. To grow accustomed to taking unpopular positions, he told her, was ultimately empowering.[26] Local politics gave her millenarianism a more prosaic focus, especially the Skipton by-election caused by the death of the sitting Conservative MP in late 1943. Labour activists chafed at the electoral truce underpinning the Conservative–Labour wartime coalition and when Joseph Toole, former Labour MP for Salford South, defied the party leadership and announced he was going to stand, Dower struggled to reconcile her socialist convictions with her recognition that the Labour Party was the only viable vehicle for their promotion: 'Nationally, I believe the Labour Party for all its faults & short-sightedness is the only real basis of organisation of all us left-wingers & that only by some coalition of all left-wing parties under the aegis of a rejuvenated L.P. shall we be able to defeat the old order.' The 'Russian example', she concluded, demonstrated that the party had been correct to expel Toole because notwithstanding his credentials as a representative of working-class voters, 'extreme discipline inside the Party is absolutely essential for real victory over capitalism'.[27]

Despite moving towards the left of the Labour Party, Dower's position was complicated by the appeal of the Common Wealth Party, a political grouping established in July 1941 by the amalgamation of the '1941 Committee', a dissenting group of liberal-left politicians and thinkers who advocated a more robust approach to post-war planning, and the Christian 'Forward March', led by the Liberal MP Sir Richard Acland. Despite her professed atheism, she admired Acland, whom she considered unconstrained by party politics, a particular virtue in her eyes; and it is easy to imagine why she was attracted to a party convinced an alliance between working and middle-class people who had to earn their living – and, indeed, between Christian Socialists and Marxists – was essential to building a socialist Britain.[28] The Common Wealth Party candidate duly won the Skipton by-election and until the end of the war the party maintained its status as the rallying point for middle-class Labour and Liberal voters frustrated by the party-political stasis imposed by coalition government. John encouraged Dower's support for Common Wealth, though she continued to crave a more idealist politics, ruminating on how Common Wealth and the young communists might inject the necessary energy and ideological commitment into the Labour Party that would ensure it did not lose young voters. If Common Wealth was a temporary response to the war, she speculated, might the Communists be a 'force for the future rather than the L.P.'.

By January 1944, when John was embroiled in arduous Whitehall debates about the acceptance and publication of his report, Dower reassured her father she would not do anything to 'invalidate' her husband's 'position' or 'break up the family's life'. She now questioned her tendency to judge 'everything by the criterion of Russia's achievements' and admitted she must learn to 'study objectively what is happening in the world'. Still, she remained unreconciled to the role of a respectable wife of a distinguished public servant. She wondered if her father, like her, also sometimes felt 'a sort of logic of despair, or of impatience' that led him to hope the 'Capitalist New Order' that would emerge from the war ('Kindly imposed, of course, by UNRRA & other philanthropic media!') would 'work out its own ruin till the bloody revolution it must engender in all countries blows it sky high for ever'. When the time came, she was ready to play her role, 'if possible doing the blowing up', and were she blown up along the way, she jauntily looked to 'some post-life existence' that would enable her to 'live in the only order worth living in!'.[29]

No attempt need be made to explain away Dower's wartime enthusiasm for the Soviet Union and Stalinism. Her father's political preferences influenced her receptiveness to pro-Russian sentiment and her views were common enough on the Left at this time. But Dower's letters indicate that she understood the extremity of her politics as partly symptomatic of the protracted emotional and psychological burdens imposed by the war, including her husband's attitudes and, less directly, his illness. She habitually related her rejection of conventional thinking to a lack of social contact, conscious of how much she brooded on the ideas encountered in books. Her husband's failure to take her seriously strengthened this tendency. 'I don't think he's ever thought much of my brain-capacity', she wrote to her mother.[30] The pull of the Left helped to meet a psychological or emotional need for a firm place from which to make sense of a disturbingly complex world; her impassioned outbursts – that yearning to escape present burdens for the immolation of revolution – suggested the ultimate avoidance strategy. She had three small children and it seemed their father – her husband – was working himself to death. 'This account may sound a bit off-hand & perhaps taken too lightly,' she explained to her mother when writing of John's deteriorating condition, 'but I find I just cannot talk about the poignancy of a man of John's rare capacities living with this growing sense of struggle against disease, & it is better to keep to bald facts in reporting his condition.'[31]

During the war, Dower wrote of how John's mood had oscillated between being 'dreadfully depressed & anxious' and then 'cheerful and confident again'; the completion of the Hobhouse Report over the harsh winter of 1946 left him 'content and confident', seemingly without 'worries or anxieties'.[32] John died the following October, aged 47. Obituaries celebrated his extraordinary contribution, and it is perhaps not too glib to imagine he found some peace in the completion of this great work, confident that national parks would take their place in Attlee's 'New Jerusalem'. For Dower and the children, grief-stricken and plunged into mourning, the sense of loss can scarcely be exaggerated. Photographs from the period show Dower's emotional exhaustion written across her face. Shortly after John's death, she and her sons spent a night with John's parents. They scattered his ashes on Ilkley Moor. Some comfort was found talking about John with his parents. That night, she slept soundly for the first time in months.[33]

The Commission Gets Started

Two years after the publication of the Hobhouse Report, parliament passed the National Parks and Access to the Countryside Act, legislation that came out of the same social democratic or democratic socialist thinking that gave the UK the National Health Service a few years earlier. It is no coincidence that the national parks system was created by a Labour government, but the park authorities envisaged by the legislation were significantly weaker than those proposed by the Dower and Hobhouse Reports. The government was reluctant to take away powers extended to the county councils as recently as 1947, and it was mindful of considerable political resistance to the national park agenda particularly from the landowning and agricultural community. There would be no national body with authority over the new parks and, in the main, the new authorities would be committees of the county councils and would lack full planning powers. The principal task of the commission, then, was to follow the recommendations of Hobhouse and designate parks, for which ministerial approval could be expected to quickly follow, and then to act as advocate for the parks at all levels of government.

The inaugural meeting of the National Parks Commission was held at the Ministry of Housing and Country Planning on 4 January 1950. 'Mrs. John Dower, J.P.' was recorded as present, along with the chair, Sir Patrick Duff, the deputy chair; the other commissioners; Will Nally, the junior minister; and officials. Also of note was her status as a Justice of the Peace. Her appointment stemmed from the initiative taken by her father as Lord Lieutenant of Northumberland, who hoped a public role might help bring her out of mourning. His instincts seem to have been sound. Dower also embraced Anglicanism during this period, which quickly consolidated into a lifelong commitment. Her conversion was part of a longer process. She had attended Quaker meetings during the war and had dallied with Christian sects in the aftermath of John's death, but it was through the more formal structures of Anglicanism that she satisfied the spiritual yearning that had underpinned something of her wartime mental turbulence, and came to terms with widowhood. Indeed, there was a congruency between the work she did for the church and for the National Parks Commission. Like many a Trevelyan and a Dower, she derived satisfaction from public service in institutional settings aligned with her progressive commitments.

As Lewis Silkin explained to the new commissioners, his task was to mark the significance of the occasion ('the culmination of long years of battling for National Parks'), clarify the scope of the legislation, and advise the commissioners on what they might prioritise; he reassured them of their significance despite the apparent shortcomings of the 1949 Act. Silkin explained what was already widely known. The government had not been prepared to reduce the powers conferred on local authorities by the 1947 Local Government Act, the consequence being that the new park authorities would not be independent planning authorities, but county council boards, or joint boards if a park crossed a county boundary. He conceded that the commission's role, in contrast to Hobhouse's recommendations, was 'advisory' rather than 'executive', but he insisted they could exert 'influence' across Whitehall, having 'great authority' with respect to all that happened in the parks.[34]

The commissioners should take their lead from the Dower and Hobhouse Reports, particularly the latter, but should not feel bound by their recommendations. Among those recommendations Silkin questioned was whether Hadrian's Wall, the South Downs or much of the Yorkshire Dales really were suitable for national park designation, the last because it had been made subject to significant agricultural development. Silkin thought the commissioners should consider Weardale or the Cheviots instead. Dower later became deeply embroiled in the Hadrian's Wall question. Silkin advised the commissioners to identify priority areas, such as the Norfolk Broads, given its degraded 'physical condition', and the Peak District, because there was 'great public demand for more access', these contrasting reasons reflecting the dual purpose of the 1949 Act. But Silkin also wanted an uncontroversial, high-profile success, and recommended that the commission turn its immediate attention to the Lake District. For similar reasons, he was keen to see long-distance footpaths established, such as the proposed Pennine Way and the Thames Towpath, and the designation of Areas of Outstanding Natural Beauty, perhaps starting with small 'local beauty spots'. Like any politician, Silkin hoped for some early successes.

He also offered a warning. The commissioners should use their 'great influence with circumspection and responsibility', seeking to always take 'a really balanced view'. Ultimately, a designation was a ministerial act, and controversial recommendations would mean bad press and politically difficult decisions for the minister. Duff responded with mild remonstrance. Staffing levels would determine the commission's early priorities and they could only be the 'shock troops in this stage of the battle' and might well require the 'big guns' in the minister's arsenal. In other words, Duff reminded the minister, the intentions of the 1949 Act would only be fulfilled if the minister was prepared to invest some of his political capital in its implementation. A separate note stated that the commission might engage a secretary on a pay scale between £1,320 and £1,700 if a man and between £1,160 and £1,550 if a woman.[35]

Silkin retired before the general election in February 1950, narrowly won by Labour, and was replaced by Hugh Dalton. Housing and Country Planning was not an obvious posting for a former President of the Board of Trade (1942–5) and Chancellor of the Exchequer (1945–7) – Evelyn Sharp later described the ministry as a 'wretched little backwater' – but Dalton embraced his 'light departmental assignment'. He expected the Labour Party to lose the next general election and was too old to expect a senior ministerial position in a future Labour government. As Dalton's biographer Ben Pimlott explains, with 'personal ambition behind him, he could perform his duties with fewer signs of nervous strain', demonstrating 'how much difference a major politician in a minor department could make'.[36] He found responsibility for establishing the national parks system particularly congenial. As chancellor he had established the National Land Fund, an ill-fated attempt to secure culturally significant land property for the nation as a memorial to the dead of the Second World War, and in 1948–50 was President of the Ramblers Association.

These moves reflected long-standing commitments and connections. Dalton was very much a part of Dower's world. An Etonian, a Cambridge graduate, a professed socialist and a protégé of Charles

Trevelyan, he had enjoyed invitations to Wallington and the Man Hunt, and when he entered parliament in 1929, inheriting his wife's seat, it was for the north-east constituency of Bishop's Auckland. Brief diary entries from May 1928 evoked the excitement of 'Trevelyan's Man Hunt', noting changing mores along the way:

> Hunting. Good fun and, except 27th, which is misty and rainy, good weather. Sing songs at night. Beer obtainable. This is new! The party, much of which only sees each other at Hunts, fits together surprisingly well.
>
> I grow a blister on my left heel which quite disables me on the third day. I become a very lame hound indeed. But no matter![37]

Some 20 years later, and shortly after taking on his new ministerial responsibilities, Dalton was once again in Northumberland, enjoying the Whitsun weekend walking the 'lovely country, with long green shepherds' tracks' of the Cheviots. He stayed the night at Cambo, where Charles Trevelyan, now 81, 'bent, but very friendly and effusive', showed him photos of the Hunt from 1911, 1912 and 1913. Dalton found himself to have been 'a smooth-faced young man with hair smoothly parted in the middle', feted for catching G.M. Trevelyan on two occasions.[38] These continuities, lubricated by Cambridge and shared political convictions, can hardly be gainsaid. Note who else formed that Whitsun walking party. Arthur Blenkinsop, elected Labour MP for Newcastle upon Tyne in 1945, was a determined advocate for national parks and conservation; Geoffrey de Freitas, another Cambridge graduate, was elected Labour MP for Nottingham Central in 1945; George Chetwynd, of working-class background, was elected Labour MP for Stockton-on-Tees in 1945, dislodging Harold Macmillan, and acted as Dalton's Parliament Private Secretary; Barbara Castle, Oxford graduate and rising star of the Labour Party, was elected MP for Blackburn in 1945; and Fred Willey, also Cambridge, was elected MP for Sunderland in 1945 and for

THE TIMES

LONDON
WEDNESDAY
FEBRUARY 22 1967

NO. 56,872
PRICE 9D
ROYAL EDITION

DR. BORG OLIVIER FOR LONDON

Early talks on new offer to Malta

Bribery charge by Mr. Wilson

'Rhodesians tried to get conference papers'

Lady Sayer stands in the landing path of an army helicopter yesterday during her protest on Dartmoor.

Two accused of drug theft and killing girl

THE QUEEN'S ILLNESS — Duke of Kent takes over investiture

Woman on the warpath at Dartmoor

MR. JAY IS CALLED TO NO. 10

'No knowledge of such operation'

ON OTHER PAGES

1. During the military training exercise on Ringmoor Down in February 1967, Sylvia Sayer transformed her right to access Dartmoor's commons into her greatest publicity stunt. The press photographer on hand caught this dramatic image. It proved irresistible to the picture editors at *The Times*.

2. The Ringmoor Down training exercises left a deep impression on Sayer. Here she captured the disturbance they brought to the moor. Dartmoor ponies, adopted as a symbol of the national park, are seen to embody its essence, a place we can all go feral.

3. John Singer Sargent's portrait of Octavia Hill (1898) was commissioned to mark her 60th birthday. Henrietta Barnett wrote that the 'beauty' of Hill's face 'lay in brown and very luminous eyes, which quite unconsciously she lifted upwards as she spoke on any matter for which she cared'.

4. As co-founder of the National Trust in 1895, Hill was especially keen that the organisation acquire land for public access within easy reach of towns and cities. Ide Hill was one of several breezy heights commanding magnificent views of the Kentish Weald whose purchase she helped enable.

5. Hill hoped others would follow the example of Mr and Mrs Richardson, who donated Toys Hill to the National Trust in 1895 as a memorial to their nephew Frederick Feeney. Like other National Trust sites in the area, Toys Hill now forms part of the Greensand Way crossing Surrey and Kent.

6. Beatrix Potter found fame for her Peter Rabbit books and contentment and privacy as Mrs William Heelis, fellswoman and wife of a local solicitor. She used much of her substantial personal fortune to acquire land in the Lake District, in time becoming the National Trust's single most important benefactor.

7. Hill Top Farm in Near Sawrey was Potter's first Lake District purchase. Following a childhood and young adulthood dominated by the expectations of her parents, in these exquisite surroundings she asserted her independence. For readers familiar with the Peter Rabbit books, it is an especially enchanting place.

8. Potter sought to preserve the agricultural regimes that had produced the Lake District and she believed that Herdwick sheep were the quintessential Lakeland breed. Although proud of her success as a breeder at local competitions, some fellsmen grumbled that she relied more on cash than judgement.

9. 'Uncanny, a place of silences and whispering echoes.' In 1923, Potter acquired Troutbeck Park Farm, one of the Lake District's largest enclosed farms. Here she could manage things as she wanted them. She maintained a hefted flock of Herdwicks, employed whom she liked and wandered its magnificent solitudes.

10. Following agricultural college and a little dallying at art college, Pauline Trevelyan was set to take on some responsibility for her father's estate at Wallington in Northumberland when she met John Dower. 'Matrimony cut across a great many professions,' commented her mother.

11. The Dower marriage became strained during the war. This study in modernist alienation, taken at Byland Abbey in Yorkshire, captured those difficult times. John, caught up in his work and plagued by illness, seemed an increasingly distant figure to Pauline, who found solace in new political commitments.

12. Dower helped drive the process that led to the designation of Northumberland National Park in 1956. This windswept scene hardly captures the awesome sweep of the county's most celebrated landscapes – the great rolling hills of the Cheviots or the brooding presence of the Roman Wall – but well might she have taken pride in the handsome boundary stone.

13. Dower painted and drew throughout her life, especially when on holiday or travelling. Her sketchbooks show the debt she owed the Impressionists, and the bold strokes and bright colours of this Northumberland scene reflected her own outlook on life.

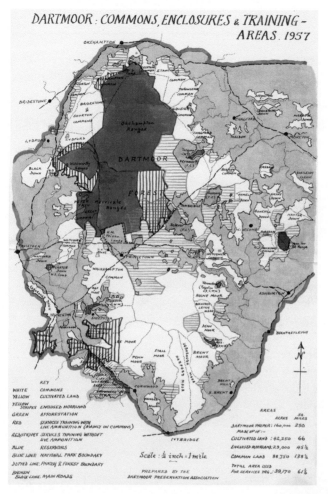

DARTMOOR: COMMONS, ENCLOSURES & TRAINING-AREAS. 1957

14. Sylvia Sayer often used visual means to get her arguments across. This map, produced by the Dartmoor Presentation Association for the Royal Commission on Common Land in 1957, gave vivid expression to the complex pressures shaping the landscapes of Dartmoor National Park.

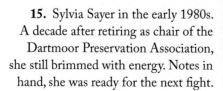

15. Sylvia Sayer in the early 1980s. A decade after retiring as chair of the Dartmoor Preservation Association, she still brimmed with energy. Notes in hand, she was ready for the next fight.

Sunderland North in 1950. Willey was particularly caught up in national park politics in the 1960s when he served as minister for the short-lived Ministry for Land and Natural Resources (1965–7). Dalton, then, was accompanied to Northumberland by prominent members of the 1945 Labour intake, including three North-East MPs, who were prepared to walk 50 miles over three days, accompanied by the 'pressmen and photographers', providing the new minister 'pretty good publicity', all of whom then stayed the night at Cambo.[39] Much of Dower's time on the commission was spent under Conservative governments, but that Whitsun weekend testified to the continuing importance of Wallington and the Trevelyans as a focal point for Labour politicians in the north of England.

And it was to Dower that Dalton communicated his enthusiasm for the task facing the National Parks Commission.

> There seems to be some misconception, both in my Department and in the National Parks Commission, of my relationship to the latter. I have no intention of waiting inertly for their recommendations. I wish to engage in an active two-way traffic in bright ideas, positive purposes and eager prodding! I want to put the N.P.C. on the map as soon, and at as many scenic points, as possible.[40]

Dalton need not have been concerned. In February 1950, the first meeting of the commission decided to make the designation of a Peak District National Park its priority on account of its proximity to major population centres and importance to the industrial working class of the north of England. Relatively speaking, the case for designating the Peaks rested less on its scenic, archaeological or ecological value – Hobhouse considered the Lake District and, in certain respects, Dartmoor and Snowdonia, superior – and more on its exceptional amenity value.

During her first months in post, Dower found herself on five subcommittees. Meetings could keep her in London four days a week.

A morning spent on Long-Distance Footpaths could be followed by an afternoon discussing the Countryside Code with representatives of the National Farmers' Union (NFU) and the Country Land and Business Association. Commission business took her to Oban in Scotland, to the Norfolk Broads (where she stayed with the Traffords at Wroxham Hall), to Somerset (where she stayed with Garnet Wolseley at Nettlecombe, another Trevelyan estate) and to Snowdonia, where she was the guest of Clough and Anabel Williams-Ellis, doughty campaigners for the protection of the Welsh countryside.[41] Her greatest responsibility, however, was her role as chair of the sub-committee responsible for designating the Peak District National Park. It was an arduous process of negotiation and renegotiation. A site visit was planned for May and a draft map was published shortly after; comment was sought from the local authorities and the CPRE, the Joint Committee Peak District, the Limestone Federation, the National Trust, the Nature Conservancy, the Forestry Commission and the Ministry of Agriculture and Fisheries. Further visits consequent on those comments were undertaken in October; in November local authorities were invited to a series of conferences to make the case for proposed revisions to the draft map that the commission had not accepted; the draft map was duly revised, the commission approved the designation order which was passed to the minister for confirmation, and the minister, recognising the strength of objections, called a local public inquiry.

A week or so before the inquiry was due to take evidence, Duff wrote to assure Dower of the commission's faith in her abilities and her right to take any necessary decisions. His letter, caught somewhere between kindly and sexist, invoked Henry V:

> What I am moved to write now is only this. You are so good and so willing in all the work that you undertake for the Commission that, although I may have some idea of the spirit in which you undertake it, I sometimes have heart searchings, as now, lest you

are shouldering an unfair part of the burden. There is no possible doubt that you will do your part in the Inquiry better than anyone else could: and I can imagine that you may not quite realise yourself how well equipped you are! But I still feel when I think of you going to stand in the breach at Buxton, like 'The gentlemen of England now abed/ Who held themselves accursed they were not there' and am wondering if there is anything one could do to help you?[42]

Dower replied once she had met the commission's counsel, J. Ramsey Willis, whom she quickly took to, and her characteristically upbeat letter captured something of the commission's pioneering spirit and idealism, as well as her own determination to live up to her late husband's legacy.

It was so encouraging to get your nice letter – thank you very much for it. I wanted to wait until I had met Mr Willis, before replying. I do not think you could possibly have chosen anyone better as our Counsel – he is much our type of man, & is thoroughly interested in the work & had a real 'eye' for country, so that 'beating the bounds' with him was a pleasure. With him & the Secretary to back me, I am not alarmed at the prospect of facing a critical, perhaps hostile, hall-full of objectors. But we shall all be glad when the first Inquiry is over & we can see how serious the antagonism to National Parks may be. It really is rather exciting, this carrying into effect, for the very first time, of so fine an ideal; we have no precedents, and our responsibility as a Commission is therefore, I think, the greater, to see that we are not frightened into overmuch compromise by the hostility of other interests. . . . It really is encouraging, the confidence you express in my judgement; I feel it is a high responsibility & great honour to represent the Commission at this our first real public 'action'.[43]

A few days before the inquiry was due to begin, Dower wrote to her mother from a hotel in Buxton, keen to impress upon her the hours worked, the complexity of the commission's task, and the camaraderie animating the team. Long days on site visits were followed up by evenings spent with case papers and maps strewn about the room. She worked with Willis, a small team from the commission and a Treasury solicitors' clerk but enjoyed the 'restful' time alone at the hotel.[44] She was not wholly at ease with her brief. Land west of Chesterfield, included on the forceful recommendation of Tom Stephenson, commission member and long-time secretary of the Ramblers Association, was not up to scratch. Her appraisal tells us something about the commission's thinking. Land to the north of Horsleygate Hall might be found 'charming country, partly open bracken-covered rough pasture' but Barlow and Brampton parish ends were 'not at all the sort of the country we should normally include in a N.P.'. It was 'high-lying agricultural land, a good deal of it cultivated', some under plough and some recently reseeded, 'with no attractive features, and almost no trees'.[45] She wished she'd taken a firmer stand before the commission finalised the boundaries. Duff sympathised, writing crossly of Stephenson's 'pretty poor show', but he reminded Dower that she had to represent the commission's 'corporate view'; she might concede some decisions were not fully supported by every commissioner, but the boundary represented the commission's settled opinion. For 'good or ill', personal preferences must be set aside and her job was to defend the commission's decisions to the best of her ability.[46]

As counsel, Willis would present the commission's position and cross-examine the objectors; Dower attended as witness to the commission's decisions, meaning the objectors, most likely through their counsel, had a right to cross-examine her. She could be questioned on anything the inquiry's chair felt admissible. Her proof of evidence, a formal document presented to the inquiry, attempted to see off some likely criticisms by explaining her role as a commissioner, the commission's statutory purposes, and the procedures it followed, particularly with respect to consultation and review. As she reminded objectors, the commission took its lead from the Addison, Dower and Hobhouse Reports, long in the public domain and parliament's reference point during the legislative process, which meant the commission's recommendations broadly reflected the will of parliament. Throughout the process, rhetorical strategies and techniques familiar from the criminal court were deployed to catch her out and expose inconsistencies or muddled thinking on the part of the commission, but Dower's and Willis's thorough preparation served them well. Their notes comprised a typed document running to 67 double-columned pages. On the left-hand side were extensive notes to be used by Willis – he would do most of the talking – and on the right were the justifications and explanations that might be offered by Dower.[47]

Willis opened his remarks by reminding the inquiry that the commission existed to implement government legislation. 'Parliament has said that there shall be National Parks,' Willis said, 'and the choice of the Peak District would appear to be the obvious one.' Nor was the inquiry an opportunity to make the case that the designation did not go far enough, a comment directed at Major Haythornthwaite, a prominent member of the national parks lobby and the CPRE. Instead, their concern was with 'matters of detail'. Willis rightly anticipated that many objections would concern what implications inclusion would have for land use. He explained that the designation had no effect on rights of land ownership and would not 'sterilise' included land from development, but it would establish a new planning authority, the Peak District Joint Board, to represent the five planning districts affected.[48]

The cases Dower was called upon to justify during the three-day inquiry reveal much about the mindset of the commission and its opponents and something of the pressures brought by her public role. Several objections were made with respect to the inclusion of 'agricultural land', by which objectors meant either enclosed or improved land rather than open moorland or rough grazing, prompting Dower to offer her fullest remarks with respect to the commission's overall purposes:

> The Commission are asked by statute to determine what areas are, in their opinion, of such beauty as to merit inclusion in a National Park. Thereby they secure for such areas greater protection from drastic change of use and preservation as national assets and agricultural land is clearly such an asset. Though it may not be access land it will still be visible from roads and from footpaths for the enjoyment of the public.[49]

She was repeatedly forced to explain that including pockets of agricultural land indicated no presumption with respect to public access but often did reflect the land's positioning with respect to areas, including footpaths, where the public did have access. Preserving the view from access lands or rights of way was part of the commission's purpose. Dower also explained that where possible national park boundaries were drawn along existing administrative boundaries (of rural or urban district councils) or roads, rivers and 'public footpaths of old standing'.[50] This approach followed the recommendations of the Dower Report and the advice of Hugh Dalton, who reminded Dower of the 'need for speed' and, therefore, the 'need to stick to existing administrative boundaries wherever possible, so as not, by arguing about inconsequential [sic], to lose the substance for the shadow'.[51] When pointedly questioned about how the general public would know they had entered a park, Dower replied:

> There are two ways; one is the obvious way to put up a map and hope that the public can read it, and the second way is to choose land in such a way that its quality shows itself as being National Park land. That is what we have tried to do in most cases so that as one comes up against what is actually the boundary on the map

you can often tell by the quality of the land over the edge that that is the edge, that it is of National Park standard.[52]

This opened her up to the challenge that the landscape quality of included land was not always sufficient and Dower had to repeat that there were no hard-and-fast rules. For example, the commission did not doubt that Wildboarclough warranted inclusion on grounds of landscape quality, but it was easy for Mr Isaac, representing the water undertakers of the borough of Macclesfield, to ridicule the decision to follow the administrative boundary between the civil parishes of Wildboarclough and Sutton because it passed through Trentabank Reservoir and Macclesfield Forest, a Forestry Commission plantation. Dower was briskly dismissive when asked if she'd brought her bathing costume when visiting the site.[53] More contentious were sites supposed to already have sufficient protection. Lyme Park, a country estate turned country park, was an important consideration for Stockport and its satellite towns and villages. It was managed for public access through an arrangement between the local authorities and the National Trust, and the objectors feared that 'interference' by the new National Park Authority would demoralise the local volunteers the park relied upon.[54] Similarly, the farmers of Leek objected to the inclusion of a large stretch of enclosed land to the east of the town, arguing that the wooded river valleys of the Manifold and Dove were already adequately protected by the National Trust. Once again, Dower argued the case on landscape quality grounds, adding that the National Trust could only benefit from having the commission support its preservationist and access priorities. With respect to Leek, she might have added that the Derbyshire Dales, an extensive stretch of enclosed land, was included in the park and that the boundary at Leek followed the River Morridge, a 'natural' boundary.[55] Some 'mapping questions' were determined by practicalities.[56]

Much the most forceful questioning came from the counsel representing industrial interests. J.K. Boynton, representing Derbyshire

County Council and a string of urban and rural district councils, provided the lowest and, inadvertently, the highest moment in the proceedings. His questioning of Dower began with a memorable exchange. Boynton asked, 'I think there are a number of male members of the commission, Mrs Dower, but they are sheltering behind your very capable self this morning?'. Dower replied, 'No, it just happens that I am the Chairman of the sub-committee that deals with this'.[57] Boynton pressed on, seemingly unabashed.

The boundary west of New Mills was particularly contentious. It took into the park relatively open land north-west of Chapel-en-le-Frith and east of New Mills, but excluded the River Sett, industrialised since the nineteenth century. Rather awkwardly, the boundary ran eastwards near the south bank of the Sett and then, east of Hayfield, westwards along the north bank of the Sett, excluding the river, the railway line to Hayfield, and Hayfield itself, a small town that grew in the nineteenth century on the back of its cotton mills and calico-printing industries.[58] The boundary hemmed in limestone quarries at New Mills (the same applied to the Bee Low limestone quarries near Buxton). Boynton tried to prove that the boundary was arbitrary and embarrass Dower into admitting that there was nothing the commission could do to protect the landscape that was not already within the capabilities of Derbyshire County Council. So pushed, Dower insisted that the new park authority could provide additional protections exceeding existing provision, and in response to a lecture about the social and economic significance of the industry, she did not shy away from saying that the inclusion of land in the park registered a hope that the commission would have a say in its later development. The new planning authority, she said, might well 'interfere' in the development of the limestone quarries in the future.[59]

This was an important moment in the proceedings. Dower had been repeatedly pressed on the significance of national park designation and had repeatedly played down its significance, saying designation would have no 'immediate effect'. This was no more than the truth, but designation would subject the landscapes of the park to a new Joint Planning Committee with active responsibilities to improve public access, such as by developing facilities like car parks and public conveniences, but much of its anticipated role would be responsive, either to private planning applications or larger developments. So, although there was little scope for positive management, and lines of questioning did expose the limited significance of designation, Dower also drew attention to the new authority's obligations towards the existing population:

> One of the characteristics – one of the important things in describing National Parks – in making a definition of a National Park has always been that the local way of life shall be respected and shall be carried on in its essentials. Though one of the reasons for the existence – for the making – of National Parks is that these finer stretches of country shall be preserved for public recreation as natural assets for future generations, that does not mean that the local people are going to be overrun by people from the towns and their own life spoiled by this. That is one of the major duties of the planning authority of a National Park – to hold the balance between the two.[60]

This quotation demands some unpacking. Who would decide what constituted 'the local way of life'? By the 1950s, quarrying and mining had long been an aspect of upland economies, whether limestone in the Peak District, slate in the Lake District and Snowdonia, or granite and china clay on Dartmoor, and yet Dower admitted that the new authority might seek to restrict the further expansion of these industries. Who would decide what constituted a 'natural asset' and on what basis would this be determined? Dower had mainly spoken in terms of scenery, hence the emphasis she placed on the importance of including non-access, agricultural land on the fringes of the park, but the new authority would have virtually no power with respect to how land was farmed. The commission's general position that designation would not have a negative effect on agriculture failed to foresee the impact agricultural intensification, often state-subsidised, would have on park ecologies. That challenge, and the inevitable arguments about the purpose of the park authorities, would take at least another decade to come into focus. Finally, what of these visitors? Here, Dower implied, was the positive case for national parks. If increased mobility, mainly thanks to the rise of mass car ownership, led to increased visitor numbers, then local people should surely welcome a new authority established to manage the likely influx. Like Hill before her, and sometimes Potter, Dower was part of a progressive tradition that considered access to countryside as good for the wellbeing of the people and that to deliver the means of securing that wellbeing was an obligation on all.

In her matter-of-fact way, Dower took to the stand to explain a set of decisions predicated on a visionary attempt to reconfigure the relationship between the landscape and the people. Heroics, rhetorical flights of fancy, grandstanding, all were unnecessary. Her case was scaffolded by statute and legitimised by the democratic mandate afforded by parliament. But in a lengthy letter to her mother, Dower gave a more personal account of proceedings and how she found her own performance. She described the layout of the room, reckoned on there being upwards of 200 people present, and told of her pleasure at being introduced as Charles Trevelyan's daughter and John Dower's widow. 'Then the first objector came to the table opposite, and the fun began.' She grappled with broad Cheshire dialects, 'big & very able business men', and severe questioning from the young solicitor employed by Derbyshire County Council, but her preparation saw him off. Pressure from the quarrying interests was intense, but she refused to budge on the most contentious question, the inclusion of 'the most exquisite bit of detailed limestone country' she knew, near a village called Meadow, 'as lovely as its name'. A 'little friendly banter' saw off businessmen, button-holing her at the end of the day, and she found herself more 'confident' with powerful interests, with whom she could be 'quite firm and frank . . . and they know it', than with 'the nicer & less intelligent farmers & local authority men'. She knew the territory; she knew the legislation. 'Absolutely first rate' read the note slipped her way by the commission secretary as she sat down following an especially tough grilling.[61] Dower had found her voice. Dalton confirmed the designation order on 19 April 1951 and Britain's first national park came into being.

At Work

Dower travelled constantly, relying not on hotels but a fat address book and a wide circle of friends and contacts. For instance, at the start of the summer holidays in July 1952, she gave a talk on the Country Code as part of Children's Hour on the BBC Home Service; a month later, she attended the Town Planning Institute summer school, during which she acted as the voice of the National Parks Commission, emphasising the difficulties the commission faced in implementing legislation 'based on a new way of thinking about the countryside'. Misconceptions were widespread, she explained, instancing 'the motormower firm that wrote to the commission applying for the contract to cut the grass in its parks' and 'the pathetically naïve fears of farmers who thought all the land in a national park was nationalised and thrown open to public access'. When questioned about mining and quarrying in the new parks, she explained that it was time the national assessment of mineral needs and resources, begun in 1948, was published, implying that the national interest did not preclude the expansion of the extraction industries in national parks. She was also asked about agriculture in the parks and, as a harbinger of later controversies, was quizzed on whether the commission would interfere with agriculture.[62]

In February 1958, Dower and Lord Strang, the new chairman, represented the commission at the public inquiry into the siting of a nuclear power station on Trawsfynydd Lake in Snowdonia. Dower expressed their opposition in visual terms, objecting to 'a huge over-mastering imposition, a creature utterly out of scale and character with that of the landscape around it', but local voices, including the NFU spokesperson, objected to her lack of consideration for the socio-economic needs of a poor Welsh rural community.[63] Preservationists were often accused of this. A decade later, Dower represented the commission at the public inquiry into the General Electricity Board's application for a 400kv line to carry Yorkshire's surplus electricity across the Pennines from Bradford to Darwen. Of the three routes identified, coded blue, red and green, the commission favoured the most expensive, which avoided Wadsworth Moor (blue) and the Brontë village of Haworth (red), and instead passed near the built-up areas of Brighouse, Elland and Ripponden. 'Trying to construct for oneself the "feel" of the Brontë country,' she said, 'would become almost impossible with so flagrant and omnipresent an intrusion cutting across a view.'[64]

The proposition that developments could destroy the 'feel' of a place influenced Dower's response to the most contentious question the commission faced in the 1960s, the Draft Manchester Water Order of 1965. Manchester Corporation, the water undertaker for the city and the surrounding region, was obliged to meet the water supply needs of industry and some 1.35 million residents. Enabling legislation passed in 1879 and 1919 allowed Manchester Corporation to develop Thirlmere and Haweswater lakes in the Lake District into impounding reservoirs and to build the necessary infrastructure needed to carry the water to the urbanised North-West. In the 1950s, future projections demonstrated that existing supplies would not meet increasing demand, which was expected to almost double to 480 million gallons a day by 2000. In 1961, Manchester again turned to the Lake District, placing before parliament a private bill seeking permission to extract water from Ullswater. It would be pumped to Haweswater via new piping, allowing a greater volume of water extraction from the reservoir. The scheme was hugely controversial and duly thrown out by parliament in 1962. The minister then instructed Lord Jellicoe to investigate Manchester's predicament, and his subsequent report upheld the Corporation's case with respect to need and investigated a range of options, including the Ullswater proposals, but did not make a firm recommendation.[65] Ullswater, then, was still on the table and, buoyed by Jellicoe's sympathetic but inconclusive report, Manchester pursued the case again, proposing in 1965 a scheme to pump water from Ullswater and Windermere to Haweswater. The increased supply would feed the Corporation's aqueduct system. The opposition in 1965 was no less fierce than it had been in 1962 and, perhaps inevitably, this led to a public inquiry.

Dower represented the commission. Her argument rested on several observations and a significant proposition. The first was that implementing the scheme would place the watersheds of Thirlmere, Ullswater and Windermere 'under control as a source of water', further strengthening Manchester Corporation's position in the Lake District.[66] If the minister confirmed the Water Order, the influence of Manchester's ratepayers in the Lake District would appreciably increase. Second, the proposal might be 'the easiest, the cheapest, the most attractive means of obtaining water' but this was not 'the standard of judgement to apply to a National Park'; as Dower reminded the inquiry, there was a statutory obligation to protect the 'national' interest vested in the Lake District, which could not be casually trumped by important urban needs if viable alternative solutions were available.[67] That 'if' is crucial, for this was not a question of absolutes but of the need to reconcile the obligations of two statutory bodies, namely the national park authorities and a water undertaker. In essence, she asked the inquiry to consider if the interest the British people now had in this landscape, as created by the designation of the Lake District National Park, would be reduced in value if the sectional needs of Manchester were met in this way. Finally, she emphasised the scheme's considerable 'unused capacity', meaning that the limits imposed by the draft order might one day be lifted, leaving open the possibility that Ullswater could be dammed and developed into a reservoir at a later date.[68]

Dower's claim that to approve the scheme would effectively extend the territorial reach of Manchester Corporation, partially transferring control of Ullswater from the nation, as enabled by the national park system, to Manchester's ratepayers, had force if the case for protecting Ullswater was persuasive. Manchester Corporation, after all, had to meet its statutory obligations, and extracting water from marginal upland agricultural landscapes was not inherently objectionable. For a century or more, the uplands had been the obvious solution to the growing water needs of urban Britain, and the case clearly highlighted how national park provision created new sites of contention by narrowing the options available to rival statutory bodies. Thus, Dower could not hope to win the argument by seeking to demonstrate that water should not be extracted from national parks on principle; instead, she had to make the case for Ullswater's exceptional qualities and demonstrate why this particular scheme would harm them. Quantitative means, such as the current vogue for 'natural capital', had not yet been developed to give expression to the value of the natural landscape, whether to humans or non-humans. Instead, the currency at Dower's disposal was principally affective, and her purpose was to rouse subjective or emotional responses. Her task was to convince the inquiry of the magnitude of the harm threatened, rendering it unconscionable that they would approve the scheme.

The setting of the lake surrounded by the great hills, in a land-scape astonishingly little altered during the last 150 years to judge from old prints, the fields sloping gently to the water's edge, the fringe of self-sown alder, ash and willow along the shore, the variety of detail, with the little beaches of fine grey shingle set among the trees, the rocky outcrops, the smooth green fields, even the winding road which meanders so casually along the western shore, all combine to give a sense of changelessness, of rural simplicity and a genuine local life unaffected by urban pursuits, extraordinarily refreshing to experience.[69]

Evocative though this passage is, the tropes it deploys, and the argument they carry, were characteristic of the parks lobby. The force of the argument relies on the distinction drawn between rural continuity and urban disruption. The former was of psychological benefit to those relentlessly assailed by the latter: the value of 'genuine local life' was not so much inherent as found in its broader utility. Tourists did not need to be entertained, for Ullswater 'provides its own attractions': a car can be easily parked just off the road; children can safely paddle in the lake. Recalling aspects of the arguments once made by Octavia Hill, Dower did not evoke Ullswater as untamed wilderness, but as easily accessible and family-friendly, a landscape that embodied national park principles and the democratising effect of mass car ownership. Her argument would have been weakened had she presented Ullswater as a form of natural beauty accessible only to the particularly intrepid or able-bodied. Domesticating Ullswater was not diminishing. She developed her argument further, drawing on a long tradition of political argument about landscape, and particularly the commons, that reified the rural as a site of freedom of movement and authenticity in contrast to the artifice of mechanised urbanity.

There is nothing here to remind the townsman of any of the restrictions or artifices of urban life. The landscape is entirely rural, the lake waters uncontrolled, access to the lake free and unquestioned. Ullswater enshrines the freedoms which are so difficult to safeguard in our crowded, restricted and highly-mechanised life; freedom to come and go as one likes, freedom from control, from noise, from overcrowding.

To see work in progress on the pumping station and pipeline, evidence that this lake was after all to be controlled and that

191

thereafter public access to its shores and public recreation on its waters would be by grace of Manchester Corporation, and not as now unchallenged and unexamined, would gravely reduce the value of this peerless place.[70]

As this passage develops, it becomes clear that Dower believed bodily freedom and psychological uplift were not only integral to each other but peculiarly susceptible to perceptions of place. If visitors became conscious that the lake was being made subject to control and that public access was by permission rather than by right the psychological benefits of exposure to rurality would be diminished. To diminish the freedoms of the rural, including the agency of the lake, was a form of urbanisation. Thus Dower asked: should Ullswater, currently rural, be permitted to become urban, a site of control and regulation? This argument recalled Dower's concern about the loss of 'feel' in Brontë country, ballasting her consistent concern with what contemporary planners referred to as 'visual amenity' or what today's commentators sometimes refer to as the 'sense of place' (*genius loci*) or 'placeness'. Aesthetic judgements were always entangled with cultural signifiers – the Brontë factor – that gave places psychological and emotional resonance. Parliament eventually found against Manchester Corporation and Ullswater was 'saved'. The arguments she made shaped her role on the commission over the course of its existence, not least with respect to its most idiosyncratic park, that designated in her home county.

Northumberland National Park

Northumberland is a large, sparsely populated county on the border with Scotland with a long North Sea coastline. As today, in the 1950s much of the county was undeveloped upland, long cleared of tree cover, used primarily to graze sheep and cattle. Rural Northumberland remains dominated by large estates, tenanted farms and small villages with little common land. As a tourist destination, it was best known for its coast, which boasts long sandy beaches punctuated with picturesque castles, such as Bamburgh, Alnwick and Dunstanburgh, as well as bracing North Sea waters. Even on warm days, strong easterlies can carry a cold bite. The southern reaches of the county, to the north of the Tyne, are bisected by Hadrian's Wall, built by the Romans in the second century AD to help manage the northern reaches of the Empire. Twenty or so miles north of the wall are the Cheviot Hills, which straddle the Anglo-Scottish border and peak with the Cheviot at 815 metres, the highest point in Northumberland. Those who develop their landscape tastes in the Highlands of Scotland, the mountains of Wales or the fells of Lakeland might find the Cheviot unprepossessing, more hill than mountain, but it nonetheless commands magnificent open views north and south. As one commissioner put it after a site visit:

> The Cheviot area . . . was considered unanimously by the inspecting party to have an exceptionally high degree of natural beauty. Its blend of colours of heather and grass, which is probably at its best in September, is something which I have seen in such great extent nowhere else. The hills are cut by deep valleys in which run burns of unusually clean water. By comparison with most of the Pennines the airs and the rocks are clean.

By some measures, the Cheviots even surpassed the Lake District because they suffered less the effects of industrial pollution. Parts of the Lakes received 'visible smuts from the nearby blast furnaces of Barrow'.[71] More than any other county in England, Northumberland is characterised by wide open country, and to stand at almost any high point is to be impressed by its sheer expanse. This is 'scenery' on a grand scale, exposed rather than intimate, hilly rather than mountainous, horizontal but undulating, a tranquil landscape of rolling breakers rather than crashing waves.

How, then, to designate a national park that included Hadrian's Wall, the Cheviots and the coast? The Dower and Hobhouse Reports recommended that the Wall should be the basis of a Northumberland park, with the Cheviots and adjacent Rothbury Forest having a lesser status. The commission broke with this: COU 1/597, the file containing the designation papers in the National Archives, was initially titled 'Cheviot National Park Designation' and in October 1953 the commission duly recommended the minister designate a Cheviot National Park. This would be a small park, some 200 square miles in total, and would comprise land from Pawston Hill on the Scottish border to the Simonside Hills in the south and the edge of the Cheviot moorlands in the east. This approach was consistent with existing practice, whereby designation was based on – if not largely determined by – geological and geographical features. The landscape itself seemed to dictate the existence of national parks for the Peak District (1951), Lake District (1951), Snowdonia (1951), Dartmoor (1951), Pembrokeshire Coast (1952), North York Moors (1952), Yorkshire Dales (1954), Exmoor (1954) and Brecon Beacons (1957). In each case, the precise boundaries of the parks were subject to dispute, but the broad reach of each was apparently determined by natural features. At first glance, this seems to be a straightforwardly anthropic process, an imposition of meaning onto the landscape by human actors, but by responding to the natural features of the land-scape the commission responded to deep time, implicitly recognising the agency of nature. For the proposed Cheviot National Park, however, the dictates of deep time were undermined by the Anglo-Scottish border, which cuts diagonally on a south-west/north-east axis across its western reaches, and the distance of the Cheviots from a significant conurbation. The Exmoor, Peak District and Lake District parks straddled county boundaries but the 1949 Act only included England and Wales: there was no provision for a park boundary that straddled the Anglo-Scottish border. The dense tracery of pink contour lines that describe the Cheviots on the OS map could not determine the extent of the park.

Proposing a Cheviot National Park saw the commission sidestep two challenges. The first was that the commission did not consider the land immediately north of Hadrian's Wall to be of high landscape value, particularly that south of Redesdale, including the relatively developed – by Northumberland standards – stretch of country along the North Tyne between Hexham and Bellingham. Second, and more seriously, the Forestry Commission's largest holdings were in Northumberland, especially in the great south-west expanse of the county at Kielder and Wark. Here, coniferisation was in progress on an unprecedented scale, producing the largest timber reserve in England, and second by extent in the UK only to the commission's less concentrated plantings at Galloway in Scotland. By the 1950s, the Forestry Commission held some 84,000 acres of plantable land at Kielder, Wark and Redesdale, of which approximately 59,000 acres had been planted with Sitka and Norway spruce, and some Scots pine and Douglas fir.[72] This was commercial forestry on a vast scale.

John Dower had advocated Kielder's inclusion in his proposed Roman Wall National Park, envisioning a park on a large scale, but the commission was inhibited by both the Forestry Commission's expansionist plans and the conventional wisdom that large-scale commercial forestry was at odds with national park principles. Including Kielder also raised complex issues of governance and the commission feared the new park authority would be vulnerable to criticism for forestry developments over which it had no control. Designating a Cheviot National Park meant taking the line of least resistance, avoiding the dual challenge of an expansionist forestry sector and the Cheviot–Wall–Coast problem. The commission's cautious approach was also evident in the reassurance it provided Northumberland County Council. The administration of Dartmoor

National Park might have cost £7,500 per annum, but the cost of a Cheviot National Park was unlikely to exceed £1,000 per annum.[73]

It was not to be. Northumberland County Council was not satisfied. Like Devon County Council, but unlike most other county councils, Northumberland was a park enthusiast. The proposed park was too small to justify the new administrative burden and could not meet the council's hope that national park designation would put the county on the map as a tourist destination, raising its status with respect to its all-conquering western neighbour. To confine the park to the county's far north, distant from the Wall, the coast, and urban Tyneside, was hardly auspicious. As the county council explained to the commission, a larger park 'would do much to dispel the ignorance which exists elsewhere in the country of the extreme beauty of the County's scenery and the great interest of its antiquities'.[74] Press reports revealed that the county council intended to propose a larger park which would include the Ministry of Defence artillery range in Redesdale and Forestry Commission land at Kielder, Wark and Redesdale. These proposals envisaged a park of 570 square miles, making it smaller only than the Lake District, Snowdonia and the Yorkshire Dales national parks.[75] If the new Northumberland National Park was to compete with the Lake District, it needed to capture the imagination and that meant a bold, maximalist designation, not a cautious act of confinement.

Including MOD land in a national park was contentious but not without precedent. Large sections of Dartmoor National Park, particularly in the northern quarter, were occupied by the military, and access there had to be carefully managed, although this was not always successful. As on Dartmoor, in Northumberland the retention and expansion of training areas had been a pressing political question in the immediate post-war years, not least because the authorities were aware that territories suitable for battlefield training were among those likely to attract national park designation. On both Dartmoor and in Northumberland a new military settlement evolved in parallel to the national park designation process. In both cases, the War Office sought to consolidate holdings recently acquired through a combination of purchase and requisition before national park designation, but in practice it would prove to be a long process of feint and counterfeint as a new landscape settlement was gradually formalised. External forces, most obviously the UK's long-term strategic interests, invariably trumped local concerns, and new weapons systems requiring larger ranges could create local pressures in the broader context of contraction.

In the case of Redesdale, originally leased by the War Department in 1911, the most contentious terrain was the wartime requisitions to the east and north of the River Coquet, which had extended the pre-war range into country considered of high scenic and amenity value. At the end of the war, it could not be assumed that the status quo ante would be restored, and G.M. Trevelyan had been quick to write to *The Times* to explain the importance of this terrain. He cited the Roman camp at Chew Green, 'an outpost on the uttermost edge of the Roman Empire', evoking the area's romantic associations, and noted the popularity of the upper waters of the Coquet as 'a splendid field for sport and exercise for the considerable population of industrial Tyneside' and the importance of the area to the proposed Cheviot National Park and the Pennine Way.[76]

New training needs brought by developments in long-range field artillery ensured the War Department sought to retain their new holdings, including three gun-sites at Elishaw (120 acres), Shittleheugh (190 acres) and Holystone Priory (200 acres), and extend its southern reaches eastwards into the Harbottle Hills and Holystone Common. This was unacceptable to Dower and the commission. As *The Times* had argued in December 1945, it was plausible to claim that the pre-war range did not have high amenity value but extending these boundaries to the south-east and north-east of the Coquet was much more intrusive.[77] Not only are the nucleated villages of Coquetdale among the county's most attractive and easily accessible by car, but they were also home to long-established rural communities. According to the CPRE, the landscape was of 'first-class importance', most particularly Holystone Common, Billsmoor Park and the Grasslees Burn, the last of particular ecological value.[78] The War Department, slowly coming to terms with national park thinking with respect to visual amenity, accepted that the southern boundary would be withdrawn to the skyline west of Holystone and instead prioritised the acquisition of six additional gun-sites that would allow firing into the range from outside. Following a local public inquiry in June 1948, the War Department's plans were approved in March 1949, but restrictions were imposed, not least thanks to a direct intervention by Lady Trevelyan, Dower's mother. In her capacity as chair of the Northumberland and Newcastle Society, the local branch of the CPRE, she wrote directly to the prime minister asking for assurance that the War Office would not be permitted to develop the disputed areas east and north of the Coquet without consulting the County Planning Committee. Much to the frustration of Northern Command, and breaking with all convention, Attlee replied to the effect that this would indeed be the case.[79] Trevelyan influence could still be felt in the higher reaches of the Labour Party.

The fate of the Elishaw, Shittleheugh and Holystone Priory sites was not decided by the inquiry, though it was understood that occasional use of the Holystone site would continue because it was easily accessible by heavy vehicles. In December 1953, the commission was informed that the War Department considered the retention of the three gun-sites essential and would now seek planning clearance. With the commission now focusing its attention on designating a national park in Northumberland, it found there was little it could reasonably say about Elishaw and Shittleheugh. Both were a little outside the proposed Cheviot National Park border. Holystone, though, was in, and Dower was not about to let it become permanent War Department property without a fight. She suspected the War Department's plan for the gun-site was the first step in a larger programme of acquisition. If it were to 'get a lease for this site, unopposed by us,' she wrote, 'they will almost certainly eat back towards the main block of the Range, and recover all that they were forbidden to have in the Inquiry.' As we will see, Dower could be quick to suspect the motives of rival government bodies. The National Parks Commission, she added, must not oppose the acquisition 'out of spite' but on the grounds that 'Holystone is a very charming, quiet, tiny village, absolutely unspoilt, and that if this area becomes a regularised War Dept. holding, it *must*, whatever the present conditions, eventually affect the character of the place'. Anticipating that the War Department would highlight the commission's apparent acquiescence in its current use of the site, Dower made the procedural point that the department's attempt to 'regularise' use was the first time the commission was given a formal opportunity to lodge an objection.[80] The Northumberland and Newcastle Society agreed, and Dower encouraged Claud Bicknell, its honorary secretary, to declare their opposition. Rev. R.G. Bell of Otterburn Hall feared an enhanced military presence at Shittleheugh would harm the local community, threatening its water supply (a natural spring), the well-being of the local school, and tourism. Otterburn also boasted three hotels which, as Bell cannily observed, made it 'a small holiday centre near to the Cheviot National Park'.[81] Spurred on, the commission resolved to oppose the War Department's attempt to achieve a permanent hold over all three sites. It was not the last time the commission would adopt a stronger position in response to outside pressure.

Forcing the issue was not in the interest of the War Department and it allowed the uncertainty to continue. Only with the publication of Duncan Sandys' Defence Review White Paper in 1957 were all parties compelled to tackle the issue. Substantial cuts were planned for Britain's territorial forces, reducing its need for large training grounds, and notable territories to be given up included Stobs in Scotland, the Trawsfynydd range in Snowdonia, half of the 26,000 acres held at Fylingdales in Yorkshire and the East Merrivale Range on Dartmoor. Paradoxically, these concessions elsewhere intensified

199

pressure on Northumberland. Increased use of Redesdale was a consequence of the decision to give up Stobs, but the military assured the commission that the eastern side of the range, including Upper Coquetdale, would continue to be used only for infantry manoeuvres. Ameliorative gestures were also made with respect to an old bugbear of Dower's, namely the military's lackadaisical attitude towards taking down the red warning flags when the range was not in use – also a long-standing problem on Dartmoor – but it remained reluctant to let go of the Holystone site. Horse-trading followed. The Northumberland and Newcastle Society, retaining its principled objection to the military's presence in Redesdale, pushed for the three sites to be relinquished and sought a public inquiry, whereas the commission, with Holystone the main prize, was ready to treat them separately. The military authorities insisted that the three were a job lot, but its veiled threat that losing Elishaw and Shittleheugh would necessitate firing into land north of the Coquet revealed a chink in its armour. Bicknell recognised the way the wind was blowing and wrote to the CPRE to explain that he was not unduly worried about Shittleheugh and Elishaw but wanted the military off Holystone Common and Grasslees Burn Valley preserved from any military activity.[82]

Agreement was finally reached at a cordial meeting in August 1958. The military agreed to minimise its presence in Coquetdale. There would be no live firing east of the Coquet, allowing public access to the valley at all times; extraneous huts and other military buildings would be removed; a new military road to bypass Otterburn village might be constructed; and military activities in the Grasslees Burn Valley and in the vicinity of Holystone Beacon would be minimised. In a gesture that reflected more the anxieties of the times than a likely prospect, the military undertook to ensure there was 'no use of nuclear weapons' at Redesdale. And the Holystone gun position was to be given up.[83] The commission claimed a modest victory, congratulating itself on its tenacity, but Dower was not content.

Looking to a time when Redesdale would be given up altogether, she shared local concerns that established rights of way, reduced by the military's presence to permitted footpaths, might not be restored. Continued vigilance was needed. Perhaps a legal guarantee could be made, mused a military contact, but it is not clear that anything came of this.[84]

For now, Holystone had been saved, but over the following decade Coquetdale would become the most contested site in the new national park, with Dower often deeply engaged in the argument. Before looking at her role in these conflicts, we must return to the designation process and the second challenge the county council had set the National Parks Commission, namely the inclusion of Kielder Forest in the new national park.

The Forestry Commission intended to declare Kielder a forest park, but to successfully make the case for its inclusion in the new national park would accord the specific site a higher status and challenge the assumption that coniferised landscapes were at odds with national park principles. Consequently, the debate this aspiration provoked proved to be among the most historically significant to accompany the designation of any national park. If plans for a Cheviot National Park were off the table, this meant the parameters of a putative Northumberland National Park were far from evident. Deep time could not provide the answers. Instead, Northumberland National Park had to be imagined into being, and if an amalgam of distinct landscapes could be imagined as a national park, could the interventions made by commercial forestry be reimagined as having a positive impact on the landscape? Dower played a pivotal role in these discussions, and in the following years worked to uphold the integrity of their outcome.

In July 1954, the commission descended on Northumberland for a couple of days. Dower hosted a party that included Lord Strang, Brunsdon Yapp and Brigadier P.B.E. Acland of Devon County Council. They came with two purposes in mind. First, to establish the attitude of the Forestry Commission to the inclusion of the Kielder, Wark and Redesdale forests in the new park, and second, to decide for themselves whether Kielder, the largest and most established of the three, was 'worthy' of inclusion. Sir Henry Beresford-Peirse, Deputy Director-General of the Forestry Commission, and Mr Connell, Forestry Commission Conservator, showed them around, grasping the opportunity to make the case for Kielder's social and cultural value and its legitimacy as a National Park landscape. They admitted that in the early years of the plantation rapid progress was prioritised and rides were driven straight up and down the hills, making them unappealing to walkers and unsightly from a distance, but recent planting took 'amenity' into consideration. Rides now followed contour lines, greater care was shown for preserving 'vistas and panoramas', and 'amenity flats' in the valley bottoms were achieved by mixed planting. The Forestry Commission was keen to see the British public become 'forestry-conscious' and visitors were now encouraged, enabled by excursions organised by British Rail and the new youth hostel at Kielder village – the Border Counties Railway was closed to passengers in 1956. If the amenity value of forestry was recognised, they argued, apparent differences in priority between the interests of the Forestry Commission and the National Parks Commission would dissolve.

Strang later reflected on the visit. He was ready to accept the strength of the Forestry Commission case. Kielder might not be 'conventionally attractive', but it was not inferior to the north-western part of the Peak District National Park and, as we have already seen, pragmatic judgements rather than absolutes had often guided the commissioners. Moreover, Strang understood the practical advantages of inclusion for Northumberland County Council. Dealing with the Forestry Commission, whose ambitions reached beyond Kielder, would be easier with a single administrative structure and the support of the National Parks Commission. The real question, then, was whether the commission should 'break fresh new ground by including the largest forest area in England and Wales in a National Park'. His fellow commissioners duly wrote up their conclusions.[85]

The county council's favourable position on the inclusion of Kielder and the positive response by the Forestry Commission left Dower concerned that the reputation of the National Parks Commission would be harmed if it rejected both overtures. Resisting cooperation with the Forestry Commission might also damage relations in the future, not least given its current 'offer to stand down on their own plan for the National Forest Park, and to accept instead our cover for the whole of their Kielder area'. She was also impressed by the Forestry Commission's efforts to improve the amenity value of the plantations. She presumed that if Kielder were incorporated into the new park 'the present scheme of view-points, open rides and areas left unplanted' would be 'systematically developed'. The National Parks Commission might even learn from the Forestry Commission's experience 'running information centres, camping sites, and a system of trained wardens'. Like Strang, she also acknowledged that for administrative reasons and to create a coherent geographical space, the commission had already included in national parks land of low scenic value or land where there was little prospect of delivering public access on account of how it was farmed. She was also susceptible to the positive case for inclusion made by the Forestry Commission:

> I found myself, against all expectations, much impressed by Kielder. Its scale is bigger than I had remembered; due to the grand scale of this country, its great sweeps of hill give opportunity of wide views from vantage points. Not all of this area is 'spoiled' by afforestation; where the rides in the plantations are allowed to follow the contours and not driven in straight lines up to the horizon, and where the species of trees are mixed, especially where such mixing is of deciduous trees with conifer, the landscape is sufficiently varied to be interesting and often quite fine.

THE WOMEN WHO SAVED THE ENGLISH COUNTRYSIDE

> There is no doubt that it is most interesting to see this very bleak upland country being put to a new use, with the introduction of new village communities.

Brunsdon Yapp agreed. A zoologist from Birmingham University and the most original thinker on the commission, he urged Kielder's inclusion for several reasons. First, the commission should take the lead in challenging 'prejudice' against coniferous plantations, which he put down to the relatively unappealing nature of spruce plantations in their first decades and the pervasive idea that they were 'non-native'. Yapp maintained that such thinking was often dubious, citing both accidents of geography – human interventions could accelerate what might occur naturally – and outmoded romantic sensibilities of nineteenth-century origins. Second, Yapp challenged the assumption that Northumberland's open hills were more natural than its afforested terrains. Kielder had been sheepwalk before the arrival of the Forestry Commission, but this dated back only as far as the introduction of sheep by the Cistercians in the thirteenth century. According to the Forestry Commission, Kielder had formerly been covered with birch, alder and oak, but Yapp went further, suggesting that Scotch fir also once thrived in these uplands. So it was not entirely fanciful to argue that there was a natural history case for inclusion. If Kielder was included in the new park, Yapp argued, the commission must recognise that here forestry was 'the basic form of land use, just as sheep farming is in the Lake District', accepting that its 'natural beauty' was 'based on woodland not bare moor, and its enhancement . . . achieved by special care in planting and felling'.

Dower's colleagues were less convinced. Acland thought the British needed to learn to love their forests rather as the Germans did theirs but remained sceptical with respect to the Forestry Commission's motivations. He suspected they looked to strengthen their hand elsewhere by using Kielder's inclusion as a means of proving that coniferous plantations were not at odds with national park principles.[86]

L.J. Watson, the field officer, admired the professionalism of the Forestry Commission's work at Kielder, and acknowledged its necessity given it had been hounded out of the Lake District, but he could not understand why the commission would seek to include in the new park a large district of low-quality land undergoing intensive development over which it could expect to have little or no influence.[87] Senior members of the Forestry Commission were now also concerned. Lord Radnor dispelled the idea that the Forestry Commission had a settled view on the question, despite the impression given by the local representatives.[88] Privately, Yapp toyed with the idea that the National Parks Commission should disregard these concerns and include Kielder in the designation, though in meetings with the Forestry Commission he was conciliatory, insisting they would respect its priorities at Kielder. Radnor's position was hardening quickly. The Forestry Commission could only contemplate inclusion if the National Parks Commission agreed to make no objection to afforestation between Hadrian's Wall and Redesdale.[89] This confirmed the fears of the commissioners, chiming with ongoing efforts to protect open views from the wall. Dower was now concerned. She feared that the National Parks Commission would look weak if it had to accept too many conditions.[90]

Parallel concerns were at work in the Forestry Commission. Beresford-Peirse, impressed by the enthusiasm the national park commissioners had shown for the forestry work at Kielder, argued that the 'disadvantages' of inclusion were 'more imaginary than real', but the Forestry Commission leadership now doubted whether inclusion was in its interest. Some 25,000 acres remained unplanted across Kielder, Redesdale and Wark, and although the legal position suggested that the Forestry Commission's plans would be unaffected by inclusion, it was concerned that the county council would feel empowered by the designation and cause difficulty in the future. Evelyn Sharp, permanent secretary at Housing and Local Government, feared the National Parks Commission, taking its lead from the county council, might designate Kielder in the face of the Forestry Commission's opposition. Wishing to avoid an open breach, a messy public inquiry and a difficult dilemma for the minister, she summoned representatives of both commissions to Whitehall.

The meeting achieved a modest breakthrough when an official made the simple suggestion that the inclusion of the Forestry Commission land at Wark Forest would make the park continuous between the Cheviots and the Roman wall, diminishing the need to include Kielder. 'Eureka!' moments in Whitehall minutes tend to take the form of all parties noting their willingness to begin a new round of consultations. Things now moved quickly. Carter Bar, the viewpoint where the A68 crosses the Scottish border, became the starting point for drawing the south-west border of the park. Pencils were sharpened, maps scrutinised, roads and rivers closely examined: boundaries were suggested by the A68, the forestry road running south from the mouth of Blakehope Burn, the Chirdon Burn, the Tarset and the North Tyne. The proposed park would have a wide foot, taking in the most striking reaches of the Roman wall, and a narrow waist, squeezed in the west by Kielder Forest and in the east by the more developed areas of the North Tyne – a tight belt strapped in place between Falstone and Bellingham – before the great broadening north of Otterburn embraced the Cheviots. A draft map was agreed. The commissions agreed to simultaneously announce the designation of the Northumberland National Park and the Kielder Forest Park.[91] Sharp had got her way. There would be no complications for the minister.

For the National Parks Commission, the publication of a designation map was always a moment of celebration and anticipation. Objections were inevitable, but they proved modest. Henry and Helen Myles, siblings living at Shittleheugh Farm, Otterburn, wrote to explain that the proposed boundary excluded 90 acres of their 514-acre farm. They wanted a further 24 acres excluded, reflecting recent costly land improvements on the grounds that enclosed land tended to be excluded from the designation. Theirs was a diplomatic letter. They did not oppose the designation and presented their request as a corrective to a minor anomaly, ensuring their enclosed land was not made subject to different regulatory regimes. Moreover, visitors were already inclined to park in their drive and drop litter, which they feared would be encouraged by inclusion. Dower took the minutes at the commission meeting that granted their request, and Henry Myles wrote to thank the commission.[92]

Less straightforward were the objections raised by the National Farmers' Union. Although the NFU opposed the designation of the park on principle, its outlook was pragmatic, focusing its objections on three sites on the margin of the proposed park. Each site included enclosed agricultural land on the edge of open land – echoes here of the Peak District inquiry. It looked for the exclusion of a strip of land north of Akeld, but soon dropped the demand, and the exclusion of a series of small plantations amounting to approximately three square miles at Alwinton and Clennel. More contentious was the NFU's request for the exclusion of Elsdon and the moorland south-east of the village, running north to King's Dod and south to the watershed at Steng Cross.[93] It would include the string of farms that punctuate the rough road east of Elsdon that end with Eastnook, one of England's most isolated houses.

The County Planning Office did not think the NFU could be brought around, and the commission was ready to grant the exclusion, but Dower refused to acquiesce, notwithstanding a rather patronising letter from Strang reminding her that 'it is part of the Commission's duty to do their best to smooth away opposition to Parks, and try by reasonable concessions to obtain the good will of our opponents'. Accepting the Elsdon 'adjustment' did not entail 'sacrificing anything fundamental', Strang argued, and would avoid a public inquiry, which would draw attention to the NFU's more thorough-going objection to the scheme.[94] Dower wrote at length to explain why a firm line should be taken on Elsdon. The NFU did not have good cause to seek the exclusion of unenclosed grouse moor, so they must have an ulterior motive. The answer surely lay with the Forestry Commission. It did not have an established interest in the land proposed for exclusion, but the land was contiguous with Harwood Forest, and she was sure a failure to designate the Elsdon moorland would be rapidly followed by planting. Dower's feelings were raw. Immediately east of the excluded area was Harwood Farm. Her father had sold it to the Forestry Commission, and it was now afforested. Shortly before the Wallington Estate was passed into the hands of the National Trust, he had also leased Fallowlees and Redpath farms, immediately to the north of Harwood, to the Forestry Commission. She remembered that the transaction was conducted with 'extreme diplomacy', implying that her father had acted in an underhand way, leaving the National Trust, the Northumberland and Newcastle Society and the CPRE unable to object. Her uncle, G.M. Trevelyan, had been 'sick at heart' to witness, in her words, 'the obliteration of the moors of his boyhood, which he had hoped to have seen saved for all time'. Dower shared her uncle's view, and now anticipated the plantation encroaching further westwards onto open moor.[95]

She did not consider the moors of great significance. What mattered was the view. Harwood Forest had obscured 'fine views' to the Simonside Hills, and now more important scenery was threatened. The Elsdon moors, she explained, were 'the foreground of a view known through all the North, the view from the Watershed at Steng Cross, north to the Cheviots, West across Redesdale to the Border Hills, South to the Pennines and East to Rothley Castle and the sea'. G.M. Trevelyan had described the region in *The Middle Marches* (1935) and the site itself also had a 'macabre interest' for here stood – as it still does – a replica of Winter's Gibbet.[96] In 1791, William Winter and two sisters, Jane and Eleanor Clark, were convicted of the murder of Margaret Crozier; they were hanged in Newcastle, and William's corpse was then suspended in chains from the gibbet in sight of Crozier's cottage. Sir Walter Trevelyan erected the replica gibbet in 1869. This survived a further 150 years, and was then replaced in 2014 by the National Trust.

It is a chilling spot, and the commanding view north does render this section of the proposed park thrilling. Strang, impressed by Dower's local knowledge, had key passages from her letters extracted for circulation. Dower now bowed out, saying her personal involvement meant the decision should be left to colleagues. Strang, however, made further enquiries in response to Dower's confidential suggestions. The Forestry Commission denied it had plans to acquire Elsdon but admitted the land was ideal for planting and was under consideration for the future. A site visit was duly planned. Commissioners Watson, Yapp and Strang made the journey to Steng Cross. Duly impressed, J.B. Ross of Northumberland County Council was tasked with reopening negotiations with the NFU. The NFU gave way, and in response Dower urged that the commission concede the Alwinton objection as a gesture of goodwill. It was a characteristic balancing move.[97] The commission had its map, had avoided a public inquiry, and confirmation could be sought from the minister. Northumberland National Park came into being on 5 June 1956.

Case Work

It is something of a truism that the National Parks Commission and the new authorities had little power to resist developmental pressures in the first decades of the system's operation. As we'll see in the next chapter, the ink was barely dry on the Dartmoor National Park confirmation order before the new authority had to respond to the BBC's plan to erect a transmission mast on North Hessary Tor at Princetown. On the eve of confirmation, Northumberland National Park faced a challenge at least as significant. Northumberland County Council, Tynemouth Corporation and Newcastle and Gateshead Water Company, acting together, proposed the construction of an impounding reservoir in the Coquet Valley to help regulate the volume of water available for extraction downstream. They looked to dam the valley five miles upstream of Harbottle in order to flood some three miles of Coquetdale as far as Carshope. The existing road would be submerged, as would Windyhaugh Farm and the small hamlet of Barrowburn.

Surprisingly, the surviving archival material leaves no trace of Dower's involvement in the conflict, but her previous stance on the military's presence in the valley makes it impossible to imagine she did not have a view. Initial reports prepared for the commission indicate that it believed new infrastructure could be an improvement on existing agricultural structures and landscapes. The loss of the hamlet and the farm would remove 'a number of existing disfigurements', including some 'very unsightly' buildings, and the commission was unconcerned by the recommendation that the submerged road be replaced by developing Clennel Street, then a bridleway, or the loss of moorland judged to be low quality agricultural land.[98] Rather than lodge an objection, the commission supplied the county council with practical suggestions. A good landscape architect, among other design experts, was needed; local stone should be used in the construction of the dam; the 36-inch pipe, which would run the length of the Coquet, should be buried or concealed; the effect on Usway Burn should be investigated; the siting of the filtration works should be looked at again; and access should be taken into account.[99] The county council gave provisional approval to the scheme, and it would be considered at the first meeting of the new National Park Planning Committee on 19 October 1956.

In the event, the committee proved less supine than the commission, proving that national park designation could disrupt the plans of developers. In the new year the scheme was in abeyance and the promotors investigated extracting water nearer the mouth of the Coquet. Claud Bicknell of the CPRE now raised fresh concerns. The new scheme required a small reservoir upstream, once again threatening the valley of Grasslees Burn. Bicknell's reading of the valley geography led him to conclude that it would be flooded from somewhere near Hepple Woodside to Billsmoor Park. A decade after the public inquiry ensured that the military could not make use of the valley, Bicknell again had to make the case for its importance. It was 'not a typical Cheviot Valley', he wrote to the county council. Its 'green bottom, scrub woodlands and rugged banks of heather and gritstone' contrasted Grasslees with the tributary valleys of the Coquet above Harbottle, making it 'one of the special beauties of our beautiful county'.[100] Ross was equally pleased that the large reservoir scheme had been abandoned, thus preserving the 'beauty and accessibility of that delightful valley', and he too insisted that Grasslees must not be lost as tribute.[101] With Grasslees ruled out of bounds until all other possibilities were examined, the CPRE transferred its concern to Usway Burn, which flowed from the southern reaches of the Cheviots into Coquetdale, stating its preference for the damming of Barrowburn just to the west of Alwinton.[102] Brushing aside the reservations of the Nature Conservancy, Ross successfully persuaded the Park Planning Committee to accept Barrowburn, claiming a small reservoir would 'lend interest to an otherwise unexceptional landscape'.[103] As modern maps show, nothing further came of this development.

Not every issue the commission faced was as contentious, involving issues of high principle, or prospecting large-scale landscape change, but the commission's fear of the cumulative effect of small developments meant that even modest proposals invited careful consideration, as preservationists and public access campaigners insisted. Low-key case work constituted much of Dower's day-to-day work, evidence of how, from the moment of their inception, the national parks became contested sites of modernity. Sometimes these processes exposed the relative weakness of the park authorities in the face of competing state interests, but outcomes could equally reflect the basic expectation that statutory bodies pursuing distinct goals needed to reach an accommodation. Some examples follow.

Greenlee Lough is three miles north of the Sycamore Gap, one of the most iconic sites on Hadrian's Wall. It is currently managed by the Northumberland National Park Authority and Northumberland Wildlife Trust as part of the Roman Wall Loughs Special Area of Conservation, as designated under the European Union Natura 2000 framework. Things were rather different in the 1950s. In July 1957 Northumberland County Council brought the commission's attention to the Greenlee Boat Club. The club already made use of Greenlee Lough but wanted permission to use hydroplanes, the latest craze among boating enthusiasts and, seemingly, sought retrospective planning permission for a roadway, gangway and slipway. Northumberland County Council and the park committee considered the club an asset to the park but sought the commission's view on its judgement that use should be restricted to sailing boats and the summer months to prevent disruption to migratory birds, as local naturalist groups demanded.[104] Dower was keen to see for herself and she made a site visit with a small group of officials. The existing structures were found to be insignificant, little visible from Hadrian's Wall and the Roman site Borcovicium; the scenic value of the site was low, but noisy hydroplanes would still be 'quite out of keeping' in a quiet isolated spot accessible only on foot or by a farm track off a minor road. Sailing during the summer was 'a good and suitable recreation on that open water'.[105] The boat club's request was turned down.

In 1958, the proposers unsuccessfully appealed, seeking permission to use motorboats with silencers, but when the Westwater (Northumberland) Lakes Society, as the Greenlee Boat Club now styled itself, later sought permission for additional buildings and a chemical toilet, Dower was again ready to tolerate the developments. Her principal worry was that work might be done in concrete when 'the character of all work should be entirely simple and rural'. The commission was reassured. Walling around the edge of the jetty would be in stone and permission to continue using the lough would be granted until 1970 on the condition that the lough would be restored to its previous condition if permission was then with-drawn.[106] Photographs from the 1970s suggest that the club thrived, but it did not survive the advent of a more accessible club at Derwent Water, and in 1990 was reclassified as part of the Roman Wall Loughs site of special scientific interest.[107]

A similarly minor question arose in relation to a nearby site. In 1964, the Post Office Engineering Department identified Hopealone Farm on Henshaw Common as the best site for the last of 'backbone' installations required for national television transmission, connecting the mast at Pontop Pike in north County Durham to Carlisle and the mast at Sandale at the Caldeck Fells in Cumbria to Tyneside. In essence, the transmitter mast would carry ITV east to west and BBC west to east. A small transmitter mast was erected at Hopealone in 1951, so the siting of the mast was not particularly controversial, but a taller, more substantial mast would have a greater impact on the scenery. In essence, the commission was asked for its opinion on the submitted designs for the mast, which included two lattice structures and a solid concrete structure. Surprisingly, following a field inspec-tion with county officials, the commission favoured the concrete structure: 'Northumberland is a county of big scale, the Wall itself is the epitome of this vast landscape. The solid tower is a more truthful statement of function, though its profile would need to be carefully designed'.[108] Quite why a 'solid tower' was more 'truthful' than a lattice tower is baffling, rendering this nod towards the modernist aesthetic that form should follow function pretty spurious. Dower was unconvinced. The recent concrete tower that had been erected near Oxford suggested that the same at Hopealone would be 'horridly obtrusive'.[109] In August, Dower made a site visit with local officials and her report made the visual case against a concrete tower. Whereas people had become used to large lattice towers, hardly registering their presence, a solid concrete structure would be 'far more eye-catching, more arresting', and she did not think it credible to claim that its 'solidity' would be 'associated with the Roman Wall'. Moreover, the nearby forestry fire-watch tower, a lattice construction, would render another lattice structure less conspicuous. This 'protuberance' must be 'an abhorrent intrusion in any landscape', that much she did not doubt, but whereas the appearance of a concrete structure would have 'a horrible permanency', a lattice mast would allow a 'spark of hope' that the thing might one day be dismantled. 'No such hope is given by the inexorably dominating solidity of the concrete tower.'[110]

Dower was rarely this hyperbolic, but she was quite right to argue that the commission could change its mind without any significant loss of face. Strang drily authorised J.R.B. Ferguson to inform the county council that the commission would not dissent from a lattice construction. Two months later it offered no comment on the detailed plans submitted to the county council; the park committee approved the plans on the condition that base building was faced with 'natural random rubble stone'.[111] And so the lattice mast was built.

The problem raised by the final section of the Pennine Way was more intractable. Long-distance footpaths had been envisaged by the 1949 Act and served a dual function. They enabled access, being the product of numerous access agreements, and they managed access, functioning to confine walkers to certain parts of the parks. There is little doubt that establishing long-distance footpaths created a new kind of physical challenge, encouraging walkers to embark on ambitious but safe journeys, ensuring they ventured further afield, encountering unfamiliar landscapes. They were central to the purposes of the parks and had been discussed since at least the 1930s. The Pennine Way, brainchild of Tom Stephenson, was the highest-profile of these initiatives, charting a course from Edale in Derbyshire to the Scottish border. Much of the planned route passed through the Peak District, Yorkshire Dales and Northumberland National Park, taking in iconic sites like Kinder Scout and the Cheviot. There can be no doubt that routing the Pennine Way through Northumberland National Park significantly increases the park's visitor numbers. The significant economic beneficiary is Haltwhistle, which lies just south of the park boundary. Using recycled paving stones to mark the way helps walkers easily traverse boggy moorland and minimises the harm likely to be caused to the landscape by thousands of footsteps, particularly along the stretch hugging the Anglo-Scottish border.

The route was approved by Dalton in July 1951. Seventy miles of new rights of way were needed, raising the prospect of objections and a more protracted process, but it was clear that the minister was firmly behind the initiative.[112] Unexpectedly, the most contentious section of the route proved to be the six miles or so that passed over Blakehope Common to the east of the Redesdale Forest in Northumberland. Sir Charles Morrison Bell, holder of the baronetcy of Otterburn, reached an agreement with the county council granting permission part of the way, but Lord Northbourne, holder of the James baronetcy of Langley Hall, Berkshire, would not give permission for the way to pass over Blakehope Common and into the Rede river valley beyond Kellyburn Hill. This is fascinating country, rich with evidence of long human settlement, whether it be the remains of the medieval village of Evistones or the village of Rochester, rich in Roman associations, including Bremenium Roman Fort. It is easy to imagine why Stephenson wanted the Pennine Way to pass through this country.

The problem was not resolved prior to the designation of the park and Dower thought it best to visit Northbourne and his son at Evistones if she was to understand the difficulty. She discovered that the disputed land was a mix of open fell and lower 'intake' fields, in the main largely unimproved rough grazing used as pasture for cattle. For a large part of the year James followed local practice and ran his bulls, a Galloway and a White Shorthorn, with his cows. He was absent much of the time, and this approach meant that the work could be left to 'an unskilled kind in his absence'. James feared that the county council might pass a byelaw prohibiting the running of bulls where there existed a right of way, thereby rendering, in Dower's words, the 'whole system of stock farming . . . impossible'.[113]

Dower was sympathetic, but Stephenson and the Ramblers were not about to give way. Somehow a route had to be found through to Blakehopeburnhaugh but the issue was complicated by the proximity of the Redesdale Forestry Commission plantation. The choice was between an alternative moorland route, which would not resolve the access issue, or a route through the plantation along a forestry road. Largely thanks to Dower's sympathy for the agricultural argument, the commission came down on the side of the latter. Arthur Blenkinsop, one of the MPs who joined the Whitsun hiking weekend of Labour MPs in 1950, got wind of this and complained to Dower that the proposal would mean the 'grim prospect' of an eight-mile stretch of metalled roads. Dower put a positive gloss on the compromise. Much of the forestry road was grassed and there was little prospect of this changing in the foreseeable future, making it 'a quite reasonable walking route . . . never badly beset by cars'. This was 'the most sensible solution', she wrote, to 'a sore problem of many years standing'. To her fellow commissioners, she conceded that it would be 'foolish' to give way to pressure from Blenkinsop or the Ramblers because this would entail a 'fight for every yard of path', though she feared the 'stinging rejoinder' that she 'cared for landowners more than for ramblers'.[114]

The Ramblers did not give way. Working with other lobby groups, they proposed an alternative route that accepted the commission's compromise route across open country to Brownrigg Head but rejected the adoption of the forestry road to the west, proposing instead that the route would continue north across open land into the Wind Burn Valley and then up to Blackwool Law and down to Deadwood on the Rede. The issue rumbled on until, finally, the county council created two rights of way, the forestry route and the Wind Burn Valley route. This provoked appeals, necessitating a public inquiry and a decision by the minister.

This takes us to March 1964, a full 13 years after Dalton approved the route. Yapp represented the commission, but its position was essentially derived from Dower. The Wind Burn Valley route did not resolve the right of way issue or the question of bulls; moreover, there were no existing paths or tracks on this route and the Forestry Commission was concerned that the prevalence of molinia grass posed a fire risk. The inquiry largely dismissed these concerns on the grounds that such conditions were found elsewhere on the Pennine Way and bulls run with cows were not thought dangerous. The real issue was whether the minister should confirm a new right of way. The inquiry acknowledged the strength of the Ramblers' case because it aligned with conventional thinking about what constituted good walking and who constituted a good walker: the Wind Burn route offered fine views and its 'hard going' over 'marshy land' would attract 'only well shod and experienced walkers', persons likely to 'respect the rights of landowners and farmers'. Less experienced walkers would gladly take the forestry road, or so the inquiry supposed. Both routes should be approved.[115]

This was not the conclusion reached by Sir Keith Joseph, the Minister of Housing and Local Government. In one of his last acts before the dissolution of parliament and the 1964 general election, he took the commission line and approved the forestry route. Blenkinsop spoke out against this 'ridiculous' decision, but, as the OS Explorer map for Kielder Water and Forest (OL 42) testifies, the decision held.[116] The Pennine Way charts a route from Brownrigg Head into Redesdale Forest, following the Kielder Forest/Northumberland National Park boundary to Byrness, before the long last section along the Anglo-Scottish border to Yeltholm. Nothing on the map encourages walkers to head into the valley and up to the trig point at Blackwool Law.

This time, the farmers, supported by Dower and the commission, had got their way. It was not always the case. When the Duke of Devonshire refused to permit the Pennine Way to be routed through his Bolton Abbey Estate, Dower advised him to make a generous public gesture, for the commission would otherwise exercise its powers and declare a right of way. She took a particular pride in the success of this manoeuvre.[117]

Outweighing these individual issues was the continued expansionism of the Forestry Commission. Designating the Kielder Forest Park had not placed a territorial limit on its ambitions and by 1960 the Forestry Commission was looking to reach agreements with several park authorities with respect to afforestation. They attempted to apply a formula developed on Snowdonia. Working with the park authority, the park would be mapped according to different afforestation 'presumptions', namely whether with reference to the afforestation of specific sites the authority was either against, against but open to negotiation, or accepting but requiring consultation. The issue was especially tense on Dartmoor where the existence of a large expanse of common land, effectively off limits for planting, confined the Forestry Commission's operations to relatively small areas of the park. Common land was not the issue in Northumberland, but the Forestry Commission considered virtually the whole park suitable for afforestation, clearly not a situation acceptable to the park authority. The key issues in Northumberland stemmed from the fact that in the 1950s and 1960s it made economic sense for landowners to sell derelict or uneconomic farms to the Forestry Commission, or have them dedicated for planting, which brought distinct tax advantages.[118]

Dower had her ear to the ground, reporting in May 1960 on her visit to a chipboard mill on the Tyne. She was impressed by what she saw. Chipboard was the future. Germany had 60 plants, Russia planned 400 but Britain only had four. The plant on the Tyne mainly processed wood from Finland but the maturing of existing plantations at Kielder meant a new facility would soon be needed. She considered this to be part of the Forestry Commission's broader plans for Northumberland, including their 'move' on Wooler Common, plans for the Cheviots, and reluctance to agree to discuss their county policy.[119] When the Forestry Commission, the County Council and the park authorities finally met at County Hall that July, Dower attending on behalf of the commission, the main issue concerned the balance between agriculture, forestry and the preservation of the landscape. Dower reminded the meeting that the park had been designated on the assumption that the Forestry Commission would not want to afforest the Cheviot Hills with 'Kielder Forest type of planting', though shelter belt planting might be a good thing, but the Forestry Commission's desire to map the landscape meant that the focus quickly fell on specific sites. Talk of Greenlee Farm on Henshaw Common, Batailshiel Haugh and the Usway Burn in Upper Coquetdale (west of the Forestry Commission's Kidland Forest), the Ingram Valley and Wooler Common Farm immediately indicated how important detailed local knowledge was to these discussions. Greenlee would extend Wark Forest south and was not particularly contentious, providing planting did not unduly under-mine the openness of Greenlee Lough, but Dower did not want to see Batailshiel Haugh or Usway Burn planted and she reminded her colleagues that the area had only been recently released from live firing by the War Department 'and is a much used and favourite route to the hills and the border'. The opposition of the park planning committee to planting the small field on Brough Law in the Ingram Valley, a popular spot with visitors on the eastern edge of the park, was also shared by Dower and the commission. Wooler Common Farm, a 500-acre site, had been approved for planting by the Ministry of Agriculture, but plans had not yet been presented.[120]

Batailshiel Haugh demonstrated in microcosm how the interests of the Ministry of Agriculture, Fisheries and Food (MAFF) and the Forestry Commission could align. Now that Batailshiel Haugh was no longer subject to live firing, the farmstead could be restored, but this would cost £8,000, and farm labour, chiefly shepherds, would have to be found. The Forestry Commission, ready to exploit the declining value of upland farms, was well placed to relieve MAFF of a liability. A land grab was in the offing and it was evident that the

Forestry Commission did not consider the Cheviots out of bounds.[121] In January 1961, the focus fell onto the Harbottle Hills near Holystone. The Forestry Commission submitted a land acquisition request for 800 acres with the intention of coniferising all of it. The park authorities and the county council opposed; the commission had 14 days to object. Dower insisted they must, for the scheme was 'entirely unacceptable'.[122] The park planning committee took a less hard-line view. Although the proposed planting would impair the visual amenity of the site, causing 'the characteristic craggy hilltops to the south of the village being submerged under tree planting', seriously affecting the 'appearance and setting' of this 'attractive village', it would consider a 'modified scheme' that preserved the 'existing characteristic skyline and upper slopes' to the south of the village.[123] G.B. Ryle, the Director of Forestry for England, claimed that the park planning committee had given the impression that it was not unduly concerned by afforestation west of the Coquet, and the Ministry of Agriculture, approving the plan providing the tenant retained use of the better-quality land, made the case for the importance of forestry as a means of providing employment and arresting rural depopulation.[124]

In the meantime, Dower heard that the Forestry Commission also had its eye on a 1,171-acre site at Kirknewton on the northern edge of the park. Afforestation here was no more acceptable than at Usway Burn and she was clearly angered by the Forestry Commission's tactics, writing in no uncertain terms to her colleagues at the commission:

You know that up here the F.C. work through their Acquisitions Officer who does all the negotiations and contact with the local authorities. Selby, this officer, who has been in the region a long time, has no good word for National Parks, being himself a 100% F.C. man; so the climate of afforestation work and feeling on any hill-country application is tense and unhappy. The F.C. do not notify the County as soon as they do us (this Kirknewton case came in to us much sooner than it did to the County) but fortunately our relation to the County is good, and they trust us never to let them down.[125]

Ferguson replied in rather cool terms, explaining that although the agreed map classified these sites according to the 'presumption against' rubric, the commission's position was that each case had to be dealt with on its own terms.[126] A site visit was necessary and Dower willingly obliged.

Dower's detailed report, a page of single-spaced typescript, almost certainly written late at night from her study at Wallington, opens with a description of the site, at once an exercise in evocation and a form of technical writing:

Approaching up the valley road from east we entered the area from the north-east, coming into a large amphitheatre of moorland, surrounded by a ridge of high moor. Three rights-of-way footpaths cross this land, and, combined with the sweep of moor to the west, it makes a stretch of fine walking country, much enjoyed by holiday-makers, and very popular as a short, rough moor walk for families at weekends. It is clearly valuable as hill grazing-land, the more level centre of the area being well sheltered by present Forestry Commission acquisitions, all of which are, or are to be, planted up to the fence-line. On the south, the planting will dip over the edge of the skyline (rather a pity from the landscape point of view) but this acts as an effective shelter belt for the lower land.

Seen from the open road just west of Harbottle village, the moor-edge stands as one of the finest Cheviot heather moor views. If all this hillside were planted up, it would 'make Harbottle into a Forestry Village' as one of the County Council representatives said.[127]

A lot is at work in this passage. Emphasis is placed on the visual amenity of the site. Terms like 'ridge', 'sweep', 'stretch', 'edge' and 'skyline' are simultaneously everyday words and drawn from an established lexicon of landscape description, as are more value-laden terms like 'fine', 'valuable' and 'sheltered'. Dower's strong visual sense has already been discussed, and here it functions to make the case for the status quo. Equally notable are the claims made about the use of the site, be it recreational or agricultural. She knew that a local man ran his sheep and cattle on the hills, using land on the 'Park' system of yearly rentals, but her claims about the land's recreational value were devoid of any statistical ballasting. Statutory bodies often made their case on an essentially impressionistic basis. Note, too, how Dower's perspective entirely lacked any ecological judgement. Was grazing necessarily more beneficial to nature than afforestation? This was not a question she asked.

She then tackled what the Forestry Commission rather modishly had started to refer to as 'the sociological point of view'. Twenty-eight local men were employed on forestry work in the area, but the Forestry Commission's acquisitions were almost fully planted up and thinning operations would not begin before 1970. Sustaining current levels of employment required more acres. A Forestry Commission district officer freely admitted to Dower that he'd happily afforest the whole of the National Park, though 4,000 acres would meet their current needs. Ryle said much the same at an earlier meeting, Dower quoting him to the effect that he 'would like to turn the whole of Cheviot into another Kielder'. Any farm that came onto the market, or any owner that could be persuaded to sell, would be 'snapped up' by the Forestry Commission. Nearby farms at Alwinton and Clennel were in their sights, as were farms in the north. The Kirknewton sale fell through because the vendors withdrew but the implications were clear. The strategy of the Forestry Commission was to acquire farms in the north of the park to create a large forestry block.

County council officials shared Dower's assessment of the Harbottle scheme and although initially rattled by the 'sociological' argument came to regard it as spurious.[128] E.P. Harvey, clerk to the council, argued that the population of Rothbury Rural District Council was stable and that the most significant factor in maintaining rural population was the availability of council houses. Forestry was an important employer in certain areas, but it accounted for just 2 per cent of rural employment, and Harvey rejected the notion that forestry policy should be directed towards maintaining employment rather than the production of a timber crop.[129] Frustrated by these obstacles, the Forestry Commission sought a high-level fix. Lord Radnor wrote to Lord Strang. He emphasised forestry's importance to rural employment, local support for the industry's further expansion and the difficulty the Forestry Commission faced in the area because of the shortage of land between the Rede and the Coquet on account of the military training area.[130] A further Forestry Commission document explained the predicament more fully. Kidland Forest, a substantial forestry block north of Harbottle, employed 26 people with 30 dependants, including 15 children. Planting began at the site in 1953, but no thinning was necessary until 1978–80, and to sustain current levels of employment 250–300 acres were needed for planting per year. Current land reserves would last until 1970, but to sustain levels of employment until the 1980s required an additional 2,500 acres. A further 1,000 acres would help absorb into the workforce redundant farmworkers or school-leavers, including the children of forestry workers.[131]

Such arguments were not easily dismissed. The Forestry Commission was established in 1919 in response to long-standing anxieties about timber supply that were intensified during the First World War. The UK's timber security was vulnerable thanks to its unsustainable approach to forestry and consequent reliance on overseas suppliers, including Russia, Scandinavia and North America. In essence, the UK harvested its own supply but did little replanting, a dynamic intensified during the First World War with the 'devastation' of a significant proportion of remaining supplies. To this day, the UK is exceptionally dependent on imported timber. The principal purpose of the Forestry Commission as a statutory body was to guarantee Britain's timber security by acquiring or dedicating land for planting in marginal agricultural landscapes; secondarily, significant hopes had always been attached to forestry's capacity to arrest rural depopulation and deprivation by developing the industry. The Forestry Commission never had a free hand, facing opposition from amenity groups in the 1920s and 1930s, but it had significantly increased its footprint across Britain's uplands and elsewhere. As the Harbottle controversy demonstrated, successful forestry required long-term planning and continuous land acquisition and management.

National Park designation severely stymied the Forestry Commission's activities. It created a competing state body, largely focused on the same resource – marginal upland landscapes – which, despite Brunsdon Yapp's unorthodox thinking, was principally valued for its openness and relatively high degree of public access. For much of the national park lobby, industrial forestry was and would remain anathema and, as has been shown, the designation of Northumberland National Park had come to be predicated on containing the Forestry Commission, particularly with respect to the Cheviots.

This was the context in which Radnor contacted Strang. Both men chaired statutory bodies, not lobbying organisations, and they had to reach an accommodation. Both also had statutory obligations to fulfil, and the case threw into sharp relief how the designation of national parks posed a quite fundamental challenge to the Forestry Commission. Dower's anger was understandable, for the Forestry Commission did not seem to be acting in good faith, but in truth the decision to designate separate parks or agree the forestry map were highly contingent responses to immediate political pressures and bound neither the hands of the Forestry Commission, the National Parks Commission or the park planning committee. Leading figures in both commissions – Strang, Dower, Harold Abrahams, Ferguson, Radnor and Ryle – met in March, but this became an opportunity to recapitulate their positions rather than reach an agreement. This, then, would be a decision for the minister. Both sides now drafted their advice.

A visit was planned. Representatives from the two commissions and the two ministries – Housing and Local Government and MAFF – would make the journey to Harbottle. Dower and Radnor would attend, along with two junior ministers, Lord St Oswald (MAFF) and Major Fred Corfield (Housing and Local Government), and G.J.L. Batters, Northeast Conservator for the Forestry Commission. No officials would be present. Dower broke her ankle shortly before the visit, necessitating the cancellation of a meeting in Barnstaple and a conference in Bristol, but assured Strang she could 'think & speak perfectly effectively' though was willing to give way to a colleague if Strang felt 'such an occasion should not be marred by the inevitable unconventionality of my being half-immobilised'. In the event, Dower joined the visitors for a pub lunch in Otterburn.

She duly reported on the meeting:

Our luncheon party at Otterburn consisted of Lord Radnor & Lord St Oswald, Major Corfield from the Ministry of Housing, Mr Batters, Northeast Conservator, & myself. They had reserved all discussion until they met me, which I thought most kindly of them, & over lunch & coffee afterwards we thoroughly discussed the whole question of Harbottle, with maps (I had brought my own, marked up to make the point of Forestry Commission & War Office range ownership completely cutting off all the surrounding hill land from public access); the talk ranged much wider, as both Lord St Oswald and Major Corfield had a good deal to ask about farming & other aspects of rural life up here. Altogether it was a very pleasant occasion; you would have enjoyed it, so I feel sure, & Lord Radnor was so kind & thoughtful.

Even when the archaisms are set aside ('luncheon', 'most kindly'), it is still hard not to read this as an 'establishment' set piece. Titled gents and a high-born woman meet in a country pub to straighten out a matter of state. The local authorities have been side lined, denied the opportunity to represent themselves, courtesy and conviviality will not be marred by the dispute that necessitated the gathering. For a time, the chaps attentively lean over the woman's map, fascinated by the state's carving up an obscure piece of landscape, but soon they will return to London and a host of other decisions. What, then, of Harbottle? Dower wrote:

> My feeling was that the general opinion veered towards letting Harbottle go for afforestation, though I also felt that our case was entirely right to put, & that there was much to say for it. The chief thing is that we have been given all possible opportunity to put our point of view, & I felt that the whole question was being most objectively and thoroughly considered, & that whatever decision is come to will be arrived at after very full consideration, & in such a friendly spirit that no rancour should be felt. I was so glad I went to this luncheon.[132]

How different in tone to the letter complaining of Selby's underhand tactics. And this is the key issue. That Dower found the company and setting agreeable should not obscure the emphasis she placed on the commission's point of view getting a fair hearing. Her position was pragmatic and professional, and she understood the forces at work in the process. Two statutory bodies, the Forestry Commission and the National Parks Commission, each charged with fulfilling their statutory obligations, had entered into a negotiation in good faith. This meant that however strongly she valued the Harbottle Hills in their existing state, the openness with which the process had been conducted ensured a legitimate outcome.

It went as Dower predicted. Corfield explained their decision in a succinct if somewhat muddled letter. Had landscape been the only consideration, he should have come down against afforestation, but there were other factors to consider. He claimed the plantation would not ensure a 'loss of amenity', then conceded that the forest walks would 'present less variety', making the rather odd claim that the 'charm' of local walks would be undermined if they became more popular, but the new forest walks would allow more people to enjoy the area 'without destroying the feeling of seclusion'. As for the village, it would be changed but leaving the in-bye land unplanted would mean it was not 'shut in'. He went on. Agricultural opposition to planting was usually a key factor in these decisions, but not so here, and Corfield argued that if the grazing and heather-burning ceased, which was possible given the relatively unproductive nature of the land, the hills would 'revert' to birch scrub, 'hardly preferable to careful afforestation in its effect on the scenery'. Finally, he turned to the 'sociological argument'. Forestry was the only industry that stood between Harbottle and 'decay'. The loss of this 'thriving community' would have a 'depressing effect' on the whole area.[133] The deep plough soon began.

'Such an Interesting Life'

The decision to replace the National Parks Commission with the Countryside Commission came as a shock. All but two commissioners were sacked. Fred Willey, Minister of Land and Natural Resources, wrote apologetically to Dower in June 1966, explaining that the new Countryside Commission would be chaired by Lady Wootton, a criminologist with a reputably remarkable intellect, and there was no scope for a deputy. Willey could not see how Dower could be kept on.[134] This was mealy-mouthed stuff, for Dower could have been invited into the new commission. She responded coolly, outlining the extensive field work completed by the commissioners and the time it took to prepare for public inquiries. Noting that Willey had announced at a press conference that the new commission would be smaller but with a larger staff, she said that it was hard to imagine how a smaller commission could carry out the work.[135] As deputy chair, Dower found herself in the invidious position of writing to the other commissioners and interested parties to explain her fate and that of the commission. In essence, the government had decided to expand the remit of the National Parks Commission to take a more expansive and integrated approach to managing countryside leisure. Designating country parks within easy reach of towns and cities was the new priority. The letters she received in response lamented how 'shabbily' she had been treated, particularly the short notice, and expressed disbelief that, of all the commissioners, she was not being kept on. In many ways, these letters provide the strongest testimony we have to the value of her work. Strang described her as the 'linch-pin' of the commission and he hoped she would find in the CPRE 'a field for powerful action and influence'. Harold Abrahams, the first secretary of the commission, wrote that he knew she would not 'feel bitter' but must 'feel hurt', for nobody 'could have done more for National Parks than you'; another commissioner, accepting that at 72 it was right for him to retire, felt 'very strongly indeed that a Commission without your very great knowledge, experience & contacts with our local authorities will be an absolute cripple' and he wished her to know of his 'unbounded admiration' for her 'as our deputy leader'; and Francis Ritchie, who had also served on the commission since the beginning, expressed his 'shock' at the news but could not help think that the coming changes meant they were best out of it.[136]

Brunsdon Yapp was furious at what he regarded as the Labour Government's failure to advance the National Park agenda, particularly with respect to increasing funds and strengthening the park authorities.[137] In a 'scorching letter' to Willey, he outlined these grievances, lamenting a government 'more interested in creating massive picnic areas, within easy reach of the big cities, touched up by landscape artists, complete with motor cycle tracks and funfairs'. There was nothing necessarily wrong with this, he conceded, but the broader context was a government seemingly 'quite happy to give the go-ahead to every application for industrialisation' in the parks and 'leave effective control to the landowners'. Yapp's letter was quoted in the *Sunday Telegraph*'s 'Mandrake' column, whose coverage of the story had the ludicrous headline 'Purge of the long-haired preservationists'.[138] J.B. Ross, clerk of Northumberland County Council, and long an ally of the commission, felt Dower's 'retirement will be specially severely felt in Northumberland because we all realise that the creation and development of Northumberland National Park owes far more to you than can ever be learned from printed reports'.[139]

Yapp's frustration and Ross's testimony capture something of the reality of the commission's 16-year existence. As we will see, environmental activists often found the commission wanting, lamenting its caution and unresponsiveness, and later critics thought it amateurish and lacking any meaningful ecological agenda. These criticisms are not without some justification. Dower did focus principally on preserving visual amenity and enhancing rights of access, and, notwithstanding her open-mindedness with respect to the Forestry Commission's transformation of Kielder, little she did or said questioned the broad assumption that agriculturalists, including lowland arable farmers as well as upland pastoralists, were the rightful custodians of the countryside. They produced the charismatic landscapes that provided stressed urbanites with vital psychological and spiritual refreshment. Dower's preoccupations and assumptions reflected her broad expertise, and in this they were typical of the preservationist milieu. Attempts by the wildlife charities and the Nature Conservancy to steer the debate in an ecological direction had made little headway and it was not until the 1970s that political pressure began to mount against the environmental degradation caused by state-subsidised agricultural intensification. For this to happen, it was necessary to recognise that modern agricultural landscapes are not necessarily good wildlife habitat. That slow revolution in thought continues to this day.

And yet, while Britain's national park system may be flawed, the 70th anniversary of the 1949 legislation testified to the foundations laid by Dower and her fellow commissioners. With few financial resources and a small staff, they designated 10 national parks, establishing a territorial footprint that remains the basis of the system today. Dower worked hard. She spent many a late night at her desk and travelled constantly, juggling tasks in a manner instantly recognisable to us today. And her career in public life did not end with the dissolution of the commission. She continued to act as a magistrate, fulfilled multiple roles for the Church of England and served as a long-term member of the British Waterways Board. Whether her work for the commission was more or less important to her than the other obligations she shouldered is difficult to say, but her younger son Robin notes her determination to see her husband's legacy fulfilled and says her Christian faith was powerfully motivating. Her sons felt similarly drawn, and both Michael and Robin followed in their parents' footsteps. Michael was the national park officer of the Peak District (1985–92), director-general of the Countryside Commission (1992–6) and YHA Vice President from 1996. Robin trained as an architect, worked closely with the National Trust on the care of Wallington, and served as a ministerial appointee to the Northumberland National Park Authority (1978–81) and member of the Countryside Commission (1981–90). Perhaps Dower and her sons have worked to a pattern established by John Dower, but to recognise that Dower saw her work in these terms does not diminish her concrete achievements any more than it does her children's. These persist, whether we see them as the response of an educated and energetic woman to widowhood or to her children growing up or to those deep Trevelyan commitments.

Dower's gender, however, was always with her. In October 1958, the *Newcastle Journal* reported on her visit to Allendale in her capacity as the 'chairman' of the Northumberland Rural Community Council. Allendale had been named Northumberland's best-kept 'large' village and Dower was to present the prize. Her next stop was Belsay, where she was due to give a talk to the Women's Institute. The article headline read 'A grandmother stays active', and Dower was described as one of 'Northumberland's most active grandmothers'.[140] She was just 53 and would live for another 30 years. Irrespective of her contribution to public life, she could not escape the apparent primacy of her reproductive role.

The personal fulfilment she derived from her work should not be underestimated, nor how strongly this contrasted with the dark days of the Second World War when she struggled to find satisfaction in her marital and maternal obligations. In May 1959, she wrote to her mother about the National Parks conference at Bakewell. The chair had to excuse himself because his 'gammy leg' was playing up and Dower found deputising 'huge fun'. She did not attempt to 'imitate his position or seniority' but wrote openly of how much she enjoyed planting a commemorative tree, helping to receive the minister, and responding on behalf of the commission to points raised from the floor in response to his tape-recorded speech ('the modern manner').[141] Early in 1960, she wrote again, this time from Exeter. 'Now I'm going out to the early service at the Cathedral, then b'fast, then meetings all day. Such an interesting life. Ten years ago, who would have dreamt that I would be discussing the rebuilding of Princetown Prison!!'.[142]

SYLVIA SAYER

Segregating Dartmoor

Sylvia Sayer
Segregating Dartmoor

'My Unconscionable Impatience'

Dartmoor is one of the few wild, uncultivated areas of comparatively unspoiled natural beauty now left in the South of England.
Its traditional usage, as the great hill-grazing, stock-rearing reservoir of store cattle and sheep in Devon, goes hand in hand with
its incalculable value to the nation as an area of free recreation,
exploration and exercise for those whose mind and bodies need
the refreshment of natural beauty and of those elementary 'tough'
conditions now so increasingly hard to find. Dartmoor still offers
the essential challenge of human endurance and initiative, and
the silent treasures of nature study and prehistory, which are of
paramount importance in counteracting the artificial conditions
and influences of modern life. There are very few such reserves of
natural recreation in Southern England. Dartmoor is the greatest
and best-loved of them, and the most severely threatened.[1]

So wrote Sylvia Sayer, chair of the Dartmoor Preservation
Association (DPA), to Sir Patrick Duff, chair of the National Parks
Commission, on 11 May 1950. In her capacity as chair and then patron
of the Association, she wrote numerous such letters to members of the
commission, government ministers and officials, and senior figures in

statutory bodies. She never hesitated to address the man at the top, a sign both of her confidence and the strength of her convictions.

Sylvia Olive Pleadwell Sayer (1904–2000) was not born into such grandeur as Pauline Dower, but she was firmly placed within the English middle classes. She inherited her political commitments from her grandfather, Robert Burnard (1848–1920), founding member of the Dartmoor Preservation Association, but her social standing and the ease with which she dealt with male officials surely reflected the record of distinguished naval service on her father's side. Richard Cleveland Munday (1867–1952) entered the Royal Navy in 1890 as a surgeon and retired as a Major-General.[2] He proposed to Olive L. Burnard (1873–1960), Robert Burnard's eldest daughter, at a Plymouth Athenaeum excursion to Tavy Cleave on Dartmoor in July 1891; they were married in 1895.[3] They had two daughters and a son.[4] Sayer was educated at Princess Helena College, established in 1820 to educate the daughters of naval officers who served the Royal Navy in the Napoleonic War, and the Central School of Art in London, before marrying Guy Bourchier Sayer (1903–85), a Royal Navy midshipman, in 1925. Her parents kept a house in Plymouth and many years later Sayer recalled the journey by train to Princetown and then by pony and trap to her grandfather's home at Huccaby House, Hexworthy, in the heart of Dartmoor. In 1925, the Sayers bought a dilapidated Dartmoor cottage at Old Middle Cator near Widecombe-in-the-Moor for £150, where they lived when not away on service; in 1930 they had twin boys, Oliver (1930–94) and Geoff (1930–2013).

Guy Sayer had been educated at Highgate School before joining the service in 1916. During the Second World War, he was on the staff of the Commander-in-Chief, the Nore, and had the command successively of HMS *Ludlow* and HMS *Cleveland*, before joining the Admiralty naval staff. He commanded an assault force during Operation Zipper in 1945, the first stage of the aborted attempt to recapture Singapore, and was a flag officer during Operation

Musketeer, the disastrous assault on Port Said during the Suez Crisis in 1956. Promoted to admiral commanding the Reserve Fleet in 1958, he retired in 1959, upon which he was knighted. Henceforth, Sayer was Lady Sayer, a title that did her profile no harm.[5]

The subject of Sayer's letter to Duff was the need to expedite the designation of Dartmoor National Park. She reminded Duff that the Hobhouse Report of 1947 had declared Dartmoor a priority, and the Dartmoor Sub-Committee of the county council – Sayer was a member – had already formally requested that the process be accelerated. Numerous amenity organisations had followed suit. As Sayer explained, during the intervening period the sub-committee did not have sufficient clout to prevent harmful developments by powerful, government-backed interests. She was acutely aware that the armed services and the Forestry Commission were consolidating their hold on Dartmoor, her anxieties mirroring the challenges Dower faced in Northumberland. She worried that agreements reached between the War Office and the commoners with grazing rights on the open moor would entail the permanent curtailment of public access. The DPA's position was that 'no definite or irrevocable decision should be made on any of these proposals until after Dartmoor has been designated as a National Park'. Equally concerning was the proposed extension of the vast china clay mining operation at Lee Moor on the southern edge of the proposed national park. Sayer acknowledged that the industry was an important 'dollar-earner' at a time when the government was endeavouring to increase the UK's exports and improve its balance-of-payments position, but again alluding to the apparent hiatus created by the designation process, she questioned the justice of 'claim-staking while the going is good and the opposition weak'. What was more, meetings between the china clay interest, Devon County Council and the Dartmoor Sub-Committee were closed to the press, keeping the public uninformed of likely developments. Speedy designation was needed.[6] Duff and Geoffrey Clark, Director of Planning at Devon County Council, shared Sayer's worry about 'untoward developments taking place in the interval', including modest commercial initiatives at accessible sites. For example, at Widecombe-in-the-Moor, a village known for its spectacular setting and the tall tower of the parish church of St Pancras (the 'cathedral of the moor'), an entrepreneur wanted to open a café 'out of keeping with the village' as a base for running 'an undesirable bus service across the moor'.[7]

Like Northumberland County Council, Devon County Council was keen on designation, but in contrast to Northumberland, there was little need to debate the would-be park's parameters. Dartmoor had been long established in the public mind as a singular entity. As the greatest of the granite bosses that punctuate England's south-west peninsula, Dartmoor comprises a vast, largely unenclosed upland, much of which is peat bog and sometimes referred to as High Dartmoor, and numerous beautiful river valleys, such as those formed by the Teign and the Dart to the east and the Tavy to the west. For many, the source of Dartmoor's enduring fascination are the granite tors that break the moor's surface, and, notwithstanding its notorious reputation for high winds and cold rains, it frequently enjoys a fresh Atlantic breeziness and the balmy caress of the Gulf Stream. The major designation questions concerned its edgelands, particularly the hinterlands of Plymouth, Exeter and Tavistock.

The designation process was uncontroversial because the National Parks Commission accepted the recommendations made by Devon County Council even when it doubted the value of certain inclusions 'on landscape grounds'. South Zeal and South Tawton, villages to the north of Dartmoor, or Roborough Down, north of Plymouth and vulnerable to future development pressures, did not impress the commission. Excluding the china clay country to the south and Bovey Tracey, an attractive small town to the east notable for its light industry, caused little dissent. Pauline Dower, fresh from the Peak District public inquiry, was on the commission team that visited Dartmoor in May 1951 and it is likely her experience informed the commission's readiness to accept local recommendations. Concessions at the edges of the park did not compromise the integrity of the whole and to include Plymouth's 'playground', ensuring its likely preservation, sent a positive message about the new park to the inhabitants of that city.[8]

In August 1951, Duff wrote to tell Sayer that designation was imminent. He looked forward 'with every confidence to seeing England's green and pleasant land grow more green and more pleasant, and its healing gifts find their way to the hearts of more people'. Sayer was delighted but already anticipating the next fight. 'I will try now to curb my unconscionable impatience, which you so delightfully forgive,' she wrote, 'though I fear it will now give me a little trouble until at last the *local* administration of the Dartmoor park is on the right footing!'[9] Sayer was more combative when interviewed by *The Times*. Powers were now available to protect the moor 'but they must be vigorously and effectively used, and it will be up to the independent preservation and "out-of-doors" societies to make certain that they are'. She continued:

> Miracles will not happen, nor will the threats to its beauty and freedom be at an end; but the forces of vandalism and encroachment will not in the future be able to 'get away with it' quite so easily as they have in the past; the armour of defenders will be stronger now, and their weapons of heavier calibre. Those who love Dartmoor – and how many of us there are – may therefore, with tempered optimism, rejoice, as would those great pioneers of Dartmoor preservation who worked and battled so stoutly in the past, and to whom we owe it that the National Park of Dartmoor is yet so lovely, so free, and so unspoiled.[10]

Prior to the passage of the 1949 Act, she had been quick to discern attempts to 'sabotage' the Hobhouse Report by local authorities unwilling to yield planning control over national park territories to new authorities. As she had told readers of *The Times* in 1948, it was impossible to imagine Devon County Council exercising control over how Dartmoor was used by the Duchy of Cornwall, the Admiralty, the War Department or the Forestry Commission. A powerful national body was needed.[11] Sir Henry Slesser, former Labour MP and appeals court judge, county councillor and future chair of the Dartmoor Standing Committee, took Sayer to task for wishing to take control out of the hands of locals.[12] Sayer was quick to respond that the Hobhouse proposals did exactly the opposite, leaving half the members of the proposed new authorities to nominated locals. Local authority control, she insisted, would mean no control at all.[13] In the event, the government approved Devon County Council's proposal that oversight should be vested in a new Dartmoor Standing Committee (hereafter 'Dartmoor committee'), to which the county council's director of planning might refer planning proposals that would affect the park but over which the existing county planning committee would retain the power of decision.[14]

Sayer was dissatisfied with this arrangement. It failed to provide the necessary powers required by the new authority if it was to live up to her somewhat instrumentalist commitment to the national park ideal. She hoped Dartmoor's designation would enable its preservation in its present form and, in some respects, her outlook and priorities were rather narrow. She was not much interested in other places, including other parts of the national park system, and readily urged developments threatening Dartmoor be enacted elsewhere. But she should not be seen as parochial or intolerant. As we will see, Sayer's case for the preservation of Dartmoor drew directly on contemporary political, aesthetic and cultural agendas; similarly, her leadership of the DPA saw it deploy sophisticated activist tactics, often aimed at Whitehall and the parliamentary lobby, that sought to compensate for the limited powers of the new park authority. There is little doubt that her preservationist politics arose from a deep, and seemingly unshakable, conviction that the landscapes of

Dartmoor must be protected against almost all forms of change, but the case she made for their importance did not arise merely from instinct or personal affection.

Sayer's preservationism was premised on her belief that Dartmoor's natural characteristics gave it an essential purpose as grazing land or pasture, primarily pursued through the exercise of common rights, which had to be protected at all costs. Dartmoor's secondary purpose, to which she was no less committed, was its delivery of 'health and happiness' through the provision of extensive access land. As a result, Sayer opposed virtually all forms of enclosure or disturbance to the existing surface of the moor, including ploughing for agricultural or forestry purposes and any impact caused by the military's use of the moor as a training ground. She was also wary of traditional land management techniques like burning (known on Dartmoor as 'swaling'), whose use she believed had come to be excessive and therefore harmful. In essence, Sayer believed Dartmoor provided a single essential resource – rough grazing – and with it benefits to the public – health and happiness – and it should not be exploited in any other way.

Dartmoor's First Preservationists

Sayer's beliefs rested on her understanding of Dartmoor's history, and in particular the sense of Dartmoor's past that had been established by her grandfather Robert Burnard's generation of topographers, archaeologists and preservationists in the late nineteenth and early twentieth centuries. They included such Dartmoor luminaries as R.N. Worth, W.F. Collier, Sabine Baring-Gould, William Crossing and, of course, Robert Burnard himself, all of whom were part of a rich voluntarist associational culture that included members of the Plymouth Institution (founded 1812), the Teign Naturalists' Field Club (1858), the Devonshire Association (1862) and the Dartmoor Preservation Association (1883). The *Transactions of the Devonshire*

Association attests to the high seriousness of this work, particularly with respect to the archaeological exploration of Dartmoor.

Burnard's generation was animated by four main interests. First, and perhaps principally, was their interest in Dartmoor's surface antiquities, the plethora of stone rows, circles and monuments, as well as enclosures and hut circles of various types, that make Dartmoor an exceptionally important repository for evidence of the late Neolithic and early Bronze Age. As a scholarly or epistomological community, they took pride in their cautious scepticism and empirical methods, strongly identifying against what they took to be the fanciful speculations of their antiquarian predecessors, a tradition that had culminated in Samuel Rowe's extensive – and in certain respects deeply learned – *A Perambulation of the Ancient and Royal Forest of Dartmoor* (1848). Little inclined to consider Dartmoor antiquities as sites of paganistic ritual and orgy, reading them instead as early evidence of farming and domesticity, the preservationists tended to dismiss the Druidical theories propagated by antiquarians like Rowe. They recorded more than they speculated; essays published in the *Transactions of the Devonshire Association* were characterised by the careful descriptions of sites, including detailed measurements and diagrammatic representation.[15]

The work of the DPA can now be best accessed through Burnard's *Dartmoor Pictorial Records*, published in four volumes between 1890 and 1894 (republished in 1986 with a foreword by Sayer). This remarkable work brought together Burnard's pioneering interest in photography as a representative medium with extensive textual topographical and archaeological comment drawn from DPA reports, including accounts of the association's archaeological projects and preservationist achievements. The book runs to several hundred pages, and Burnard explained its purposes in terms of how photography, as part of his empiricist agenda, could help correct earlier traditions of Dartmoor representation and preserve existing evidence for future students of Dartmoor's past. 'Dartmoor literature has hitherto been adorned with illustrations which have either been too imaginative or too sketchy in their character,' he wrote, whereas 'Camera pictures are true in every detail.'[16] It is tempting to link Sayer's later use of photography to record damage inflicted on the moor, particularly by the military, to Burnard's pioneering work.

Second, Burnard and his friends were greatly interested in how Dartmoor had been governed in the past, particularly since the Norman Conquest, including how these systems of governance generated rights and responsibilities. They sought to understand the history of common rights on Dartmoor and how the stannary courts meeting at the village of Lydford managed the tin mining industry. Incidentally, Sayer later objected to plans to widen Lydford's roads ('gashed open') to accommodate a new bus service because it was one of 'the very few Saxon towns in England not destroyed by modern development' – a characteristic charge.[17] By the early nineteenth century, the stannary courts were redundant – what little remained of the industry functioned according to modern commercial practices – but a bastard form of common rights still determined how the moorscape was exploited.

The third great interest of the Burnard generation were the material precipitates of the medieval and early modern periods. Structures like the famous clapper bridge at Postbridge, which the antiquarians were prone to misdate to earlier periods, were appealing, but of greater interest was how Dartmoor's religious history intersected with secular uses of the moor. The stone crosses marking medieval and early modern trade routes were of enduring fascination; the Celtic design motifs of the crosses making them an exotic and much reproduced symbol of Dartmoor's pre-modern past. Similarly fascinating were semi-mythic grass trackways like the Lich (or Lych) Way, the route along which the dead were carried from Dartmoor's tenancies to St Petroc's at Lydford. Linked to this was interest in folksong and stories, as collected by the Revd Sabine Baring-Gould, prolific author, squire of Lewtrenchard and Anglican parish priest.[18]

Finally, more immediate questions were raised by modern developmental pressures, which ranged from small-scale incremental steps to large infrastructural developments. In part, the DPA had been formed to oppose 'encroachments' on the Dartmoor Commons allowed by the Duchy of Cornwall, the principal landowner. Burnard highlighted this in 'Plundered Dartmoor', his landmark lecture of 1895, published shortly afterwards by the DPA.[19] Partly thanks to the catchy title, Burnard's lecture achieved an iconic status among later preservationists. It confirmed the shift in sensibility away from the optimism of Dartmoor's agricultural improvers and industrial speculators that characterised much writing about Dartmoor in the early nineteenth century towards the more defensive outlook of the preservationists, generating a discourse dominated by the language of 'spoliation' and 'encroachment', in which the 'newtake' – granite-walled fields cut from the edges of the common – symbolised all that was wrong with modern Dartmoor. Some newtakes were on a modest scale, representing the opportunism of local commoners, but others were more deliberate, reflecting new ideas. Burnard's enclosure map provided a powerful visual commentary on the extent of enclosure in the central part of the Forest of Dartmoor in the early nineteenth century when the agricultural improvers, enabled by the Prince of Wales, were most active. The establishment of Princetown, a Dartmoor 'new town', and the prisoner of war depot – later HMP Dartmoor – during the French Revolutionary and Napoleonic wars, helped drive this dynamic. This 'spoliation', Burnard argued, cut off access between the moor's northern and southern quarters, undermining the integrity of the Forest of Dartmoor as common land. As we will see, Sayer was particularly exercised by the fragmentation of Dartmoor's 'wild country'.

Burnard was also exercised by more imminent threats, for which he proposed radical solutions. In the early 1890s, London County Council alighted on the possibility that Dartmoor might provide the city with a reliable water supply, piped to London along Brunel's great London to Penzance railway line. This was not as outlandish as it might at first seem. Parliament had enabled Birmingham and Liverpool to acquire large tracts of land in Wales as water catchment areas, dissolving common rights along the way, and in the 1880s Manchester Corporation converted Thirlmere Lake in the Lake District into an impounding reservoir. In the event, the private bill London County Council placed before parliament was withdrawn for technical reasons and the city turned its attention to Glamorganshire. During the controversy, Burnard and the Quaker radical W.G. Collier proposed that Devon County Council should purchase the Duchy's Dartmoor holdings on behalf of the people of Devon.[20] The proposal attracted some local attention, particularly when linked to the need to protect Devon's water security, and chimed with the 'purchase to preserve' agenda underpinning the preservationist strategies of Octavia Hill and the National Trust. Burnard's proposal not only echoed London County Council's decision to buy Epping Forest on behalf of Londoners, but also talk in the late 1890s about the Trust or the government buying the Muckross Estate in County Killarney and opening it as a national park on the US model.[21] Burnard reverted to this theme in 'Plundered Dartmoor', insisting that it was only a matter of time before Dartmoor was 'grabbed by some distant powerful municipality'. If local water supplies were to be maintained 'pure and undefiled', the people of Devon must acquire the Forest of Dartmoor for themselves. It was a question of 'sanitation and self-preservation'.

Acquisition by the county council would allow unsustainable practices undermining Dartmoor's value to be addressed. If traditional peat cutting already undermined Dartmoor's capacity to retain water, risking turning Dartmoor's rivers into 'rapid torrents' in winter and 'dry water courses' in summer, efficient forms of commercial peat extraction threatened Devon's future energy security by diminishing its capacity to harness Dartmoor's hydropower. 'In the hands of the County,' Burnard wrote, 'electric power derived from Dartmoor streams may in a few years to come be a valuable and a revenue-earning asset of no mean importance.' More conventionally, Burnard complained that common rights and rights of access were undermined by the convict prison at Princetown (a 'hideous incubus' that stigmatised the moor, according to Sayer) and the expansionist ambitions of the War Office, which leased training grounds from the Duchy in the north quarter. Burnard thought prison labour could be put to better use on harbour work – the intractable nature of the moorscape meant that the prison farm was never efficient. Purchase promised other benefits. If Dartmoor was owned by the people of Devon, 'the public would possess the grandest park in England', 'pre-historic monuments' would be preserved, common rights and customary uses maintained, and the pernicious effects of 'rack renting', a recent development, reversed. Burnard even hinted that a degree of ecological restoration might flow from the purchase. Deer might be encouraged back onto the moor, 'fur and feather' numbers increased, and hunting revived as a popular pastime.[22] Enthusiastic commentary in the press emphasised the public-interest aspects of Burnard's case, as when the correspondent of *Trewman's Exeter Flying Post* commended Dartmoor's health-giving qualities as early as 1896:

Dartmoor seems by nature to have been given as a health resort in the south-west of the island; in a relaxing and enervating climate, it provides that tonic which braces the system, and gives therewith moral impetus as well. It is said that consumption is unknown on the moor. What is certain is that, if taken in time pulmonary weakness may be prevented from development and decline may be arrested, by the pure air and the peat smoke; and that in cases of nervous prostration the invigorating air, the brilliant light, revive the patient in an extraordinary manner.[23]

The possibility of purchase soon faded from view, and Sayer's generation of preservationists did not revive the idea, but nor did they prove sanguine when Devon's water needs did press on Dartmoor in the post-war years. Although Sayer shared her grandfather's belief that Dartmoor preservationism must be based on the public interest, she often found the local interest to be antithetical to her aims, and it was for this reason, if no other, that she championed the national park ideal.

The Silent Remembering Moor

Sayer's first major statement about Dartmoor, her short booklet *The Outline of Dartmoor's Story from the Earliest Times to the Present Day*, was published in 1951 to coincide with the designation of the park. Illustrated by her own drawings, *Outline* ran to some 50 pages, and was characterised by the elegance and concision of her prose as well as her evident proficiency as a commercial artist. A reader with a decent knowledge of the literature on Dartmoor could not but recognise how effectively the *Outline* synthesised the work of the Burnard generation.

Outline was not a guidebook or a detailed history but was intended to help visitors 'see the Moor with new eyes'. Notwithstanding a few popular beauty spots, Sayer thought visitors were inclined to see Dartmoor as 'bare and barren', a part of Devon that had 'unaccountably stayed wild', a place without 'any very interesting history'. Principal among the non-seeing were 'some of those who travel across Dartmoor by car or by coach', an echo there of Potter's contempt for the day-tripper and a common enough trope among preservationists. To teach a tripper to see was to make an ally. Dartmoor's relative lack of development, Sayer explained, meant it preserved evidence of human history 'from man's first days of cattle-minding when the world was new' to 'our own mechanized, materialistic, destructive twentieth century'. Alarmed by the depredations of modernity, Sayer did not promote a comfortable narrative of continuous human history that chimed with national myths propounded during the Second

World War, but instead a narrative of decline that traced Dartmoor's transition to modernity, albeit a transition Dartmoor's numinous qualities could still defy. Sayer was not the first preservationist to imagine her favoured place could be still pulled back from the brink of irrecoverable destruction. Human history was:

> all here, written in the hills and valleys and the little border villages of the silent, remembering Moor. And it's because of this long unbroken continuity of evolution, and the grandeur of its lonely beauty, that Dartmoor possesses a magical quality impossible to describe. Some people fear it and find it sinister. Others find their hearts captured by it and held for ever.[24]

The *Outline* reveals the debt Sayer owed to Burnard's generation, particularly the work of William Crossing (1847–1928), the greatest of Dartmoor's modern chroniclers, from whom she derived much. But the booklet was equally post-war, anticipating the arguments W.G. Hoskins made in *The Making of the English Landscape*.[25] Hoskins's enormously influential book described the depth of the human time signature on the English landscape through the metaphor of the palimpsest. Just as medieval parchments were reused, criss-crossed with later script, so too was the English landscape layered with evidence of past human activities that the work of later generations never fully erased. Hoskins did not present the landscape as solely anthropic – that is, largely the product of human agency – or present it as a hybrid co-production of human and non-human nature, as some modern critics do, but instead taught his readers to recognise how modern landscape usages were patterned or structured by the medieval and early modern past. Sayer did not express herself with the same historical sophistication – she pitched her history as a story, and her tone could be faux naïve – but she too endeavoured to tease out the complexities of Dartmoor's history, transforming this apparently barren 'space' into profoundly anthropic 'place'. And like

Hoskins – and Burnard and Crossing before him – she tended to see the modern period as a fall from grace, disrupting the harmony between humanity and nature enjoyed in the pre-industrial period.

Sayer began with deep time, when the earth was a 'fiery ball' and Dartmoor formed by a 'great up-boiling of molten granite'.[26] She described Dartmoor's 'clitter', the rocks that lie at the base of its tors, as the remnants of former mountains; iconic sites like Bowerman's Nose near Manaton (illustrated against a starlit sky) remained after softer rock was washed away 'by the rains and frosts of millions of winters'.[27] The earliest humans, when Britain was a part of continental Europe, did not ascend the cold bare heights of Dartmoor, but after the last ice age, when rising waters and temperatures made Britain a temperate island, Neolithic migrants from continental Europe, skilled cattle herders, headed for the sunny uplands. Their flints and hut circles are evidence of a sophisticated civilisation, later enhanced by intermingling with Celtic tribes skilled in working bronze. Sayer illustrated these developments with a jolly village scene of strong healthy folk, domesticated animals – dogs, chickens and cattle – and sophisticated hunting weapons, all safely bounded by a dry stone wall. Sheep were a later Mediterranean import. Antiquities, like the Grey Wethers, a stone circle near Fernworthy Reservoir (constructed in 1942), had many purposes. People assembled, the stones marked the graves of great men, and there were 'strange rites of worship' where – she hedged her bets – 'sacrifice probably took place'.[28] The first people to till the land and grow corn, she pointedly observed, tended to settle in the valleys: grazing remained the predominant occupation in the uplands. That continuity was one of her great themes.[29]

The Romans did not venture west of Exeter, or so popular understandings of Roman Britain had it, leaving the Celtic inhabitants of Devon and Cornwall undisturbed. The ancient laws and customs of the Dumnonii ('the tribal name for the mixed people of the region') saw no disruption until the arrival of Christian missionaries from

Ireland. Churches dedicated to Celtic saints, Sayer was sure, were built in the border villages of Widecombe, Harford, Lydford and South Brent. Despite waves of invasion by rivalrous Celtic tribes during the 'Dark Ages', the pattern was set until the Saxons drove the Dumnonii out. Saxon place names (e.g. Hexworthy, Foxworthy, Ponsworthy, Scorriton, Okehampton, Sourton, Uppacot) 'tell the tale of this very thorough conquest'. Reading history through place names was a characteristic preservationist method – the English Place-Names Society was established in 1923 to promote the study of toponymy. The Danes, all 'horror and bloodshed', prompted the remaining men and women of ancient Dartmoor to flee, some beyond the Tamar into modern-day Cornwall, but those who remained either 'took refuge on the Dartmoor heights' or were enslaved or intermarried. One is reminded of the mural at Wallington. Local 'pixie' legends, and the mythic 'Wish Hounds', she speculated, might well refer to the 'fierce and cunning ... little native people of the Moor' hiding out in the hills.[30]

If life was hard on Saxon Dartmoor, it was also a place of busy activity, 'shaping along lines we could recognise today'. Manor courts were established, commoners' rights were defined, churches were built (and Roman Catholic rites adopted), tin streaming developed, and watermills and forges were built. All of this was disrupted by the Norman Conquest and the decision to place Devon under strict forest law, meaning only the king could hunt the hart, the hind, the wolf, the boar and the hare; in 1204, she exclaimed, striking a radical note, 'the people's liberties were ... restored' when all but Dartmoor and Exmoor were deforested. It cannot be repeated too many times that Dartmoor's status as a 'forest' was a legal claim rather than a description – it was briefly a 'chase' in the thirteenth and early fourteenth centuries.[31] Henry III presented the Manor of Lydford, comprising much of High Dartmoor, to his brother Richard, the Earl of Cornwall. On 24 July 1240, an iconic date in Dartmoor history, '"twelve loyal knights"' (cue another charming illustration) made 'a perambulation of the boundary between "the forest of Dartmoore" and the lands of "the knights and free tenants" adjoining it', establishing a boundary which retains legal status to this day. A century or so later, in 1337, Edward III granted 'The Castle and Manor of Lydford ... with the Chase of Dartmoor' to his young son, Edward the Black Prince, the Duke of Cornwall. It has remained part of the Duchy of Cornwall, and the patrimony of the Prince of Wales, ever since.[32]

Sayer offered a jaunty if imprecise account of common rights, reminding the reader of her own status as a commoner, but given the importance of common rights to Sayer's politics it is necessary to describe more clearly what her nineteenth-century predecessors had established. The central area of upland that forms much of Dartmoor National Park comprises the Forest of Dartmoor and the Commons of Devon. Largely contiguous with the parish of Lydford, the Forest forms the central mass of the Dartmoor upland, and the Commons of Devon are the smaller commons that belong to the parishes that encircle the Forest and the Commons. The Forest and the individual commons of Devon are not fenced but indicated on the ground with occasional stone markers and only faintly inscribed on the OS map. The rambler or rider happily passes from common to common or in and out of the Forest unaware of the numerous boundaries they've crossed.

Percival Birkett, solicitor, and associate of the Commons Preservation Society (CPS) and the DPA, explained in a Devonshire Association lecture of October 1885 that three types of rights holders made use of this land. They were the holders of the ancient tenements, the venville tenants and the wider tenantry of the county of Devon.[33] The ancient tenements were farms that lay within the forest boundary and are clustered near the East and West Dart in the east and south quarters.[34] Historically, the holders of the ancient tenements could graze their beasts in the forest providing they could overwinter them in their tenancies. This was known as levancy and couchancy. For a fee known as agistment, the holders of the ancient tenancies admitted to the Forest the livestock of down-countrymen from throughout the county who drove their cattle up to the moor for summer grazing. This is known as transhumance.[35] The venville tenants occupied farms in the parishes bordering the commons and grazed their stock on their respective parish common. For a fee, they could graze their stock on the Forest provided they could be taken off the Forest at night; they, too, could pay for summer grazing on the same basis as the stock-raisers of Devon. Additional rights enjoyed by the commoners included the right to take anything off the moor that the household could use, except vert (vegetation supplying food and shelter for deer) and venison, including turf for fuel (the right of turbary), wood, reeds, heather and bracken (the right of estover), and fish from ponds and streams (the right of piscary): nothing the commoner took from the moor could be sold to a third party.

By the late nineteenth century, practices had begun to change, partly with the complicity of the commoners. Duchy middlemen played a larger role in the management of summer grazing, displacing the holders of the ancient tenements (who retained their grazing rights); availability of commercial products made rights of removal (turbary, estover and piscary) increasingly redundant; and the principle of levancy and couchancy was overlooked as year-round grazing was enabled by the introduction of hardy Scottish sheep breeds. Burnard's generation advocated the revival of traditional common rights and their corollary, the restoration of traditional grazing regimes, as the means to recover Dartmoor's status as a shared asset in Devon's agricultural economy. Sayer thought this was unrealistic. She argued that summer grazing by the commoners of Devon was no longer sustainable – the right was 'too widespread and unwieldy' and had been 'forgotten' – but she insisted that 'local or native Dartmoor rights' remained 'essential to the true Dartmoor economy'. Recalling the methods of the CPS, Sayer keenly asserted her rights as a venville tenant, particularly when she opposed novel uses of common land, such as by the military, for which she had not given consent.[36] New practices, however, needed to be regularised, and again she registered her technocratic faith in the potential of new systems of management and oversight. Setting a hare running, she hoped that the National Parks Commission, working with the Duchy, would 'sponsor' 'a determined effort to redefine, record and re-establish these ancient rights'. This was no longer just a question for the Commoners. The 'preservation of these ancient common rights' reflected the interests of visitors, for they guaranteed the 'freedom of the Moor' by ensuring 'unfenced access land where one may walk without let or hindrance'.[37]

Sayer was not a political scientist, and her language was imprecise. To follow David Matless's characterisation of early twentieth-century critics of the development of the landscape, she was a 'planner-preservationist' rather than an 'organicist' but her perspective is perhaps best understood as segregationist.[38] Her supposition that ancient rights could be at once preserved and redefined and yet remain ancient rights was not altogether plausible, particularly if those redefined rights allowed overwintering of stock on the moor and excluded the right of the commoners of Devon to summer pasture on Dartmoor. She would have understood that the development of Devon's road infrastructure, particularly the busy trunk roads connecting Exeter to Okehampton and Plymouth, had cut across the old drovers' roads, rendering summer grazing for the commoners of Devon near impossible. Implicitly, she accepted that year-round grazing, supported by the headage payments provided by the farm subsidy system, was now the norm, though she could not countenance any ploughing of moorland to produce seeded grassland. As such, she did not advocate the major restructuring of Dartmoor's agricultural economy which was required if commoners were obliged to exclusively farm traditional Dartmoor breeds, hold only stock they could overwinter on their farms and supplement their income with agistment payments. However, she did advocate reform of how the commons' inadequate governance allowed large stockholders, particularly those who increased the size of their herds by taking full advantage of headage payments, to exercise increasing control over the commons, squeezing smaller rights holders like herself.

Key to understanding Sayer's position are the phrases 'local or native Dartmoor rights' and 'the true Dartmoor economy'. Although Dartmoor stock-raising could only function as part of a wider agricultural economy – Dartmoor livestock was fattened off the moor – Sayer tended to represent Dartmoor as a distinct place rather than as an integral part of Devon, the West Country or the wider nation-state. Her enthusiasm for national park status, which placed exceptional value on Dartmoor's unique characteristics, and her insistence that the park's governance should be placed on the correct footing, stemmed from her segregationist outlook. Rather than seeing park status as inviting unwarranted interference, as commoners tended to, Sayer saw it as a means of sealing Dartmoor off from the surrounding country and broader national pressures. The fact that her purposes relied on protections provided by national government meant that the seal could not be absolute. Paradoxically, her segregationist approach to Dartmoor depended on an integrationist approach to the management of landscape by the nation as a whole. In later campaigns against the exploitation of Dartmoor's natural resources by what she regarded as outside forces, Sayer repeatedly legitimised the exceptional claims she made for Dartmoor in terms of the public or national interest. She emphasised Dartmoor's exceptional health-giving properties, physical and psychological, thereby linking public access to the maintenance of common rights and aligning the broader public interest with that of the commoners.

What, then, to make of her phrase 'local or native'? The use of 'native' smacks of essentialist claims about the right of certain people to certain places, and it undoubtedly connotes exclusion, for any use of 'native' implies that there must be non-natives. There is little evidence that Sayer had thought very deeply about 'native' as a racial or ethnic signifier that implied a line of descent to which rights-based claims could be attached. Nonetheless, as we've already seen, the *Outline* was suffused by a casual racialism, partly in terms of how she referred to the character of Dartmoor people, but most obviously evident in her account of the waves of migration that had shaped Dartmoor's history. Again, this owed much to the work of the late nineteenth-century preservationists. Sayer's predecessors might have rejected the 'fanciful claims' of the antiquarians but they were strongly influenced by late nineteenth-century racial science, writing about long-headed Iberians, round-headed Celts and the like.[39] Sayer did not get embroiled in these speculations, but took for granted the broad outline they established, including the notion that Dartmoor had been peopled by folk with distinct physical characteristics. Its Neolithic people, for example, were 'small, dark-haired and short-limbed' whereas the Celts were 'taller, round-headed and lighter-haired';[40] still, her reference to the Celts rather than the Saxons as 'the little native people of the Moor' suggests she used the word 'native' very loosely.[41] Add to this Sayer's clear sense that common rights were attached to property rather than people and we should be wary of making too much of this; nonetheless, her defence of 'native' rights as the wife of a senior naval officer at the beginning of a decade in which British foreign policy would be dominated by wars of colonial retention can hardly be overlooked.

Equally slippery was her claim that 'the *true* Dartmoor economy' was based on pasture. Just as Hoskins wrote favourably of pre-modern uses of the landscape, Sayer offered a positive account of tin mining in medieval and early modern Dartmoor; to reify the tinners as people of the moor made Sayer a typical Dartmoor enthusiast. She described the tinners' working methods, evoked their hardy independent culture and explained how the consequent fifteenth-century prosperity was made manifest in enlarged or rebuilt churches. This was of a piece with those parts of *Outline* that combined a lively social history of Dartmoor's 'busy communal life' with short accounts of certain Dartmoor personalities, salted with detail on religious life and the region's role in major political events like the Civil War. Mindful, perhaps, of the influence of Baring-Gould's collection of folk traditions and the broader market enjoyed by popular retellings of old tales, she noted the decline of superstitious beliefs. As a public figure, Sayer evinced no interest in folksy aspects of popular impressions of Dartmoor. Her picture of the moor was duly completed by a damning account of the prison ('grisly excrescence'),[42] and a paean to Dartmoor ponies, whose purity was now threatened by alien stock, resulting in 'clumsy, hairy-hoofed hybrids painful to behold'.[43] Her activism included ardent support for Dartmoor pony breeders and their wish for controls over the livestock that could be grazed on the moor.[44]

As this suggests, Sayer's account traced the transition to modernity, and in the best preservationist tradition she offered a mordant account of nineteenth-century 'speculators'. Tin mining succeeded tin streaming, which in turn become largely defunct by the First World War.[45] More aggravating were the 'money-making ambitions of the Industrial Revolution', which attracted to Dartmoor agricultural improvers (cue failed attempts to cultivate grain, flax and hemp at Princetown), peat and naphtha factories, the tin mine at Vitifer, granite quarrying, the Princehall plantation, the Cherrybrook gunpowder mill and the Sourton ice works. Granite was quarried until the last years of the twentieth century, but Dartmoor remained intractable – another preservationist shibboleth – and 'old Dartmoor could swallow or defeat' these efforts 'with comparative ease'. Sayer must have taken from Crossing the notion that the people of the Moor carried 'on quietly with the right and traditional usage of their land', watching 'the failure of the speculators without emotion and without surprise'. They knew better than the 'many "progressives"' who forget, 'and still forget' that Dartmoor was 'designed by Nature to be above all else a summer pasturage for cattle and sheep (and that one can't dictate to Nature with impunity)'.[46]

Dartmoor now had to 'compete with the Twentieth Century'. The individual speculator had been replaced by a far more 'powerful and damaging' force, the state. The Moor 'endures', she wrote, but 'with some difficulty'. The War Department had long used the northern quarter for artillery practice, but, as in Northumberland, had appropriated further land after the Second World War for 'live ammunition' training. With the collusion of the Duchy, the Forestry Commission enclosed thousands of acres of hill pasture and ploughed it up 'for doubtful experiments in commercial conifer-production'; and this was to say nothing of the china clay works and water impounding reservoirs 'detrimental' to Dartmoor's 'natural character', the latter re-engineering its river systems. At the same time, Sayer could scarcely conceal her contempt for the 'suburban-type villas upon its perimeter', the traffic congestion caused by 'giant motor-coaches' and private cars, the 'shoddy cafes, plaster gnomes and Birmingham-made souvenirs', and the 'ice-cream cartons and paper bags strewn like dirty snow along its roadsides; the broken bottles hidden in the heath'.[47] In an odd coinage, she once described motorists as 'crowdomaniacs', whereas in a hilarious letter to *The Times* she cannibalised this line of rhetoric by comparing the fate of Widecombe, one of Dartmoor's honeypots, with that facing Ayot St Lawrence in Hertfordshire following the death of George Bernard Shaw and the opening of 'Shaw's Corner' to the public.[48] Still, as on Dartmoor, when the holiday season comes to an end 'the beleaguered village becomes its true self again'.[49] Much here recalls Potter's acerbic remarks in the 1930s, the difference being that Sayer gave public utterance to what Potter tended to confide to private letters.

Dartmoor's communities were not entirely resilient. As farms changed hands, there was no guarantee that newcomers understood 'Dartmoor farming'; young men were less inclined to take up farm work, leading to the labour shortages that contributed to declining stock numbers and more rabbits and 'mongrel ponies', a sure sign of decay to the agriculturalist; and the old pieties were gone, the churches full only on special occasions.[50] Still, Sayer was not without hope. Once the tourist season was over, 'the villages became their true selves' – that modifier again – 'and voices are raised cheerfully, argumentatively, critically, amicably in the parish hall, the village square, the Women's Institute and the inn'.[51]

Thus Sayer's attempt to make Dartmoor known ends on a somewhat disconcerting note. The visitor remains 'other', and to them Dartmoor is unknowable, because its resident communities – perhaps its 'native' population – necessarily adapt their behaviour in their presence because they depend on the service economy. Notions of authenticity should never be accepted uncritically, and rural communities often sustain dubious notions of the 'local' that serve old hierarchies and cultures of deference, but the end of the tourist season does see spatial regimes transformed and voices recovered. For the resident population, less congested roads, shorter queues in shops, perhaps recovering that favoured place at the bar, are conjoined to less deferential, more expansive ways of being and freer, sometimes louder speech. University towns experience something similar during the vacation when things become less gown than town.

That Sayer was committed to the notionally 'true' Dartmoor, that *Outline* was obviously not a work of critical anthropology or sociology, and that Sayer's confidence that she could see all sides might be treated a little sceptically, did not mean that she and the DPA were necessarily reactionary. The evidence they presented in April 1956 to the Royal Commission on Common Land, chaired by Sir Dudley Stamp, struck a remarkably progressive note. Once due deference was paid to the DPA's founding aims and principles, Sayer insisted that Dartmoor should not be treated as a 'museum piece'. Things had changed. Account must now be now taken of the amenity interest – integrationism again – especially by sectional interests like the Dartmoor Commoners' Association (DCA). Sayer considered the DCA, established in 1952, as largely representing the interests of the larger commoners, particularly with respect to its desire to resolve the tension between ancient rights and modern usage in favour of the latter. She feared that the Royal Commission might succumb to the DCA's push to see the Forest and the Commons of Devon formalised as distinct entities, which she judged would make them vulnerable to enclosure by allowing the strong farmers to buy off the rights of others, farm by farm, until they could take complete control of the common in question. Collier, writing in the 1880s, had argued that the liberty of feral ponies to wander at will across the commons was proof that for all practical purposes the common had always been treated as a unity – so potent is the association of the Dartmoor pony with the landscape's freedoms that it was later adopted as the symbol of Dartmoor National Park.[52] Further enclosure of the Dartmoor commons, Sayer argued, would diminish the freedoms of the British people. To allow that to happen would be at odds with the public interest.

> The agricultural value of Dartmoor – and we say this quite boldly – is not its main value now, and still less is it likely to be so in the years to come. The major importance of Dartmoor and the other national parks to this overcrowded country is as its last strong-holds of physical and mental recreation. We hold very strongly that health and happiness are Dartmoor's best exports. It is important that Dartmoor should produce better cattle, ponies and sheep; it is more important still that it should help to produce better human beings.[53]

Untethering the DPA from Big Agriculture was a bold but shrewd move. Small venville tenants, like Sayer herself, might find the pres-ervationists useful allies, but the old preservationist commitment to the maintenance of traditional common rights was no longer a tenable basis on which to mount a defence of Dartmoor's existing landscape qualities. Moreover, the big commoners had a powerful ally in the Ministry of Agriculture, Fisheries and Food and the National

Farmers' Union. The National Parks Commission, a marginal body with a small staff and a meagre budget, did not have the statutory powers to challenge how land within national parks was farmed. Sayer seems to have quickly understood that the DPA could amplify the commission's voice in government only if it became an effective activist body that represented broad public interests. As we shall see in the next section, what she determined constituted the public interest was formed at the intersection of her own sensibilities and the broader debates animating post-war development.

Rural Subtopia

On 20 August 1951, Geoffrey Clark wrote to Duff. He had just heard that the BBC planned to erect a 750-foot television transmitter mast at North Hessary Tor, overlooking Princetown. This was 'the first major proposal from a statutory body ... likely to alter the landscape of the heart of the wildest part of the moor'. The development was 'bound to create a disturbance among the purists'.[54] He was right, and the ensuing conflict proved to be Sayer's first major foray into activist politics, as well as her first high-profile defeat – recalling the seminal effect the loss of Swiss Cottage Fields had on Octavia Hill. In the process, she got to grips with the technical issues, found herself at odds with the Dartmoor committee, helped the commission assemble its case against the mast for the public inquiry, which included helping persuade the Dartmoor Preservation Association to provide substantial financial support for the campaign, and generally inserted herself and the association into the debate. According to a DPA memorandum, likely drafted by Sayer, she steeled the organisation against adopting an 'attitude of resentful but helpless resignation'.[55]

The progress of the conflict has been traced in detail elsewhere, including the BBC's technical case for locating the transmitter mast at North Hessary, but no account of Sayer's activist career can overlook this early bloodying or the arguments she helped mobilise against the mast.[56] By identifying alternative sites she helped the commission place the BBC under pressure to conduct further tests and explain its preferences more fully. These moves were largely tactical, for her case against the mast was absolute and rested on a set of arguments based on the exceptional status of Dartmoor that set the tone for her and the DPA's opposition to other developments throughout the 1950s. But these arguments were also part of a larger national debate. The DPA's newsletter, the bulk of which Sayer wrote, showed how she was part of a broader post-war culture of complaint about the negative impact of modernity and materialism on the built and natural environment. Sayer was strongly influenced by Ian Nairn's notorious *Outrage* special edition of the *Architectural Review*, and subsequent publications by the Architectural Press, including Sylvia Crowe's *Tomorrow's Landscape*.[57] Sayer's politics were reactionary in the sense that she largely opposed change, but her outlook was not parochial.

This early foray into the heady world of activism saw Sayer relish her developing skills as a rhetorician. The television mast would 'destroy, and destroy for ever, the wild and natural character of a very wide area of ancient hill-country landscape'; the mast would 'dominate the surrounding country with inescapable ubiquity'; its 'alien presence and associations would be a perpetual reminder of that modern "civilisation" which most people come to a national park to forget'; 'buildings of the well-known BBC-type – flat-topped rectangles like petrified railway carriages – would crown the tor in place of its natural rocks'; it would be 'landscape-slaughter on a more than usually impressive scale'; 'No other feature of landscape value [the tor], or such a beloved viewpoint, has ever been deliberately destroyed for a *luxury*'.[58] Sayer could barely comprehend the suggestion that the fabric of the tor itself would be lost to the installation. Of her alternative site suggestions, she exclaimed: 'Even local interests, even materialists, even rabid all-out TV viewers might be able to see that their *best* advantage might be gained in this way, rather than by the destruction of Hessary Tor as a "short-term grab".[59] Was there a touch of humour here? Following an apparently intemperate outburst during a telephone call with the commission, she sought to explain her reference to 'Coronation TV hysteria'. She was not 'denigrating the enthusiasm we all feel for the Coronation itself' – she was an unabashed royalist – but the BBC's attempts to use it as a pretext 'to "cash in" on that clamour'.[60] Sayer was prone to place colloquialisms in speech marks, another way she indicated her disdain for contemporary ways. Following the decision to approve the site with some mitigations – the mast would be sited just off the tor and the cables buried – Sayer presented Duff with a painting of the tor, 'almost the last representation of that landscape that can be made while it is still unshadowed and unspoiled'.[61]

Other controversies provoked a comparable onslaught. When Torquay Corporation proposed a reservoir in the Avon Valley, on the east side of the national park upstream of Didworthy and South Brent, she hurled questions at readers of the DPA newsletter about whether alternative sites or solutions had been sufficiently considered before inveighing against a water engineer who allegedly claimed that no one could mind because the site was 'right off the beaten track': 'It has never occurred to him that the beaten track is not what we want to save on Dartmoor.' This apparent failure to understand what people like herself liked most about the moor prompted an assault on the 'urban mind', and a brief tour of its degradations.

> we get the untidy litter near the dam at Fernworthy and the stark white villa at its entrance road, the staring white buildings and concrete erections on the skyline at Prewley Moor, the square concrete box and iron railings in the lovely Cowsic valley, the pipes and tunnels at Swincombe, the brick-and-concrete building at the intake works that already disfigures a whole reach of the river Avon, and similar glaring incongruities.[62]

The water board 'mentality' meant 'the painfully suburban white concrete kerbstones of the new access road, now ribboning incongruously beside the river',[63] part of the transformation of 'the landscape ... from one formed by Nature to one fabricated by man'; only those who preferred the 'artificial to the free' could imagine everything soon looking 'lovely in the Avon valley'.[64] Who was to blame? 'Parliamentary indifference' and votes won by 'handing out material advantages to a clamorous electorate' rather than by 'endeavouring to ensure that some untamed country, some solitude, some beauty and quiet shall be saved for posterity'. Posterity had no votes, Sayer wrote, and so 'the last thing on which public money need be spent, for which sacrifices need be made, is the preservation of national beauty. It is, unfortunately, as simple as that'.[65]

In October 1955, the *DPA Report and Newsletter* was headed with a note explaining that enclosed was a leaflet describing 'a most courageous, stimulating and outspoken book'; 'It is also horrifying, but this nation needs to be shocked out of the complacency and blindness with which it is allowing the destruction of the loveliness of its land'. That book was Nairn's *Outrage*. Even members of the DPA, 'in the front line of the battle against Barbarism', would find it a 'revelation'. 'Its brilliant, stinging phrases provide first-class ammunition for use by our side in the fray.'[66] *Outrage* lived up to its title thanks to Nairn's pugnacious literary style and use of the visual medium. Stinging prose and forcefully uncompromising arguments were reinforced, following the *Architectural Review*'s visual style, with numerous photographs, piling up examples of what Sayer would call incongruities, forcing the argument home. And when reality did not quite deliver the visual argument Nairn needed, specially commissioned drawings provided either parody or prophecy, contrasting ideal types. Nairn's 'outrage' was provoked by an England 'reduced to universal Subtopia, a mean and middle state, neither town nor country, an even spread of abandoned aerodromes and fake rusticity, wire fences, traffic roundabouts, gratuitous notice-boards, car-parks, and Things in Fields'.[67] *Outrage* might have been pitched against the homogenising consequences of post-war planning, but much Nairn found objectionable originated in the apparently untrammelled developments of the inter-war period and the legacies of wartime. In this respect, he was an inheritor of Clough Williams-Ellis, and Gillian Darley notes the peculiar preoccupation of Nairn and his associates with the inter-war period, including John Cowper Powys, the extraordinary if now neglected novelist.[68] Disused aerodromes particularly preoccupied Nairn. Barbed-wire fencing and admonitory signage made them an exceptionally visible example of reduced public access to the countryside.[69]

Nairn was at his most effective when railing against the uniformity brought by what Joe Moran describes as 'quite small phenomena', like road signs, railings, advertising hoardings, street furniture and other amenities, condemning a landscape of 'clutter', 'squalor' and, yes, 'subtopia'.[70] Like Sayer's *Outline*, albeit more literally, Nairn's intention was to teach people to see, to sensitise them to the accumulated effect of small interventions. But the ambition of his broader critique should not be missed. Nairn decried the lamentable effect of the growing network of arterial roads, subtopia's basic infrastructure, insidious in the homogenising visual effect it had on the countryside and a further inducement to subtopia's spread. *Outrage*, therefore, built its argument by following the A34 from Southampton to Carlisle. 'Ribbon development', equally despised by Hoskins, was at odds with Nairn's fundamental commitment to the development and maintenance of a high-density model of urban life in which architectural modernism was reconciled to local traditions and clear boundaries were drawn between the rural and the urban. More particularly, he argued, architecture must serve civil society, whereas suburbia, in Lewis Mumford's words, 'offers poor facilities for meeting, conversation, collective debate, and common action – it favours silent conformity'. Subtopia made men 'mean – a meany'.[71]

Much of this chimed with Sayer's outlook, and it was clear she relished Nairn's bracing prose. His brief detour into the Lake District can only have strengthened Sayer's sense of the relevance of his argument. Much there displeased him, compounding his political purpose: the same street furniture suffered by the towns of the A34, the same ill-considered architecture. His furious description of the attempt to turn Helvellyn into 'the foothills of the Carpathians' through coniferisation, 'visual sadism at its worst', indicated just how broadly subtopia could be conceived.[72] Sayer's reference to 'painfully suburban white concrete kerbstones' at the Avon reservoir development was surely inspired by this section of *Outrage*; more explicit was the DPA's report titled 'Subtopia on Central Dartmoor' published in October 1956. It was Sayer's most Nairnian intervention and drew on Nairn's particular disdain for subtopian lamp posts designed according to the precepts of 'Municipal Rustic' and identical whether planted in town, country or suburb. Sayer began: 'Princetown, now in possession of extra electric power, wants a new street-lighting scheme.' Historians have examined the electrification of rural Britain as a modernising process, and this observation reminds us that improved infrastructure was enabled by increased energy supply.[73] The establishment of the National Grid and the construction of a new network of power stations facilitated improvements to Princetown's street lighting. The same statist impulse to improve and regularise water supply saw regional water undertakers turn to Dartmoor, later provoking Sayer's most iconic campaigns. She continues: 'Fair enough; its present lamp posts (neglected and unpainted, lamps bent, glass shattered and gas mantles gone: have the convicts had a go at them?) certainly need better maintenance and new electric bulbs. There could be no objection to that.' Here was evidence of the shortcomings of the post-war recovery: decay, neglect and disrepair still evident in the 1950s. Here too was a reminder that rural electrification was mainly a phenomenon of the 1950s and 1960s. An aging infrastructure needed repair and updating, but the local authorities wanted to take things further: 'But what is now proposed by Lydford Parish Council (in whose area Princetown lies) is something very different.' Lydford Parish Council is unusually large, but this does not sound like faceless bureaucracies doing their worst. Local people might well have supported the proposals. What were they? 'It is a *sodium* street-lighting scheme, with new tall posts, to be carried right out of the village centre to the borders of the Moor itself.'

Here Sayer makes two Nairnian observations. One, the posts are disproportionately tall and two, they blur the distinction between town and country. Urban needs bleed into the rural, compromising the distinct character of both. Sodium lighting might look appropriate in Pimlico, Ealing or bordering the Kingston Bypass, she ventured, 'turning night into hideously artificial day', but it was 'grossly ill-chosen for a small village high up on the Dartmoor plateau'. Sayer's insistence that the ascendancy of 'Nature' is Dartmoor's key feature made 'artificial' the key word here. She then argued that the 'exaggerated blare of light in the dark and silent hills would be as great an intrusion in the Dartmoor night as the television mast is in the violated landscape by day'. Here 'exaggerated' is the key term, clarifying her case that the problem is not light itself but its intensity. Notice too her use of 'blare', a word also associated with noise, and how she contrasts the light effect with the 'dark and silent hills'. She takes a dig at the decision made by Two Bridges Hotel to install sodium lights as a vulgar, materialist intrusion ('garish self-advertisement'). Nairn, of course, despised advertising hoardings; Sayer recognised the different forms advertising might take.

For all that post-war British governments promised managed development, local government was responsible for street lighting, and statute provided minimal extra provisions to account for Princetown's position within the national park. Rather than consult the Dartmoor committee, Devon County Council approved the scheme 'without batting an eyelid'; the Ministry of Transport did consult the Dartmoor committee before approving the loan, but the committee, lacking the requisite planning powers, could do no more than ask the parish council to think again. The DPA and the Campaign for the Protection of Rural England (CPRE) apprised the commission, the transport ministry and Housing and Local Government (HLG) of their discontent and raised the issue with the Royal Fine Arts Commission, for this was a question of good design. As Sayer explained, all that was needed was 'a scheme reasonably suited to a country village': 'ordinary electric bulbs, and not mounted on concrete sky-hooks like the new atrocities at Yelverton, but on ordinary lamp posts such as are in use now at Alphington or Chudleigh or a hundred other Devon villages; and *not* a flaring burst of sodium light, like suburb come to Dartmoor.'[74]

Hope was offered by the publication of *Dartmoor: Building in the National Park*, a 64-page booklet published for Devon County Council by the Architectural Press in January 1956. As Sayer explained, the booklet offered advice on siting, design and materials in order to avoid the further spread of houses and bungalows of 'sadly "subtopian" design'.[75] She does not appear to have contributed directly to the booklet's production, but Lord Strang, the chair of the National Parks Commission, wrote the introduction and he certainly sympathised with her point of view.[76] More broadly, its content is worth examining for three main reasons. First, it suggested much about preservationist subjectivities in the 1950s, including the basis on which certain practices and aesthetic preferences were judged 'traditional' and to be maintained; second, it exhibited the strong tendency, so characteristic of the *Architectural Review*, to be both prescriptive and unapologetically judgemental about other people's preferences; and, third, it demonstrated a determination, in spite of all this, to insist that the present should be guided but not bound by the past. The case made was coherent and persuasive, but also exceptionally rigid and somewhat authoritarian. That might seem a stern judgement, but it can be justified by a close look at the booklet. Moreover, to treat the booklet as a historical document, as the product of its time, helps elucidate subjectivities more clearly. What was found objectionable to the preservationist-planners in the 1950s might now seem rather innocuous.

The booklet's purposes were delivered – and perhaps made palatable – through elegant design, blending unaffected photographs, romantic or picturesque illustrations, effective captions and admirably lucid prose. The cover, however, was bold and arresting, invoking the confrontational style of *Outrage*. It showed grazing ponies in an upland landscape dominated by a tor but shaped by long, sloping moorland horizons. Superimposed in bold graphics on this peaceful, if gloomy, black and white photograph were four square, boxy houses of differing styles and a large red question mark. The hard edges of the houses contrasted with the gently undulating lines of the natural environment, and the booklet's opening statement argued that jarring contrasts like these had become common on Dartmoor during the previous 200 years. Before then, Dartmoor buildings had 'harmonised perfectly' with the landscape, growing 'naturally out their surround-ings', but since then '"residential villa" type' houses, built from 'cheap manufactured materials', 'often coloured as blatantly and sited as conspicuously as possible', and indifferent 'to local building traditions and to architectural good manners', had proliferated. This now familiar historical argument, Wordsworthian in its origins, but reinforced by Williams-Ellis and recalling Potter's grumbles, was typical of the preservationist milieu. It was now possible to reverse the trend thanks to the 1947 Town and Country Planning Act. By nationalising land use rights with respect to building, planning authorities now had the opportunity to impose more direction on future developments.

The booklet began its argument with the front endpapers. They showed two OS maps of south Devon inscribed with the national park boundary and anticipated the advice given by the booklet, namely that planning applications for buildings that '*look as if they belonged* to the Dartmoor region' were more likely to be approved. The first map was titled 'Administration' and showed the boundaries of the park's rural and urban district councils; the second was titled

'Geology', and indicated that the bulk of the park sat on 'igneous granite', with some variation on the fringes, including the Culm Measures (sandstone and shale) of the north-east and the Upper Carboniferous slate of the south-east and south-west. Building materials should align with Dartmoor's natural characteristics, particularly its geology, and would ideally be extracted from the moor itself. Proposals that utilised granite and thatch were therefore preferable, except in the Culm Measures where proposals in sympathy with white-washed cob were more likely to find favour. Criteria for siting, design and colour were also adumbrated in terms of pre-modern practices, providing the basis on which plans could be judged to reflect 'traditional principles'. Although these principles were segregationist, once understood and accepted, 'the possibilities of successful and original design' were 'unlimited' and did not preclude modern designs or materials. Any such prohibition would have been at odds with the modernist precepts of the Architectural Press. What Darley and McKie say of Nairn equally applied here. 'Nairn valued, above all else, that harmony of Man's work with Nature's that he saluted wherever he found it throughout his working life. He wanted at all times to see the local and the different prevail over the centrally ordered and mass produced'.[77]

As the booklet's discussion of siting showed, the argument was both aesthetic and moral. Locating a house on the skyline might secure a lovely view for the owner but the negative impact this decision had on the views of others made it not just a selfish act but at odds with the public interest. A well-sited Dartmoor building would 'sit firmly and securely on the ground and seem to grow naturally out of it, fitting in with natural slopes and levels, and never appearing to shoot vertically upward from them'. Trees grouped about the house would 'help it to settle into the scene'. In villages, this must mean a 'neighbourly relationship with existing buildings' in order for the village to retain 'cohesion, character and beauty'.[78] Integration, not disturbance, should be the intention, each new building a communal act rather than an assertion of independence or dominance. To achieve this, equal care needed to be taken with the design, the keystone of which on Dartmoor should be its '*horizontal emphasis*'. Buildings should be long in proportion to width, roof lines should 'harmoniously repeat the long contour-lines of the uplands', and there should be 'no ornamentation, no fussiness, no striving for effect'. The Dartmoor longhouse was clearly the archetype, but the booklet encouraged vernacular idiosyncrasies, such as large porches, sometimes with a second storey, thought to characterise Dartmoor's seventeenth- and eighteenth-century houses. Because they were granite-built and dating from the period just before the apparently external imposition of modernity on Dartmoor they were acceptable. Modern examples that adhered to these principles included the Lutyens house at Stone Cross, Drewsteignton in the Culm Measures and, at a pinch, certain council houses in Bovey Tracey.[79] Slate-hanging, a technique of later vintage, provided a practical defence against the weather and was therefore also judged to provide a traditional cue. Good examples at Princetown were noted. Pebble-dashing, the quintessence of suburbia, was 'never satisfactory'; like decorated wrought iron gates, it was 'utterly alien to Dartmoor'.[80]

Granite could be substituted with concrete blocks, provided they were not very smooth or rusticated but instead of a 'rather coarse texture'. Dressed granite, like that used to build London Bridge, was for export and not for Dartmoor. Granite-faced concrete offered an acceptable cheap alternative to granite. Alternatively, a granite effect could be achieved by colour-washing concrete, and the booklet provided examples of suitable colours and local suppliers. The attractive palette of muted colours included Mist Grey, Tavistock Slate Grey, Moorland Buff, Granite, Lichen Grey, Upland Grey, Old Granite and Trowlsworthy Granite. Granite itself, however, should never be colour-washed and in general upland Dartmoor was not a place for white-washed cottages or 'over-bright colours' or, indeed, for red or pink brickwork or asbestos tiles ('utterly foreign').[81] Of these injunctions, the preference for concrete over brick was most redolent of its time, or perhaps most emblematic of the role played by the Architectural Press in the production of the booklet. The same might be said of the favourable notice given to granite-faced concrete. The injunction against corrugated iron was unrealistic in post-war rural Britain.

In October 1956, Sayer reported in subtopian terms on the positive effect of the booklet. In the early 1940s, the Forestry Commission built a row of foresters' houses at Bellever, one of its largest Dartmoor sites. As relatively affordable freehold properties in an extraordinary setting and charmingly redolent of a previous age, the cottages now represent a very scarce commodity, but Sayer pronounced them 'well-known White Elephants' placed in 'standard formation on the hillside, looking from a distance like rows of china clay outcrops in quite the wrong place'. Perhaps their proximity to Cator caused her most offence. In any case, the Forestry Commission had them 'colour-washed' in 'Granite' and 'Old Granite' and they now looked like '*Dartmoor* cottages, not like new council houses from Anywhere at All'.[82] In the same issue of the DPA newsletter, Sayer promoted Sylvia Crowe's *Tomorrow's Landscape*, another Architectural Press publication, particularly the chapter on 'Open Country', 'burningly applicable to the Dartmoor situation'. Crowe's publication prompted her to comment: 'Although the great mass of the public, sunk in its welfare state of mind and glued to its "telly", remains indifferent to the growing blight of Subtopia, the thinking minority are becoming more active in opposition to it every day'. An obnoxious outburst by any standards, but Sayer was nonetheless right to admire Crowe's 'brilliant book ... as a constructive attempt to show how the blight can be arrested by prompt, resolute and creative action'.[83] Apart from this endorsement, textual evidence suggests Sayer was directly influenced by Crowe.

Axiomatic to Crowe's argument were questions of scale, particularly with respect to the relative impact developments could have on the 'small landscape patterns of most parts of Great Britain'. Increased population densities in the cities and towns created demands that required infrastructural developments that could only be met on a scale that challenged British landscape characteristics, whether they be urban, where 'man is indisputably dominant', rural, where the 'hand of man' is 'guiding rather than dominant', or wild, 'where nature is indisputably dominant, although man, on nature's own terms, may still make his living from it'.[84] Like Nairn before her, these categories – urban, rural and wild – were important to Crowe, for only by recognising different landscape types could the impact of developments be fully anticipated and factored into planning decisions.

Crowe was unusually conscious of the ecological consequences of developments and she emphasised how easily human interventions could, on the one hand, disrupt the delicate balances that sustained ecosystems and particular plant communities, or, on the other, to take two examples, transform 'natural woodland' into 'urban grove' or 'meadowlands' created by good husbandry into a 'neglected pasture of thistles, scrub and tussock'.[85] Crowe could strike a subtopian note, observing that the addition of safety railings could see a 'wild stretch of coast ... pass swiftly into the suburban category',[86] but modern developments were often necessary and could be successful from a landscape perspective if their implications were fully recognised.

Power stations, hydro-electric schemes, huge mineral workings, factories, gasometers and vast areas of conifer forests are all on a scale totally divorced from that of our geologically varied and intimately humanized landscape. We have to accept these new colossi, but in doing so we are faced with the alternatives of either linking them by siting and design with the existing scale or of creating around them a new landscape related to their own scale.[87]

From the perspective of the early twenty-first century, the only site on Dartmoor where a new landscape has been created on a scale to accommodate modern infrastructure is at Burrator, where the Victorian reservoir, with its fine masonry dam, is now surrounded by mature conifer plantations with attractive mixed planting at the edges. Thanks to the undulating road circumnavigating the reservoir, Burrator is a popular leisure site, particularly attractive to cyclists seeking somewhere safe to complete demanding laps. The passage of time, especially with respect to the forestry works, has allowed a degree of naturalisation to occur, making this closely managed land-scape a distinctive habitat.[88] But the setting also adds to the positive effect. The reservoir is enclosed by the surrounding tors and the highest point, Sharpitor, is almost 200 metres above the surface of the water; the six peaks have been kept clear of tree cover. As Crowe allowed, forestry in the valleys could often have a positive visual effect, and Burrator might now be thought to constitute a 'magnifi-cent composition',[89] rather like the Elan Valley in Wales, whose 'scenic beauty' Crowe thought had probably been enhanced by the great reservoirs and dams serving Birmingham that 'none the less removed it from the category of the wild into a region where the impact of the city can be sensed'.[90] Forestry, then, was not necessarily objectionable if the individual needs of particular landscapes were not ignored by 'our mass-produced civilisation'.[91] Of conifer planta-tions in two sites in the Brecon Beacons, Crowe observed that what would despoil steep escarpments might 'absorb the jarring elements and restore a feeling of peace' to the already busy valley floor.[92]

In general, though, Crowe's chapter on 'Open Country', which she sometimes referred to as 'wild country', sounded a warning that chimed with Sayer's thinking and broader preservationist ideas that dated back at least as far as Octavia Hill's earliest interventions in the Open Spaces debate. Industrialisation intensified the human psycho-logical and spiritual need for 'wild' landscapes, which posed an espe-cial planning challenge in the national parks. Enabling access meant new car parks, public toilets, accommodation and signage, and risked spreading elsewhere the urban 'holiday camp atmosphere' already evident at Windermere in the Lake District.[93] Such concerns were continuous with Sayer's objections to villa-style housing. Like new housing, tourist infrastructure imposed urban needs on wild country.

More threatening, however, were the extractive demands of the city, which pictured the uplands as a resource. If wildness was not to be lost altogether, it was vital for planners to take account of the peculiar scale effect achieved by British upland landscapes where the 'feeling of grandeur' was 'out of all proportion to the true size of their hills'.[94] Planning in 'Open Country', Crowe argued, had to be largely negative, preventing 'all intrusion of the city element'.[95] Vast human structures that reified the sublime scale of the mountainous regions of Switzerland or the USA served only to expose the diminutive scale of British landscapes. These arguments recalled Sayer's objections to the erection of the television mast at North Hessary Tor; she had been concerned that it was not possible to capture the importance of North Hessary Tor in a photograph. It was 'deceptively unspectacular', she wrote, 'having no startling crags or beetling precipices', and although on a clear day a good photograph was possible, this was no substitute for 'personal observation'.[96] As Crowe argued, ill-conceived interventions served 'as a measuring rod to dispel the magic of illusion': 'as soon as the proportion of man's handiwork is great enough to challenge nature's supremacy, the spell of the wild is broken'.[97] Crowe made this crucial point repeatedly. Human structures in 'wild country' that served 'local needs' generally did not break the 'spell of the wild' because their scale was proportional to the populations they helped sustain.[98] Writing from a Marxist perspective, Raymond Williams made a similar argument that contrasted the scale of the environment made by a family farming over generations to meet its needs and the vast transformations brought about by the exploitative practices of a wealthy landowner establishing an elegant country estate.[99] By contrast, 'the category of works whose scale and purpose belong to the city' had a disproportionate effect on the landscape because these works served the new materialism of scaled-up urban populations, including energy and water supply, as well as consumer products.[100] Crucially, the expectations of the urban consumer could be met only if large extractive demands were made on non-urban places. Crowe's most arresting formulation concerned mineral workings, which equally applied to the impact of the china clay workings on Dartmoor and recalled London's designs on Dartmoor in the 1890s. Forestry could make a 'constructive addition to the landscape' whereas mineral workings transferred 'the wealth of the hills to the cities': its 'object' and 'manner of working' was 'wholly urban'.[101]

Sayer continued to beat the subtopia drum. In early 1959, she directly framed 'the work of preservation' in terms of the questions roused by *Outrage* and its successor, *Counter-Attack Against Subtopia*, which provided copious examples of contrastingly good and bad design. She felt public opinion was increasingly with them. The Civic Trust was a good augury; it was established in 1957 by the Conservative politician Duncan Sandys in response to *Outrage* to challenge the 'characterless urban sprawl which is disfiguring both town and country'.[102] She was also pleased that a series of articles in the *Field* entitled 'Campaign for the Countryside' included favourable mention of the DPA. Still, they could not afford to be complacent. 'As long as the statutory planning machinery continues to creak through faulty design and operation, so long will the Association's work continue at a high tempo.'[103]

The prospect of a general election in 1959 saw Sayer warn readers against the materialist promises of the politicians. The electorate would be 'stunned and deafened by promises of more and bigger roads, bombs, TV stations, sputniks, cars, sports stadiums, and all the other bribes intended to capture the maximum numbers of votes, whether of criminals or countesses'. From a 'cash and comfort point of view', she wrote, 'we have never had it so good', alluding to Harold Macmillan's famous speech, but 'the beauty of the countryside has never had it so bad'. Politicians of all parties needed to be asked the same questions. What would their party do 'to prevent the spread of

Subtopia?'. Does it favour amending statute to strengthen the National Parks Commission? Does it favour spending money to save 'beautiful woodlands', bury 'ugly cables', and 'save lovely old buildings from demolition'?[104]

These were good questions. In the late 1950s, attempts by backbench MPs to strengthen the statutory powers of the national park authorities and improve their finances were not supported by the government.[105] Instead, as the 1950s gave way to the 1960s, the 'tempo' of the DPA's work would ratchet up considerably. The threat from 'subtopia' faded from view as the training demands of the armed forces, the expansionist ambitions of the Forestry Commission and the needs of Devon's water undertakers provided Sayer with the fights that defined her career as an activist and established her reputation on the national stage. Throughout, she insisted – often successfully – that organisations like the DPA had a right to be heard in disputes that affected the use of private land.

Locus Standi

Locus standi is the right or ability to bring a legal action to a court of law. To claim *locus standi* an individual must have a 'sufficient interest', or legal right in the matter at hand, that will be violated if the decision goes a particular way. A private individual cannot legally contest a private action solely on the grounds that they find the action concerning. Conversely, unless expressly provided by statute, a private person cannot bring an ordinary civil action to assert a right owed to the public generally; only the Attorney General can assert a legally established public right through an ordinary civil action. In other words, once a public right is established in law, it is the responsibility of the government to ensure that a private or public actor does not violate that right.[106]

The principle of *locus standi* is also applied to the right of an individual or organisation to petition against a government order. Such orders might arise from the successful passage of private bills, but government orders also became an essential development tool of post-war governments, and on numerous occasions amenity societies contested development orders through the petitioning mechanism, forcing the government to look again. It thus came as a shock in 1967 when the petition submitted by the DPA and other amenity organisations against the order to establish a reservoir in north-west Dartmoor was ruled inadmissible by parliament on the grounds that the amenity societies did not have sufficient interest in the valley to claim *locus standi*. As will be shown, the subsequent debate in the Lords established that the ruling was technically correct, but influential voices urged that standing orders be amended because this interpretation cut across their spirit and – with respect to the amenity societies – customary practice established since 1910. Proponents of reform claimed that a rigid interpretation of *locus standi* was at odds with the necessary role civil society organisations played in a democratic society, particularly one in which the government made frequent use of statutory instruments to enable significant infrastructural developments.

A less technical or legalistic understanding of *locus standi* also provides a way of making sense of the campaigns led by Sayer and the DPA. Her opposition to the establishment on Dartmoor of new reservoirs and conifer plantations, and her attempt to see greater controls placed on the military's use of the moor as a training ground, saw her effectively claim *locus standi* on behalf of the DPA. Although briefly a technical question with respect to the reservoir controversy, in the main this was not the case, and the degree to which the DPA established itself as an organisation that official bodies had to take account of reflected the determination and commitment of its activists. Sayer was foremost in this regard and her capacity to help set the terms of the debate infuriated officials; their private responses to her effectiveness often evidenced how highly disruptive her activism could be.

277

Her tactics were simple but effective. She spoke to the press, and in her capacity as chair of the DPA submitted memoranda to multiple government agencies including the National Parks Commission. By deploying her very considerable ability and through sheer force of will, Sayer made herself a person of consequence. Just as the commission, impressed by the coherence of the DPA's position, often requested the Forestry Commission, the water undertakers or the armed services answer her charges, so too senior figures in those agencies sought assurance from juniors acquainted with the situation on the ground that Sayer's claims might be rebutted. Government agencies looking to exploit Dartmoor could reasonably expect to take account of the views of the park authorities, but for the commission to become the mouthpiece for Sayer and the DPA, or to insist that her views were taken into account, was an extraordinary achievement.

Legal specialists, including specialists in environmental law or parliamentary proceduralists, might object to this loose use of the meaning of *locus standi*. It is certainly less precise and more meta-phorical than formal legal uses, but whatever the particular focus of environmental activism in the immediate post-war decades – Sayer retired as chair of the DPA in 1973 – always at stake was the claim, dating back at least as far as Octavia Hill's activism, that the natural environment was a form of public good whose protection must be assured. By 1939, the extractive needs of the Forestry Commission and the regional water companies were already being met by Dartmoor, but as these needs intensified in the 1950s and 1960s, so confrontations between Sayer and a string of statutory organisations and private interests became common. More charac-teristic still was the vigilance with which she and the DPA moni-tored the use of Dartmoor as a training ground by the armed forces. The degree to which she set the terms of the debate now seems scarcely credible, but the evidence is in the government files. In each case, she effectively claimed *locus standi* on behalf of the DPA as a body representing the national park interest, which she understood to be the interest not of 'cranks or fanatics but ordinary, hard-working, well-balanced, reasonable people'.[107]

The Reservoir Battles

Much of Britain's water supply originates in the uplands, and Devon is no exception. The rivers Dart, Teign, Tavy, Okemont, Walkham, Meavy, Avon and Plym have their origins in High Dartmoor, and as long as there have been human beings in Devon attempts have been made to harness these apparently inexhaustible supplies. The modern use of Dartmoor's water began in the late sixteenth century with the cutting of leats (small canals), important to the development of Plymouth, but most iconic today are Dartmoor's reservoirs. Just as Manchester's and Birmingham's growing demand for water made the Lake District and the Welsh uplands sites of preservationist conflict, so Plymouth and the Torbay area did the same to Dartmoor. A string of reservoirs was established on Dartmoor between 1861 and 1957, the two most iconic being Burrator (established 1898, enlarged 1929), which supplies Plymouth, and Fernworthy (1942), which supplies Torquay; a handful of others mostly supply the Torbay area (Tottiford, 1861; Kennick, 1884; Venford, 1907; Trenchford, 1907; and the Avon Dam, 1957).[108] Storage reservoirs regulate seasonal water flow in order to ensure that a sufficient volume of water can be extracted from the rivers downstream. This has significant ecological effects, not least on migratory fish species; to use Sayer's preferred term, each reservoir 'denatures' the rivers, establishing what Sara Pritchard calls a new envirotechnical regime.[109]

When the Avon Dam was approved in the teeth of DPA opposition, Sayer scolded the 'enterprising water engineer' and belittled the 'average official mind' for regarding Dartmoor's rivers as 'no more than useful water conduits provided by a thoughtful Providence solely as material for enterprising exploitation'.[110] As the disputes of the 1950s gave way to the high-profile conflicts of the 1960s, Sayer increasingly framed her critique of officialdom in terms of its techno-cratic materialism and inability to recognise Dartmoor's unique quali-ties. Sayer's contempt could carry a gendered subtext, impugning the masculinity of the small-minded, middle-aged male official uncom-prehendingly encountering the moor in the wrong clothes and shoes, an enfeebled urban counterpart to his rural brethren – an echo here of Potter's disdain for overweight women wearing inappropriate foot-wear. Still, Devon's 'water undertakers' did not always get their own way. When Torquay sought permission to pipe water from the North Teign and East Dart to Fernworthy Reservoir, a rare show of unity by the DPA, the National Farmers' Union, the Dartmoor Commoners' Association and local government representatives convinced the government to reject the proposal. By contrast, the DPA's opposition to the North Devon Water Board's decision to extract water from the underground lake at Taw Marsh near Belstone in north Dartmoor was to no avail. In both cases, the DPA emphasised the negative ecological consequences of the schemes, namely reduced water flow in the two rivers and a lowered water table at Taw Marsh. When the yield at Taw Marsh proved just a third of that hoped for and high levels of radiation – a consequence of Dartmoor granite – necessitated an aeration plant that emitted radon gas, this meant that the water board had to look elsewhere if it was to meet its needs.[111]

The DPA gamely floated the idea that shallow aquifers might be the solution, as had been adopted by the South Devon Water Board at Totnes. It was unlikely that the North Devon Water Board scoured the DPA newsletter for advice. Instead, the board's favoured solution was a storage reservoir and, after examining various sites on the West Okemont, it settled on the valley at Meldon in the north-west corner of the national park. Objections to the board's plan to make explora-tory boreholes prompted Keith Joseph, Minister of Housing and Local Government, to call a local public inquiry, which was held on 1 January 1963. Bad weather prevented witnesses from attending – 'a routine farce', according to the DPA – and Joseph duly approved the plans.[112] During the summer of 1964, the board applied to Joseph for the order and Devon County Council for planning consent. Labour's victory in the 1964 general election slowed these processes down, but in January 1965, Richard Crossman, Joseph's successor, ordered a local public inquiry.

Opposition to the reservoir scheme united the DPA, the CPRE, the Devon River Board and, most importantly, Devon County Council and the Dartmoor committee. Sayer represented the DPA and, like other objectors, emphasised not just the irreplaceable natural beauty of the valley, but also its 'wildness and splendour', what another DPA witness called its 'primitive' character. The inquiry report acknowledged these arguments, accepting they had to be weighed in the balance, but the more significant achievement of the objectors was their promotion of Gorhuish, north-west of Okehampton, as an alternative site. After much procrastination, Crossman signed the order, got a very bad press and, following legal advice, objections were lodged by the CPRE, the Commons, Open Spaces and Footpaths Preservation Society, the Ramblers' Association, the Youth Hostel Association, the Dartmoor Rambling Club, the Exeter Rambling Club, the Dartmoor Rangers and the DPA. The Meldon Appeal Fund was quickly established, for the amenity societies would need to hire counsel if they were to have any chance of success before a parliamentary select committee.

It was at this point that the right of the amenity societies to claim *locus standi* was denied. In essence, the board sought a ministerial order for the compulsory purchase of the land, but it was not clear on what basis the amenity societies could claim they would be 'injuriously affected' by the decision. In parliament, Lord Molson, a close ally of the amenity societies, took up their cause. Conservative MP for High Peak (1939–61), Molson had enjoyed a ministerial career before being made a life peer; he was also chairman of the CPRE's Standing Committee on National Parks and later acted as the organisation's chair and president. On 4 April 1967, he asked that the compulsory purchase order be annulled on the grounds that denying the amenity societies a hearing was in breach of parliamentary standing orders. His intervention was successful, and the order was withdrawn until the procedural question was settled.[113]

During the subsequent debate in the Lords, Molson argued that the decision to deny the amenity societies a hearing went against precedents dating back to 1910. He cited numerous occasions when the *locus standi* of the amenity societies had been accepted without demur.[114] Molson got a sympathetic hearing, though some peers took the opportunity provided by the debate to comment on the individual case rather than the procedural principles. Take as an example Lord Clifford of Chudleigh, 12th baron, direct descendant of the Norman invader and inheritor of Ugbrook House and Estate. He was keen for restrictions to be imposed on the DPA's right to be heard. The association was a nuisance: 'these people oppose anybody planting a tree. There is a continual abuse of Her Majesty's Services. There is a perpetual irritant to the public services and local government officials.' It is always instructive when a hereditary peer, whose views on most issues can be preserved in *Hansard* should they so wish, objects to others being heard in the public square. 'So far as we in Devon are concerned,' he continued, 'the joke of the year was when we heard that somebody was complaining that this society had not been heard. We never get a moment's rest from hearing about them.'[115] How their Lordships must have chuckled, but Sayer would not have been displeased by this further evidence of the DPA's effectiveness.

Lord Listowel, Chairman of Committees, sympathised with Molson's position but explained that the decision had been correct. The matter came down to a technical distinction between an order made following the passage of a private bill, for which the *locus standi* of a petitioner only had to be established if challenged by the promoter, and a Special Procedure Order, which required that the chair of the select committee scrutinising the bill establish that each petitioner had *locus standi* by acting in a local representative capacity.[116]

The Meldon order fell into the latter category, meaning the decision to deny petitioners a right to be heard did not break with precedent but instead reflected the different standing orders that applied to these orders. With respect to private bills, promoters rarely invoked the principle of *locus standi*, likely because governments indicated that they did not take kindly to being required to adjudicate on who might be heard in a private bill process. In any case, the most striking aspect of these proceedings was the readiness of the government to amend the standing orders of both Houses so the same procedures applied in both cases, thereby making it less likely that *locus standi* would be denied to the amenity societies. Just a month later, motions were duly passed in both Houses, and although Molson regarded them as a stopgap, these procedures had the desired effect.[117]

The reason for dwelling on these arcane matters is this. The debate about the *locus standi* of the amenity societies exposed how the planning apparatus, from local public inquiries through to petitioning against a government order, was predicated on local rather than national interests, and these local interests were generally assumed to be material in nature. What impact would a development have on local economic interests? Molson claimed in a letter to *The Times*, however, that the interests of the amenity societies could be 'injuriously affected' by an order, though he did not state explicitly that to make such a claim meant accepting a more generous notion of what constituted 'interest'.[118] One thinks of Sayer's scathing account of the etiolated gaze of the engineer onto the landscape, but more importantly was the national significance statute attached to national park landscapes. When Sayer wrote up the DPA's account of 'The Meldon Story', the most substantial text the association has ever produced, she drew attention to the absence of local opposition to the scheme, citing the indifference of the smaller local authorities and 'the farming community of Devon', who 'appear to regard wild moorland almost with hostility'.[119] The amenity societies had an essential role to play, therefore, if national park principles were to be upheld. Despite this, and notwithstanding the personal politics of some MPs and peers, both Houses accepted that the amenity societies did have a right to be heard. When the Lords examined the problem again in 1972, it was generally accepted that the amenity societies did represent a significant tranche of public opinion and had an important role to play in a democratic society committed to greater 'public participation' in decision-making processes. As Lord Sandford observed, these questions had become pressing because the increased provision of universal services by the state (electricity, gas, roads, water) made great demands on the land and had seen the private bill gradually superseded by the creation of statutory instruments that empowered ministers to make compulsory purchase orders.[120]

Being heard, of course, was no more than that. There would be further twists and turns to the Meldon story. The amenity societies did succeed in persuading the nervous select committee to require that the water board investigate the Gorhuish site and the DPA caused further delays by raising concerns about the presence of arsenic in the soil, a legacy of nineteenth-century industry, but when Devon County Council withdrew its opposition following the publication of the order and the coordination of statements of support for the proposal by the local rural, urban and borough councils of North Devon in August and September 1968, confirmation was near inevitable. Works began in March 1970.

Meldon was the most significant single defeat suffered by the DPA during Sayer's long service as chair of the DPA. The *locus standi* of the amenity societies had been established, but the valley was lost. Photographs in *The Meldon Story* comparing the before and after effect of the dam are moving. Affecting in a different way was the decision to personify the process by reproducing a photograph of the chair of the water board, dressed for the city, being interviewed for television. The camera and sound operators are in sharp focus, busy with their modern equipment, the 'primitive' valley is blurred in the background. Those city clothes are intended to signify ignorance of

Dartmoor, and Sayer sarcastically described this 'little Water Board Napoleon' celebrating 'his moment of triumph by pressing a button and blowing up a tree'.[121] Nothing, alas, alters the fact that in 1972, a decade after the board had turned its attention to Meldon, a valve was closed, and the valley was converted into a water storage container.

This small but momentous gesture came in the aftermath of Sayer's greatest victory. Such was the anger at the Meldon decision that when the water undertakers for Plymouth and South-West Devon turned their attention to Dartmoor, lodging a private bill for the creation of a reservoir at Swincombe in the heart of the moor in 1969, the political atmosphere could not have been less friendly. Burrator Reservoir, Dartmoor's largest, has a surface area of 150 acres; the Swincombe scheme proposed a reservoir with a surface area of 745 acres. The amenity societies, local and national, were stunned by the ambition of the scheme but soon set to work as might be expected. Official opinion was also perturbed, and the strikingly emotive response to the proposal by a regional planning officer, which touched on technocratic considerations but concluded that an intervention on this scale would be morally wrong, presaged the eventual decision made by the parliamentary select committee. The bill was thrown out in December 1970, and much credit was afforded to Sayer's performance before the select committee, modest compensation for what many took to be the UK's disappointing response to Europe's first 'Year of Conservation'.[122]

For Dartmoor aficionados, it is scarcely conceivable that the Swincombe decision could have gone any other way. Nothing in the intervening period has invalidated the planning officer's judgement that Swincombe is 'magnificent in its forbidding qualities and uncompromising in its attitude'.[123] But Swincombe is a harder sell than Meldon. Sayer might have been amazed by the failure of the 'old men' in the council, those 'utter barbarians', to see that Swincombe was one of Dartmoor's 'loveliest valleys', but it did not always make a particularly favourable impression on journalists.[124] Whereas the river valleys of Dartmoor's peripheries are accessible, conventionally beautiful and popular with visitors, Swincombe is a vast shallow bowl, often referred to as an 'amphitheatre', dominated by molinia grass with hardly a tor in sight. 'Part swamp, part showing residual traces of tin mining,' wrote one journalist, 'it is mainly moorland speckled with sheep, sheeps' carcasses, cattle, and wild ponies.'[125]

Nonetheless, a reservoir on this scale at Swincombe, including new roads and other infrastructure, would have constituted a vast concrete eyesore and gross inconvenience, radically disrupting passage by foot or horseback across this part of the moor. These are subjective judgements, of course, that reflect ways of valuing the moor at odds with what Sayer considered the materialism of the water boards, but to follow Sylvia Crowe's prescriptions, it seems plausible to argue that a colossal intervention like the proposed reservoir could not have been integrated into the existing landscape according to existing aesthetic conventions. It was out of scale. Only the transformation of the landscape itself would prevent the reservoir remaining a vast incongruity. In 1970, it was likely that commercial forestry would be considered the best means to bring this about, but rather than the compact form of the reservoir-forestry complex at Burrator, Swincombe's transformation would be on the vast sprawling scale since seen at Kielder Water in Northumberland. Such a high modernist transformation would be at odds with national park principles, and it is no coincidence that Kielder Water is in a forest park rather than a national park. Such a transformation would also have been contrary to the general direction of travel with respect to commercial forestry on Dartmoor.

In December 1979, a *Guardian* journalist recalled Sayer's performance before the select committee, replete with map showing encroachments on the moor, writing that she saved Swincombe 'almost single-handed'. That might be an exaggeration, but it also overlooks the fact that the air of finality associated with the 1970 decision had come to seem in doubt. In April 1978, Sayer rose to the defence of

Swincombe one more time. Like Stengator, near Black Tor Copse in the West Okemont Valley, it was among the sites proposed by South-West Water for a new reservoir. Another protracted process, another agonising wait, another ministerial decision. In 1983, Roadford was selected, a site to the west of Okehampton and outside the national park. It is an open question whether any government really could have chosen Swincombe or Stengator, but the vast austerities of Roadford Lake, little softened by landscaping, tell something of Swincombe's fate had things gone the other way.[126]

Forestry

In the face of stiff resistance from the DPA and other amenity organisations, the Forestry Commission secured a firm foothold on the moor during the 1930s through the acquisition of two substantial sites on High Dartmoor, the Duchy's 800-acre plantation at Fernworthy and the ancient tenement at Bellever, duly coniferised in the 1930s. At the end of the war, the commission leased, fenced, deep-ploughed and planted Soussons Down and took over the management of the Plymouth Corporation planting at Burrator Reservoir.[127] Little did the Forestry Commission know that Soussons Down would prove to be its last major acquisition on Dartmoor. Not only did the establishment of the national park subject the Forestry Commission's every move to scrutiny by the Dartmoor committee, but the extraordinary tenacity of Sayer, the DPA and its allies ensured that apparently marginal decisions about Dartmoor forestry became questions for the National Parks Commission and occasionally government ministers. No other group of senior officials were more infuriated by Sayer than the regional and national leadership of the Forestry Commission. By helping generate adverse publicity for the commission's determination to expand its Dartmoor footprint, she successfully inserted the DPA into the debate, strengthening the association's symbiotic relationship with the National

Parks Commission and disrupting the cosy complicity between the foresters and landowners.

At issue was the Forestry Commission's renewed sense of purpose, as enabled by the tools placed at its disposal by the Forestry Act 1947. The first tool was the old one, namely the acquisition of new free-holds on which new conifer plantations could be established. On Dartmoor, the extent of common land radically narrowed the Forestry Commission's options, but energetic forestry officers sought out such opportunities, negotiating with landowners who might be ready to sell unproductive land. The second tool proved more efficacious. The Forestry Commission could persuade private landowners to 'dedicate' in perpetuity suitable parcels of land, including existing woodlands, to forestry. Once the commission and the proprietor agreed a plan of operation the proprietor became eligible for planting grants, including 'scrub clearance' grants (1953–63), and an annual management grant. Outweighing these incentives, however, were related tax breaks. As Sayer came to understand – and as D.C. Nicholls argued in an essential paper based on research undertaken in the early 1960s – income tax concessions were of greater importance than government grants in incentivising forestry expansion, without which many proprietors would not have embarked on timber production. Losses incurred through forestry operations and management could be set against other incomes while further incentives made the sale of timber virtually tax-free. Crucially, these tax incentives were of significant value only if the landowner had sufficient income from other sources to offset against forestry losses. As Nicholls argued, a proprietor paying the highest rate of income tax and the surtax could receive a tax rebate of up to 17s 9d (89p) for every pound invested, rendering the effective cost of reforestation about an eighth of its actual cost – Sayer quoted the same figure in a letter to the press in 1960.[128] In Devon and Cornwall, where commercial forestry was undeveloped, the general pattern was not afforestation but the application of plans of operations to existing forested areas, mostly affecting the management of what foresters considered poor-quality, over mature or scrub hardwoods. Sometimes these woods were thinned but more typically policy incentivised clear-felling, the sale of existing woodland timber and its replanting with fast-growing softwoods.

To the purveyors of 'economic forestry', Dartmoor was ripe for exploitation. Private forestry companies brought a new dynamism to these processes by forming alliances with businesspeople and landowners, traduced in Sayer's lexicon of evil as 'syndicates'. Wistman's Wood, the relict dwarf oak woodland on High Dartmoor, looms large in the public imagination as the quintessential Dartmoor woodland, but it was the potential locked up in the river valley woodlands fringing the high moor that most excited speculators. Usually some combination of oak, ash, beech, birch and chestnut, these woodlands had generally suffered decades of neglect and were considered ripe for 'dedication' by the commercial interest. The priorities of the Nature Conservancy obviously differed, but it too considered Dartmoor's most ecologically valuable woodlands sorely in need of management. Local authorities could restrain forestry operations by placing tree protection orders on individual trees, but compensation was owed if this prevented a dedication, and the Forestry Commission needed the permission of the Dartmoor committee to proceed with new planting or a dedication, but officials were generally well-disposed towards enabling use of the 1947 Act. Like agricultural operations, forestry operations were not subject to planning controls and, outside of the national park context, were largely at the discretion of the landowner. If the Dartmoor committee agreed, and the National Parks Commission did not object, coniferisation could take place, but when there was no agreement, the minister might order a local public inquiry, at which point non-statutory bodies like the DPA and the CPRE, as well as members of the public, could expect their views to be heard.

Sayer opposed the clear-felling or coniferisation of any part of Dartmoor. Forestry provoked her strongest segregationist instincts.

As early as June 1949, she described to readers of *The Times* how she saw 'with grief and anger the alien works of man – the Forestry Commission's State-regulated conifer reserves – whose creeping advance is insidiously changing the whole aspect, character and ancient usage of the moor'.[129] She was also exasperated by the narrow use that could be made of the Forestry Commission's expertise. When it refused to take over the management of a woodland site at Bovey Tracey at the request of the Dartmoor committee, she decried its refusal to do anything 'other than the cutting-out from normal hill-country life of considerable acreages in which pasturage, commoners' rights, and free access come alike to a gloomy and sterile end'.[130] The commonplace view that coniferisation was of foreign inspiration found expression in her claim that most people wanted Dartmoor, the Lakes and the Peaks to 'remain identifiable as themselves, and not be disguised as hybrid imitations of Switzerland or Germany'.[131] And when in 1952 Dudley Stamp had the temerity to suggest that the best use for Dartmoor might be recreation and forestry, Sayer retorted that 'there is as much opportunity for recreation in a close-set conifer plantation as there is in a railway tunnel'.[132] Particularly provoking was the DPA's 1954 memorandum, 'Suggested Woodlands Policy for the Dartmoor National Park', copied to the Duchy, the Forestry Commission, the Nature Conservancy and the CPRE. It argued that all new planting and clear-felling should cease because it caused erosion and flooding, harmed the 'natural living conditions' of the park's flora and fauna, partly by lowering the water table, inhibited free access and destroyed hill-farming, Dartmoor's 'most ancient and appropriate' use. In bad-tempered private responses, the Forestry Commission rejected these claims, but senior figures were quick to recognise that Sayer needed careful handling. Their written response went through several drafts before senior figures were happy that it was sufficiently conciliatory.[133]

The DPA was not easily pacified. It raged against 'licensed arboricide' when private landowners felled 'hedgerow trees', complained repeatedly that the Forestry Commission planted on antiquities, and amplified rumours – dating back to the 1930s – that the commission aspired to connect the Fernworthy and Bellever plantations through a new programme of planting and then connect this vastly enlarged plantation to Moretonhampstead by cutting a new road across open moorland. Sayer, however, was always ready to acknowledge the benefits of cooperation and once the rumours were scotched and an agreement was reached on leaving antiquities exposed – some existing conifers were felled – the DPA trumpeted a new age of cooperation.[134] This proved short-lived. Tempers at the Forestry Commission began to fray when DPA lobbying helped rouse the National Parks Commission to thwart Forestry Commission plans to coniferise three ancient enclosures at Cuckoo Bell, Swine Down and Trendelbere Down.[135] As had been the case in Northumberland, the foresters thought site visits by senior officials might convince the park interest that mature plantations were an asset. The requisite politesse was deployed, but differences were unresolved. Senior Forestry Commission officials privately agreed that the park authorities would need to be fought on a case-by-case basis.[136]

Opposition to the proposed clear-felling and coniferisation of Buckland Woods, a 300-acre woodland clothing the Dart and Webburn valleys above Holne Bridge, made it a cause célèbre. As Sayer explained to readers of *The Times* in January 1959, the site had recently been bought by a firm of timber speculators, and the Dartmoor committee had responded by placing a tree preservation order on the woods, subsequently withdrawn, allegedly following pressure from the industry. With the clear-fell of 300 acres of oak and beech and the significant thinning of a further 150 acres imminent, Sayer called on the public to demand a ministerial intervention.[137] Frank Hayman, Labour MP for Falmouth and Camborne and one of parliament's most faithful Dartmoor preservationists, prodded Sir Henry Brooke, the minister, to report on the number of protests received opposing the proposed developments. Five organisations and 180 individuals, came the answer, including seven petitions signed by 437 people. Hayman followed up several weeks later by demanding a public inquiry; Lord Chorley brought the issue to the attention of the Lords.[138]

New members and donations flowed into the DPA, which publicly criticised the 'defeatist' park committee for again demonstrating that 'it simply does not represent amenity interests in Devon'. On-site meetings between officials indicated that the park committee did not plan to rescind the felling licence, raising the prospect of the National Parks Commission breaking with the park committee.[139] In the event, the commission opted for compromise, requesting that the size of the clear-felled area be reduced, and the basis of the replanting be 40 per cent hardwood. Brooke was keen to make an irritating problem disappear and approved the plan on the basis of a 15 per cent hardwood replanting, eventually raised to 25 per cent, prompting the DPA to scorn 'ministerialese' and lament the 'sacrifice' of 'the essential character and beauty' of Buckland Woods: '800 acres of lovely mixed woodlands will be exchanged for one enormous conifer expanse (with a sad little fringe of beeches here and there)'.[140]

Sayer's hostility to 'syndicates' intensified. Official language, the DPA argued, obscured realities. Exploiting tax incentives was euphemised as 'investing in forestry', Dartmoor's oak forests were labelled 'scrub' fit only for firewood, and woodlands valued by the Nature Conservancy needed to be 'regenerated' or 'rehabilitated'; the 'commercial forestry expert', standing beneath the shade of a beech or an oak, was mocked for claiming that the land was unsuitable for growing hardwoods. Companies like Foxbury Estates Ltd, Fountain Forestry Ltd, and above all Economic Forestry Ltd, and their specialist agents, joining forces with established lobby groups like the Country Landowners' Association and the Timber Growers' Organisation and a secretive new generation of landowners – bankers and industrialists – cared nothing for the natural beauty of Dartmoor or national park principles. The DPA emphasised the London addresses of the commercial forestry groups, their wide-ranging financial interests (which included, but were not limited to, the timber industry) and the role played in their management by accountants and financiers.[141]

Signs that the government might reconstitute the Forestry Commission so it could promote commercial forestry *and* conserve and manage 'amenity woodlands' were warmly received, but a Treasury veto and new threats from syndicates chasing dedications put an end to that momentary optimism. A notional compromise was reached over three adjacent sites in the south of the moor – permission was granted for the coniferisation of two – but the felling of mature decid-uous woodland or the planting of moorland always registered as a loss for the preservationists.[142] Once again, the DPA saw a precious resource being squandered at the behest of a government that did not under-stand its value. Whitehall mandarins might see moorland as 'marginal land', but the fundamental position of the preservationists remained that its utility could not be expressed in monetary terms. Sayer linked the issue to contemporary concerns. Politicians concerned by the state of the nation's youth might talk of the need for 'adventure training', for 'open-air recreation'; they might even claim that 'open-air recreation' might combat delinquency ('boredom', it was alleged, 'is the worst enemy of the law'), but if the UK's 'wild uplands' were further industri-alised or 'denatured' the character-building challenges to be met on Dartmoor would become no greater than 'a picnic on Wimbledon Common'.[143]

Forestry Commission attempts to repair the reputational damage caused by these conflicts, not least by appointing Sylvia Crowe as its first landscape architect in 1963, could not obscure how the dedica-tion system and government incentives ensured it remained in hock to private commercial interests. When Sayer publicly claimed that Economic Forestry Ltd had contravened the wishes of the planning authority and the Ministry of Works by coniferising an Iron Age hill camp, planting within three feet of a prehistoric stone circle, over-planting two prehistoric hut circles and running a wire fence through a prehistoric village, a senior Forestry Commission official felt moved to establish that her claims were false. 'Knowing Lady Sayer by repute I can imagine that her statements are not too rigidly related to the truth,' H.A. Turner wrote to Alan Connell, Forestry Commission South-West Conservator, 'but it would be useful if you could tell me.'[144] Connell duly assured his boss this was indeed so, a response typical of the official encounter with Sayer, but she was not to be so easily dismissed, as Connell discovered to his cost over the course of the 1960s.

Connell feared that the preservationists had made Dartmoor forestry so difficult that it was likely that landowners and investors would simply turn their attention elsewhere, significantly narrowing the terrain on which the Forestry Commission could fulfil its statutory obligations. Despite pressure from the National Parks Commission and the amenity societies, the Conservative government, like future Labour governments, remained unwilling to subject forestry to formal planning processes, demonstrating its ideological commitment to voluntarism by supporting the 'gentlemen's agreement' of January 1961 that required the park authorities and the Forestry Commission to work together to agree all dedications. The 'gentlemen's agreement' was soon in disarray when it transpired that Pudsham Down, a 173-acre site north of Buckland Woods, bought by Fountain Forestry before the agreement was made, would not be approved for dedication by the National Parks Commission. There was talk at the Forestry Commission about a high-level fix on the grounds that Fountain Forestry had acted in good faith – perhaps Mr Ryle could have a chat with Sir Henry? – but it was hard not to see a degree of denialism at work here. Fundamental differences could not be so easily resolved.[145]

And so it proved. Connell's pursuit of an agreed Afforestation Survey for Dartmoor, emulating their successful promulgation in the Snowdonia and Northumberland national parks, proved just how difficult this terrain had become. As elsewhere, the purpose of the survey was not to establish a clear plan for afforestation but to minimise the likelihood of future controversy by identifying those parts of Dartmoor sites where public bodies could agree that forestry might be acceptable. On this basis, the Forestry Commission hoped it could secure freeholds or agree dedications without becoming repeatedly locked into fierce local conflicts. Whereas in Northumberland the survey had been quickly agreed, only for Dower to oppose further dedications, on Dartmoor the agreement process itself proved contentious and protracted. Sayer, the DPA and the CPRE kept the pressure on, charging the Forestry Commission with placing the park committee under undue pressure to significantly extend Dartmoor's forestry acreage. 'This is madness in the national park,' Sayer told the local press. 'Open land is becoming more and more valuable for recreational use as the country becomes more overcrowded.'[146] When she successfully lobbied for a meeting with officials in London, internal Forestry Commission correspondence suggests officials were rather pleased with their performance. Sayer left apparently convinced that her concerns about antiquities were misplaced and assured that the forestry industry had been scared off Dartmoor by the conflicts of the late 1950s and early 1960s.[147]

Connell completed his draft map in 1965, agreeing with the park committee that 2.2 per cent of Dartmoor fell into category A, where there was a strong presumption that afforestation was acceptable; 41.5 per cent, mainly unplanted enclosed land including the enclosures on High Dartmoor in the Princetown area, fell into category B, where the presumption was against afforestation, but a proposal might be acceptable; and the remainder fell into category C, mainly common land, where there was a strong presumption against afforestation. Senior figures at the Forestry Commission heralded the figure for category B as a remarkable achievement, though the wording was such that it is hard to see it as a significant concession, and it was certainly naïve to suppose that 'certain loud noises' anticipated from the DPA once public consultations began would be managed away by the National Parks Commission and the CPRE. However, the response from the Country Landowners' Association and the Timber Growers' Association confounded the expectations of the foresters. Both rejected the survey as an unacceptable challenge to private property rights. Common land was untouchable, that was accepted, but they demanded either that additional lands were shifted into category A or that the wording of category B be made less prohibitive. Predictably, the National Parks Commission pulled in the other direction. It took three more years of wrangling before Connell's survey was finally approved.

On the publication of the draft, Sayer had obligingly provided *The Times* with a good quote, saying the Forestry Commission planned to afforest 15,000 acres, including Yelverton golf course and 'people's back gardens'. She also co-wrote the DPA's lengthy response to the survey, supplied to Fred Willey, Minister of Land and Natural Resources. Repeating arguments made many times before about the negative impact of coniferisation, it cuttingly dismissed the quality of Connell's work, and emphasised the survey's tactical purposes and the fact that government policy had effectively conceded that commercial forestry was not economically viable. In the event, the landed interest was assuaged by the rewording of category B but this did little to commit the Dartmoor committee, and the survey was finally signed off in January 1969. Sayer fired off another well-formed critique, but in retrospect it is evident that the long survey process served only to demonstrate that the Forestry Commission was in retreat, at least on Dartmoor. In September 1968, Connell was ready to move on, signing off as conservator with a defensive letter denigrating the DPA as 'an amateur pressure group of no status' and insisting he had always acted according to ministerial instruction.[148]

Connell's dismissal of the DPA as 'an amateur pressure group of no status' denied it *locus standi* and implied that questions of forestry should be settled between statutory bodies whose conduct should enable each to carry out their allotted tasks. To substitute 'voluntary' for 'amateur' as a description of the DPA, thereby taking account of the expertise the DPA could leverage, places Connell's complaint in a different light. The logic of Connell's position, however, rested on a defensible but somewhat *étatist* definition of democratic accountability, whereby a public body acted legitimately when it exercised the powers conferred on it by the legislative process, powers which in this case were counterbalanced by those of the National Parks Commission.

Similar strategies of exclusion characterise how the commission presents its history. G.D. Rouse's *The New Forests of Dartmoor* (1972) traced the progress of an essential industry peaceably committed to providing the nation with an essential resource – timber – and bringing economic prosperity and environmental improvement to a neglected rural upland. This narrative allied the 'sociological argument' familiar from the Kielder debates of the 1950s to nineteenth-century languages of improvement. Woodland owners who introduced conifers to 'waste land' or 'derelict' oak coppice were 'enlightened', forestry brought jobs to the rural economy, and no reference was made to clear-felling in the river valleys or the controversies that had dogged the commission's every move. Tax incentives are strangely absent from the story. It was not plausible to claim that antiquities on Fernworthy had been 'sedulously preserved', though by the early 1970s Rouse could claim with some justice that antiquities in the woodlands now stood out clearly on 'a fine carpet of fallen needles' whereas those on reserved land at Lakeland near Bellever were hard to discern due to 'rank growth of heather, willow, bramble, rushes and purple moor grass'. Similar arguments have been made in recent years about the growth of purple moor grass caused by lower grazing pressures.

It was certainly disingenuous to cite Connell's survey as evidence that the commission took seriously fears that 'uncontrolled afforestation might upset the balance of land use', but more telling was the description of the survey as an agreement between the Forestry Commission, 'in consultation with the Timber Growers' Association and the Country Landowners' Association', and the Dartmoor committee, 'which consulted the appropriate amenity societies'.[149] The privileging of propertied interests is obvious here. The DPA was not to be named and, at least according to Connell, it did not have a legitimate role to play, yet the Forestry Commission happily worked with landowner and industry bodies, whom the dedication scheme made both the commission's partners and their dependants. The emphasis might be reversed: propertied interests happily exploited their statist enablers to take advantage of generous tax breaks. In any case, the Forestry Commission continues to write contestation out of its history. The official history of its centenary blithely describes the 1960s as a period of 'consolidation and confident expansion', the tropes shaping the narrative being those of technological advance, greater efficiency and growing ecological awareness.[150]

Sayer, of course, refused to accept the Forestry Commission's view that, in her words, 'the right way to decide the future land use of national parks is by striking some kind of balance between opposing claims'.[151] To reject the idea that claims by statutory bodies could be balanced fundamentally challenged their modus operandi and the vested interests of those whose tax affairs stood to benefit from these compromises. Did the devastation of 300 acres of deciduous forest at Buckland, a net loss of irreplaceable natural habitat, reflect balance? Sayer's opposition to forestry policy on Dartmoor sought to disrupt the state–property–fiscal nexus, seeking to establish a legitimate, non-materialist public interest in private land.

Military and Access

Field artillery experiments were first made on Dartmoor in the 1860s and in August 1873 large-scale military manoeuvres were conducted on Dartmoor – the Prussian defeat of the French forces in 1870–1 focused minds – and over time the temporary camp at Okehampton took on a permanent character, particularly during the 1890s. The main training grounds were the Okehampton Range (20,000 acres) and the Merrivale Range (19,000 acres), both leased from the Duchy, and from 1900 the Willsworthy Range (3,200 acres), which the War Office bought from the Calmady-Hamlyn family for use as a rifle and field-firing range. All entailed complicated agreements with the commoners. In 1901, the War Office toyed with buying the whole of the Duchy's Dartmoor holdings, but its budget fell short of the Duchy's asking price. The next 40 years saw motorised vehicles replace horses, moorland tracks developed into simple roads and 18-pounders pummel the landscape, but the military did not extend its territorial claims on the moor. It remained confined to the northern quarter, Dartmoor's harshest and most challenging terrain. The outbreak of war in 1939 led to the militarisation of a much larger proportion of Dartmoor, as John Somers Cocks explained:

> By agreement or under the defence regulations most of the Moor north and west of Tavistock–Two Bridges–Moretonhampstead road was used as a firing range; another rifle range was made on the flank of Rippon Tor; much of the south-eastern sector of the Moor, known loosely as Scorriton, became an area for training with rifles, machine-guns and anti-tank weapons; an airfield on Roborough Down and a hutted camp at Plaster Down were built; Penn Moor and Ringmoor Down were used for further training. Finally, an area around Haytor and Houndtor was set aside towards the end of the war to train troops for service in the Far East.

Add the hundred-foot Air Ministry aerial erected on Laughter Tor – Dartmoor's contribution to the Gee radio navigation system operated by the RAF – and the full extent of Dartmoor's militarisation is realised. In the run-up to D-Day, 'virtually the whole of the moor was used in preparation for the invasion of Europe'.[152]

The DPA and other preservationist organisations accepted this encroachment as a temporary necessity, but the end of the war and the prospect of national park designation created the expectation that the status quo ante would be quickly re-established and, in time, the military use of Dartmoor brought to an end altogether. Attitudes at the War Office and the Admiralty were rather different. Emerging Cold War threats, new technology and Britain's wars of colonial retention created new training needs, and the armed service ministries tended to assume that their room for manoeuvre on the moor would not be significantly inhibited by peacetime pressures. Behind the scenes, the government tended to support the services, but, as seen with respect to Northumberland, pressure from below ensured that the services had to publicly justify their needs. The same occurred with respect to Dartmoor. The Admiralty's peremptory announcement that it intended to retain the use of wartime sites in the southern quarter like Ringmoor Down and Penmoor (4,850 acres), Scorriton (11,200 acres), Rippon Tor, Plaster Down and Laughter Tor, excluding the public completely from Scorriton and partially from Penmoor, provoked a swift response from the local authorities and grassroots campaigners. The services, Devon County Council and the government pulled together a provisional agreement which was then examined at a public inquiry. Consequently, live ammunition could only be used on the pre-war ranges and, in addition to these areas, the military could restrict access only to the small hutted camp at Plaster Down and the RAF Gee station at Sharpitor. Land south of the Tavistock–Two Bridges–Moretonhampstead road could be used for 'dry' training, but only insofar as this did not interfere with access and common rights. Contentious issues remained unresolved, particularly with respect to vehicular access and the digging of foxholes on Ringmoor and Roborough Downs, which continued despite Devon County Council's insistence that this was forbidden under the 1947 agreement. The War Office and the Admiralty stuck to their guns, insisting tracked vehicles and foxholes were needed on Ringmoor and Roborough. At the subsequent public inquiry in October 1950, their emotive appeal about the importance of these sites to the training of soldiers who served in the recent war in Korea helped public relations, but it was always likely the inquiry would not go largely their way. Sayer, attending as representative of the Ramblers' Association, lamented another 4,000 acres of 'unspoiled Dartmoor' doomed 'to ordeal by tracked vehicle and spade'.[153]

In short, despite the 1947 agreement and subsequent public inquiries, on the eve of designation great uncertainty remained concerning use of Dartmoor National Park by the armed forces. Live firing had been confined to the north quarter ranges and the withdrawal from Scorriton had some significance, but the maximalist audacity of the military's initial demands was likely an opening bid in a process that ultimately left them a great deal of latitude in the south quarters. Little suggested that the government intended to subordinate the military's training needs to national park principles or, indeed, that the military's behaviour would be made subject to civilian oversight. None of this was very surprising. The military remained largely self-regulating and was given every reason to be confident that its needs would take precedence at the highest levels of government.

Sayer was unbowed by these setbacks and the following dozen or so pages evince her extraordinary tenacity on this issue. Her actions suggest that she had grasped a simple truth. Despite the weakness of the commission's formal powers, it had a set of statutory responsibilities with respect to national parks which meant, at the very least, that it could not be entirely ignored within government or Whitehall. Sayer and the DPA therefore took it upon themselves to monitor and record the behaviour of the military so the commission could be kept fully informed of what was going on. She was particularly keen on documenting the military's misdeeds using photography, and the archive preserves these remarkable visual records, carefully mounted, and annotated in Sayer's distinctive hand. These were generally sent to Harold Abrahams, secretary to the commission, who received regular letters on the subject from Sayer throughout the 1950s and

1960s. Her vigilance encouraged the commission to seek resolutions, which Sayer endeavoured to help along by making concrete suggestions, such as proposing alternative sites when military needs changed.

The commission was responsive from the off. Following the 1950 public inquiry focused on Roborough and Ringmoor, Sayer complained to Abrahams that she had been unaware that it was acceptable for witnesses to offer alternative sites. Had she known this, she would have drawn the inquiry's attention to several sites, including Plaster Down, where there was already the hutted camp; the northern leg of Roborough, used during the war as an aerodrome and now semi-derelict; Crownhill Down and Heddon Down, south of Lee Moor, where tungsten and other mining works already dominated; and Hanger Down, above Ivybridge, a landscape she felt to be of little significance. In contrast to Ringmoor, none of these sites possessed important antiquities. Abrahams dutifully raised her suggestions with the ministry, which eventually responded that among other reasons these sites were 'too small and cannot be combined'.[154]

Grassroots activism or campaigning did not lead to a significant reduction in the presence of the armed services on Dartmoor. The gradual scaling back that had occurred by the 1970s, and the establishment of the basic settlement that pertains to this day, reflected the UK government's broad geo-strategic interests. A good example of this arose in May 1955 when the War Department informed Devon County Council that it proposed developing the hutted camp at Plaster Down into a permanent barracks for an infantry battalion rather like those at Larkhill and Bulford in Wiltshire. Devon County Council opposed the development and was already in discussion with the government when Sayer got wind of the possible development in March 1956 and prodded the commission into action. Internal correspondence indicates that the commission was not convinced by Sayer's claim that the agreement of 1949 forbade the development of permanent barracks on the site, but it nonetheless dutifully inserted itself into the discussion. In December 1957, when the War Office finally informed the commission of its decision to abandon its plans, it was emphatic that it had not been swayed by pressure from the national park lobby: 'The change of plan is due to the reduced requirements for accommodating the Regular Army of the future in the United Kingdom.'[155]

Sayer did help ensure that the military was forced to explain its needs and could not simply retain its established position without justification. Plaster Down again provides a good example. In the early 1960s, the military did 'give up' Plaster Down because it was no longer needed, but the actual decision to relinquish the site, rather than passively retain possession, was partly thanks to pressure from Sayer.[156] In other words, Sayer and other national park lobbyists disturbed the complacency of the military by helping to ensure they did not retain control over assets they did not own and were not presently needed. That marked a quite significant shift away from wartime culture and towards the domestication of the armed services and its gradual submission to civilian priorities. All of this, of course, was not achieved by Sayer alone. She and the DPA worked with other pressure groups, most notably the CPRE, but their local knowledge was crucial. An unsung hero of this story is H.G. Godsall, clerk of Devon County Council, later described by Sayer as a 'man of humanity and fairness' who 'was not always able to guide the Council or the Authority in the right direction . . . but he invariably tried'.[157] Almost every issue Sayer pursued by letters to the commission, ministers or the media was mirrored by the vigilant Godsall. His behind-the-scenes diplomacy ensured that the military eventually cleared up unexploded mortars dating back to wartime training, repeatedly writing of the risk this neglect posed to the general public exercising rights of access.[158] Godsall's attitude towards Sayer's skills as publicist was generally one of weary forbearance, but he could bridle at the DPA's criticism of the county council, and was occasionally minded to remind officials that the DPA was simply an organ of public opinion, did not have any official standing and should not be treated as representative or as having a formal political status – *locus standi* once again.

More specifically, Sayer and the DPA played a central role in the agitation that ensured that the military came to treat Dartmoor with greater care and took greater account of civilian needs. The need for reform was made pressing by the death in April 1958 of Henry Whitfield, a schoolboy killed by shrapnel near Cranmere Pool when out hiking with his parents. Whitfield's death renewed attention to the long-established complaint that the army was not assiduous in lowering the red warning flags when live training was not in progress, making the flags an unreliable indicator of whether it was safe to enter the ranges. With its arrogance and complacency horribly exposed, and not helped by insensitive ministerial statements in the Commons, the military faced a major public relations challenge. Captain E.L. Carter appeared before the National Parks Commission and was duly despatched to Devon on what would now be called a 'listening exercise'. Thereafter, the range boundaries were marked with evenly spaced red and white posts, newly designed leaflets outlining the risks were widely distributed, and a large number of local people and organisations were informed in advance of firing times, allowing them to be further publicised.[159]

In quick succession the DPA submitted several memoranda outlining the military's sins of commission and omission. In private correspondence with the War Office, Godsall admitted that these complaints could not be ignored.[160] The DPA raised objections to the use of tracked vehicles on Mary Tavy Common (not part of the ranges), the damage caused to rocks and tors by firing (used as targets), the night-time battles with blank ammunition in the Postbridge area (which kept people awake at night), military litter (a perpetual complaint) and abrogation of the agreement with the CPRE to keep people informed of planned exercises outside of the ranges.[161] Frustrated by the unresponsiveness of the SW District Command, Sayer took up these issues with the War Office, but her principal complaint concerned the lack of consultation that now characterised the military's dealings with the amenity societies. She was particularly angered by the construction of new military roads in northern Dartmoor, '*where, in the national interest, the peace, remoteness from motor traffic, and "challenge" of this part of the national park ought to be most strictly to have been preserved*'. It was now easy to traverse Dartmoor terrain previously only accessible on horseback and by the most determined hikers. The military road became more contentious still when motorists discovered that nothing stopped them from driving that way. Reports of picnickers, transistor radios and parked cars at tors were especially provoking. Perhaps the least appealing outburst of her entire career was quoted in the *Observer* newspaper: 'Like a tin opener; in go all the cars; little spivvy children opening the gates make £1 a day.'[162] Getting the military to take responsibility for access to the road was a battle to come. For now, she was aggrieved by the decision to hold motorcycle trials on the open moor at the Willsworthy Range and lay a telephone cable by cutting up its surface, and by the service food tins and cartons found hidden in all manner of places, including at Childe's Tomb, built on the site of a prehistoric kistvaen. If nothing was to be gained by taking up their complaints with District Command, she warned, they would have no choice but to take their grievances to local MPs and the press.[163]

The War Office duly wrote to SW District Command listing Sayer's complaints. The response was as revealing as it was unapologetic. The work on the roads was simply repairs, albeit repairs to improvements made during the Second World War, further evidence that the war had shifted the baseline, and though the improvement of the old track at Yes Tor for Land Rover use was new, it was necessary to facilitate access to the warning flags. As for Sayer's other complaints, the motorcycle training was 'authorised', they had no knowledge of the cable laying and action had now been taken to tidy up the litter.[164] As far as SW District Command was concerned, that was that. Sayer was not done. On 11 June 1961, she helped coordinate a gathering at Crockern Tor, once the site of the tinners' 'parliament', to petition for the release of Dartmoor from military use. The amenity societies turned out in force.[165] Another DPA memorandum followed, which Lord Chorley submitted to HLG. Rather than a litany of complaints, the DPA set out its view that ministers should commit to withdrawing the military from Dartmoor, ideally by 1970, and calibrate its use of the moor accordingly. There should be no further investment in military infrastructure; military roads should be restored to their original state as rough trackways; obsolete or disused buildings and other 'works' should be removed; live missiles or explosives littering the ranges should be cleared away; and a commitment made to scrupulously avoid causing any further damage to Dartmoor's antiquities, the tors or other natural features.[166]

When Lord Jellicoe, minister at HLG, visited Dartmoor that November, Abrahams was surprised he had not seen Sayer's memorandum, but Jellicoe admitted 'mopping-up operations' were needed. Brigadier Acland duly reported on progress to Abrahams, apparently having been provided with a list of things to deal with, including 45 specific complaints by the DPA. Of Yes Tor, Sayer complained: 'Civilian car and motor cycles now found their way to the top of the Tor on non-firing days. There is no sense of achievement now for the walker in getting to the summit.' Worse still was the situation on Okemont Hill, 'once a wild moorland hill which was a challenge for walkers and an achievement to reach.' 'Now,' she wrote, striking a subtopian note, 'it is like a municipal car park. A portable wireless was blaring from one of these cars when this photograph was taken. Litter was strewn everywhere.'[167] That subtopian note was there again, four years later, when she was quoted in parliament:

Motor vehicles scattered widely over open landscape dominate and denature the whole scene. With their shiny surfaces and glittering windscreens they impose all the associations of urban life on scenes which should be free, natural and wild. Even the solitary car or motor cycle perched high on a ridge or tor, or parked in a remote valley, can destroy the whole essence and inspiration of wild landscape. And they often leave disfiguring track marks and deposits of litter, some of it dangerous to children and cattle and all of it unnecessary and disgusting.[168]

Sayer's persistence scored a political hit. Jellicoe was rattled. Writing to Abrahams for an update, he explained that the army had been given five months to complete the clear-up, Chorley was bound to raise the issue in the Lords and he did not want to be seen to have been prompted into action. When Acland contested some of Sayer's claims, Abrahams was congenial in response:

I thought dear Sylvia had probably got something wrong somewhere; she never does worry much about her facts! Indeed, the last letter I had from her I replied that I would give her an opinion as soon as I had ascertained the facts and, of course, when we looked into them they were somewhat different from what she had asserted. Still, I would not be without her for worlds. She tells me that she has just become a grandmother and that her granddaughter is very attractive. I wonder if my successor will have to deal with her in 30 years time.[169]

Abrahams let Jellicoe know that the army seemed to have done a good job, though he doubted the DPA would be satisfied, wryly commenting that they probably surveyed the range daily. Sayer kept on, writing to the commission about the Franco-British paratrooper exercise carried out on Ringmoor Down and Ditsworthy Warren during that year's lambing season and the Marines and RAF camps established outside the training areas for months at a time.[170] Remarkably, the Standing Committee on National Parks and a host of amenity organisations issued a memorandum effectively repeating the demands of the DPA memorandum calling for the phased withdrawal of the military from Dartmoor by 1970.[171] The *Guardian* newspaper took up the call in an editorial, but it quickly became evident that the prospect of a phased withdrawal was not on the cards.[172] The War Office's public response contextualised the position on Dartmoor in terms of international developments, including the loss of training areas in Egypt following the Suez debacle, and emphasised the reduction of the military's footprint on Dartmoor since 1945 (4,000 acres at Merrivale East was now being let go) and its adoption of better practices, particularly with respect to littering and unexploded ordnance. Decolonisation increased the pressure on training grounds in Britain. Where else could they find 28,000 acres uninterrupted by residential housing, public roads or railways?[173]

For all that Abrahams handled Sayer with a degree of irony, at least when corresponding with fellow officials, he nonetheless sought her response. She was unimpressed. Given that the military used much of the park's access land, relinquishing Merrivale East, where live ammunition was not permitted, was no more than 'window-dressing', and given the inefficient use made of the existing ranges, she thought the 28,000-acre claim was meretricious. She was equally unconvinced by the War Office's claim that disfigurements caused by training were temporary: 'nature rapidly assists in recovery and permanent damage to natural beauty is not caused by military activities'. 'This astonishing assertion is quite untrue', Sayer wrote.

> The craters, trenches and ruts caused by military use in many parts of Dartmoor are of course permanent, as could only too easily be shown; and these have a secondary long-term effect in producing erosion and leaching of the soil, which if allowed to continue must increasingly alter the character and destroy the beauty of large areas of the national park.
>
> The damage and fracturing of the tors, prehistoric menhirs etc caused by using them as targets are also unfortunately permanent, and beyond the 'assistance of nature' rapid or otherwise.[174]

The controversy rumbled on. The DPA relentlessly documented the military's misdeeds. In early 1964, another DPA report, on the 'Misuse of a National Park', attracted press coverage because it was partly prompted by the complaints of holidaymakers.[175] Sayer kept up the pressure for the rest of the year, highlighting the Royal Marines' use of Burrator Reservoir – a 'new incursion' – but Plymouth Corporation, the landowner, permitted 25 training exercises per year ('escape and evasion exercises' and 'ambush drills') for up to 50 men, including two nights' camping, provided there was no live firing and no more than one exercise per week.[176] Intensified use of the Merrivale Range meant further hardened tracks onto the Common, and military road extensions, hard or soft, were either in prospect or completed at Baggator Gate, Holming Beacon, Great Mis Tor, Hangingstone Hill and Whitehorse Hill. Sayer claimed that the prehistoric hut circles on Conies Down, a site about to be scheduled as an ancient monument, had been used for target practice ('plain vandalism' and 'wanton destruction', as she told the *Guardian*); attempts to fill in craters using heavy bulldozers and earth movers at Great Mis Tor did further damage, leaving behind deep rutted tracks; and the motorcycle trial held at Okehampton for 72 participants over a 12-mile route churned up the surface of the moor.[177] Again, the commission acted, raising complaints with the War Office, eliciting weary if relatively constructive responses, and writing a memo on the need to restrict civilian traffic on military roads.[178]

In October 1964, Sayer and Somers Cocks sought the sponsorship of the commission for yet another statement, only this time it took a slightly different tack. 'National Land Use and the Dartmoor National Park: The Case for the Removal of Damaging Military Training' was projected as a constructive response to the creation of the short-lived Ministry of Land and Natural Resources and the prospect that land use would now be made subject to national planning. The operative word in the title was 'damaging' – readers were referred back to the DPA's pamphlet 'Misuse of a National Park' – and the statement drew a distinction between 'adventure training' – arguing that no 'natural training ground for initiative and endurance could be finer' than Dartmoor – and existing training regimes, with their accompaniment of 'the military roads and installations, the random military vehicle-driving, the bombing, firing, digging and helicopter flying', and the 'very ugly' camp at Okehampton. Removing the training base to Scotland seemed the obvious solution, and Sayer was always ready to recommend shifting the military from Dartmoor to Scotland, not least because this would modestly address the problem caused by the overpopulation of the south and the underpopulation of the north.[179]

The commission did not take Sayer's advice on military training altogether seriously, but an official still thought the pamphlet 'the most reasoned and sensible document yet produced by Her Ladyship'. Sayer's honorific was often a source of private merriment among her interlocutors, but the official nonetheless made it clear that she deserved the commission's 'approval and backing, in this instance'.[180] Sayer kept up the pressure over the course of 1965 and 1966. In September 1966, the MOD informed the commission that further motorcycle trials had been cancelled, but another new track had been bulldozed into the turf at Little Mis Tor; further damage was done to antiquities at Great Kneeset and Dinger Tors, and a new Royal Navy camp at Foggintor near Princetown was among the complaints fuelling another DPA pamphlet. Sayer now accused the Duchy of failing to ensure that the covenants agreed with the War Office were upheld, and she took exception to the new map of Dartmoor's military roads. Mapping the roads would create a sense of permanence, lowering the barriers to the development of rough tracks (not distinguished on the map from more developed military roads), and encouraging civilian motorists. The tarmacking of the road at Dinger Tor, which she thought contravened earlier agreements, roused her to a particular fury.[181]

Readers following this chronicle of Sayer's tenacity will not be surprised that in July 1966, representatives of HLG, the National

Parks Commission and the Ministry of Defence (MOD) met to discuss the 'increasing volume of Ministerial correspondence on the topic of military training within National Parks and especially Dartmoor' (read: 'increasing volume of Ministerial correspondence generated by the vigilance of Lady Sayer and the DPA'). Could regular meetings between HLG, the MOD and the commission be instituted as a means of diminishing these pressures and ensuring the responsible officials were kept up-to-date on the issues? That was one way to kick the can down the road, though firm plans were not made because Whitehall considered these to be local issues to be dealt with through effective communication between local park committees and military representatives. It was the unresponsiveness of the military that led Sayer to make these issues the concern of Whitehall. Moreover, as the meeting acknowledged, ministers were obliged to respond to the issues raised by the commission's annual reports. In any case, the segregationist basis of the DPA's case was brilliantly missed by the proposal that effective recreational planning might be the answer. If visitors were kept happy elsewhere in the park, it was imagined, the clash of interests that arose in training areas might be avoided.[182]

In September 1966, accompanied by her husband, Sayer ventured onto the Royal Marines training range during a live firing exercise to inspect a prehistoric stone that she feared had been damaged and to take photographs. 'Firing Stops for Lady Sayer' ran the headline in *The Times*.[183] In February 1967, she made the incursion onto Ringmoor Down during a helicopter training operation that saw her photograph on the front page of *The Times* and a story headed 'Woman Who Defied an Army'.[184] These stunts produced good copy, but like Sayer's relentless harrying of government and officials, they would soon be overtaken by larger questions. The Duchy leases were due for renewal in 1970, creating a once-in-a-generation opportunity for the preservationists and the amenity societies to get the armed services off the moor. The DPA, like the Dartmoor Livestock Protection Society, took its place in the ranks alongside the CPRE,

311

the Commons, the Open Spaces and Footpaths Preservation Society, the Ramblers' Association, the Youth Hostel Association and their local branches, to address a petition to the Prince's Council asking that the leases not be renewed.[185] The Duchy, acutely conscious of public opinion, not only took their opposition seriously, but in private correspondence made clear its preference for removal and lack of readiness to simply sign another 21-year lease. The Countryside Commission, successor body to the National Parks Commission, took a firmer position still. To the government's proposal that there be a break clause at seven and 14 years, Lady Wootton's team responded that there should be a phased withdrawal to 1975, with significant restrictions placed on use in the meantime. Low-flying aircraft were not suited to a national park, helicopters should be confined to the firing areas in the north and only light vehicles should be used on the open moor. On withdrawal, the military roads should be restored to their former condition. The National Trust was firmer still, saying it could no longer accept training exercises on its land in the southern quarter.[186]

The cosy complicity between the National Parks Commission and the armed services had been broken; the united front shown by the Dartmoor committee, chaired by Lord Roborough, the Countryside Commission, chaired by Lady Wootton, and Sir John Winnifrith, the Director-General of the National Trust, had to be taken seriously in government, not least because the credentials of the new countryside agency could not be undermined from the start. Hints that the Duchy was ready to compromise were criticised by the *Western Morning News*. The MOD enjoyed the tacit support of the government, but it had a case to make. As it wrestled with possible easements, such as giving up some lands and curtailing operations at weekends and during the holiday season, the gist of its position boiled down to the critical importance of the Dartmoor training grounds to Royal Marine Commandoes, whose training bases were in Devon. To lose Dartmoor would necessitate finding new training grounds elsewhere, the transfer incurring high capital costs and fresh controversies. There was unlikely to be much appetite for this in government. Key to the eventual resolution of the problem was a surprising low-profile move, the downgrading of Dartmoor from a 'major training area' to a 'local training area' in April 1969. Henceforth, its use would be largely confined to forces based in the south-west, with training conducted by officers with an intimate knowledge of the terrain. Classes already given to recruits by Lady Aileen Fox, the eminent archaeologist based at Exeter University, would continue.[187]

Sayer, who had done so much to shape the conditions in which the armed services operated, demanded the question be settled publicly. She wrote to Gwyneth Dunwoody MP to propose a judicial inquiry, a suggestion Dunwoody passed on to the MOD.[188] It was a minor intervention by her standards, but not entirely at odds with the resolution. Leases would be renewed for 14 years, with a break clause after seven, and a review at five. It was somehow fitting that the review was conducted by Baroness Sharp, Permanent Secretary at HLG, 1955–66, and the first woman to hold this rank in a ministry. Once again, the MOD took the process seriously, though they had reason to feel confident. Sharp's terms of reference were strictly limited. Her job was to review existing arrangements and make recommendations, but ministers made it clear that the intention of the review was not to bring into question the MOD's need to main-tain a training presence on the moor. A jaunty letter between two major-generals during the build-up to the public hearings suggested that they felt little jeopardy beyond managing the public relations aspect of the process. Concerning Sayer, their 'most well known and vociferous adversary', some old prejudices surfaced. Her powers might be waning, local gossip suggesting she was now 'utterly unpre-dictable' with 'absolutely no regard for the truth', but her ability to generate press should not be underestimated.[189]

Baroness Sharp took Sayer rather more seriously, quoting her at length in her report.[190] It cannot have escaped their notice that they were women of the same generation who had thrived in worlds dominated by men. Perhaps they were dimly aware that almost 25 years before, another woman of their generation, Pauline Dower, had defended national park principles for the first time in a public forum at the Peak District public inquiry. Sharp was not tasked with establishing whether training and national parks were incompatible on principle, but to examine this specific case. Her conclusion was blunt. Military training on Dartmoor was 'exceedingly damaging to the national park'. It was a question of scale. At 365 square miles, Dartmoor National Park was small, and much of its 'wildest and finest scenery' fell within the military training areas, mostly the live firing ranges. There are echoes here of arguments made by Sylvia Crowe, another brilliant woman of that generation. Training curtailed rights of access, the noise caused great disturbance and the scenery was spoiled by warning signs, flags, notices and observation posts. 'And perhaps worst of all the heart of the northern moor is invaded by cars, both military and civilian, using the military road and trucks.' Dartmoor was simply too small to absorb the damage.[191] Little of consequence flowed from Sharp's report, but Sayer had been right all along.

Wild Country

Sayer chose to step down as chair of the DPA at the AGM in May 1973. She was 69 and her husband was keen on the idea.[192] Henceforth, she planned to work 'free-lance – with the emphasis on lance', and this she did until her death in 2000.[193] In August 1971, *The Times* wrote that to merely mention the name of this 'elegant grandmother' and 'militant conservationist' in parts of Devon 'is enough to make men throw their beer in your face'. The key to her success as a campaigner, she explained, was 'homework', and the journalist described her study as 'packed with files on Dartmoor battles past, present and future' and her copying machine, the crucial tool of any campaigner in this period. She understood that she was disliked, even considered an 'arrogant fanatic' for her refusal to play the 'meek preservationist', but she was proud that the DPA was now a 'force to be reckoned with ... no longer scornfully dismissed as "those amenity people"'.[194]

At that moment, she was preparing for the public inquiry into the proposed expansion of china clay mining on the edge of Dartmoor, but this account of her period as chair of DPA can be rounded off by looking at her general principles. These were captured in *Wild Country*, the address she delivered on the future of the uplands to a conference jointly organised by the Country Landowners' Association and the Northern Pennines Rural Development Board in 1970 and from which she drew in her statement to the Sharp inquiry. Slightly different versions of the address were published by Sayer herself and the Standing Committee of National Parks, but the version drawn on here is the DPA reprint of 2000, which included material from both.

Recall Sayer's enthusiasm for Crowe's chapter on 'Open Country' in her *Tomorrow's Landscape*, for it is immediately obvious how strongly this influenced *Wild Country*. Sayer dismissed quibbling about whether landscapes were 'natural' or 'man-made' as a form of false sophistication generally used to 'disarm opposition' – she had a point – and instead distinguished wild country from 'truly virgin land' as places where humans lived and worked but 'nature is still manifestly dominant over man'.[195] As Sayer's *Outline* had made abundantly clear, she judged Dartmoor's value in anthropic terms and on this she was entirely consistent. Like Crowe, she emphasised questions 'of scale, of use and of material', arguing that work done by physical labour, rather than machines, and using natural materials close to hand, such as stone and wood, could be assimilated by nature, so the 'essential wildness still survived'.[196] These arguments chimed with her favourable reception in the 1950s of the park authority's *Dartmoor: Building in the National Park*. Modern heavy machinery

– the earthmovers and concrete mixers – allowed humans to transform landscapes, demolishing mountains and raising mountains of
industrial waste.[197] Her 'own small national park' could not assimilate
the 'artificial works of man'.[198]

Much that was familiar from the Sayer playbook made it into the
address. She was smarting at the outcome of the Meldon battle, so the
councillors and the men of the water board did not escape unscathed.
She distinguished those able to see that on the moor was 'written the
history of our race' from those whose 'barren minds' and 'municipal
eyes' found the landscape 'empty and featureless'.[199] Well might she
harp on these themes, but this should not obscure how her argument
made a number of claims now commonly associated with ecocritiques
of industrial modernity. As she argued, to some people, wild country
was a 'challenge to their sense of human dominance and power', it
must be tamed, made productive, the 'might of man' must not be
failed, the 'god of Progress' must be assuaged.[200] Others, living in 'car-
jammed . . . built-up conurbations',[201] 'experience a sense of liberation
and renewal' in wild country, and she insisted that this applied across
the generations and classes, vigorously rejecting any suggestion that
her cause was that of 'backward-looking selfish middle class reaction-
aries suffering from fossilised minds'.[202] To Sayer, it was self-evident
that the preservationists were not 'cranks or fanatics but ordinary,
hard-working, well-balanced, reasonable people'.[203]

Aspects of this discourse have strong conservative connotations,
carrying echoes of the distinction between the deserving and the
undeserving poor, but Sayer's use of terms like 'well-balanced' and
'reasonable' also reflected the criticisms often faced by pressure
groups. Striking an intentionally progressive note that aligned her
with Crowe's prescriptions, she said preservationists did not oppose
planning, land management, house building, tree planting or farming.
Nor did she deny that inflation should be tackled, and, despite her
irony of tone, she conceded that mainstream political priorities –
industrial expansion, restoring the balance of payments, improving

the country's dollar-earning capacity – were necessary, but she saw no reason why the pursuit of 'Growth' made the protection of the environment a 'triviality'.[204] Her whistle-stop tour of modern illusions even took in 'Common Marketry', though this was in the context of her argument that the subsidies paid to upland farmers should be used to revive 'small-scale traditional husbandry', thereby securing the 'age-old dual use of hill-grazing and access', restoring to hill-farmers their traditional role as conservers of landscape. The 'horse-riding farmer' should replace the 'mechanised cowboy' and traditional grazing regimes should be restored, putting an end to outwintering livestock on the moor.[205] Only through the restoration of traditional agricultural practices and increased controls could the national parks deliver their most valuable product, the 'health and happiness' of the people.[206] She observed ironically:

No doubt arguments such as these render one liable to the charge that they are the views of a romantic idealist – a woman, of course – who is clearly unable to assess or appreciate the fundamental importance of these issues of growth and expansion, or the seriousness of the financial situation of a country that has for years been living beyond its means.[207]

Epilogue
Fifty Years On

L ooking back from the third decade of the twenty-first century, it might seem absurd to imagine that Octavia Hill, Beatrix Potter, Pauline Dower and Sylvia Sayer saved the English countryside. Even if treated as representative of larger environmental movements, as they can be, this is surely an implausible proposition. Yet to think about the four historically invites a different kind of question and a more generous answer. What did they think the English countryside needed to be saved *from*? The activist lives of the four provide similar answers. The countryside needed saving from the developments associated with industrial modernity, whether this took the form of new housing, tourist infrastructure, commercial and industrial interests or the voracious appetites of the modern state. What did they think the English countryside needed to be saved *for*? All four believed access to the countryside, whether Hill's 'open spaces' or Sayer's 'wild country', brings about human health and happiness and that this is a right, perhaps even a God-given right. Society is therefore obliged, whether through voluntarist or statist means, to find a way to guarantee this right. To save the countryside was to save something essential to human wellbeing.

As the shared priorities of the four indicate, the century that takes us from Hill's embrace of the Open Spaces movement in the 1870s to Sayer's retirement as chair of the Dartmoor Preservation

Association in 1973 has a historical coherence. Viewed in this way, the achievements of their activist lives become clearer. They translated that rights-based claim into a meaningful and often successful environmental activism. In the twenty-first century, their reasons for saving the countryside remain as potent as ever, but what it needs saving from has changed significantly. The early 1970s saw a palpable shift away from the preservationism characteristic of their activist careers and towards an environmentalism more strongly predicated on nature conversation, ecology and the shared vulnerabilities of all life on Earth.

Debates about population growth, the future scarcity of natural resources, particularly oil, animal extinctions and collapses in soil health stoked fundamental fears about the sustainability of human and animal life on earth long before global warming, climate change and the sixth great extinction began to dominate environmental debate. By the 1970s, amenity societies like the DPA did not always appeal to those seeking an effective response to these systemic problems. A new generation of environmentalists felt compelled to join Friends of the Earth (established 1969), Greenpeace (1969) or the People's Party (1972), forerunner of the Green Party (1990), or subscribe to magazines like the *Ecologist* (1970) or the *Vole* (1977–80). High-profile campaigns by transnational environmental organisations suggested that international agreements, brokered by the United Nations, could prevent the threatened extinction of charismatic megafauna like whales, pandas and tigers or prohibit the use of an unnecessary chemical pollutant like CFCs.[1]

Although Sayer's segregationist campaigning did get later outings thanks to the attempt by the china clay industry to expand its operations (a notable win in 1978) and the long battle over the routing of the A30 Okehampton bypass (a loss in 1985), new approaches adopted by the British government began to change the context in which the preservationists worked. The year before Sayer retired, the Conservative government under Edward Heath strengthened the national park committees as part of its wider reforms to local government. Granted the power of planning authorities, the new park authorities were tasked with protecting the parks, developing tourist infrastructure and improving the quality of life of residents. This moment of renewal reflected the successful promotion of national park principles by Dower, Sayer and a host of campaigners. Heath's government effectively conceded that the provisions of the 1949 Act were too weak to uphold the principles it sought to promulgate. Winning the argument, however, weakened Sayer's brand of political activism, not least because the new National Park Authorities, tasked with producing 10-year management plans by 1977, sought to institutionalise consultation as a means of diminishing conflict ('management by agreement').[2] These strategies, combined with the emergence of salaried conservationists, often university-based but working with partner organisations like the Wildlife Trust, ensured that long-established amenity societies like the Dartmoor Preservation Association lost influence.

Also challenging the preservationists was how the environmentalist injunction to 'think globally, act locally' played out in the English countryside with respect to the negative effects of modern agriculture. The most significant threats to the national parks were now identified as coming from within rather than without. That marked a significant change, which could leave the amenity societies not just seeming parochial but also awkwardly placed with respect to agricultural interests. Disquiet in the 1950s and 1960s developed into major conflict in the 1970s as a new suite of problems became apparent. The grubbing up of hedgerows to create larger fields, allowing greater efficiencies by using heavy machinery, and the application of toxic pesticides, herbicides and fertilisers, was common throughout the countryside, but in the uplands two distinct controversies threw into sharp relief the problems caused by state-subsidised agricultural intensification. On Exmoor and the North York Moors rough grazing and heath was ploughed and planted with agronomic seed, reducing the footprint of the terrain that had originally justified their designation as national parks; more generally, overgrazing was a problem on almost every upland as agricultural subsidies incentivised overstocking with sheep and cattle. These problems were the unintended consequence of a range of policy initiatives that flowed from the Hill Farming Act of 1946, which made grants available for the 'improvement' of hill pasture, and the Agriculture Act of 1947, which established the pattern of post-war agricultural subsidies long before the UK joined the EEC in 1973.

Changing sensibilities were thrown into sharp relief by the decision taken by Balliol College in the 1950s to sell the Buttermere estates it had purchased in the 1930s. A.D. Lindsay's retirement as Master in 1949 was probably a factor in the decision, for the annual September visits to the Lake District were something of a burden and there was little incentive to retain the properties in the absence of their principal champion. Evidence also suggests that the college thought the designation of Lake District National Park rendered its guardianship null – in any case, once sold the land would remain subject to the covenants agreed with the National Trust. Keen to maximise the value of its investment, the college went to considerable efforts to help the tenants enter into grant-aided management agreements under the 1946 Act. Not all were willing because the agreements were thought to require the tenants to relinquish something of their independence, but the college's efforts eventually paid off and in 1959 the estates were ready for the auction house. Quite how much value the management agreements added to the land is hard to say, and in any case the tenants managed to raise the money to collectively buy out their holdings at auction. Still, the college could be satisfied that it had discharged the new obligations of a responsible landlord.[3]

At a distance of 60 years, it is striking that no thought was given to whether the agricultural 'improvement' of the holdings was at odds with the college's custodianship. Things had changed by the 1970s. The idea that 'improved' agriculture produced desirable national park landscapes was now less widely accepted. It was one of the issues examined by the National Parks Policy Review Committee between 1971 and 1974, chaired by Lord Sandford, though a closing of the ranks by the landed and agricultural interest diverted attention towards the negative effects of tourism, particularly the motorist. The principal findings of the Sandford report were boiled down to the Sandford Principle, promulgated across Whitehall but not given statutory force until the Environment Act 1995. Where the public enjoyment of the countryside could not be reconciled to conservation, it stated, then conservation should be prioritised.[4] That hardly subdued critics, and public pressure plus the obligation to implement EEC directives obliged successive governments to act, but the policy debate came to focus on the narrow question of how existing provisions under the Sites of Special Scientific Interest (SSSI) designation could be strengthened. After an arduous parliamentary process, the passage of the Wildlife and Countryside Act in 1981 left few on the conservation side of the debate satisfied.[5] The Act enabled the enlargement of the territorial footprint of the SSSI archipelago, especially in the national parks, largely putting a halt to ploughing and reseeding of heath and moor, but calls for the strengthening of the park authorities with respect to managing agriculture went largely unheeded.

A slew of texts lamenting the state of the countryside and the weakness of environmental regulations were published in these years. Just three give a sense of the changing shape of the debate. Marion Shoard's seminal *The Theft of the Countryside* (1980), published at the height of the tense parliamentary process that led to the passage of the 1981 Act, had the most impact, attracting much newspaper commentary.[6] As a broadside against the destructive effect on the countryside of state-subsidised agricultural intensification, Shoard rehearsed arguments made a century earlier by Hill about the people's proprietorial interest in the land, the destruction of which constituted the 'theft' of her title. Of particular importance to Shoard was time spent at play in nature to the development of happy, healthy children. But whereas Hill had been alarmed by the encroachment on common land and rights of access by private developers, for Shoard the enemy was agricultural intensification. Her observation that some upland areas 'reposed contentedly in the protection they do not need, while lowland England is ravaged' challenged the working assumptions of the national parks lobby. Protected areas, like Sayer's 'wild country', mainly included areas where the socio-economic barriers *against* protection were lowest.[7] Shoard gave Hill's pioneering interventions a more overtly radical twist; her formulation that landowners were too easily able to 'dispossess the rest of us of what we value in the countryside' neatly captured her fundamental claim that land ownership was a form of custodianship on behalf the community.[8]

Malcolm and Ann MacEwen's *National Parks* (1982) presented its argument over 300 closely argued but entirely lucid pages. As a synthesis of a great volume of material and data, the book remains important, but it is most arresting as a coruscating assessment of the performance of the national parks system, particularly in the 1970s. Its critique ranged from a damning appraisal of the 'amateurism' of the National Parks Commission to in-depth treatments of a host of subjects only too familiar to Dower and Sayer. The MacEwens were an interesting team. As Ann MacEwen's obituarist suggests, 'readers were seduced by Malcolm's combative journalism' but 'persuaded by Ann's rigorous arguments', an observation that nicely captures the effectiveness of their book.[9] Ann MacEwen (née Radford), born in 1918, was a third-generation socialist, a member of the Communist Party, and a leading town planner. She worked for the landscape architect Geoffrey Jellicoe before joining London County Council in 1949. In 1961, she became the only woman member of Colin Buchanan's small team preparing the landmark study 'Traffic in Towns' (1963) for the Ministry of Transport, and in 1964 became founding partner of the consultancy Colin Buchanan and Partners, spending the rest of the decade doing battle, sometimes successfully, with traffic engineers determined to cut roads through Britain's towns and cities. In 1947, she had married Malcolm, a *Daily Worker* journalist, and both broke with the Communist Party in 1956 when the *Worker* refused to report the truth about the Soviet invasion of Hungary. He joined the *Architectural Journal*, successfully leveraging his wife's expertise. They moved to Exmoor in 1968, where Malcolm combined membership of the Exmoor National Park Committee with active membership of the Exmoor Society, the local branch of the CPRE – an echo here of Sayer's multiple roles in the 1950s, and he could be just as provoking, especially to his property-holding opponents, who made much of his background as a left-wing activist. MacEwen remains an emblematic example of the intersection of the red and the green that gives environmentalism much of its energy.[10]

By the 1980s, the MacEwens argued, the uplands were 'threatened, less perhaps by the local cataclysmic changes made by vast new engineering works (such as reservoirs and roads) than by the insidious widespread incremental changes wrought by modern farming and forestry'.[11] Brunsdon Yapp, Dower's cerebral colleague at the National Parks Commission, agreed, though he was not overly impressed by their book. He can hardly have appreciated such a high-handed dismissal of the work he and his colleagues undertook as commissioners, and he may well have been further irritated because Ann MacEwen was part of the planner-preservationist milieu he considered to have weakened the system from the start. As he explained in 'Real National Parks', a short polemical essay published in 1984, the system had been maimed from the start.[12] By prioritising recreation rather than nature conservation and sidelining the case made for land acquisition by conservation organisations, the Addison Committee set the agenda from which John Dower, Hobhouse and the 1949 legislation did not divert. To specialists, none of this was news, though it might not always be obvious to the public. As we've seen, Dower could emphasise the weakness of designation in order to mollify local interests, just as Sayer never ceased to complain about the supine attitude of the Dartmoor committee and later the National Park Authority. But whereas Dower and Sayer tended to see the problem as one of execution rather than of fundamentals, Yapp had come to see the system as misconceived. The only solution was land acquisition and an effective programme of nature regeneration.

According to Yapp, the park system had been enfeebled, first, by official ignorance of national parks as a global phenomenon, according to which acquisition by the state was the norm, and second, the commitment of the park authorities and the amenity organisations to the preservation of 'established farming use' as the proper way to produce valuable habitat in the uplands. In effect, the propagation of a pastoral ideal – cattle and sheep grazing on moor and heath – ensured that the national parks agenda, and its open spaces component, was captured by the agricultural interest from the off. This ideal could only be sustained by agricultural subsidies, which in some cases reversed farm abandonment, effectively preserving a pre-modern industry on land that could be put to better use for nature conservation and recreation. Yapp's recommendations were clear enough. Section 84 of the 1949 Act requiring that regard be shown for the needs of agriculture and forestry should be repealed because it contradicted national park purposes. Moors, lakes and woods should be brought into public ownership. A revived National Parks Commission should start by requisitioning the vast estates of the National Trust, whose management Yapp considered conventional and often slovenly. Further land could be purchased using the National Heritage Memorial Fund. If £2 million could be spent saving a Poussin for the nation, he asked, why not save 8,000 acres of the Lake District or Exmoor from the plough or spruce? Given that the 'climax community' model of ecological development was now rejected by ecologists, he argued, nature recovery would need to be managed by professional ecologists, as occurred elsewhere in the world. Once sheep were removed, deciduous tree planting could begin.

Yapp's critique was published in a specialist journal, and he could hardly expect to make much political traction during the Thatcher years, but it took its place as part of the broader appraisal of the environmental impacts of industrial agriculture. Policy initiatives did follow, but the most significant driver of change was not environmental concern but outrage at the colossal waste and market distortions caused by EEC subsidies – the wine lakes and grain mountains of lore – leading eventually to reforms of the incentive structures that shaped how farmers used – or did not use – their land. A dizzyingly complex story can be pieced together about the development of subsidy regimes since the late 1980s – what Ann-Christian Knudson calls 'farmers on welfare' – including the introduction of relatively modest sums to finance agri-environmental schemes in agriculturally marginal uplands. The basic effect of these payments was to lower grazing pressures, but this could result in smaller commoners being driven out of business, allowing larger commoners to consolidate their businesses by buying up small farms.[13] Yapp, one imagines, would have despaired at this halfway-house approach, and critics now lament the consequences of 'undergrazing' which led to the colonisation of great stretches of upland with molinia grass.[14] In some uplands, the restoration of peat bogs by 're-wetting', effectively reverse-engineering drainage systems, is beginning to have a positive effect by stabilising bogs as carbon stores, rebooting their capacity to further sequester carbon, and seeing improved plant and insect biodiversity.[15] These schemes, however, hardly change the basic facts. Notwithstanding some iconic local success stories, the authoritative State of Nature Reports have made it abundantly clear that these measures have not reversed the precipitous and continuing decline in the UK's biodiversity.

Declining biodiversity was just one component of the growing sense of environmental crisis that engulfed humanity in the first decades of the twenty-first century. Global warming and climate change, the ubiquity of plastic waste, especially in the world's oceans, mineral extraction, population growth, declining soil health, collapsing populations of pollinators, all pointed to an existential threat to human and non-human life on earth. The scale of the problem could seem overwhelming, although the old environmentalist injunction to 'think globally, act locally' held promise for some. With respect to the land-scapes examined in this book, the most influential book of recent years was George Monbiot's *Feral*.[16] Monbiot enthralled and riled in equal measure, ensuring that the principles and practices of 'rewilding' went from being a fringe component of conservation science to a matter of national debate. Talk of species reintroductions, especially wolves, lynx and beavers, provoked a fierce reaction from the farmers but excited parts of the wider public.

The brilliance of Monbiot's intervention was twofold. First, he challenged romantic impressions of the UK's uplands by insisting they were 'sheepwrecked', teaching his readers to see the uplands they gloried in as ecologically diminished, monocultural sheep runs, as 'green deserts'. As Monbiot often observes, the International Union for Conservation of Nature, a United Nations agency, had to create a new category so that the UK's nature-depleted national parks could be included in its listings. Second, Monbiot placed the human expe-rience of nature at the centre of his argument. Rewilded nature would re-enchant the human relationship with the natural world, making for greater health and happiness and the greater ecological awareness needed to rescue life on earth. Much discussion about what consti-tutes 'self-willed' nature has followed, and conservation specialists often queried whether nature conservation initiatives described as 'rewilding' deserved the moniker, but there can be little doubt that 'rewilding' captured the imagination as a signifier for a more diverse, more unruly and less managed nature. The term quickly became an established part of everyday conversation among those concerned with such things.

Social media was central to the popularisation of Monbiot's ideas, but it should not for a moment be supposed he had things all his own way. His opponents were vocal and often aggressive. Monbiot is easily traduced as part of the 'metropolitan elite'. More subtle pushback to the general critique of upland farmers was also evident on social media. Most influential was James Rebanks, Cumbrian sheep farmer, Oxford graduate, UNESCO advisor, consultant and author of *A Shepherd's Life* (2015). This global bestseller narrated his family history, chronicling his working life on an upland farm, and traced his own acceptance that the Lakes are a 'form of national property'. Presented in a fragmentary way, written one imagines in the snatched moments allowed by work on the farm, *A Shepherd's Life* exemplifies how technique can convey authenticity. Other sheep farmers followed suit, notably Amanda Owen, 'the Yorkshire Shepherdess', whose string of books about family life at Ravenseat in the Yorkshire Dales was soon the subject of a charming fly-on-the-wall television documentary series. Rebanks engaged more directly in the debate about the future of the uplands, but if *A Shepherd's Life*, like his tweeted images of sheep, border collies and children, constituted the case for the defence, it was mounted primarily through affective means.[17]

Attempts to renew the public's affection for the pastoral ideal was challenged by another book published in 2015 and another debate. Mark Avery's *Inglorious. Conflicts in the Uplands* did not concern farming but the management of grouse moorlands and the illegal persecution of raptors. Avery had worked for the Royal Society for the Protection of Birds for many years but grew disillusioned with its cautious approach to the driven grouse shooting industry, which he considered consistently acted in bad faith. Pugnacious though industry representatives are, a blood sport associated with affluent 'guns' that requires huge stretches of dreary upland monoculture maintained by subsidies tends not to get good press. Intimidation is not uncommon, as Chris Packham found when he successfully led a legal challenge against the unlawful killing of several bird species in 2019.[18] A city trader in rural fancy dress shouldering a shotgun is a tougher sell than a hardy sheep farmer in an old raincoat with a collie and a crook, but both are kept afloat by subsidies, including those intended to finance developments that enhance biodiversity.

Monbiot was outraged when the British government successfully bid to have UNESCO declare the Lake District a World Heritage Site in 2017; making heavy weather of the role Rebanks Consulting played in the campaign, he polemicised against its official designation as 'a Beatrix Potter-themed sheep museum'.[19] The enduring cultural appeal of that pastoral ideal has certainly proven resilient, though Rebanks too can be numbered among those questioning the farming methods inherited from his father's generation.[20] *English Pastoral: An Inheritance*, his 2020 successor to *A Shepherd's Life*, offered a different kind of conversion narrative. Part three, 'Utopia', explains Rebanks's attempts to restore lost biodiversity to his farm through a series of interventions that include 'rewiggling' the ghyll running through the valley bottom and taking actions to restore soil health. Central to the Rebanks case is his strong critique of global food systems and his conviction that upland grazing regimes remain important to high-quality, nature-friendly, animal-welfare-orientated food production. The narrative emphasises the external pressures that have incentivised farmers to act in environmentally harmful ways (little is said about the power of the NFU as a lobby), the sense of loss felt by older farmers as they reflect on the plants and wildlife they remember from their youth and the growing acceptance by some upland farmers that they have something to learn from environmental experts previously regarded as interfering or ignorant of upland ways. Lucy Butler of the Eden Rivers Trust is one of *English Pastoral*'s quiet heroes. Rebanks speculates that of the fellsmen and women he knows, a third are starting to adopt new ways of working, a third would like to but cannot afford to and a third remain wedded to the old regime, regarding the new thinking as fanciful nonsense. One old fellsman laments the environmental harm he has inflicted on his own fields, making of them a 'green desert', though Monbiot's influence on the development of this discourse goes unacknowledged.[21]

Questions of ownership are crucial to the Rebanks story. His father was a tenant farmer and Rebanks's conversion narrative begins when he inherits his grandfather's freehold, 185 acres in Matterdale. Security of tenure has always been a factor in the readiness of farmers to 'improve' their land. This applies as much to current attempts to restore biodiversity as it did to earlier attempts to make land more productive according to the strictures of modern industrial farming. 'If we had a chance of holding on and doing anything good,' Rebanks writes, 'then it would be on our own farm in the hills.'[22] Inadvertently perhaps, Rebanks reminds us of how environmental debate is haunted by the fundamental that structures out society: the line that divides the propertied from the people without property. Few environmentalists, however effective their campaigning, have the environmental or ecological agency of a landowner. This fundamental was thrown into sharp relief by the 'wilding' experiment conducted at the Knepp Estate in Sussex, an extraordinary experiment in enlightened self-interest that has earned numerous environmental plaudits.

In 1985, when he was 22, Sir Charles Burrell, 10th Baronet, inherited a 3,500-acre estate (with John Nash 'castle'). With his wife, Isabella Tree, Burrell was determined to modernise the farm, intensifying production, taking what subsidies and incentives were on offer. At enormous cost, and a huge overdraft, they got their milk yields up, but the process was chemically dependent and unsustainable. The heavy Sussex clay would not yield. A fortuitous encounter indicated that Knepp might be eligible for financial support under the Countryside Stewardship Scheme, the means by which the UK government channelled the European Union's agri-environmental payments to British landholders. In 2000, Burrell and Tree decided to stop. They sacked 11 employees, sold off equipment and stock, let some land lie fallow, and made the rest available to contractors as they figured out what to do. What followed constitutes the most remarkable experiment in lowland farming conducted in Britain in recent times. This complex story is described in Tree's *Wilding. The Return of Nature to a British Farm* (2018), a terrific book about the remarkable place that Burrell and Tree have created in partnership with natural processes and a host of experts – accommodating rights of way along the way. They succeeded by leveraging a great deal of cultural capital, deploying a keen business sense, and benefiting from Knepp's location in the South-East. Burrell and Tree receive substantial subsidies, sell meat, and market 'Knepp safaris' and nights in a yurt on site, but their single largest source of income are the business units they rent.[23]

By the late 2010s, land ownership and subsidy remained the prime determinants of land use in the uplands and the national parks. These fundamentals were not challenged by the new agricultural settlement in prospect following Brexit, though the government did announce that future financial support paid to landholders will be predicated on the principle that public money should only be paid for public goods. The government's agriculture bill, whose parliamentary passage was delayed by the Covid-19 pandemic, will replace the current system of agricultural payments with a system of incentives paid on the basis of how far the system of farming adopted will deliver biodiversity gains on the basis of new environmental land management schemes. As had been the case during the 1980–1 parliamentary process, environmental organisations, particularly those dedicated to sustainable food production, worked hard to ensure that the legislation promised environmental gains. Debates about rewilding or grouse moors, the kind of stuff that excites social media pugilists, were peripheral to a process dominated by professional interests from across the agricultural and environmental spectrum working within parameters largely set by the government.

This reminds us of the need to distinguish between particular and systemic developments. Activists still have the potential to prevent individual developments or seek ameliorations, but they struggle to get traction over the evolution of systemic processes already captured by vested interests. Octavia Hill's decision to focus her energies on the National Trust reflected just this problem. Protecting common rights had significant achievements to its name but if the state was not prepared to redefine common rights as public rights then only ownership could provide the absolute inalienable protections she felt were the people's birthright. Purchase was a pragmatic necessity. Potter was less motivated by a sense of the collective good, but she too purchased to preserve, relying on covenants to guarantee her wishes in perpetuity. She would have been happy to see the Lake District's valleys and fells entirely in the Trust's ownership provided they were obtained through conventional market mechanisms. As a property owner, Potter was quick to see the nefarious influence of the Left in any role the state might play in the regulation or acquisition of private property. Notwithstanding her wartime radicalism, Dower regarded the Trust and the regulatory processes overseen by the National Parks Commission as happily coexisting, though her time as a commissioner largely pre-dated the period when agriculture itself came to be considered the fundamental problem. Sayer was fervent in her commitment to the national parks ideal. She did not just work within the framework provided by the 1949 Act but was vocal in her support for its first principles. If Dartmoor was accorded the treatment warranted by the national significance of its landscapes, the foundational essence of which lay in the exercise of common rights, then virtually all encroachments on its integrity were preventable. The problem was less the theory than the practice.

It is striking, therefore, that some rewilding enthusiasts now toy with the idea that only by purchasing land can the natural regeneration of celebrated British landscapes be brought about. On several occasions, the marketing of a substantial piece of common land on Dartmoor has generated a flurry of excitement on social media at the possibility that the purchase price could be crowdfunded. This energy and enthusiasm can be infectious, as social media posts rapidly accumulate, but wiser heads quickly prevail. Unless parliament is willing to dissolve the common rights – highly unlikely – there is next to nothing new owners could do with the land.

These moments reflect how new circumstances and new agendas have made Dartmoor fashionable again. The popularity of Devon's prettiest towns and villages among those 'escaping to the country' is nothing very new, though this intensified in the early twenty-first century as a fashionable rusticity took hold of the well-heeled liberal-left, but the renewal of interest in Dartmoor can only partly be explained by this gentrified rurality. Just as Dartmoor's vast commons exercised the imaginations of the 'improvers' in the nineteenth century, so they now intoxicate the rewilders of the early twenty-first. Why other uplands do not speak to the imagination in quite the same way is an interesting conundrum. The Lake District seems less malleable, perhaps because the National Trust's holdings are so extensive, perhaps because the strength of the Wordsworth–Potter–Rebanks nexus makes it seem more fixed, and perhaps because it just seems impenetrably northern to southern metropolitans. There is no Totnes in Cumbria. Whatever the explanation, for people frustrated by the apparent failures of the parks system to deliver ecological diversity, purchase can seem the only answer, just as it did for Hill. For those of a more progressive idealistic bent, collective ownership is especially appealing, not least because it is at odds with the secretive nature of land ownership and its concentration in fewer and fewer hands. To many, it seems remarkable that we know Britain faces a crisis of biodiversity, but we don't know who owns much of the land on which this crisis occurs. Guy Shrubsole's *Who Owns England? How We Lost Our Land and How To Take it Back* (2020), like Marion Shoard's *This Land is Our Land* (1987), has helped put land ownership back on the agenda, not least because he has revealed as much about what is *not* known to the public as what is.

But as the politics of our four champions shows, land ownership has never been just about whose name is on the title deeds. It has also always been about access. The four, of course, understood this only too well. So did Shoard: an aim of the new social contract between landowners and the landless she advocated was the repeal of the law of trespass to deliver a general right of access to the countryside – a radical step explored in her *A Right to Roam* (1999). Kate Ashbrook, Sayer's protégé, in her capacity as first the president of the Ramblers Association and more recently the general secretary of the Open Spaces Society, has dedicated her working life to the vigilance and campaigning needed to maintain and extend the public's right of access. Her website is a good starting point for anyone wanting to start piecing together a history of access politics since the 1970s.[24] During the Covid-19 lockdown of 2020–1, access came sharply into focus again. For the millions of people confined to their homes, the daily exercise permitted by government regulations became a vital part of their lives. Many discovered the footpaths near their home, and there was much talk about the healing power of nature as the glorious spring of 2020 gave way to a pleasant summer. Podcasts like Melissa Harrison's 'The Stubborn Light of Things' and much journalism helped bring the changing moods of the country to people confined to the town or the city. Some agonised about whether it was insensitive or uplifting to write about the privileges of your local patch or post photographs on social media of nearby beautiful places; either way, it was hard to dispute the basic premise that lockdown made the possession of a small garden or living within walking or cycling distance of the countryside a privilege. Britain being Britain, this was manifest in a rural property boom. Ableist assumptions abounded, though for a small group of aficionados the Twitter account run by the Dartmoor Collective, a group of amateur photographers, got the balance right. During the first lockdown, at 7 p.m. each day, under the hashtag #my400, people from all over the world were invited to post a photograph from that day's permitted exercise taken from within 400 metres of home.[25]

It took little, however, for the tensions that animate early twenty-first-century country life to come to the surface. Any indication that the metropolitan wealthy were escaping the city for second homes generated fury and much pontificating about the inadequacies of the rural NHS. Most, however, followed the rules, notwithstanding some high-profile transgressors and a couple of political scalps. More contentious was the low-level conflict caused by attempts by some landowners to close rights of way (illegal) or permissive footpaths (a grey area), claiming this was justified by the pandemic but rousing the suspicion among many that the pandemic was just the excuse the rural propertied were looking for. Clever things were said about the country always perceiving the city to be a source of contagion, but in most cases the tension was caused by radically intensified local use. When I was confronted by a Northumberland farmer for following a right of way that passed through her land and some 20 metres from her front door, it was hard not to think about the pavement that passed directly past my front door. I have no more right than she to prevent people from passing by my front door, but spatial politics are always relative.

A historical gloss can be put on this. The sharp distinction felt today between footpaths, bridleways, lanes and roads is relatively modern. To reimagine today's fragmented network of footpaths and bridleways as an essential means of getting around, it must be recalled that lanes and roads were once more hospitable to pedestrians and riders than they are today. With these tensions thrown into sharp relief by the government's plan to criminalise trespass, Nick Hayes's *The Book of Trespass. Crossing the Lines that Divide Us* (2020) struck a chord. Gorgeously illustrated by the author's woodcuts, it charts the history of access politics as means of contextualising Hayes's own dalliances at the edge of access law – as befits an early twenty-first-century work of 'creative non-fiction', personal experience leavens the historical narrative. One thinks of Hill refusing to be intimidated by landowners in the Kentish Weald, of Potter figuring how best to manage access to land, of Dower negotiating the routes of long-distance footpaths with awkward landowners, of Sayer asserting her right to walk on Ringmoor Down, of Ashbrook's work for long-established civil society organisations, wire-cutters in hand, and of Hayes's countercultural activism. They all share the same basic commitment to extending the limited rights of every citizen.

Lockdown also brought to the fore old anxieties about how people behave in the countryside. The government's tendency to announce restrictions just a few days in advance sparked a rush to take advantage of the last chance to enjoy favourite spots. Local news reports revelled in overcrowding, the ecological harm caused by illegal campfires and littering on a massive scale. Cheap camping equipment treated as single-use consumer goods brought the grotesque wastefulness associated with music festival culture to the countryside. Octavia Hill's plea for imaginative sympathy has its limits, and these modern 'beanfeasters' were certainly reprehensible, the clean-up often falling onto local volunteers. How Sayer would have blogged! More telling than the short-term problems was what it exposed about the UK's outsourcing of mass holidaymaking. If the millions who head each summer for the Mediterranean, with its extensive tourist infrastructure, are confined to the British Isles, then where are they to go? Holiday cottages, already scarce in the busy months, are too expensive for many families, and there are too few campsites to accommodate the greater demand. Summer 2020 brought home the material consequences of what we already know. A fortnight's family holiday in Greece, Italy or Spain can be cheaper than finding accommodation for a week in St Ives or Robin Hood's Bay. Pietistic pontificating by the well-heeled about the pleasures of staycationing will not make an adequate tourist infrastructure spring up overnight.

Class still matters, a statement as banal as it is true. In a democratic society there is a collective responsibility to ensure that rights can be enjoyed by all. Rights can be established in law, but the freedom of all citizens to exercise these rights is limited by economic, social and cultural constraints. Most obviously, access to the health-giving, joy-inducing qualities of the countryside is dependent on mobility and free time, which reflects not just income and employment type, but also caring responsibilities and physical health.

People's capacity – mental, physical or material – to exercise rights are an index of their freedom. Much of the division between Right and Left of course is predicated on the degree to which it is believed that society should intervene to ensure that those rights and freedoms can be enjoyed by all. But to reduce the question to its material component offers only limited insight into the question. If we are convinced that time spent in open or green places is good for an individual's wellbeing, and that this is one reason to preserve those places and access to them – as Hill, Potter, Dower and Sayer all believed – then what obligation falls on those apprised of these benefits to help others less well placed to see how they might similarly benefit? Of the four, Hill was most sensitive to the possibility that material disadvantage did not just limit experience but narrows an individual's capacity to know what they're missing.

For citizens who regularly exercise their rights of access, enjoy the benefits that flow from this and are firmly committed to the maintenance of these rights, it is hard to grasp the idea that their fellow citizens can find rambling culture 'middle class' and underpinned by unfamiliar and opaque behavioural norms, including dress codes.[26] The decision to include the injunction to 'enjoy your visit, have fun, make a memory' in the April 2021 update to the Countryside Code ensured the sensible list of dos and don'ts chimed with contemporary social media culture. My reaction to the advice that visitors 'be nice, say hello, share the space' was initially a bit scornful until a friend suggested I could just concede that saying 'hello' to strangers is the norm in the country but not the city (true) and that women often feel shunted to one side on footpaths.[27] As Kerri Andrews examines in Wanderers. *A History of Women Walking* (2021) – following in the footsteps of Rebecca Solnit – walking is a highly gendered activity. Exercising freedoms men take for granted can constitute a form of radical self-fashioning by women.

Just as access to the countryside is agitated by questions of class and gender, neither is it immune to other currents of political protest and concern. At the heart of the Black Lives Matter protests and the spectre of institutional racism are grave concerns about whether political, social and cultural structures uphold the rights of every citizen, irrespective of class, colour or creed. Again, just as it takes a little 'imaginative sympathy' (Hill again) for the middle-class rambler to appreciate why members of the urban working class might feel excluded from the rural environment the former comfortably occupies with their sturdy boots and OS maps, so should the same effort be made to appreciate why people of colour might feel similarly alienated, especially when their experience is compounded by their class position. Is the countryside as welcoming a place for people of colour as it is for those who are white? Do people of colour feel able to freely exercise their rights as citizens without let or hindrance? Do white people without British accents also feel at ease?

These questions have been brought to the fore by the tension at the heart of the National Trust's 'Colonial Countryside' research project. On the one hand, the project has highlighted the connections between the UK's great houses, imperialism and the proceeds of slavery and, on the other, it has begun the process of recovering a historical understanding of the presence of people of colour in the countryside, particularly through literary sources. The findings published in the project's 2020 interim report partly drew on the UCL 'Legacies of Slavery' project, which in 2012 made information about the compensation payments to slave-owners following abolition available through a free online database. The report highlighted the roles played by successive Trevelyans at the highest levels in the imperial administration and drew attention to the £27,000 – a colossal sum – awarded to Trevelyan family members as compensation for the freeing of 1,004 people they owned following abolition.[28] The report's publication was met with a predictable and disheartening backlash, particularly from the right-wing press and Conservative MPs, who accused the National Trust of adopting the 'woke' agenda, linking the Colonial Countryside project to the 'Rhodes Must Fall' campaign at the University of Oxford, and the toppling by protesters of the statue of the slave-trader Edward Colston in Bristol in June 2020. Some claimed, implausibly, that the project does not align with the Trust's statutory obligations, and ominous noises were heard from the government benches about whether this might be consistent with the Trust's charitable status. Much fire was drawn by Corinne Fowler, literary scholar and the project's academic lead, whose *Green Unpleasant Land. Creative Responses to Rural England's Colonial Connections* (2020) adds to the sizeable bibliography on the countryside as a site of political conflict. Fowler has begun to tease out how the English countryside has been produced by imperial and colonial processes rarely associated with its apparently peaceable historical continuities.

Fowler's work foregrounds recent literary engagements with the English countryside by Black British and Asian British writers. Some of this work tackles directly the experience and legacy of racism, other work offers a subtle challenge to questions of belonging. Elizabeth-Jane Burnett's *The Grassling* (2019) is a striking example of the latter. Much of *The Grassling* is characteristic of early twenty-first-century nature writing. Burnett explores her childhood domain – the village of Ide near Exeter – through local histories, old maps and historical vocabularies, tracing her family's long presence in the area and invoking her solitary experience of the landscape's numinous qualities. This genealogical dialogue with the loamy soils of mid-Devon might appear nativist, and perhaps a little too susceptible to that old antiquarian investment in the truths told by place names, but all is inflected by Burnett's part-Kikuyu background. Her mother is Kenyan, and she met Burnett's father when he was teaching in Kenya in the early 1960s. The migratory journeys of swifts from the Congo to Devon give her pause and she reflects on the linguistic particularities of Swahili, one of her mother's languages. 'Sometimes', Burnett writes, 'to hear one thing we must block out another', but still the colonial dimension of her Devonian pastoral will be heard.[29]

Anita Sethi's *I Belong Here. A Journey Along the Backbone of Britain* (2021) is more direct. It describes how the author, a Mancunian, was the victim of a racist hate crime on the TransPennine Express and began to find solace and healing by walking the Pennine Way. Dower helped make this possible. Sethi addresses the trauma caused by racism and how this is compounded by well-meaning denials, by the suggestion that perhaps she misconstrued something innocent as racist. She asks us to consider how these experiences intersect with being the only 'brown woman' on the trail, in a village, in a pub, and the unthinking way people feel free to point this out. However often she is called a 'P***', or reminded she is regarded as 'other', Sethi is a Northerner who needs open spaces like everyone else. Of her first visit to the Lake District, she writes:

> I breathed more deeply than I ever had done before and, for the first time I could remember, it was a joy to breathe and feel the oxygen flowing through my lungs, around my body, lifting my heart, clearing my head . . . . it felt right to be. I felt strong as if, like that tree, I would be able to withstand any fierce gale that may come battering. My heart was opening, growing, becoming as vast and deep as those lakes, as wide as those woods.[30]

Hill, Potter, Dower and Sayer sought to preserve precisely this right to be.

NOTES

Introduction

1. *The Times*, 22 Feb. 1967; Second Report of the Countryside Commission, 30 Sept. 1969 (NA [National Archives]/HLG [Ministry of Housing and Local Government], 127/1200).
2. Kate Ashbrook's account of the day can be found at https://campaignerkate.wordpress. com/2019/12/24/huccaby-memorial-to-dartmoor-campaigners/ (accessed 30 Sept. 2021).
3. Sayer played a similar role in Dartmoor to Ethel Haythornthwaite in the Peak District and Esmé Kirby in Snowdonia. See Melvyn Jones, *Protecting the Beautiful Frame. A History of the Sheffield, Peak District and South Yorkshire Branch of the Council for the Protection of Rural England* (Sheffield: Hallamshire Publications, 2001) and Teleri Bevan, *Esmé: Guardian of Snowdonia* (Talybont: Y Lolfa Cyf, 2014).
4. Not so long ago, a distinction tended to be drawn between Women's History, which sought to recover knowledge and understanding of women's past lived experiences, and Gender History, which emphasised how men's and women's experiences are shaped by conceptions of gender that are determined culturally, rather than biologically, and constructed discursively. This distinction now seems too sharp. Historians are still in the business of recovering past experiences, and this book contributes to that fundamental historical endeavour, but it is also interested in how experiences are embodied, and the role played by feelings and sensations alongside more conventional explanations of political change. Political developments cannot be satisfactorily explained according solely to 'rational' factors and their 'material' coordinates, and such accounts are now enriched by work on 'embodiment', 'emotional regimes' and 'structures of feeling', and a broader interest in 'subjectivities'.
5. *The Times*, 30 Aug. 1971.

Octavia Hill

1. Robert Whelan (ed.), *Octavia Hill's Letters to Fellow-Workers 1872-1911: Together with an Account of the Walmer Street Industrial Experiment* (London: Kyrle Books, 2005), p. 663.
2. National Trust, Report of the Council [hereafter NTR], 1903–4, p. 3; NTR, 1907–8, p. 5.
3. *The Times*, 2 July 1912; Whelan, *Letters to Fellow-Workers*, p. 663.
4. Octavia Hill to Mrs Senior, 3 Aug. 1875 in C. Edmund Maurice (ed.), *Life of Octavia Hill as Told in Her Letters* (Cambridge: Cambridge University Press, 1913, 2010), pp. 332–3.
5. Paul Readman, 'Octavia Hill and the English Landscape', in Elizabeth Baigent & Ben Cowell (eds), *'Nobler Imaginings and Mightier Struggles': Octavia Hill, Social Activism and the Remaking of British Society* (London: Institute of Historical Research, 2016), pp. 163–84.
6. Maurice, *Life of Octavia Hill*, p. 539.
7. *The Times*, 2 July 1912.
8. Hill to Canon Rawnsley, 22 Mar. 1897 (Octavia Hill Letters, NT [National Trust]).
9. Hill to Robert Hunter, 11 Apr. 1902 (Octavia Hill Letters, NT).

10. Hill worked to inspire generous giving by developing innovative fund-raising strategies. For example, when the National Trust campaigned to raise £12,000 to purchase 700 acres of fell country in Ullswater in the Lake District, Hill told readers of *The Times* that a donor had pledged £50, to be paid if 20 others agreed to do the same. Shortly afterwards another unnamed donor pledged £100, to be paid if nine others agreed to the same. *The Times*, 20 June 1905; 21 Nov. 1905.

11. Stefan Collini, *Public Moralists. Political Thought and Intellectual Life in Britain 1850–1930* (Cambridge: Cambridge University Press, 1991), p. 65.

12. Hill to Rawnsley, 25 Nov. 1898 (Octavia Hill Letters, NT); Hill to Mrs Senior, 3 Aug. 1875, Maurice, *Life of Octavia Hill*, pp. 332–3.

13. From a speech given in June 1888. Quoted in Paul Readman, *Storied Ground: Landscape and the Shaping of English National Identity* (Cambridge: Cambridge University Press, 2018), p. 125.

14. Paul Readman, 'Walking and Environmentalism in the Career of James Bryce: Mountaineer, Scholar, Statesman, 1838–1922', in Chad Bryant, Arthur Burns & Paul Readman (eds), *Walking Histories, 1800–1914* (London: Palgrave Macmillan, 2016); William Whyte, 'Sunday Tramps (act. 1879–1895)', 2007, ODNB online: https://doi.org/10.1093/ref:odnb/96363 (accessed 5 Nov. 2021); Hill made this point when lecturing on 'Open Spaces' to the National Health Society, *The Times*, 10 May 1877.

15. *The Times*, 25 July 1898 (Hornsey Urban District Council, Middlesex County Council, London County Council, and Islington and St Pancras Vestries).

16. *The Times*, 2 July 1912.

17. Indispensable recent works include Gillian Darley, *Octavia Hill: A Life* (London: Constable, 1990, revised as *Octavia Hill: Social Reformer and Founder of the National Trust* (London: Francis Boutle, 2004)), and Baigent & Cowell', 'Nobler Imaginings'.

18. Elizabeth Baigent, 'Octavia Hill, Nature and Open Space', in Baigent & Cowell, 'Nobler Imaginings', pp. 142–7.

19. *The Times*, 2 May 1877.

20. Christopher Ferguson, 'London and Early Environmentalism in Britain 1770–1870', in Bill Luckin & Peter Thorsheim, *A Mighty Capital Under Threat. The Environmental History of London, 1800–2000* (Pittsburgh: University of Pittsburgh Press, 2020), pp. 88–110.

21. Since 1980, they have been part of the Greensand Way which follows a 108-mile route between Haslemere in Surrey and Hamstreet in Kent.

22. Hill to Hunter, 12 Oct. 1889, 20 Oct. 1889, 7 Jan 1890 (Octavia Hill Letters, NT).

23. For an excellent overview of the development of the area focused on Sevenoaks, see David Killingray, 'Influences shaping the human landscape of the Sevenoaks area since c.1600', *Archaeologica Cantiana*, 130 (2010), pp. 35–64.

24. He is buried, with other members of his family, at Holy Trinity, Crockham Hill.

25. Hill to Hunter, 7 Jan. 1890 (Octavia Hill Letters, NT).

26. For the Leveson-Gower family tree, see: https://theweald.org/N10.asp?ID=314093 (accessed 10 March 2021).

27. NTR, 1972.

28. William Stevenson, *General View of the Agriculture of the County of Surrey. Drawn up for the Board of Agriculture and Internal Improvement* (London: Phillips, 1809), p. 463.

29. For a copy of local Byelaws, see http://www.kentwildlifetrust.org.uk/sites/default/files/2018-06/commons_bye-laws.pdf (accessed 8 Nov. 2021).

30. Darley, *Octavia Hill*, p. 198.

31. Hill to Mrs Blewitt, 3 Oct. 1900 (Octavia Hill Letters, NT).

32. Quoted in Darley, *Octavia Hill*, p. 199.

33. NTR, 1903–4, p. 3.

34. NTR, 1907–8, p. 5.

35. See 'The Kent Compendium of Historic Parks and Gardens for Sevenoaks District': http://www.kentgardenstrust.org.uk/research-projects/Sevenoaks/Larksfield.pdf (accessed 16 Aug. 2017), and the website of the National Gardens Scheme: https://www.ngs.org.uk (accessed 16 Aug. 2017). Incidentally, Larksfield remained home to the 'intellectual aristocracy' for a period after Yorke died in 1930. The house was bought by Nathaniel Bishop Harman (1869–1945), Fellow of the Royal College of Surgeons and highly regarded ophthalmic surgeon and reformer; he married Katharine Chamberlain of the great political dynasty; his daughter Elizabeth married Frank Pakenham, later Lord Longford. She became a very successful historian and, with her cousins, formed an influential literary dynasty. Elizabeth's brother, John Harman, another physician, was the father of Harriet

Harman, the Labour Party politician and former cabinet minister: http://livesonline.rcseng.ac.uk/biogs/E004151b.htm (accessed 16 Aug. 2017).

36. John Newman, *The Buildings of England. Kent: West and the Weald* (New Haven, CT: Yale University Press, 2012), p. 206.
37. Elizabeth Baigent, 'Octavia Hill: "the Most Misunderstood . . . Victorian Reformer"', in Baigent & Cowell, *'Nobler Imaginings'*, p. 8.
38. Darley, *Octavia Hill*, p. 314.
39. *The Times*, 29 Nov. 1930.
40. Edward Royle, *Robert Owen and the Commencement of the Millennium: The Harmony Community at Queenswood Farm, Hampshire, 1839–1845* (Manchester: University of Manchester Press, 1998), pp. 68–72.
41. R.K. Webb, 'Smith, (Thomas) Southwood (1788–1861)', *Dictionary of National Biography*: https://doi.org/10.1093/ref:odnb/25917
42. Kathryn Gleadle, *The Early Feminists: Radical Unitarians and the Emergence of the Women's Rights Movement, 1831–51* (London: Palgrave Macmillan, 2016), pp. 38–9; Caroline Southwood Hill, *Notes on Education* (London: Seeley, 1906), pp. 12–13; also *Memoranda of Observations and Experiments in Education* (London, 1860) and *Wild-Flowers and their Uses. A Book for Children* (London, 1870).
43. See Robyn M. Curtis, 'English Women and the Late-Nineteenth Century Open Space Movement', PhD thesis, Australian National University (2016), pp. 115–19; regarding Agnes and Rhoda Garrett, recent work has drawn attention to the Arts and Crafts businesses opened by lower-class women, see Zoë Thomas, 'Between art and commerce: women, business ownership and the Arts and Crafts Movement', *Past & Present*, 247, 1 (May 2020), pp. 151–96.
44. Hill to Miranda and Florence Hill, 5 Feb. 1860, Maurice, *Life of Octavia Hill*, p. 177.
45. Hill to Miranda Hill, 29 Apr. 1860, Maurice, *Life of Octavia Hill*, p. 180.
46. Hill to Emily Hill, 15 July 1861, Maurice, *Life of Octavia Hill*, pp. 197–8.
47. Margaret Todd, *The Life of Sophia Jex-Blake* (London: Macmillan, 1918); Shirley Roberts, *Sophia Jex-Blake: A Woman Pioneer in Nineteenth-Century Medical Reform* (New York: Routledge, 1993); Sophia Jex-Blake, *The Medical Education of Women* (London, 1874).
48. *The Times*, 22 June 1995, 10 Jan. 1996.
49. Caroline Morrell, 'Octavia Hill and Women's Networks in Housing', in Anne Digby and John Stewart (eds), *Gender, Health and Welfare* (London: Routledge, 1998), pp. 104–10, quote p. 108.
50. Darley, 'Octavia Hill: Lessons in Campaigning', in Baigent & Cowell, *'Nobler Imaginings'*, pp. 31–4.
51. Helen McCarthy, *Double Lives: A History of Working Motherhood* (London: Bloomsbury, 2020), p. 75; Noel Annan's famous essay of 1953 is reproduced in his *The Dons* (London: HarperCollins, 1999).
52. Martha Vicinus, *Independent Women: Work and Community for Single Women, 1850–1920* (London: Virago, 1985).
53. Quoted in Morrell, 'Octavia Hill and Women's Networks', p. 95.
54. Jane Garnett, 'At Home in the Metropolis: Gender and Ideals of Social Service', in Baigent & Cowell, *'Nobler Imaginings'*, p. 245. See also Vicky Albritton & Fredrik Albritton Jonsson, *Green Victorians: The Simple Life in John Ruskin's Lake District* (Chicago, IL: University of Chicago Press, 2016), pp. 72, 87.
55. Garnett, 'At Home in the Metropolis', p. 248.
56. Quoted in Garnett, 'At Home in the Metropolis', p. 247.
57. *The Times*, 15 July 1910.
58. Census records: https://theweald.org/P2.asp?PId=We.WarrenF (accessed 10 March 2021).
59. Octavia Hill, *Extracts from Octavia Hill's 'Letters to Fellow-Workers,' 1864–1911. Compiled by E.S. Ouvry* (London: Adelphi Book Shop, 1933). Ouvry was also long active in the Huguenot Society of London, serving as president, 1937–8, see *Proceedings of the Huguenot Society of London. Vol. XVI. 1937–1941* (London: Huguenot Society, 1941).
60. Andrea Geddes Poole, *Stewards of the Nation's Art: Contested Cultural Authority, 1890–1939* (Toronto: University of Toronto Press, 2009), pp. 121–1.
61. Planning documents (incl. but not limited to 10/03003/FUL; 12/00562/LDCPR; 14/00324/HOUSE) are available at: https://www.sevenoaks.gov.uk (accessed 9 Nov. 2021).
62. See Iain Sinclair, *London Orbital* (London: Penguin, 2003), p. 395 ff.
63. NTR, 1897–8, pp. 3–4.
64. Hill to her mother, 14 Aug. 1898, Maurice, *Life of Octavia Hill*, p. 541.

65. *The Times*, 21 July 1898; NTR, 1900–1, pp. 11–12.
66. For example, see *Sevenoaks Chronicle & Kentish Advertiser*, 28 Apr. 1967.
67. *The Times*, 25 Oct. 1913; NTR, 1914–15, p. 7.
68. *The Times*, 26 July 1928.
69. *The Car Illustrated: A Journal of Travel by Land, Sea and Air*, no. CXXXVI; Thomas Okey, *A Basketful of Memories: An Autobiographical Sketch* (London: Dent, 1930), p. 108.
70. *The Times*, 5 July 1937; NTR, 1938–9, p. 1
71. NTR, 1939–40, p. 11. The purchase by the Robertson bequest of Sutton House in London is marked with a plaque.
72. Sales were advertised in the *Surrey Mirror*, 9 June 1939.
73. NTR, 1922–3, p. 25.
74. See: http://www.hendenmanor.com/en/about/history (accessed 25 Oct. 2017).
75. Simon Mosely and Peter Moore, 'Seeing the wood from the trees', *New Scientist* (16 June 1988), pp. 59–61.
76. 'Natural development at Scords Wood, Toy's Hill, Kent, since the Great Storm of October 1987', English Nature Research Papers, 346 (2000), p. 25.
77. *The Observer*, 15 Oct. 2017.
78. See: https://www.woodlandtrust.org.uk/visiting-woods/wood/26681/ide-hill/ (accessed 25 Oct. 2017).
79. NTR, 1898–9, pp. 6–7.
80. NTR, 1899–1900, p. 20. The National Trust records Ide Hill as having been given by Miranda Hill, which appears to be incorrect.
81. NTR, 1910–11, pp. 4–5.
82. Hill to Mrs Edmund Maurice, 22 Sept. 1875, Maurice, *Life of Octavia Hill*, p. 336; Darley, *Octavia Hill*, pp. 166–8.
83. Hill to Mary Harris, 14 Feb. 1875, Maurice, *Life of Octavia Hill*, pp. 319–22.
84. P.R. Ghosh, 'Style and Substance in Disraelian Social Reform, 1860–80', in P.J. Waller (ed.), *Politics and Social Reform in Modern Britain. Essays Presented to A.F. Thompson* (Brighton: Harvester Press, 1987); J.P. Parry, 'Disraeli and England', *Historical Journal*, 42, 2 (Sept. 2000), p. 724.
85. The CPS attracted little formal support from Conservative MPs but enjoyed the patronage of MPs from across the Liberal party, including MPs of Radical and Whig persuasions, particularly representatives of metropolitan constituencies. M.J.D. Roberts, 'Gladstonian Liberalism and environmental protection, 1865–1876', *English Historical Review*, 128 (Apr. 2013), pp. 307–9.
86. Octavia Hill, 'Space for the people', *Macmillan's Magazine*, Aug. 1875, p. 328.
87. Hill, 'Space for the people', pp. 328, 330.
88. Ben Cowell, 'The Commons Preservation Society and the campaign for Berkhamsted Common, 1866–70', *Rural History*, 13, 2 (2002), pp. 154–6; Roberts, 'Gladstonian Liberalism and environmental protection', pp. 298–301.
89. Roberts, 'Gladstonian Liberalism', pp. 311–13.
90. Antony Taylor, '"Common-stealers", "land-grabbers" and "jerry-builders": space, popular radicalism and the politics of public access in London, 1848–1880', *International Review of Social History*, 40, 3 (Dec. 1995), pp. 383–407.
91. Neil MacMaster, 'The Battle for Mousehold Heath 1857–1884: "popular politics" and the Victorian public park', *Past & Present*, 127 (May 1990), pp. 117–54.
92. David M. George, 'The Plumstead Common riots of 1876: a study in mid-Victorian protest', *The London Journal*, 36, 3 (2011), pp. 195–210.
93. See Elizabeth Baigent, '"God's earth will be sacred": religion, theology and the Open Space Movement in Victorian England', *Rural History*, 22, 1 (2011), pp. 31–58.
94. Hill, 'Space for the people', pp. 328–9.
95. Hill, 'Space for the people', p. 329
96. Hill, 'Space for the people', p. 332.
97. *The Times*, 5 Feb. 1876.
98. Quoted in Collini, *Public Moralists*, p. 90.
99. William Whyte, 'Octavia Hill: The Practice of Sympathy and the Art of Housing', in Baigent & Cowell, *'Nobler Imaginings'*, p. 48.
100. Hill quoted by Ughtred Kay-Shuttleworth, MP, during the parliamentary debates on the Artisans' Dwelling bill (*Hansard*, 15 Feb. 1875, vol. 222, pp. 370–1).
101. *The Times*, 12 June 1876.

102. *The Times*, 24 Dec. 1881.
103. *The Times*, 28 Feb. 1890.
104. Altruism is a key theme for Collini in *Public Moralists*, esp. pp. 60ff.
105. Roberts, 'Gladstonian Liberalism', p. 298.
106. Collini, *Public Moralists*, p. 73.
107. Octavia Hill, 'Our common land', *Macmillan's Magazine*, Apr. 1897, p. 536; cf. Elizabeth Baigent, 'Octavia Hill, Nature and Open Space: Crowning Success of Campaigning "Utterly Without Result"', in Baigent & Cowell, '*Nobler Imaginings*', pp. 150–1.
108. John Rawls's summary of Smith's impartial spectator is helpful: 'Endowed with ideal powers of sympathy and imagination, the impartial spectator is the perfectly rational individual who identifies with and experiences the desires of others as if these desires were his own', quoted in D.D. Raphael, 'The Impartial Spectator', *Proceedings of the British Academy*, 58 (1972), p. 350. Ruskin's famous adage is quoted in William Whyte's ingenious analysis of the continuities between Hill's work as a copyist for Ruskin and her turn to philanthropic work: Whyte, 'Octavia Hill', p. 48.
109. Hill, 'Our common land', pp. 536–7.
110. Hill, 'Our common land', p. 538.
111. Hill, 'Our common land', p. 539.
112. William Cowper's Commons (Metropolis) bill 1866, which aimed to ban the further enclosure of land within the London metropolitan police district, was criticised along similar lines by radical MPs representing constituencies fringing the area. Roberts, 'Gladstonian Liberalism', p. 297.
113. Walter Houghton, *The Victorian Frame of Mind: 1830–1870* (New Haven, CT: Yale University Press, 1985).
114. Darley, *Octavia Hill*, pp. 168ff.
115. Cf. Baigent's sympathetic critique of Hill's Kyrle lecture as a 'rare attempt ... to explain her general philosophy' in Baigent, 'Octavia Hill, Nature and Open Space', pp. 152ff.
116. Octavia Hill, 'Colour, space, and music for the people', *The Nineteenth Century: A Monthly Review*, 15, 87 (May 1884), p. 741.
117. Hill, 'Colour, space', p. 742.
118. Hill, Colour, space', p. 745.
119. Hill, Colour, space', p. 746.
120. *The Times*, 31 Jan. 1887.
121. David Killingray, 'Rights, "riots" and ritual: the Knole Park access dispute, Sevenoaks, Kent, 1883–5', *Rural History*, 5, 1 (1994), pp. 63–79; for the broader context of rising tensions regarding public access to private estates, see Peter Mandler, *The Fall and Rise of the Stately Home* (New Haven, CT: Yale University Press, 1997), Knole disturbances at pp. 200–6.
122. Hunter is the least known of the three. For an appraisal of his career, see Ben Cowell, 'For the Benefit of the Nation: Politics and the Early National Trust', in Baigent & Cowell, '*Nobler Imaginings*', pp. 302–3.
123. J. Ranlett, 'Checking nature's desecration: late Victorian environment organisations', *Victorian Studies*, 26 (1983), pp. 210–12.
124. *The Times*, 17 Nov. 1893.
125. *The Times*, 17 July 1894.
126. Parry, 'Disraeli and England', p. 702.
127. Annan, *The Dons*; Annan should be read alongside William Whyte, 'The intellectual aristocracy revisited', *Journal of Victorian Culture*, 10, 1 (2005), pp. 15–45.
128. *The Times*, 17 July 1894.
129. Hill to Sydney Cockerell, 26 Oct. 1896, Maurice, *Life of Octavia Hill*, p. 538.
130. James Moore, 'The "last railway mania": The Light Railways Act of 1896 and local railway construction in Britain', *The Journal of Transport History*, 42, 2 (2020), pp. 229–53.
131. *The Times*, 10 Mar. 1896.
132. *The Times*, 14 Feb. 1896, 21 July 1896.
133. *The Times*, 23 Apr. 1896; 28 Apr. 1896; 6 July 1896.
134. Octavia Hill, 'The open spaces of the future', *The Nineteenth Century*, 46, 269 (July 1899), p. 28.
135. Hill, 'Open spaces of the future', p. 26.
136. Hill, 'Open spaces of the future', p. 30.
137. Hill, 'Open spaces of the future', pp. 32–3.
138. Whelan, *Letters to Fellow-Workers*, p. 405.

139. Hill, 'Open spaces of the future', p. 33.
140. Whelan, *Letters to Fellow-Workers*, p. 308.
141. Hill, 'Open spaces of the future', p. 33.
142. Alun Howkins, 'The use and abuse of the English Commons 1845–1914', *History Workshop Journal*, 78 (Autumn 2014), p. 123.
143. Hill, 'Open spaces of the future', p. 35.
144. Hill to Carrington Ouvry, 8 Sept 1903, quoted in Darley, *Octavia Hill*, p. 312.
145. Whelan, *Letters to Fellow-Workers*, pp. 325–6.
146. Octavia Hill, 'Natural beauty as a national asset', *The Nineteenth Century and After* (December 1905), p. 935.
147. Hill, 'Natural beauty', p. 935.
148. Hill, 'Natural beauty', p. 935.
149. Hill, 'Natural beauty', p. 937.
150. Hill, 'Natural beauty', p. 938.
151. Hill, 'Natural beauty', p. 939; cf. Baigent, 'Octavia Hill, Nature and Open Space', pp. 155–6.
152. Hill, 'Natural beauty', p. 938.
153. John Galsworthy, *The Forsyte Saga, Vol. 1* (London: Penguin, 1978, repr. 2001), p. 67.
154. Max Saunders, *Ford Madox Ford. Volume 1: The World Before the War* (Oxford: Oxford University Press, 1996), p. 90; D.H. Lawrence to Louie Burrows, 16 Oct. 1911, in James T. Boulton (ed.), *The Selected Letters of D.H. Lawrence* (Cambridge: Cambridge University Press, 1997), p. 31.
155. Paul Delany, *Fatal Glamour: The Life of Rupert Brooke* (Montreal: McGill-Queen's University Press, 2015), pp. 36–7.
156. *The Letters of Sidney and Beatrice Webb: Vol. 3, Pilgrimage 1912–47*, ed. Norman Mackenzie (Cambridge: Cambridge University Press, 2009), p. 180.
157. N. Waddell, *Modernist Nowheres: Politics and Utopia in Early Modernist Writing, 1900–1930* (London: Palgrave Macmillan, 2012), pp. 69, 88–90, 105–6.
158. Helen Smith, *The Uncommon Reader. A Life of Edward Garnett* (London, 2017); Sarah Knights, *Bloomsbury's Outsider: A Life of David Garnett* (London: Bloomsbury, 2015).
159. Jose Harris, *Private Lives, Public Spirit: Britain 1870–1914* (London: Penguin, 1994), pp. 240–1.
160. Lawrence Goldman, 'Octavia Hill, Beatrice Webb and the Royal Commission on the Poor Laws, 1905–9: A Mid Victorian in an Edwardian World', in Baigent & Cowell, *'Nobler Imaginings'*, pp. 255–74, quote at p. 265.
161. For a full account of Hill's posthumous reputation capturing its complexity, see Baigent, 'Octavia Hill: "the Most Misunderstood . . ."' in Baigent & Cowell, *'Nobler Imaginings'*, pp. 3–26; for an account of Hill's (limited) influence on the international preservationist movement, see Astrid Svenson, '"To Every Landless Man, Woman and Child in England": Octavia Hill and the Preservation Movement', in Baigent & Cowell, *'Nobler Imaginings'*, pp. 187–204.
162. *Hansard*, 17 July 1919, vol. 35, col. 770; 5 Dec. 1927, vol. 69, col. 502–3; 4 Mar. 1930, vol. 76, col. 774; 18 Apr. 1934, vol. 91, col. 633; 17 Dec. 1934, vol. 296, col. 884.
163. *Hansard*, 17 Dec. 1917, vol. 27, col. 186; 21 May 1925, vol. 61, col. 448; 7 June 1935, vol. 302, col. 2238; 4 Mar. 1946, vol. 139, col. 1023; 8 Mar. 2007, vol. 690, col. 387; 5 Feb. 2018, vol. 788, col. 1841.
164. *Hansard*, 12 Nov. 2001, vol. 628, col. 424; 11 Nov. 2020, vol. 663, col. 439–40.
165. *The Times*, 24 Jan. 1935, 28 Feb. 1935, 2 Dec. 1938, 3 Dec. 1938. A search of the *Times* digital archive suggests that journalists were particularly preoccupied by Hill between 1996 and 1998 until a click or two reveals that a racehorse went by the same name.
166. Ian Hislop, in *A Life More Noble: Reflections on Octavia Hill's Ambition of Nobility for All* (London: Octavia, 2015), loc. 152.
167. *Hansard*, 24 Oct. 2013, vol. 569, col. 152.

Beatrix Potter

1. When Brantwood, Ruskin's house, came on the market in 1932, there was talk of the Trust buying it. Potter was unconvinced: 'There are other things better worth buying; and Ruskin is at present under an eclipse – too deep a reaction – visitors have nearly ceased to ask where he lived'. Heelis to Sam Hield Hamer, 30 May 1932 (National Trust [NT] letters).
2. Potter to Bruce Thompson, 13 Apr. 1934 (NT letters).
3. Heelis to Hamer, 3 Feb. 1930 (NT letters).

4. Vicky Albritton & Fredrik Albritton Jonsson, *Green Victorians. The Simple Life in John Ruskin's Lake District* (Chicago, IL: University of Chicago Press, 2016), p. 109.
5. John Cousins, *Friends of the Lake District: The Early Years* (Lancaster: University of Lancaster, 2009), pp. 41–61.
6. Matthew Dennison, *Over the Hills and Far Away: The Life of Beatrix Potter* (London: Head of Zeus, 2016), p. 85.
7. *Miss Potter*, dir. Chris Noonan, 2006.
8. Linda Lear, *Beatrix Potter: The Extraordinary Life of a Victorian Genius* (London: Penguin, 2008), pp. 151–2.
9. Lear, *Beatrix Potter*, p. 139.
10. Amanda Vickery, 'Golden age to separate spheres? A review of the categories and chronology of English women's history', *Historical Journal*, 36, 2 (June 1993), p. 392.
11. Quoted in Lear, *Beatrix Potter*, p. 122.
12. Eve Colpus, 'Women, service and self-actualization in inter-war Britain', *Past and Present*, 238, 1 (2018), pp. 197–232.
13. Lear, *Beatrix Potter*, p. 9.
14. Lear, *Beatrix Potter*, pp. 10–14.
15. Quoted in Dennison, *Over the Hills*, p. 43.
16. Lear, *Beatrix Potter*, pp. 14–16.
17. Lear, *Beatrix Potter*, pp. 16–20.
18. The seminal intervention is Vickery's 'Golden age to separate spheres?', pp. 383–414.
19. Lear, *Beatrix Potter*, p. 21.
20. Dennison, *Over the Hills*, p. 85.
21. Quoted in Dennison, *Over the Hills*, p. 111.
22. Quoted in Lear, *Beatrix Potter*, p. 42.
23. Dennison, *Over the Hills*, pp. 96–7.
24. Lear, *Beatrix Potter*, p. 25.
25. Lear, *Beatrix Potter*, pp. 45–6, 63.
26. Lear, *Beatrix Potter*, pp. 53–4; Dennison, *Over the Hills*, p. 121.
27. Lear, *Beatrix Potter*, pp. 142–3, 145–6.
28. Lear, *Beatrix Potter*, p. 139; Albritton & Jonsson, *Green Victorians*, p. 97.
29. For 'taskscape', see Tim Ingold's seminal paper 'The temporality of the landscape', *World Archaeology*, 25, 2 (Oct. 1993), pp. 152–74.
30. Jonathan Bate, *Romantic Ecology. Wordsworth and the Environmental Tradition* (London: Routledge, 1991), p. 45.
31. Bate, *Romantic Ecology*, p. 51.
32. Paul Readman, *Storied Ground: Landscape and the Shaping of English National Identity* (Cambridge: Cambridge University Press, 2018), p. 145.
33. Kenneth R. Olwig, 'England's "Lake District" and the "North Atlantic Archipelago": A body of managed land contra a body politic', *Landscape Research*, 43, 8 (2008), pp. 1032, 1039.
34. Matthew Kelly, *Quartz and Feldspar. Dartmoor: A British Landscape in Modern Times* (London: Vintage, 2015), pp. 85–6.
35. Kerri Andrews, '"Learning the lakes": Harriet Martineau's *A Complete Guide to the English Lakes* and pedestrian authority', *Romanticism*, 27, 1 (Apr. 2021), pp. 99–108.
36. Harriet Ritvo, *The Dawn of Green. Manchester, Thirlmere, and Modern Environmentalism* (Chicago, IL: University of Chicago Press, 2009).
37. Readman, *Storied Ground*, pp. 109ff.
38. Quoted in Wendy Joy Darby, *Landscape and Identity: Geographies of Nation and Class in England* (Oxford: Berg, 2000), p. 151.
39. Quoted in Darby, *Landscape and Identity*, p. 151.
40. Readman, *Storied Ground*, p. 144
41. Albritton & Jonsson, *Green Victorians*, p. 107.
42. Albritton & Jonsson, *Green Victorians*, pp. 108–9.
43. Albritton & Jonsson, *Green Victorians*, p. 105.
44. Albritton & Jonsson, *Green Victorians*, p. 112.
45. See http://www.herdwick-sheep.com/herdwicks/about-us/ (accessed 7 Dec. 2018).
46. Frank Garnett, *Westmorland Agriculture, 1800–1900* (1912), p. 142.
47. T. Rowlandson (1869), quoted in Garnett *Westmorland Agriculture*, p. 156.

48. Garnett, *Westmorland Agriculture*, p. 152.
49. Garnett, *Westmorland Agriculture*, pp. 157–8.
50. After 1864, their annual shows were always held at the Woolpack Inn at Eskdale.
51. Garnett, *Westmorland Agriculture*, pp. 153, 157–8, 160, 162.
52. Garnett, *Westmorland Agriculture*, pp. 160, 172.
53. A story from *Bell's Messenger*, repr. in *The Country Gentleman's Magazine*, July 1869, pp. 38–9.
54. Daniel Gate, *Gate's New Shepherd's Guide for Cumberland, Westmoreland & Lancashire* (Lancaster: Brash Bros, 1879), pp. 491–3.
55. On the problems with the Spanish theory, see W.M. Dickenson, quoted in Gate, *New Shepherd's Guide*, p. 490.
56. H.D. Rawnsley, *Life and Nature at the English Lakes* (Glasgow: James Maclehose, 1899), p. 70.
57. H.D. Rawnsley, *Months at the Lakes* (Glasgow: James Maclehose, 1906), pp. 186–7.
58. H.D. Rawnsley, *By Fell and Dale at the English Lakes* (Glasgow: James MacLehose, 1911), pp. 11, 48, 50–1.
59. H.D. Rawnsley, *A Rambler's Note-Book at the English Lakes* (Glasgow: James Maclehose, 1902), pp. 208–18.
60. Readman, *Storied Ground*, pp. 136–9.
61. Kelly, *Quartz and Feldspar*, pp. 85–6.
62. Readman, *Storied Ground*, pp. 133–43.
63. Bruce Thompson, *The Lake District and the National Trust* (Kendal: Titus Wilson, 1946), pp. 42–3.
64. Hill, in Robert Whelan (ed.), *Octavia Hill's Letters to Fellow-Workers 1872–1911: Together with an Account of the Walmer Street Industrial Experiment* (London: Kyrle Books, 2005), pp. 473–5.
65. Thompson, *The Lake District and the National Trust*, p. 43.
66. Matthew Kelly, 'On Why the U.K.'s First National Park Might Have Been in Ireland', in Matthew Kelly (ed.), *Nature and the Environment in Nineteenth-Century Ireland* (Liverpool: Liverpool University Press, 2019), pp. 118–38.
67. Whelan, *Letters to Fellow-Workers*, p. 526.
68. Readman, *Storied Ground*, p. 134.
69. *NT Reports*, 1923–4, pp. 5–6, 31 & 1924–5, p. 9. On the replacement of the Fell and Rock Climbing Club memorial, see https://www.iwm.org.uk/memorials/item/memorial/3961 (accessed 15 Nov. 2021).
70. William Farrier and J. Brownhill (eds), 'The Parish of Hawkshead' in *A History of the County of Lancaster: Vol. 8* (London: Constable, 1914); H.S. Cowper, *Hawkshead (The Northernmost Point of Lancashire)* (London: Bemrose, 1899), p. 44.
71. Lear, *Beatrix Potter*, pp. 4–5.
72. Peter Mandler, *The Fall and Rise of the Stately Home* (New Haven, CT: Yale University Press, 1997), pp. 184–7; NT Report, 1926.
73. Mandler, *Fall and Rise*, pp. 187–91.
74. Lear, *Beatrix Potter*, p. 210.
75. Hunter Davies, *Beatrix Potter's Lakeland* (London: Warne, 1988), p. 60.
76. Lear, *Beatrix Potter*, p. 228.
77. Heelis Deeds, Lancashire Archives (DDN 4/9 Hill Top Farm, Sawrey, 1777–1869).
78. Heelis Deeds (DDN 4/14 Castle Farm, Sawrey, 1909).
79. Heelis Deeds (DDN 4/9 Hill Top Farm, Sawrey, 1777–1869).
80. E.H.H. Green, *The Crisis of Conservatism. The Politics, Economics and Ideology of the British Conservative Party, 1880–1914* (London: Routledge, 1995), pp. 207–22.
81. Potter to Harold Warne, 8 Jan. 1910; Potter to Edmund Evans, 28 Feb. 1910, in Judy Taylor (ed.), *Beatrix Potter's Letters* (London: Warne, 1989) [*BPL*], pp. 173–6.
82. Draft letter, 1911, *BPL*, pp. 190–1.
83. *The Times*, 4 Jan. 1912, 6 Jan. 1912, 11 Jan. 1912, 12 Jan. 1912, 13 Jan. 1912, 15 Jan. 1912, 19 Jan. 1912, 23 Jan. 1912, 2 Feb. 1912, 5 Feb. 1912, 23 Feb. 1912, 5 Mar. 1912, 15 Mar. 1912, 17 Apr. 1912, 28 Aug. 1912, 29 Aug. 1912.
84. Heelis to Warne, 13 Dec. 1911, *BPL*, p. 192.
85. *Hansard*, 4 Mar. 1912, vol. 35, col. 31–2.
86. Potter to *Country Life* [pub. 13 Jan. 1912], *BPL*, pp. 193–4.
87. Potter to Hamer, 13 June 1930 (NT letters).
88. Potter to Warne, 4 Apr. 1912, *BPL*, pp. 196–7.
89. Lear, *Beatrix Potter*, p. 277.

90. Mandler, *Fall and Rise*, p. 178.
91. Lear, *Beatrix Potter*, p. 252.
92. W.R. Mitchell, *Beatrix Potter: Her Lakeland Years* (Ilkley: Great Northern Books, 2010), p. 106; Davies, *Beatrix Potter's Lakeland*, p. 128.
93. Lear, *Beatrix Potter*, p. 273.
94. Connoisseurs of this sort of thing will be interested in the detail of the lease: the lessor reserved right to all timber and timber-like trees and underwood except reasonable hedging wood as agreed; all mines, stones & quarries, sand, gravel or other substrata and liberty to take, pay compensation for all surface damage. Right to kill and take game, sport or fish. Manure generated by the land had to be used on the land. In essence, Heelis could only use the land for grazing and could not plough, convert or deforest the land. Heelis Deeds, Lancashire Record Office (DDN 4/24).
95. Heelis to Hamer, 3 Feb. 1925 (NT letters).
96. H.H. Symonds, *Walking in the Lake District* (London: Alexander Maclehose, 1933, 1947), p. 34.
97. W.H. Pearsall & Winifred Pennington, *The Lake District. A Landscape History* (London: Collins, 1973), pp. 255–6.
98. Heelis to Hamer, 18 Mar. 1926 (NT letters).
99. Harriet Martineau, *A Complete Guide to the English Lakes* (Windermere: John Garnett, 1855), pp. 35–8. On Martineau's use of her decision to relocate to the Lake District to establish her literary celebrity, see Alexis Easley, 'The woman of letters at home: Harriet Martineau and the Lake District', *Victorian Literature and Culture*, 34, 1 (2006), pp. 291–300.
100. Quoted in Easley, 'The woman of letters at home', p. 296.
101. Quoted in 'The Lonely Hills', *The Horn Book Magazine,* vol. 18 (May 1942) and reprinted in Norma R. Fryatt (ed.), *A Horn Book Sampler. On Children's Books and Reading. Selected from Twenty-Five Years of the Horn Book Magazine 1924–48* (Boston, MA: The Horn Book, 1959), pp. 31–2.
102. This section draws on the document notifying Troutbeck as an SSSI, https://designatedsites.naturalengland.org.uk/PDFsForWeb/Citation/1002088.pdf (accessed 16 Nov. 2021).
103. Kathleen Jamie, 'A lone enraptured male', *London Review of Books*, 30, 5 (6 Mar. 2008), pp. 25–7.
104. Heelis to Hamer, 26 June 1926, *BPL*, pp. 296–8.
105. Heelis to Hamer, 24 Oct. 1929 (NT letters).
106. The process can be followed in Cousins, *Friends of the Lake District*, ch. 4.
107. Heelis to Hamer, 26 June 26, *BPL*, pp. 296–8.
108. Heelis to Hamer, 26 June 1926, *BPL*, pp. 296–7.
109. Davies, *Beatrix Potter's Lakeland*, p. 124; Mitchell, *Beatrix Potter*, p. 86; Heelis to Hamer, 4 Sept. 1930 (NT letters).
110. Davies, *Beatrix Potter's Lakeland*, pp. 149–50; Mitchell, *Beatrix Potter*, pp. 87, 96.
111. Judy Taylor (ed.), *Beatrix Potter's Farming Friendship. Lake District Letters to Joseph Moscrop 1926–1943* (London: Beatrix Potter Society, 1998), pp. 37–8, 42, 48, 55–6, 60.
112. James Rebanks, *The Shepherd's Life. A Tale of the Lake District* (London: Allen Lane, 2015), p. 258.
113. She could drive a hard bargain. In 1937, she rebuffed Moscrop's claims for higher pay, feigning shock that he could ask for £16 for the season. With wool prices being what they were, surely £15 was enough?
114. Heelis to Hamer, 7 Nov. 1930 (NT letters).
115. Arthur Ransome, *Swallows and Amazons* (1930), ch. 14.
116. At the time of writing, these plastic cases were becoming of considerable environmental concern.
117. https://designatedsites.naturalengland.org.uk/PDFsForWeb/Citation/1002088.pdf
118. Heelis to Hamer, 2 Feb. & 31 Jan. 1925 (NT letters).
119. Heelis to Hamer, 2 Feb. 1925 (NT letters).
120. Heelis to Hamer, 13 Feb. 1925 (NT letters).
121. Esther Cloudman Dunn, 'Gordon Wordsworth', *The American Scholar*, 6, 3 (Summer 1937), p. 334; NT Report, 1928–9, p. 7.
122. Thompson, *Lake District and the National Trust*, p. 53.
123. Heelis to Hamer, 16 Oct. 1929, 17 Oct. 1929, 20 Oct. 1929 (NT letters).
124. Heelis to Hamer, 28 Oct. 1929, *BPL*, p. 323; Heelis to Hamer, 25 Oct. 1929 (NT letters).
125. Heelis to Hamer, 14 Oct. 1931 (NT letters).
126. This is exemplified by Cragside, a National Trust estate in Northumberland.
127. Heelis to Hamer, 20 Oct. 1929 (NT letters).
128. Heelis to Hamer, 20 Oct. 1929, 21 Oct. 1929 (NT letters).

129. Heelis to Hamer, 13 Nov. 1930, 23 Dec. 1930 (NT letters).
130. Heelis to Hamer, 24 Oct. 1929 (NT letters). To compare the 1851 Ordnance Survey map of the Lake District with the present edition is to be immediately struck by how extended the plantations now are.
131. A rare exception was a 'one-storey slated roughcast little house' near Coniston which she conceded was 'really rather pleasing in the landscape', Heelis to Hamer, 22 Oct. 1931 (NT letters).
132. Heelis to Hamer, 23 Oct. 1929 (NT letters).
133. Heelis to Hamer, 12 Dec. 1929 (NT letters).
134. Lear, *Beatrix Potter*; Heelis to Hamer, 8 Oct. 1930 (NT letters).
135. Heelis to Hamer, 27 Jan. 1930 (NT letters).
136. NT Report, 1929–30, p. 3.
137. Heelis to Hamer, 20 June 1932 (NT letters); NT Report, 1931–2, pp. 81–2. She continued to be named as the donor in the property lists that were a feature of the NT reports.
138. Heelis to Hamer, 20 Oct. 1929 (NT letters).
139. See https://designatedsites.naturalengland.org.uk/PDFsForWeb/Citation/1002038.pdf (accessed 17 Nov. 2021).
140. National Trust sign at Tarn Hows.
141. Heelis to Hamer, 28 Oct. 1929, *BPL*, p. 323.
142. Heelis to Hamer, 2 Feb. 1930, 29 June 1930 (NT letters).
143. Heelis to Hamer, 9 Nov. 1930, 13 Nov. 1930, 9 Dec. 1930, 23 Dec. 1930 (NT letters).
144. Heelis to Hamer, 2 Feb. 1930 (NT letters).
145. Heelis to Hamer, 28 Oct. 1930 (NT letters).
146. Heelis to Hamer, 21 Dec. 1929 (NT letters). Gatebeck, purchased by Imperial Chemical Industries, was also to close.
147. Heelis to Hamer, 22 Nov. 1933 (NT letters).
148. Heelis to Hamer, 27 Mar. 1930 (NT letters).
149. Heelis to Hamer, 10 Mar. 1930, 26 Mar. 1931, 18 July 1931 (NT letters).
150. Heelis to Hamer, 30 July 1930, 17 Jan. 1931 (NT letters).
151. Heelis to Hamer, 17 Jan. 1931; Heelis to Matheson, 15 June 1934 (NT letters).
152. David Matless, *Landscape and Englishness* (London: Reaktion Books, 1998, 2016), p. 47.
153. Heelis to Hamer, 11 Sept. 1932; Heelis to Thompson, 16 Sept. 1932 (NT letters).
154. Heelis to Hamer, 9 May 1933, 7 July 1933, 12 Oct. 1933; Heelis to Thompson, 8 Aug. 1933 (NT letters).
155. Heelis to Matheson, 15 June 1934; Heelis to Thompson, 17 Dec. 1934, 29 Jan. 1935 (NT letters).
156. Heelis to D.M. Matheson, Sec of the NT, 22 Jan. 1935, *BPL*, p. 373; Heelis to Thompson, 29 Jan. 1935 (NT letters).
157. Heelis to Hamer, 31 Dec. 1930 (NT letters).
158. Heelis to Eleanor Rawnsley, 24 Oct. 1924 (NT letters).
159. Cousins, *Friends of the Lake District*, p. 29.
160. See Lake District National Reserve Committee, evidence to Addison, 17 Dec. 1929; Lake District National Reserve Committee & Fell & Rock Climbing Club, evidence to Addison, 18 Jan. 1930 (HLG 52/717–21).
161. Lake District National Reserve Committee, evidence to Addison, 17 Dec. 1929, (HLG 52/717–21), p. 5.
162. Heelis to Hamer, 11 Aug. 1932; Heelis to Thompson, 31 Jan. 1935 (NT letters).
163. Davies, *Beatrix Potter's Lakeland*, p. 218.
164. Mark David Spence, *Dispossessing the Wilderness: Indian Removal and the Making of the National Parks* (Oxford: Oxford University Press, 2000).
165. Lake District National Reserve Committee, evidence to Addison, 17 Dec. 1929, (HLG 52/717–21), p. 7.
166. Heelis to Hamer, 27 Jan. 1930 (NT letters).
167. Heelis to Warne, 22 Jan. 1924, BPL, p. 285.
168. Summary of letter from Bailey and Trevelyan, 15 Jan. 1930 (HLG 52/717–21).
169. On rubber tyres see Mitchell, *Beatrix Potter*, p. 119.
170. Trust's submission (HLG 52/717–21), p. 6.
171. *Hansard*, 21 Feb. 1930, vol. 235, col. 1747–9.
172. *Hansard*, 21 Feb. 1930, vol. 235, col. 1776.
173. *Hansard*, 15 Apr. 1931, vol. 251, cc 193, 197, 211, 231; 2 Feb. 1932, vol. 261, cc 52–3.

174. Heelis to Hamer, 15 Mar. 1932 (NT letters).
175. Heelis to Hamer, 27 Feb. 1934 (NT letters).
176. Heelis to Eleanor Rawnsley, 24 Oct. 1934, *BPL*, p. 367.
177. Heelis to Eleanor Rawnsley, 21 Oct. 1934, *BPL*, p. 366.
178. NT Report, 1934–5, pp. 3–4.
179. NT Report, 1935–6, pp. 12–13; Lindsay to Orwin, 13 Apr. 1934 (Balliol College Archives: Buttermere Papers, J-AddH-13); Thompson, *Lake District and the National Trust*, pp. 190–1.
180. Hamer to Lindsay, 2 May 1934 (Buttermere Papers).
181. Harry A. Holloway, 'A.D. Lindsay and the problems of mass democracy', *The Western Political Quarterly*, 16, 4 (Dec. 1963), p. 801.
182. Examples include C.S. Orwin, *The Determination of Farming Costs* (Oxford: Clarendon Press, 1917) and *The Future of Farming* (Oxford: Clarendon Press, 1930).
183. Trevelyan to Lindsay, 27 Apr. 1934; Carlisle to Lindsay, 20 Apr. 1934, 25 Apr. 1934 (Buttermere Papers).
184. *The Times*, 16 May 1934. Other signatories included Helen Darbishire, the Principal of Somerville, a Wordsworth specialist and trustee of Dove Cottage, who eventually moved to the Lake District; Reginald Gleadowe, the Slade Professor of Fine Art and a master at Winchester College; F.M. Powicke, old Balliol member and Regius Professor of History; Ernest de Selincourt, another academic Wordsworthian; Professor Tait; Mrs Spooner, widow of the well-known New College don; M.L. Jacks, educationalist and headmaster of Mill Hill School; Reginald Lennard, the agricultural historian; and Hugh Walpole, who lived between London and Keswick and was author of *The Herries Chronicle*, set in the Lake District.
185. 'Report on Mr. W.M.W. Marshall's Lake Land Estate', 10 May 1934 (Buttermere Papers).
186. Heelis to Mrs Miller, 13 Dec. 1934, *BPL*, pp. 370–1.
187. Heelis to Daisy Hammond & Cecily Mills, 30 Mar. 1939, *BPL*, p. 398.
188. Heelis to Bertha Miller, 13 Dec. 1934; Heelis to Caroline Clark, 19 Dec. 1934; Heelis to Esther Nicholson, 17 Nov. 1936; Heelis to Clark, 18 Mar. 1939; Heelis to Moscrop, 23 Jan. 1939, *BPL*, pp. 371–2, 380, 394, 396–7.
189. Heelis to Secretary of the NT, 22 Apr. 1936 (NT letters); *BPL*, p. 377.
190. Heelis to Thompson, 4 Jan. 1937, *BPL*, p. 382; Heelis to D.M. Matheson, 9 May 1938, *BPL*, p. 389.
191. Heelis to D.M. Matheson, 9 May 1938, 11 May 1938, 17 Oct. 1939; Heelis to Thompson, 30 Mar. 1942, *BPL*, pp. 389, 390, 409–10.
192. Heelis to Stephanie Duke, 10 Dec. 1943; Heelis to Moscrop, 13 Dec. 1943, *BPL*, p. 465.
193. Heelis to Hamer, 29 May 1930 (NT letters).
194. She did not enjoy doing the accounts, signing off on one occasion 'Depressed, but still arguing & spending!', Heelis to Hamer, 27 Nov. 1931 (NT letters).
195. Potter's will can be found at https://www.arnisonheelis.co.uk/workspace/pdfs/beatrix-potter-will.pdf
196. Beatrix Potter, 'The Lonely Hills', *The Horn Book Magazine*, vol. 18 (May 1942), reprinted in Norma R. Fryatt (ed.), *A Horn Book Sampler. On Children's Books and Reading. Selected from Twenty-Five Years of the Horn Book Magazine 1924–48* (Boston, MA: The Horn Book, 1959), p. 32.

Pauline Dower

1. *The Times*, 26 Jan. 1958.
2. Other women members included Dr Nancy Davies (1953–6), Lady Hopkin Morris (1957–8) and Margaret Davies ('Mrs Elwyn Davies'), one of the two commission members to survive the restructuring of 1966. Margaret Davies's career across a range of conservationist bodies is summarised in ch. 8 of Avril Madden, *Complex Locations: Women's Geographical Work in the UK 1850–1970* (Chichester: Wiley-Blackwell, 2009).
3. Noel Annan, *Our Age: Portrait of a Generation* (London: Weidenfeld & Nicolson, 1990).
4. Influential critiques include Ann & Malcolm MacEwen, *National Parks: Conservation or Cosmetics?* (London: Allen & Unwin, 1982) and George Monbiot, *Feral: Searching for Enchantment on the Frontiers of Rewilding* (London: Allen Lane, 2013).
5. *Manchester Guardian*, 17 Dec. 1949.
6. David Cannadine, *G.M. Trevelyan. A Life in History* (London: HarperCollins, 1992), p. 5.

7. Pauline Dower, *Living at Wallington* (Ashington: Mid Northumberland Arts Group, 1984).
8. Dower to Charles Philips Trevelyan, 15 Apr. 1941 (Newcastle University Archives: CPT/4/2/?52).
9. Charles Trevelyan to Pauline Dower, 10 Apr. 1941 (Cambo Letters). I am grateful to Robin Dower for allowing me access to his mother's papers, here referenced as 'Cambo Letters'.
10. See the National Trust's beautifully illustrated 'Your Guide to the Central Hall. Discover Wallington'.
11. See Duncan Sutherland, Trevelyan [née Bell], Mary Katherine [Molly], Lady Trevelyan, *Oxford Dictionary of National Biography*.
12. The Bells were significant Middlesbrough industrialists. Sir Hugh Bell, Dower's grandfather, entered into the family firm, Bell Brothers, and had interests in iron production, railways and steel. His first wife, Mary (née Shield), was Gertrude's mother. Widowed in 1871, he then married Florence Olliffe (1851–1930), a half-French author, social investigator and playwright. A prolific writer, her most significant work was *At the Works* (1907), a detailed investigation of Middlesbrough. Molly Trevelyan was the youngest of her and Hugh's three children. Her marriage to Charles Trevelyan thus united two great North-East dynasties. See Angela V. John, 'Bell [née Olliffe], Florence Eveleen Eleanore, Lady Bell (1851–1930)', *Dictionary of National Biography*.
13. *Leeds Mercury*, 8 Jan. 1931.
14. Cannadine, *G.M. Trevelyan*, pp. 145–6.
15. John Sheail, 'John Dower, national parks, and town and country planning in Britain', *Planning Perspectives*, 10, 1 (1995), pp. 3–4, 9–13; David Wilkinson, *Fight for it Now. John Dower and the Struggle for National Parks in Britain* (Oxford: Signal Books, 2019), esp. chs 2 & 3.
16. Dower to Charles Trevelyan, 24 Oct. 1942 (CPT/4/2/53).
17. Wilkinson, *Fight for it Now*, chs 5–9.
18. While working on the Hobhouse Report, he was unable to join Leonard Elmhirst, a committee member, on his visit to the Roman Wall, and Dower herself took the wheel, taking advantage of the 90-mile road trip to impress upon Elmhirst the importance of Roman Wall country to her husband's thinking.
19. John Dower to Lord Justice Scott, 25 Nov. 1943 (HLG [Ministry of Housing and Local Government] 93/55).
20. Charles Trevelyan to Dower, 20 Oct. 1942 (Cambo Letters).
21. Dower to Charles Trevelyan, 28 Dec. 1943 (CPT/4/2/53); Dower to mother, 27 Jan. 1943, 13 Mar. 1943 (CPT/4/2/54).
22. Dower to Charles Trevelyan, 14 Sept. 1942. (CPT/4/2/52).
23. Sidney & Beatrice Webb, *Soviet Communism: A New Civilisation* (London: Longman, 3rd edn. 1941); Charles Trevelyan to Dower, 17 June 1941, 28 Jan. 1944 (Cambo Letters). 'I find it quite impossible,' Charles wrote, 'to believe that we are going to continue to be dominated by the semi-Fascist minds of Wall Street, the City of London and the 200 families.'
24. Dower to Charles Trevelyan, 17 Dec. 1943 (CPT/4/2/?52); Charles Trevelyan to Dower, 11 Jan. 1943, 26 Dec. 1943 (Cambo Letters). In the long letter Charles wrote on Boxing Day evening, he contrasted the modest political expectations of progressives among his generation with the tremendous possibilities faced by his daughter's. Of Nehru he wrote 'a great man, possibly the foremost political mind in the world'.
25. Dower to Charles Trevelyan, 6 Jan. 1943, 17 July 1944 (CPT/4/2/52). In February 1942, Charles wrote about his Yorkshire constituents in a manner that helped make sense of his daughter's husband: 'I often think that the Yorkshire people have a greater sense of power and effectiveness under the present dispensation than any others. I always felt in my old constituency the confidence and self-satisfaction of the population at large. John has this Yorkshire quality in a superlative degree. To them all it is a good world in a grim sort of way. The working-class homes were far better than on the Tyne. I expect it is rapidly changing. But the self-reliant middle class will move last of all. On the other hand these self-respecting working men will be the quickest to ask why they shouldn't have the good life like the Russian workers are beginning to get, if they are allowed to know about it. They will have no doubt that they will be able to organise it far better than a Russian peasantry. Trust their conceit for that!', Charles Trevelyan to Dower, 7 Feb. 1942 (Cambo Letters).
26. Charles Trevelyan to Dower, 4 July 1942, 7 July 1942 (Cambo Letters).
27. Dower to Charles Trevelyan, 17 July 1944 (CPT/4/2/52).

28. For a general overview, see D.L. Prynn. 'Common Wealth – a British "third party" of the 1940s', *Journal of Contemporary History*, 7, 1/2 (Jan.–Apr. 1972), pp. 169–79. Dower also admired and knew Sir Stafford Cripps, whom she thought was 'muzzled' by party-political expectations, Dower to Charles Trevelyan, 26 Jan. 1944 (CPT/4/2/52).
29. Dower to Charles Trevelyan, 26 Jan. 1944 (CPT/4/2/52).
30. Dower to Charles Trevelyan, 4 Apr. 1943 (CPT/4/2/52); Dower to her mother, 19 Nov. 1942 (CPT/4/2/53).
31. Dower to her mother, 27 Dec. 1944 (CPT/4/2/53).
32. Dower to her mother, 24 July 1942 (CPT/4/2/53); quoted in Wilkinson, *Fight for it Now*, pp. 237–8.
33. Dower to Charles & Molly Trevelyan, 8 Oct. 1947 (CPT/4/2/53).
34. Note of a meeting between the Minister and the National Parks Commission held on 4 Jan. 1950 (HLG 92/86).
35. 'Draft for Duff on staffing on passage of the act', n/d (HLG 92/86).
36. Ben Pimlott, *Hugh Dalton: A Life* (London: HarperCollins, 1995), pp. 578–9. During the 1970s, Pimlott was a lecturer in the politics department at Newcastle University and for a few years lived in Cambo, a few doors down from Robin and Frances Dower.
37. Ben Pimlott (ed.), *The Political Diary of Hugh Dalton 1918–40, 1945–60* (London: Jonathan Cape, 1986), p. 44.
38. Pimlott (ed.), *The Political Diary*, p. 478.
39. Dalton's preoccupation with his physical condition did not abate with age: 'I had a very sore little right toe at the end, but all else sound, though I blew like a grampus going up hill with a pack on. But I raced ahead on level, or slight downward slope. Very good spirit!', Pimlott (ed.), *The Political Diary*, p. 478.
40. Dalton to Dower, 11 June 1950 (HLG 92/86).
41. Dower to her mother, 18 June 1949 (CPT/4/2/53), 10 July 1950, 17 July 1950, 26 July 1950, 1 Sept. 1950, 5 Oct. 1950, 10 Nov. 1950 (CPT/4/2/60). On one occasion, she made a point of writing on commission notepaper, keen to show it off.
42. Duff to Dower, 21 Feb. 1951 (NA COU 1/699).
43. Dower to Duff, 27 Feb. 1951 (COU 1/699).
44. Dower to Molly Trevelyan, 27 Feb. 1951 (CPT/4/2/61).
45. Note by Dower, 27 Feb. 1951 (COU 1/699).
46. Duff to Dower, 28 Feb. 1951 (HLG 93/55).
47. NA TS 527/1447.
48. 'Inquiry into the Peak District National Park (Designation) Order, 1950' (PDNPI), pp. 5–9 (NA TS 527/1448)
49. PDNPI, p. 13.
50. PDNPI, p. 52.
51. Copy of letter from Dalton to Dower, n/d (COU 1/668).
52. PDNPI, p. 51. 'I would like to know how the national parks are to be distinguished from other places. Unless there is a notice put up, or unless I have studied the map, how should I know that I am either inside or outside a national park? [...] I [...] see a farm cultivated just the same. I see the houses lived in just the same. I am glad I shall. I see everything going on just the same. I hope to see good planning there by the local planning authorities, as I hope I shall also find elsewhere. I say to myself: "Now, here I am in a national park and, it being 'national', I can go anywhere I like." The one thing I find out is that I am absolutely wrong in thinking that I can go anywhere I like in the national park any more than I can elsewhere', *Hansard HL*, 19 Oct. 1949, vol. 164. I am grateful to Nick Pepper for this reference.
53. PDNPI, pp. 58–9.
54. PDNPI, pp. 78–80
55. PDNPI, p. 56.
56. PDNPI, p. 75.
57. PDNPI, p. 103.
58. Incidentally, the branch line provided access to the high peaks and the famous climb up Kinder Scout; Bowden Bridge, where the boundary crossed the river, had been the gathering place for the famous Kinder Scout protest of 1932.
59. PDNPI, pp. 103–8, 184–5.

60. PDNPI, p. 191.
61. Dower to Molly Trevelyan, 7 Mar. 1951 (CPT/4/2/61).
62. Peter Merriman, '"Respect the Life of the Countryside": The Country Code, government and the conduct of visitors to the countryside in post-war England and Wales', *Transactions of the Institute of British Geographers*, New Series, 30, 3 (Sept. 2005), p. 340; *Manchester Guardian*, 29 Aug. 1952.
63. *Manchester Guardian*, 15 Feb. 1958.
64. *Guardian*, 6 July 1966.
65. Jellicoe, Report to the Minister of Housing and Local Government, HMSO 1963. https://ia800206.us.archive.org/20/items/op1265747-1001/op1265747-1001.pdf (accessed 22 Nov. 2021).
66. Proof of Evidence of Mrs John Dower, p. 1 (NA JH 7/4).
67. Proof of Evidence of Mrs John Dower, p. 2.
68. Proof of Evidence of Mrs John Dower, p. 3.
69. Proof of Evidence of Mrs John Dower, p. 4
70. Proof of Evidence of Mrs John Dower, p. 4
71. Note by Brunsdon Yapp, COU 1/605.
72. Note by Chairman of NPC on Proposed Northumberland National Park, August 1954 (COU 1/598); according to Forestry Commission figures, across Kielder, Redesdale and Wark, in 1954 it held 84,000 acres of plantable land of which 59,000 acres had been planted (see briefing late 1954, F18/622).
73. These issues were discussed at a meeting between NPC and Northumberland County Council, 29 March 1954, see sub-committee minutes (COU 1/598).
74. Northumberland County Council to NPC, 7 April 1954 (COU 1/605).
75. *Newcastle Journal and North Mail*, 26 Apr. 1954; *The Times*, 3 May 1954, 8 May 1954.
76. *The Times*, 27 Dec. 1945.
77. *The Times*, 22 Dec. 1945.
78. Statement by amenity societies submitted to the Local Public Inquiry, June 1949 (NA WO 32/13219).
79. Trevelyan to Attlee, 13 Apr. 1949; Attlee to Trevelyan, 29 Apr. 1949 (WO 32/13219).
80. Dower to Burbridge, 27 Dec. 1953 (COU 1/605).
81. Bicknell to Ferguson, 14 Jan. 1954; Bell to Ross, 12 Nov. 1954; Ramblers Assoc. to Ross, 23 Nov. 1954 (COU 1/605).
82. Andrews to CC Planning Officer, 22 May 1958; Bicknell to Osmond, 3 June 1958 (COU 1/605).
83. See summary by Northumberland National Park Planning Committee (COU 1/605).
84. Note of meeting, 9 July 1959 (COU 1/605).
85. See Crowe, *Tomorrow's Landscape* (London: Architectural Press, 1956), p. 48; also, the remarkable quotation on p. 41: 'The spirit of the Roman Wall country would be seriously impaired if it were invaded by the numbers which frequent Grasmere, but there at least the views are objective, and can still be enjoyed under conditions which would destroy the more subjective view of Northumberland.'
86. Acland to Strang, 3 Aug. 1954; Lubbock to Strang, 14 Aug. 1954 (COU 1/605).
87. L.J. Watson, 30 Sept. 1954 (COU 1/605).
88. Radnor to Strang, 6 Sept. 1954 (COU 1/605).
89. Record of talk with Lord Radnor, 22 Sept. 1954 (COU 1/605).
90. Dower to Strang, 16 Oct. 1954 (COU 1/605).
91. Gosling to Valentine, HLG, 5 Feb. 1955; Minuted discussion between Abrahams & Watson, 10 Feb. 1955; Gosling to Strang, 25 Feb. 1955; Ferguson to Gosling, 10 Aug. 1955; Turner (FC) to Abrahams, 26 Aug. 1955 (F 18/622).
92. Henry Myles to NPC, 22 Sept. 1955; Note for File, 5 Dec. 1955; Abrahams to Myles, 4 Apr. 1956; Myles to Abrahams, 10 Apr. 1956 (COU 1/601).
93. Ross to Dower, 3 Feb. 1956 (COU 1/603).
94. Strang to Dower, 14 Feb. 1956 (COU 1/603).
95. Dower addressed two letters to Strang in rapid succession: Dower to Strang, 14 & 15 Feb. 1956 (COU 1/603)
96. Dower to Strang, 14 & 15 Feb. 1956 (COU 1/603).
97. Strang to Dower, 16 Feb. 1956; Strang to Dower, 20 Feb. 1956; J.B. Ross to Dower, 24 Feb. 1956; Dower to Strang, 25 Feb. 1956; Strang to Dower, 29 Feb. 1956 (COU 1/603).
98. Report by Mr Mollison, 16 May 1956 (COU 1/606).

99. Ferguson to Ross, 1 June 1956 (COU 1/606).
100. Bicknell to Abrahams, 24 Jan. 1957; Bicknell to Harvey (clerk of the County Council), 9 Feb. 1957 (COU 1/606).
101. 'The charm of the valley, in my opinion, lies in its intimate scale and its rather lush appearance brought about by the brighter green of the valley bottom pastures and the profusion of trees, mostly deciduous, in marked contrast to the heather and bracken covered slopes of the fells, with the burn flowing throughout between tree lined banks.' J.B. Ross, 'County Water Scheme – Suggested site for Reservoir in Grasslees Burn Valley', for consideration at meeting of the National Park Planning Committee, 25 Feb. 1957 (COU 1/606).
102. Herbert Griffin, CPRE, to Abrahams, NPC, 16 Apr. 1957 (COU 1/606).
103. Ross to committee chair, 20 June 1958 (COU 1/606).
104. Ross to NPC, 29 July 1957 (COU 1/1085).
105. Report by Pauline Dower, 18 July 1957 (COU 1/1085).
106. Ross to NPC, 31 Jan. 1963 (COU 1/1085).
107. http://www.bonnyrigghall.co.uk/MoreOnBonnyrigg.htm (accessed 24 Nov. 2021).
108. Field Inspection with County Officials, 16 Mar. 1964 (COU 1/610).
109. Dower to Calvert, 6 Apr. 1964 (COU 1/610).
110. Dower to Calvert, 11 Aug. 1964 (COU 1/610).
111. Calvert to CPO, 28 Oct. 1964; NNP Com. approval, 20 Dec. 1965 (COU 1/610).
112. *The Times*, 7 July 1951.
113. Dower to Ferguson, 12 Sept. 1956 (COU 1/1293).
114. Blenkinsop to Dower, 4 Mar. 1959; Dower to Blenkinsop, 7 Mar. 1959; Dower to Millar (NPC), 8 Mar. 1959 (COU 1/1293).
115. The public inquiry report took the form of a letter from S.R.H. King to Keith Joseph, 20 Apr. 1964 (COU 1/1293).
116. *The Times*, 8 Sept. 1964.
117. I'm grateful to Robin Dower for this recollection.
118. Report by G.B. Ryle, Director of Forestry for England, 27 July 1960 (COU 1/1086).
119. Dower to Abrahams, 10 May 1960 (COU 1/1086).
120. NCC, NNP, FC meeting County Hall, 27 July 1960, minutes (COU 1/1086).
121. Comment by Watson in meeting, 13 Dec. 1960, at County Planning Office, 13 Dec. 1960 (COU 1/1086).
122. Dower to Ferguson, 12 Feb. 1961 (COU 1/609).
123. Extract from Northumberland Park Planning Committee, 27 Mar. 1961 (COU 1/609).
124. Ryle to Abrahams, 3 Oct. 1961 (COU 1/609).
125. Dower to Knight, 24 Nov. 1961 (COU 1/1086).
126. Ferguson to Dower, 30 Nov. 1961 (COU 1/609).
127. 'Harbottle – Visit of Inspections, December 15, 1961. Note by Deputy Chairman' (COU 1/609).
128. NNP Planning Committee, minutes 22 Dec. 1961; Ross to FC, 8 Jan. 1962 (COU 1/609).
129. E.P. Harvey to Ferguson, 21 Feb. 1962 (COU 1/609).
130. Radnor to Strang, 8 Feb. 1962 (COU 1/609).
131. FC document on employment (COU 1/609).
132. Dower to Strang, 25 Sept. 1962 (COU 1/609).
133. Fred Corfield, Parliamentary Secretary to the Ministry for Housing and Local Government, to Strang, 28 Nov. 1962 (COU 1/609).
134. Fred Willey to Dower, 10 June 1966 (Cambo Papers). On Wootton, see Ann Oakley, *A Critical Woman: Barbara Wootton, Social Science and Public Policy in the Twentieth Century* (London: Bloomsbury, 2011).
135. Draft letter, 14 June 1966 (Cambo Papers).
136. Strang to Dower, 13 June 1966; Abrahams to Dower, 22 June 1966; Gervas Huxley to Dower, 16 June 1966; Ritchie to Dower, 20 June 1966 (Cambo Papers).
137. Yapp to Dower, 19 June 1966 (Cambo Papers).
138. Mandrake. Press cutting in Cambo Papers.
139. Ross to Dower, 22 June 1966 (Cambo Papers).
140. *Newcastle Journal*, 6 Oct. 1958.
141. Dower to Molly Trevelyan, 29 May 1959 (CPT/4/2/64).
142. Dower to Molly Trevelyan, 4 Feb. 1960 (CPT/4/2/65).

Sylvia Sayer

1. Sylvia Sayer to Patrick Duff, 11 May 1950 (COU 1/449).
2. *British Medical Journal*, 2 Aug. 1952.
3. https://campaignerkate.wordpress.com/2015/02/28/encouraging-oodles-of-ouzels/ (accessed 26 May 2021).
4. Richard Burnard Munday (1896–1932) was a First World War flying ace.
5. Guy Sayer's service record can be found in the Liddell Hart Centre for Military Archives, King's College London: https://archive.is/20121223052221/http://www.kcl.ac.uk/lhcma/locreg/SAYER.shtml (accessed 24 May 2021). Guy Sayer's brother was a brigadier: Funeral notices (Arthur Pennie Sayer), *The Times*, 4 May 1962.
6. Sayer to Duff, 11 May 1950 (COU 1/449).
7. Clark to Duff, 21 Apr. 1950; Note by Duff, 4 May 1950 (COU 1/449).
8. Matthew Kelly, *Quartz and Feldspar. Dartmoor: A British Landscape in Modern Times* (London: Vintage, 2015), pp. 225–9.
9. Duff to Sayer, 9 Aug. 1951; Sayer to Duff, 13 Aug. 1951 (COU 1/449).
10. 'National Park for Dartmoor', *The Times*, 16 Aug. 1951.
11. *The Times*, 21 May 1948.
12. *The Times*, 24 May 1948.
13. *The Times*, 27 May 1948 & 9 Apr. 1949.
14. Kelly, *Quartz and Feldspar*, pp. 231–2.
15. Kelly, *Quartz and Feldspar*, pp. 17–102.
16. Robert Burnard, *Dartmoor' Pictorial Records* (Exeter: Devon Books, 1986), vol. I, pp. v–vi.
17. *The Times*, 27 Feb. 1967.
18. Material of this sort can be accessed at the extraordinary website run by Tim Sandles, https://www.legendarydartmoor.co.uk/ (accessed 26 Nov. 2021).
19. Robert Burnard, 'Plundered Dartmoor', DPA Publication No. 11.
20. On Collier, see Kelly, *Quartz and Feldspar*, pp. 202–6, 211–15.
21. Matthew Kelly, 'On Why the UK's First National Park Might Have Been in Ireland', in Matthew Kelly (ed.), *Nature and the Environment in Nineteenth-Century Ireland* (Liverpool: Liverpool University Press, 2019).
22. *Trewman's Exeter Flying Post*, 29 Jan. 1897.
23. *Trewman's Exeter Flying Post*, 15 Aug. 1896.
24. Sylvia Sayer, *The Outline of Dartmoor's Story* (Exeter: Devon Books and Sayer, 1951, reprint 1987), pp. 3–4.
25. For Crossing, see Kelly, *Quartz and Feldspar*, pp. 193–211; William George Hoskins, *The Making of the English Landscape* (London: Hodder and Stoughton, 1954).
26. Sayer, *Outline*, p. 4.
27. Sayer, *Outline*, pp. 4–5.
28. Sayer, *Outline*, p. 8.
29. Sayer, *Outline*, p. 9.
30. Sayer, *Outline*, pp. 11–12.
31. Sayer, *Outline*, pp. 13–14.
32. Sayer, *Outline*, pp. 14–16.
33. Percival Birkett, 'A Short History of the Rights of Common Upon the Forest of Dartmoor and the Commons of Devon', published as a pamphlet by the DPA with the 'Report of Mr Stuart A. Moore, and Appendix of Documents' (1889); *The Times*, 17 May 1897.
34. They include Warner, Runnage, Hartland, Merripit, Pizwell, Dury, Lakehead, Hexworthy, Sherberton, Dunnabridge and Prince Hall.
35. See Harold Fox, *Dartmoor's Alluring Uplands. Transhumance and Pastoral Management in the Middle Ages* (Exeter: University of Exeter Press, 2012).
36. Letter to *The Times*, 16 Apr. 1963.
37. Sayer, *Outline*, pp. 21–2.
38. This is one of the major themes of the brilliantly seminal David Matless, *Landscape and Englishness* (London: Reaktion Books, 1998, 2016); Joe Moran, '"Subtopias of good intention": everyday landscapes in postwar Britain', *Cultural and Social History*, 4, 3 (Sept. 2007), p. 403.
39. Kelly, *Quartz and Feldspar*, pp. 97–8.
40. Sayer, *Outline*, p. 8.
41. Sayer, *Outline*, p. 12.

42. She later described the prison as a 'morbid attraction', criticising tourists who tried to catch a glimpse of the convicts at work through their binoculars. She knew where these voyeurs gathered by the litter they left behind. *Guardian*, 29 Apr. 1969.
43. Sayer, *Outline*, pp. 36–7.
44. Letter to *The Times*, 6 June 1951.
45. Sayer, *Outline*, pp. 23–7.
46. Sayer, *Outline*, pp. 38–9.
47. Sayer, *Outline*, pp. 48–9.
48. Shaw bequeathed the house to the Trust in 1944, to be maintained as a 'literary shrine', NT Report, 1944–5, p. 13; for 'crowdomaniacs' and her view that visitors might one day have to be banned from the moor, picking up minibuses at the park's perimeters, see *Guardian*, 1 Oct. 1962.
49. *The Times*, 14 Apr. 1951.
50. Sayer, *Outline*, p. 50.
51. Sayer, *Outline*, p. 50.
52. Kelly, *Quartz and Feldspar*, p. 366.
53. 'Evidence submitted by the Royal Commission on Common Land by the Dartmoor Preservation Association', April 1956, 1238 (MAF 96/69).
54. Clark to Duff, 20 Aug. 1951 (COU 1/454).
55. DPA, Preliminary Memo, 10 Dec. 1951 (COU 1/454).
56. Kelly, *Quartz and Feldspar*, pp. 232–42.
57. Ian Nairn (ed.), *Outrage*, special edition of *Architectural Review*, June 1955 (reprinted London: Architectural Press, 1955); Sylvia Crowe, *Tomorrow's Landscape* (London: Architectural Press, 1956).
58. DPA, Preliminary Memo, 10 Dec. 1951; Sayer (to Abrahams?), 26 June 1952 (COU 1/454).
59. Sayer to Abrahams, 30 June 1952 (COU 1/454).
60. Sayer to Abrahams, 25 Nov. 1952 (COU 1/454).
61. Sayer to Duff, 30 Jan. 1954 (COU 1/457).
62. DPA, August 1951.
63. DPA, June 1954.
64. DPA, Sept. 1954.
65. DPA, Mar.–Apr. 1955. Local people were not blameless. 'Complacent landowners' permitted motorcycle trials on their land, another 'invasion'. Sayer pictured the scene: 'Then the cardboard flags go up and the motor bikes, the crowds, the cars, the coaches, the litter, the ice cream men, the purveyors of snacks, the noise, and the smell of oil and exhaust descend (generally Sunday) on the once peaceful Dartmoor scene', DPA, June–July 1955.
66. DPA, Oct. 1955.
67. This oft-quoted line comes from the Contents pages of the reprint of Nairn, *Outrage*.
68. Gillian Darley & David McKie, *Ian Nairn: Words in Place* (Nottingham: Five Leaves, 2013), pp. 365–6.
69. Moran, '"Subtopias of good intention"', p. 405.
70. Moran, '"Subtopias of good intention"', p. 402.
71. Lewis Mumford, *The City in History: Its Origins, its Transformations, and its Prospects* (New York: Harcourt Brace, 1961), p. 513; Nairn, *Outrage*, p. 367; See also Lorenza Pavesi, 'Ian Nairn, Townscape and the Campaign Against Subtopia', *Focus*, 10, 1 (2013).
72. Nairn, *Outrage*, p. 432.
73. Paul Brassley, Jeremy Burchardt & Karen Sayer (eds), *Transforming the Countryside. The Electrification of Rural Britain* (London: Routledge, 2016).
74. DPA, Oct. 1956.
75. DPA, Dec. 1955.
76. Among those Strang acknowledged were Gerald Haythornthwaite, W.A. Geenty and P.G. Laws, a trio that mixed town planning, architecture and surveying experience, as well as in Haythornthwaite's case experience as a leading national parks campaigner, alongside his wife Ethel Haythornthwaite, who had worked on the Hobhouse Report. See Melvyn Jones, *Protecting the Beautiful Frame: A History of the Sheffield, Peak District and South Yorkshire Branch of the Council for the Protection of Rural England* (Sheffield: Hallamshire Publications, 2001), p. 87.
77. Darley & McKie, *Ian Nairn*, p. 104.
78. *Dartmoor: Building in the National Park* (Architectural Press, 1956), p. 18.
79. *Dartmoor: Building in the National Park*, pp. 56–7.

80. *Dartmoor: Building in the National Park*, p. 62.
81. *Dartmoor: Building in the National Park*, p. 44.
82. DPA, Oct. 1956.
83. DPA, Oct. 1956.
84. Crowe, *Tomorrow's Landscape*, p. 13.
85. Crowe, *Tomorrow's Landscape*, pp. 19–24.
86. Crowe, *Tomorrow's Landscape*, p. 18.
87. Crowe, *Tomorrow's Landscape*, p. 15.
88. https://www.swlaketrust.org.uk/burrator
89. Crowe, *Tomorrow's Landscape*, p. 38.
90. Crowe, *Tomorrow's Landscape*, p. 43.
91. Crowe, *Tomorrow's Landscape*, p. 46.
92. Crowe, *Tomorrow's Landscape*, p. 47.
93. Crowe, *Tomorrow's Landscape*, pp. 42–3.
94. Crowe, *Tomorrow's Landscape*, p. 37.
95. Crowe, *Tomorrow's Landscape*, p. 41.
96. Sayer to Abrahams, 5 Feb. 1952 (COU 1/454).
97. Crowe, *Tomorrow's Landscape*, p. 37.
98. Crowe, *Tomorrow's Landscape*, p. 37.
99. Raymond Williams, *The Country and the City* (New York: Oxford University Press, 1973), pp. 105–6.
100. Crowe, *Tomorrow's Landscape*, p. 38.
101. Crowe, *Tomorrow's Landscape*, p. 55.
102. Quoted in Moran, '"Subtopias of good intention"', pp. 410–11.
103. DPA, Feb./Mar. 1959.
104. DPA, Sept. 1959. She was less circumspect a decade later: 'We're apolitical, I believe in voting for the man most fitted for the job. Round here, of course, they'd vote for a lamp post so long as it was wearing a blue rosette', *Guardian*, 14 May 1969.
105. For Arthur Blenkinsop's private members' bill, National Parks (Amendment) Bill, see *Hansard*, 30 Jan. 1959, vol. 598, col. 1473–92.
106. Andrew Geddes, 'Locus standi and ECC environmental measures', *Journal of Environmental Law*, 4, 1 (1992), pp. 30–1.
107. Sylvia Sayer, *Wild Country* (Dartmoor Preservation Association publication no. 13, 3rd edn 2000), p. 16.
108. For a detailed account of these developments, including the long conflict between Plymouth Corporation and Massey Lopes, the landowner, over the construction of Burrator Reservoir, see Kelly, *Quartz and Feldspar*, pp. 266–78.
109. For envirotechnical regimes, see Sara B. Pritchard, *Confluence: The Nature of Technology and the Remaking of the Rhône* (Cambridge, MA: Harvard University Press, 2011).
110. Kelly, *Quartz and Feldspar*, p. 279.
111. Kelly, *Quartz and Feldspar*, pp. 279–82.
112. DPA, *The Meldon Story* (1972), p. 4.
113. *Hansard*, 4 Apr. 1967, vol. 281, col. 915–7, 924–5, 950. The wording of the standing order (col. 919) is: 'Where any society or association sufficiently representing any trade, business, or interest in a district to which any Bill relates, petition against the Bill, alleging that such trade, business, or interest will be injuriously affected by the provisions contained therein, it shall be competent for the Select Committee to which the Bill is committed, if they think fit, to admit the Petitioners to be heard on such allegations against the Bill or any part thereof.'
114. *Hansard*, 4 Apr. 1967, vol. 281, col. 917–8.
115. *Hansard*, 4 Apr. 1967, vol. 281, col. 936.
116. *Hansard*, 4 Apr. 1967, vol. 281, col. 950–53.
117. *Hansard*, 9 May 1967, vol. 282, col. 1307–10.
118. *The Times*, 29 May 1967.
119. DPA, *The Meldon Story*, p. 6. Sayer was identified as the author in the 2000 reprint.
120. *Hansard*, 25 Jan. 1972, vol. 327, col. 287–313.
121. DPA, *The Meldon Story*, p. 47.
122. For an expression of Sayer winning the case 'almost single-handed', see *Guardian*, 19 Dec. 1979.
123. See Kelly, *Quartz and Feldspar*, pp. 296–303 for the broader significance of the Meldon and Swincombe decisions for water politics in post-war Britain.
124. *Guardian*, 14 May 1969, 28 Aug. 1968.

125. *Guardian*, 28 Aug. 1969.
126. Kate Ashbrook, among those objecting to the 'return to Swincombe', tells the tale at: https://campaignerkate.wordpress.com/2018/04/22/the-dartmoor-reservoir-saga-40-years-ago/ (accessed 30 Nov. 2021).
127. Kelly, *Quartz and Feldspar*, pp. 248–50.
128. D.C. Nicholls, 'Use of Land for Forestry within the Proprietary Land Unit', *Forestry Commission Bulletin*, 39 (London: HMSO, 1969), pp. 35–7, 68; *The Times*, 22 Mar. 1960.
129. *The Times*, 13 June 1949.
130. *The Times*, 12 Mar. 1951.
131. *The Times*, 30 July 1951.
132. *The Times*, 23 June 1952.
133. DPA memo and the FC response; Sangar to Turner, 10 Feb. 1954 (FT 18/613).
134. DPA, Mar. 1952, June 1954, Sept. 1954, June–July 1955, Mar.–Apr. 1957, Autumn 1958.
135. DPA, Mar.–Apr. 1955, Sept. 1957.
136. Abrahams (NPC) to Turner (FC), 29 Apr. 1958, Turner to Abrahams, 15 May 1958, Connell to Director, 2 June 1958; Turnball (County Planning Office) to FC Sec., 22 Oct. 1958, Dir. FC England to FC Sec., 22 Oct. 1958 (FT 18/613).
137. *The Times*, 8 Jan. 1959.
138. *Hansard*, 2 Feb. 1959, HC vol. 599; 24 Feb. 1959, vol. 600, p. 46; 25 Feb. 1959, HL, vol. 214, pp. 488–9.
139. DPA, Feb./Mar. 1959; Minutes of the Forestry Commission National Committee for England, 8 Apr. 1959 (FT 18/613).
140. DPA, Sept. 1959.
141. DPA, Dec. 1959, Mar. 1960, Apr. 1961.
142. DPA, Dec. 1959.
143. DPA, June 1960.
144. *Guardian*, 2 Dec. 1960; Turner to Connell, 5 Dec. 1960, Connell to Turner, 29 Dec. 1960 (F 18/613).
145. See papers in F 18/613.
146. *Mid-Devon Advertiser*, 28 Dec. 1963.
147. J.R. Thom, 'Note of meeting with Lady Sayer, 12/2/64' (FT 18/635).
148. Connell to the FC Secretariat, 19 Sept. 1968 (FT 18/1183).
149. G.D. Rouse, *The New Forests of Dartmoor* (London: HMSO, 1972), pp. 20, 23, 24–5, 29.
150. Ian Gambles (ed.), *British Forests. The Forestry Commission 1919–2019* (London: Profile, 2019), p. 62.
151. Sayer & Somers Cocks to Willey, 17 Sept. 1965 (F 18/636).
152. Kelly, *Quartz and Feldspar*, pp. 185–8, 216–8, 306–7.
153. Kelly, *Quartz and Feldspar*, pp. 314–5.
154. Sayer to Abrahams, 23 Oct. 1950, Abrahams to Sayer, 15 Nov. 1950, J.D.W. Jones to Abrahams, 8 June 1951 (COU 1/464).
155. The process can be followed in COU 1/980, including Sayer to Abrahams, 9 Mar. 1956, and Playfair to Strang, 9 Dec. 1957.
156. Besides its military use, Plaster Down housed Polish refugees relocated to Britain following the passage of the Polish Resettlement Act 1947, and Ugandan Asian refugees following their expulsion by Idi Amin in 1972.
157. DPA, *The Meldon Story*, p. 26.
158. Kelly, *Quartz and Feldspar*, pp. 322–3.
159. Kelly, *Quartz and Feldspar*, pp. 323–7.
160. Godsall to Andrews, 12 Aug. 1959 (WO 32/20944).
161. 'DPA Memorandum on the Services' Use of Dartmoor, July 1959' (WO 32/20944).
162. Anne Taylor, 'The Battle of Dartmoor, 1966', *The Observer*, 25 Sept. 1966.
163. Sayer to Private Sec. to the S of S for War, 24 Nov. 1959 (WO 32/20944).
164. HQ Southern Command to Under Sec., WO, 14 Jan. 1960 (WO 32/20944).
165. Copy of petition (WO 32/20944).
166. Sayer to Abrahams, Aug. 1961 (COU 1/1156).
167. Acland to Abrahams, 29 Jan. 1962 (COU 1/1156).
168. Hansard, 10 Nov. 1967, vol. 753, col. 1475.
169. Jellicoe to Abrahams, 31 Jan. 1962; Acland to Abrahams, 29 Jan. 1962; Abrahams to Acland, 2 Feb. 1962 (COU 1/1156).
170. Sayer to Strang, 7 & 13 May 1962 (COU 1/1156).

171. Signatories included the Standing Committee on National Parks, the CPRE, the DPA, the Commons, the Open Spaces and Footpaths Preservation Society, the Ramblers Association, the YHA, the Cooperative Holidays Association, the Dartmoor Rambling Club and the Dartmoor Ramblers.
172. See news clippings in COU 1/1156.
173. Vernon Bovenizer to Herbert Griffin, 17 July 1962 (COU 1/1156).
174. Sayer to Abrahams, 2 Aug. 1962 (COU 1/1156).
175. *Guardian*, 27 Feb. 1964.
176. Sayer to Bell (NPCom), 4 & 18 Mar. 1964; NPCom minutes, 17 Mar. 1964; draft 'Heads of Conditions' (Plymouth Corporation), 17 Mar. 1964 (COU 1/983).
177. Sayer to War Office, 23 Mar. 1964; Sayer to Strang, 30 Sept. 1964; Sayer to Bell, 26 Oct. 1964 (COU 1/983); *Guardian*, 19 Dec. 1964.
178. See COU/1/984.
179. Copy is preserved in COU 1/983.
180. Minute Walter Luttrell, 24 Nov. 1964 (COU 1/983).
181. Andrews, WO, to Bell, NPC, 20 Nov. 1964; Memo. by NPC 'Motor Vehicles in the Dartmoor National Park'; Bell, NPC, to Sayer, 22 Jan. 1965; Sayer to Bell, 28 Jan. 1965; Sayer to Kingsley, Duchy, 19 June & 2 May 1965; Andrews to Chesterman, NPC, 13 Aug. 1965; Sayer's observations on map, 4 Mar. 1966; Shaw, MOD, to Sayer, 14 June 1966; Sayer to Shaw, MOD, 25 June 1966 (COU 1/984).
182. 'Notes of a meeting held in Miss McNichol's room, Queen Anne's Mansions, on Friday 29 July 1966' (COU 1/984).
183. *The Times*, 16 Sept. 1966.
184. *The Times*, 22 & 23 Feb. 1967.
185. Copy in DEFE 51/91.
186. Wootton, Countryside Commission, to Denis Healey, MOD, 5 Feb. 1969 (DEFE 51/92).
187. See discussion in DEFE 51/91, especially 'Comment from HQ Southern Command on Confidential Draft on Use of Dartmoor', 22 Nov. 1968.
188. *The Times*, 9 Apr. 1969; Sayer to Dunwoody, 10 Apr. 1969, Dunwoody to G.W. Reynolds, Minister of Defence for Administration, 11 Apr. 1969 (DEFE 51/93).
189. Major-General G.L.C. Cooper to Major-General H.R.S. 'Rollo' Pain, 31 Dec. 1974 (DEFE 70/390).
190. 'Dartmoor. Report by Lady Sharp CBE to the Secretary of State for the Environment and the Secretary of State for Defence of a public local inquiry held in December, 1975, and May, 1976 into the continued use of Dartmoor by the Ministry of Defence for training purposes', pp. 27–31 (DEFE 70/215). Sayer's argument drew strongly on the lecture discussed in the next section of this chapter.
191. 'Dartmoor. Report by Lady Sharp ... into the continued use of Dartmoor by the Ministry of Defence for training purposes', 10–1, p. 77 (DEFE 70/215).
192. Personal communication.
193. DPA, Aug. 1973.
194. *The Times*, 30 Aug. 1971.
195. Sayer, *Wild Country*, p. 7.
196. Sayer, *Wild Country*, p. 7.
197. Sayer, *Wild Country*, p. 8.
198. Sayer, *Wild Country*, p. 19.
199. Sayer, *Wild Country*, pp. 8–9.
200. Sayer, *Wild Country*, p. 8.
201. Sayer, *Wild Country*, p. 15.
202. Sayer, *Wild Country*, p. 10.
203. Sayer, *Wild Country*, p. 16.
204. Sayer, *Wild Country*, p. 18.
205. Sayer, *Wild Country*, p. 22.
206. Sayer, *Wild Country*, p. 23.
207. Sayer, *Wild Country*, p. 18.

Epilogue

1. For a nuanced account, see Paul Warde, Libby Robin & Sverker Sörkin, *The Environment: A History of the Idea* (Baltimore, MD: Johns Hopkins University Press, 2018).

2. Ian Mercer, appointed Dartmoor's first National Park Officer following the passage of the 1972 Act, is a good guide to these developments. Mercer contrasts Sayer, whom he respected as a sometime adversary, with Herbert Whitley, one of the founders of the Dartmoor Commoners' Association in 1954, her 'rival in the "Dartmoor leadership" stakes'. Ian Mercer, *Dartmoor* (London: Collins, 2009), pp. 22, 321–56.

3. The process can be followed in Buttermere Papers, J-AddH-13 (Balliol College Archives).

4. I tackle these issues in 'Conventional Thinking and the Birth of the Nature State in Post-war Britain', in Wilko Graf von Hardenberg, Matthew Kelly, Claudia Leal & Emily Wakild (eds), *The Nature State. New Approaches to the History of Conservation* (London: Routledge, 2017).

5. For further reading, see Matthew Kelly, 'Habitat protection, ideology and the British nature state: the politics of the Wildlife and Countryside Act 1981', *English Historical Review* (forthcoming).

6. *The Times*, 4 Nov. 1980, 8 Nov. 1980, 13 Nov. 1980, 15 Nov. 1980, 17 Nov. 1980, 18 Nov. 1980.

7. Marion Shoard, *The Theft of the Countryside* (London: Temple Smith, 1980), p. 141.

8. Shoard, *Theft*, p. 200.

9. Chris Hall, 'Ann MacEwen', *Guardian*, 6 Sept. 2008.

10. Malcolm MacEwen, *The Greening of a Red* (London: Pluto Press, 1991).

11. M. MacEwen and A. MacEwen, *National Parks: Conservation or Cosmetics?* (London: Allen & Unwin, 1982), pp. 63–4.

12. W. Brunsdon Yapp, 'Viewpoint. Real National Parks', *Land Use Policy* (July 1984), pp. 255–60.

13. Ann-Christian L. Knudson, *Farmers on Welfare. The Making of Europe's Common Agricultural Policy* (Ithaca, NY: Cornell University Press, 2009).

14. Adrian Colston is the best guide to the questions animating the governance of Dartmoor. https://adriancolston.wordpress.com/category/dartmoor-farming/ (accessed 3 Dec. 2021).

15. On the Border Mires project in Northumberland, see the Northumberland Wildlife Trust report, https://www.nwt.org.uk/sites/default/files/2021-01/Border%20Mires%20Booklet.pdf (accessed 3 Dec. 2021) and on the Mires on the Moor project on Dartmoor, see Exeter University report, http://www.exeter.ac.uk/media/universityofexeter/research/microsites/creww/miresprojectreports/CREWW_Mire_on_the_Moors_report_2020.pdf (accessed 3 Dec. 2021).

16. George Monbiot, *Feral: Searching for Enchantment on the Frontiers of Rewilding* (London: Penguin, 2013).

17. Explaining the debate in terms of Rebanks vs Monbiot, salted with a little Potter, made good copy. See Franz Lidz, 'Britain's Lake District Was Immortalized by Beatrix Potter, But Is Its Future in Peril?', *The Smithsonian*, May 2018.

18. George Monbiot, 'Britain's countryside is dominated by bullies – as Chris Packham found', *Guardian*, 1 May 2019.

19. *Guardian*, 11 July 2017.

20. See http://icomos.fa.utl.pt/documentos/2009/WHSTheEconomicGainFinalReport.pdf (accessed 3 Dec. 2021).

21. James Rebanks, *English Pastoral: An Inheritance* (London: Allen Lane, 2020), pp. 195, 229.

22. Rebanks, *English Pastoral*, p. 198.

23. *Daily Mail*, 28 Feb. 2020.

24. campaignerkate.wordpress.com (accessed 3 Dec. 2021).

25. During the second lockdown (2020–1), the Dartmoor Collective, exhausted by the nightly regime demanded #my400, substituted it with #mycreativeweek, tempting amateur painters, sketchers and craftspeople into a little Twitter limelight.

26. Madeleine Bunting, 'The middle class have hijacked the English countryside for themselves', *Guardian*, 23 Apr. 2007.

27. See https://www.gov.uk/government/publications/the-countryside-code/the-countryside-code-advice-for-countryside-visitors (accessed 3 Dec. 2021).

28. Sally-Anne Huxtable, Corinne Fowler, Christo Kefalas & Emma Slocombe (eds), *Interim Report on the Connections between Colonialism and Properties now in the Care of the National Trust, Including Links with Historic Slavery* (Swindon: National Trust, 2020), pp. 94–5.

29. Elizabeth-Jane Burnett, *The Grassling* (London: Allen Lane, 2019), p. 135.

30. Anita Sethi, *I Belong Here. A Journey Along the Backbone of Britain* (London: Bloomsbury, 2021), pp. 80–1.

FURTHER READING

For Octavia Hill and Beatrix Potter good overviews of their lives can be found in the *Dictionary of National Biography*, to which online access is available to any holder of a local library card. For Hill, Gillian Darley's *Octavia Hill: A Life* (Constable, 1990) is the standard modern biography, published in a revised edition as *Octavia Hill: Social Reformer and Founder of the National Trust* (Francis Boutle, 2004). What we can discern of Hill's private life and attitudes is accessible in C. Edmund Maurice's *Life of Octavia Hill as Told in Her Letters* (Cambridge University Press, 1913), a carefully curated text that uses linking passages to stitch together an account of her life through extensive extracts from her letters. It's a literary genre long out of fashion. No examination of Hill's activism is complete without reference to her canonical essays, some of which were collected for publication in her lifetime and most of which can be easily accessed online. The National Trust has a cache of Hill's letters, transcribed and available to researchers. For readers wanting to know about Hill's housing work – not my focus – Robert Whelan's extraordinary edition of her letters to fellow-workers, which runs to almost 800 pages (Kyrle Books, 2005), will exhaust even the keenest interest. A full study has yet to be made of these important texts. Many articles about Hill can be found in specialist journals, but much the most useful edited collection for my purposes was Elizabeth Baigent and Ben Cowell (eds), *'Nobler Imaginings and Mightier Struggles': Octavia Hill, Social Activism, and the Remaking of British Society* (Institute of Historical Research, 2016). This is an Open Access publication and is freely available online. It constitutes a major reassessment of her work and through its largely sympathetic analysis challenges less favourable assessments of her ideological orientation.

Linda Lear's biography of Beatrix Potter (Allen Lane, 2007) is a masterpiece and readers who like to scrutinise footnotes will see that I could not have written my chapter without it. Matthew Dennison's *Over the Hills and Far Away: The Life of Beatrix Potter* (Head of Zeus, 2016) focuses on its subject's younger years, making clever use of Potter's diary to offer suggestive readings of her psychological make-up and the origins of the Little Books. Works published by the Beatrix Potter Society deserve more attention (https://beatrixpottersociety.org.uk/publications-merchandise/). With respect to Potter's relationship with the National Trust, I've tried to identify the issues that exercised her most, but anyone interested in the fine detail of her management of Troutbeck and the Monk Coniston Estate will find letters in the National Trust's archive an essential source (transcribed and available digitally on request to researchers). As I write this in late 2021, I'm conscious that in February 2022 the Victoria and Albert Museum will open a new exhibition, 'Beatrix Potter: Drawn to Nature', based on its substantial archival holdings. This will bring to public notice her less familiar drawings and paintings, though it once again reminds me of how little academic attention has been paid to this most remarkable woman. It is only a matter of time before she is the focus of a major reassessment.

Pauline Dower and Sylvia Sayer have yet to attract much attention from academics and biographers. The extraordinary Dower letters I used are part of the compendious Trevelyan Papers held by Newcastle University, but permission is needed from the family to consult materials that refer to living persons and recently deceased relatives. Dower's extensive personal papers are in the hands of the family, and they will doubtless be archived at some point. Further evidence of Dower's work for the

National Parks Commission can be found in Ray Woolmore's 'Designation History Series'. These examine the processes that led to the designation of individual areas of outstanding natural beauty, an aspect of the commission's work I overlook. The series is accessible online on an individual basis through a simple search, but this great body of work does not appear to be hosted in a single virtual space. I've written about Sylvia Sayer as part of a broader discussion in my *Quartz and Feldspar. Dartmoor: A British Landscape in Modern Times* (Vintage, 2015), and this present book revisits some of that material, particularly official papers archived by the National Archives, Kew (open to the public). Sayer deserves a dedicated biography that takes full account of her early life and later activism. This will require grappling with 130 boxes of uncatalogued material held by the Devon Heritage Centre.

No interested reader can have missed the avalanche of books published in recent years categorised as 'nature writing'. The annual longlist for the Wainwright Prize provides a snapshot of the continuing vitality of the genre. This writing tends to centre the subjectivity of the writer, keeping at arm's length the political and ideological factors at work in the production of British landscapes. Some of this literature is discussed in my epilogue, so there is no need to highlight those books here. Instead, I'll foreground some recent historical texts. All students of British landscape politics, particularly the role played by the state, are indebted to John Sheail. His formidable bibliography is too extensive to reproduce here, but as British historians take the 'environmental turn' in their research so the importance of his tremendous contribution is becoming more apparent. For the late Victorian and early Edwardian period, James Winter's *Secure from Rash Assault: Sustaining the Victorian Environment* (University of California Press, 2002) and Harriet Ritvo's *The Dawn of Green. Manchester, Thirlmere, and Modern Environmentalism* (University of Chicago Press, 2009) signalled a new wave of historical work influenced by the rise of environmental history as a distinct sub-field. British approaches, like that of this book, sit somewhere between the perspectives of environmental history, strongly influenced by the North American academy, and an older tradition of distinguished work in British landscape history. This hybridity is reflected in two stimulating recent books, namely Vicky Albritton and Fredrik Albritton Jonsson's *Green Victorians. The Simple Life in John Ruskin's Lake District* (University of Chicago Press, 2016) and Paul Readman's *Storied Ground: Landscape and the Shaping of English National Identity* (Cambridge University Press, 2018). For the early to middle decades of the twentieth century, David Matless's remarkable *Landscape and Englishness* (Reaktion Books, 1998, 2nd edn 2016) is a bona fide classic while Peter Mandler's learned yet amiable *The Fall and Rise of the Stately Home* (Yale University Press, 1997) captures the counterintuitive phenomenon its title so deftly evokes. Readers interested in the making of modern rural landscapes might consult Paul Brassley, Jeremy Burchardt and Karen Sayer (eds), *Transforming the Countryside. The Electrification of Rural Britain* (Routledge, 2016) and the essays on rural modernism I'm co-editing with Ben Anderson, Katrina Navickas and Linda Ross to be published in the *Proceedings of the British Academy* in 2022. Eagerly awaited findings from current research projects include Navickas's research on common land and Glen O'Hara and Clare Hickman's 'In All Our Footsteps: Tracking, Mapping and Experiencing Rights of Way in Post-War Britain'.

I remain attached to Raymond Williams's great work of literary criticism *The Country and the City*, and like many readers I've been haunted by these lines:

> It's fashionable to admire these extraordinarily numerous houses: the extended manors, the neo-classical mansions, that lie so close in rural Britain. People still pass from village to village, guidebook in hand, to see the next and yet the next example, to look at the stones and the furniture. But stand at any point and look at that land. Think it through in terms of labour and see how long and systematic that exploitation and seizure must have been, to rear that many houses, on that scale. See by contrast what any ancient isolated farm, in uncounted generations of labour, has managed to become, by the efforts of any single real family, however prolonged. Then turn and look at what these other 'families', these systematic owners, have accumulated and arrogantly declared. It isn't only that you know, looking at the land and then at the house, how much robbery and fraud there must have been, for so long, to produce that degree of disparity, that barbarous disproportion of scale. The working farms and cottages are so small beside them: what men really raise by their own efforts or by such portion as is left to them, in the ordinary scale of human achievement.
>
> Raymond Williams, *The Country and the City*
> (New York: Oxford University Press, 1975), pp. 105–6

Rare will be the reader who has not marvelled at a great country house, perhaps casting themselves as a Lord Grantham, a benign overseer of an 'organic community'. Williams's injunction to 'think it through in terms of labour', to contemplate 'the ordinary scale of human achievement', steadies the ego. Moreover, earlier in the passage Williams reminds us that much of this building was made possible by 'the profit of trade and of colonial exploitation'. In contrast to Hill, Potter and Sayer, only Dower, like Williams, was a Marxist, at least for a time, but all four worried about the effect capitalism, liberal, social democratic or market, had on access to green space and the development of the countryside. Irrespective of one's political commitments, to engage critically with these issues is necessarily to engage with existing power structures and the inequities and environmental destruction they entail, which the great collective endeavour that is historical research helps us to understand better.

INDEX

INDEX

Robertson, William Alexander, 37
Rouse, G.D., 297
Ruskin, John
  association with the Lake District, 78, 93
  class views of, 96
  connection with the Wallington Estate, 157
  Effie Gray, 89
  influence on Octavia Hill, 29, 30, 32, 53–4, 56
  kingly/queenly qualities argument, 32
  memorial, 102

Sackville, Lord, 59–60
Sayer, Guy, 236–7
Sayer, Lady Sylvia
  activism over the BBC transmission mast, North Hessary Tor, 209, 260–2, 274
  as an activist, 1–3, 4, 277–8, 310, 314–15
  administration of Dartmoor, 239–40
  as an artist, 247
  the blight of subtopia, 264–5, 271, 275–6, 306–7
  as chair of the Dartmoor Preservation Association, 1, 235–6, 240
  common rights on Dartmoor, 251, 252–4, 258–9
  contempt for day-trippers, 257
  defence of 'native' rights, 254–5
  designation of Dartmoor as a national park, 237–8, 247
  expansionism of the Forestry Commission, 276, 277, 287–98
  family background, 6, 236
  fragmentation concerns on Dartmoor, 243
  gendered stereotypes, 6–8, 310, 314–15
  Ian Nairn's influence on, 261, 263–6
  memorial plaque, Huccaby chapel, 2
  military training by the armed forces, 1–2, 276, 277, 278, 298–314
  national park principles, 5, 332
  The Outline of Dartmoor's Story from the Earliest Times to the Present Day, 247–58, 264, 315
  as a painter, 6
  photographic skills, 243, 301–2
  political views, 236, 261–5, 275–6, 298
  post-war debates on modernity's impact, 261–3

preservationist values, 4–6, 240–1, 248, 256, 315–17
  public knowledge of, 2, 3
  as a publicist, 1, 2, 3, 303, 311
  support for Dartmoor pony breeders, 256
  at the Swincombe reservoir select committee, 286–7
  villa-blight, 257, 262, 265, 268, 274
  water management on Dartmoor, 276, 277, 279–87
  'Wild Country', 315–17
  see also Dartmoor National Park; Dartmoor Preservation Association (DPA)
Sethi, Anita, *I Belong Here*, 340
Sharp, Evelyn, 175, 205–6, 314
Shaw-Lefevre, George, 51–2, 60, 61
Shoard, Marion, 322, 333
Silkin, Lewis, 155, 173–5
Sites of Special Scientific Interest (SSSI), 322
Smith, Adam, 53
Smith, Dr Thomas Southwood, 28
Somers Cocks, John, 299, 309
Southwark Cadet Corps, 50
Stamp, Sir Dudley, 258
Strang, William, 1st Baron, 187–8, 201, 202–3, 209, 214, 223, 224–5, 228, 267
subtopia, concept, 264–5, 271, 275–6
suburbanisation
  due to expanded road networks, 263, 264, 265
  of London's outer reaches by rail, 58, 64
  mediocre architecture of, 264–5
  Octavia Hill's fears over, 12–14
Swiss Cottage Fields, 42–5, 48, 50, 260

Tattershall Castle, Lincolnshire, 105
Thompson, Bruce, 124
Town and Country Planning Act 1947, 268
transport
  Beatrix Potter's concerns over charabancs and day-trippers, 79, 111, 127–8, 135, 140, 247, 257, 280
  car ownership and visitors to the countryside, 186, 191
  Devon's road infrastructure, 253
  objection to Lydford road widening scheme, 243
  road network's impact on the countryside, 263, 264, 265

374